PORTRAITS OF AMERICAN PRESIDENTS VOLUME VI

# THE NIXON PRESIDENCY

TWENTY-TWO INTIMATE PERSPECTIVES OF RICHARD M. NIXON

Edited by
**KENNETH W. THOMPSON**
Miller Center of Public Affairs
University of Virginia



University Press of America

Lanham • New York • London

Miller Center

University of Virginia

4720 Boston Way
Lanham, MD 20706

3 Henrietta Street
London WC2E 8LU England



Printed in the United States of America

British Cataloging in Publication Information Available

ISBN: 0-8191-6416-X (pbk. : alk. paper)
ISBN: 0-8191-6415-1 (alk. paper)

The views expressed by the author(s) of this publication do not necessarily represent the opinions of the Miller Center. We hold to Jefferson's dictum that: "Truth is the proper and sufficient antagonist to error, and has nothing to fear from the conflict, unless by human interposition, disarmed of her natural weapons, free argument and debate."

Co-published by arrangement with
The White Burkett Miller Center of Public Affairs,
University of Virginia

All University Press of America books are produced on acid-free paper which exceeds the minimum standards set by the National Historical Publications and Records Commission.

*Gratefully dedicated*

*to*

*the contributors to this volume*

*who without*

*financial or political gain*

*entered into a serious dialogue and oral history*

*seeking to help ordinary Americans*

*understand*

*a*

*controversial presidency*

## TABLE OF CONTENTS

## III. NIXON AND THE ECONOMY



## IV. THE PRESS AND THE CONGRESS



## V. THE DEPARTMENTS AND THE WHITE HOUSE



## VI. FOREIGN AND DEFENSE POLICY

# PREFACE

A pattern has emerged in the course of organizing Miller Center Forums which has led to the present volume. We have discovered that the leading authorities on particular presidents have helped the Center to draw others with common background to the University of Virginia. By "word of mouth advertising," they have encouraged their friends to come to Faulkner House. Their help has been of inestimable value to a fledgling public affairs center. It has enabled us to further presidential studies through the contributions of distinguished visitors to the understanding of contemporary presidents.

Partly by accident and partly by design, we have discovered our guests were turning the spotlight on certain American presidents. They were viewing particular administrations with shared values but different perspectives. Their differing experiences each illuminated a dimension that otherwise might have remained obscured. They helped us to understand the President they knew best. The product is a portrait, not a photograph; it helps us see the character and spirit of a leader, not the more or less important details a photograph tends to convey. It tells us what was central to his life and works, not what was peripheral. The photograph reveals what can be seen with the naked eye. The portrait shows one thing the photograph cannot reveal: the human essence of the person portrayed.

With this volume, we continue a series of Miller Center publications, *Portraits of American Presidents*. We are grateful to the University Press of America for making volumes in this series available to a wide audience. We have embarked on similar inquiries into the presidencies of Gerald Ford and Jimmy Carter. We plan to complete the series with volumes on the remaining postwar presidents. In the Introduction which follows, the editor traces the history of the Center's interest in the presidency of Richard M. Nixon.

# INTRODUCTION

The presidency of Richard M. Nixon stands apart from other postwar presidencies. Two images persist in the minds of most Americans. One is of a leader whose foreign policy may possibly have offered the best hope for peace with the Soviet Union. The other is of a President, disgraced and rejected by the people, boarding a helicopter to leave the White House forever.

To help us understand such a presidency we turned to men who served with President Nixon or sought to understand his presidency as independent observers. Among Nixon's colleagues are leaders recognized for public service in a succession of administrations. Others are associated exclusively with a President whose disgrace they are assumed to have shared. Some are among the nation's most respected governmental figures while others were imprisoned or driven into exile for reasons not fully clarified even in the pages that follow. More than with most presidents, the men surrounding Nixon are a varied lot and few if any appear to have shared his innermost thoughts or personal friendship.

Bryce Harlow, whose reflections on "The Leader and the Man" opens the discussion, is a foremost student and practitioner of government. His knowledge of executive-legislative relations is unmatched and he brought eight years of experience in the Eisenhower administration to the Nixon administration. He returned to the Nixon administration in the dark days surrounding Watergate hoping to assist the President to regain some equilibrium and control. Earlier, he had interrupted tenure in the administration when he lost confidence in the forces at work and the role he was playing. Mr. Harlow's contribution to the volume grows out of an extended taped interview in his home at Harper's Ferry.

Maurice Stans was twice chairman of the Republican National Finance Committee and chairman of the Finance

Committee to elect and re-elect Richard Nixon. He served as secretary of commerce in the Nixon administration and, in his carefully chosen words, "became very closely entangled with all the aftermath of Watergate." He was "fully absolved of any complicity in Watergate." A gracious lady, his wife Kathleen, since deceased, accompanied him in his participation at the Miller Center. Indeed we might well have dedicated this volume to loyal family members whose devotions to their beleaguered spouses never wavered. Secretary Stans' analysis of the sources of the Watergate action begins a dialogue that continues throughout the volume.

Elliot L. Richardson's active public career spans the administrations of at least five postwar presidents. His own personal background contrasts notably with that of Richard M. Nixon. That may help explain the striking detachment of his analysis and his ability to discuss the paradox of the Nixon presidency. One finds a combination of respect and an understanding of the tragic aspects of the presidency which may be missing in other discussions. Richardson offers several hypotheses to account for Nixon's downfall that are uniquely his own. At the same time, he credits Nixon with having a strategic sense of the world and a subtlety and sophistication in foreign policy that more recent presidents lack. It would be difficult to find an oral history contribution richer in content and marked by a greater measure of intellectual honesty as a participant-observer views a president.

Three close Nixon associates offer their own interpretations of the Nixon White House: H. R. Haldeman, Leonard Garment, and John Ehrlichman. The former being chief of staff saw President Nixon more frequently and was his closest associate during the first term. In Haldeman's own words: "I spent by a wide margin many more hours with him than anyone else did . . . [and] worked with him on the total range of duties of the presidency . . . ." He discusses the organization of the White House staff, the selection of personnel and the evolution of the President's use of the staff. He evaluates President Nixon's use of persons with adversarial viewpoints (Buchanan, Price and Safire as speech writers and Burns and Moynihan on domestic policy). He explores Nixon's alleged vindictiveness which is seemingly contradicted by his detachment in choosing his associates on the basis of merit. Haldeman's explanation is: "He did not view someone who was not for him as an enemy; he only viewed someone who overtly and actively carried out the role of an enemy as being an enemy." In analyzing his own role, he responds to the time honored query "how many people should have access to the President?" He offers a unique and little discussed perspective on Watergate. Finally, he compares the quality and originality of Nixon's thought on foreign, domestic and economic policy.

Leonard Garment, who had been Mr. Nixon's law partner, served as a special assistant and then acting counsel to the President responsible for civil rights in the White House. He also functioned as a "messenger in foreign policy." He sets forth the objectives of the Nixon presidency and identifies the primacy of foreign policy in Mr. Nixon's vision. President Nixon frequently said that it would take a genius to wreck the American economic system but it wouldn't take much to cause serious problems in foreign policy. In domestic policy, a President should do what was necessary to undergird a strong foreign policy. In foreign policy, he sought to achieve his objectives by recruiting Henry Kissinger, William Rogers and Melvin Laird. Mr. Garment offers a different version of Watergate than some of his colleagues. He emphasizes Nixon's leadership and the quality of his performance right up to the time of his resignation. He submits as evidence of Nixon's capacity to govern a list of the number of distinguished public servants whom Nixon brought into government.

John Ehrlichman directs attention to the White House and policy-making. His earliest exposure to Nixon as a candidate was less favorable than other contributors to the volume and some of his doubts about the candidate reappear in his current judgment of the President. Nonetheless, he agreed to participate in the 1968 campaign. His history is one of heavy involvement in the domestic politics side of the Nixon presidency serving as head of the domestic council. Ehrlichman's account of Watergate is one of the most outspoken criticisms of Nixon in the Portrait. His claim is that at a certain point the President lost the capacity to identify the truth about the controversy and that he was drawn into political intrigue as if to a magnet. Whatever the reader's reactions, Mr. Ehrlichman states his views clearly and unambiguously while acknowledging that others saw the President in a different light.*

There follow two contributions on Nixon and the economy, one by Arthur Burns who went on to become head of the Federal Reserve Board and the other by the respected economist, Herbert Stein.

Arthur Burns, like many who served in the Eisenhower administration, had a high opinion of Vice President Nixon then and now. He thought well of Nixon's intellectual ability, political courage and grasp of the issues. At the same time, he considered him a poor administrator and says he had no reason to change that judgment. Among the Presidents with whom he worked during his chairmanship of the Federal Reserve, Burns ranks Nixon worst and Ford best in the use of restraint in this sensitive relationship. Burns was also troubled by the fact that Nixon at his inauguration showed not a trace of humility and appeared already to be running for a second term. Nonetheless, Burns concludes if we should have fifty years of peace with the Soviets, Nixon because of his foreign policy will go down "in the history books as one of our truly great Presidents."

No less distinguished as an economist than Arthur Burns is Herbert Stein who was both a member and chairman of the Council of Economic Advisors in the Nixon and Ford administrations. Professor Stein observed the introduction of wage and price controls by the Nixon administration and his discussion traces some of the forces that led to this action. The main body of his essay is an exposition of the organization of the government for economic policy-making which he outlines in considerable detail.

The next section in the volume considers President Nixon's relations with the press and the Congress. Lou Cannon who is best known for his writings on Governor and President Reagan also covered the White House under Nixon. James Keogh was editor of *Time* magazine and is now Director of the Business Roundtable. He was one of Nixon's press secretaries. Clark Mollenhoff who later became Washington bureau chief of the *Des Moines Register* was special counsel to President Nixon from 1969 to 1970. Kenneth BeLieu joined Bryce Harlow and William Timmons to make up Nixon's congressional relations team throughout most of the first term. Taken together, these four presentations enhance our understanding of Nixon's relations with the press and with Congress.

There follow chapters on the relationship between leading cabinet level departments and the White House and the Congress. Robert Finch was a long-time Nixon associate and some said, the "resident liberal" in the administration. As Secretary of the Department of Health, Education and Welfare, he grappled with the difficult social problems confronting the Nixon presidency in the late 1960s and early 1970s. Earl Butz succeeded Clifford Hardin as Secretary of Agriculture and his sharp wit and pungent mode of expression is reflected in a wide ranging discussion of the President, Congress and the Departments.

Four observers to be joined by a fifth participant-observer in the concluding section analyze Nixon's foreign policy.

When we turn to foreign policy in the Nixon administration, one conspicuous difference between what precedes and what is contained in this portion of the Miller Center's history is the number of "missing chairs" in foreign policy. For their own reasons, neither Secretary Kissinger, Secretary Laird nor General Haig have seen fit to participate nor has Mr. McFarlane. CIA Director Schlesinger contributed but asked that his history be sealed for an indeterminate number of years. Some close associates have been more forthcoming and generous with their time. It will remain for historians to judge why the central players in domestic and economic policy were more willing to join in placing their views into the historical record as part of an integrated oral history.

Michael Raoul-Duval, now the managing director of the First Boston Corporation, spearheaded the advance party who sought to normalize relations with China. He spent seven years in the White House in the Nixon and Ford administrations during a difficult and turbulent period in American history. His discussion of the bureaucracy and Nixon's use of back channels, especially in forging a new China policy, is instructive in anticipating future policy-making. Duval played a role both in domestic and foreign policy and his judgment of Nixon is a measured one based on a view of the Nixon presidency drawn from varied experiences. For more than twenty years, Hugh Sidey has written the presidency column for *Time* magazine. Sidey met Nixon in the mid-1950s as vice president and interviewed or met with him regularly down to the present day. As with the late Theodore White who is quoted as saying, "Do you realize that my entire political and literary career has been based on Richard Nixon?", Sidey views Nixon as the central political figure of our times who "has probably shaped more events than any other figure, in either a positive or negative way." Sidey asks what was it about the man which gave him this place in American politics and what accounts for his grasp of foreign policy.

Helmut Sonnenfeldt is an authority on American foreign policy through public service and scholarly writing. He entered government in 1952 and left in 1977 and served with Henry Kissinger first in the National Security Council and later as counselor in the Department of State. Thus Mr. Sonnenfeldt had close relations with NSC Adviser and then Secretary Kissinger allowing first-hand participation in foreign policy. In reviewing the Nixon foreign policy, he is uniquely qualified to help reconstruct the structures and procedures by which policy was formulated and implemented. Finally, Kenneth Rush worked closely with Richard Nixon early in the President's career. He was his professor at Duke University Law School. Later Nixon was to call on Rush, who was president of Union Carbide, to become ambassador to the Federal Republic of Germany. He went on to become secretary of state *ad interim* and deputy secretary of defense. His impressions conclude the section on foreign policy.

One of the national weekly magazines published a story on President Nixon in the mid-1980s entitled: "Nixon is back," a phrase which is descriptive of various chapters in his political life. One such episode was ushered in following his defeat in the race for Governor of California. Stephen Hess who is a senior fellow at the Brookings Institution observed Nixon in exile in the period from 1961 to 1968. As was true in the mid-1980s, Nixon renewed his political standing in this period and defeated Hubert Humphrey in the race for president in 1968. Hess undertakes to describe the qualities of perseverance and resilience that continue to give Nixon the capacity for renewal.

# I.

# THE POLITICAL LEADER AND THE MAN

# THE MAN AND THE POLITICAL LEADER

## Bryce Harlow

**MR. THOMPSON:** Mr. Harlow, we hope that in this presentation we will be able to learn a little about the beginnings of your relationship with Richard Nixon, when you met him, what your initial impressions were, how you looked on him as a leader, and whether any of those views have changed over time.

**MR. HARLOW:** I first met Richard Nixon in 1947, well before he was noteworthy. By that time, I had been in Washington for nine years, having arrived there in 1938. I had spent three of those years as a Congressional secretary, five in the Army working with Congress, and in 1947, I had become a professional staff member of the Armed Services Committee of the House. So, when I met this freshman California congressman, Richard Nixon, he was the novitiate in the Congressional process, and I the veteran. We met at a rough-and-tumble evening affair. There used to be a group in the House of Representatives called The Gym Group consisting of about fifty members of the House. They would go every evening about five o'clock to the House gym and play paddleball, a game imported from the Philippines. Our ambassador to the Philippines, a former Kentucky Congressman, brought it back to the House and they all went bonkers over it. It is much like handball but played with heavy wooden paddles. They had an annual party, which one should never attend without checking his life insurance first. It was held in various places in Washington, never at the same place twice because the proprietors would not let them come back after they had been there once. This time we were at the Army-Navy Club in Washington, and that is how and where I first met Richard Nixon. He ended up sitting beside me at dinner, or I beside him, at this raucous Congressional-tribal affair. Nixon did not do anything out of the ordinary. He was in full command of himself, a rather muted dinner companion on this occasion. He was a freshman House member, remember. The Speaker of the House was there and many others of rank: the minority and majority leaders, committee chairmen and so on, so a freshman would be mindful of his manners. I was one of only four House staff allowed to attend, so even then I was apparently someone to reckon with.

What was my reaction to him? About the same as to Joe McCarthy when I first met him. Nixon was not then anything to react to as Joe McCarthy was not. McCarthy was later fashioned into a monster by the attention paid to him by Harry Truman. Richard Nixon would in time pull himself up into national distinction and later notoriety, but that was not discernable in 1947. There is a question you might want to ask, so I will do it for you: when did I first feel he was something different from a run-of-the-mill Congressman?

To answer myself, I don't know. I am never good at answering my own questions. I was working for the Armed Services Committee. He was not on it. I was with the likes of Lyndon Johnson, who was on it, and so I didn't have much dealing with Richard Nixon in the House. Then he went off to the Senate in 1950.

**MR. THOMPSON:** Several people have compared McCarthy and Nixon. They say Nixon never sat through a full committee hearing but came midway through with a well-prepared statement, which he gave to the press immediately after he had finished his remarks and then he left; in contrast, McCarthy remained throughout the hearings.

**MR. HARLOW:** People making that sort of observation are likely trying to smudge Nixon, I would surmise. Or, they are trying to say, "He's evil. He probably does bad things to people much like Joe McCarthy." Well, everybody's different. He was smarter than the pack and knowledge is power. He was more committed and energetic and he worked harder. Joe McCarthy had enormous help in becoming a national figure. The President of the United States turned him into somebody. He made it himself despite starting off on the wrong foot with the liberal left complex in the United States. They saw him as a menace to liberalism. He was tough. He liked rolling in the dust and drawing a line in the dust. In public life that takes guts, strength, courage, thick skin, and he apparently had those qualities. He started out by beating Jerry Voorhis, a California Congressman. Voorhis was a close friend of mine. He was the darling of Washington, D.C. The media, the liberals, and the leftists of the day all loved Jerry. He was a wealthy man originally who forsook his wealth and went to work in a assembly plant in Baltimore because he wanted to identify with the ordinary guy. It was a mix of economic and political philosophy and of religion. After that he went on to Congress, and then in 1946 he was beaten by Richard Nixon.

So, when Nixon came he was already marked. The Washington press disliked him before they met him. They preferred Voorhis. I'm talking about the people around the nation's capital. Next, Nixon gets another strike against him. He runs against a lady leftist from California and beats her too. In the meantime, he captivates national attention by unfrocking Alger Hiss—a most unsettling business, once again, for the liberal establishment.

The campaign against Helen Gahagan Douglas had rough behavior and cruel and unkind politics in both parties which the left likes to hang on Nixon but not on her as well. Be that as it may, he won. He came back as a senator, and now the Washington jackals had a hard fix on him. He was already the left's *persona non grata* by 1950, but now he was a national figure. Then Eisenhower comes along. He needs California. For that reason he takes Nixon. Lightning has struck. That's the way of politics' surging success or plunging defeat—a tempestuous way of life. Thus in 1952 we had a newborn national politician and a budding national leader. Richard Nixon went trooping around the country for Dwight David Eisenhower. In the beginning he got into a fund fracas much as Adlai Stevenson did. The biggest difference was that one involved the feared and hated Nixon, the other the dilletantish and intellectual Stevenson. Nixon emerged besmirched; Stevenson slightly tarnished. That's normal.

**MR. THOMPSON:** How did Eisenhower feel about him?

**MR. HARLOW:** I can't say for sure because I was not at that point an Eisenhower crony. I met Eisenhower first during the war when he was chief of the War Plans Division of the Army General Staff. I didn't have any business with him for a long time, except briefly when he became Army chief of staff, because I left the Army in early 1946. I didn't have more contact with him until I was with the House Armed Services Committee. Then I had sporadic contact with him. During that period he was head of NATO; he headed Columbia University and the Joint Chiefs of Staff briefly. Meantime, I resigned from the House Committee and returned to Oklahoma. I was completely out of contact with Eisenhower. Next I got sucked into the White House staff in 1953 against my wishes and started to know the President because I was working for him. Even so, it was a long time before I was able to say, "Mr. President, what do you think of your vice president?" So, I don't know what he thought at that time. He came to have a very high appreciation of Nixon's knowledge of Congress. He had no doubt Nixon was sharp, smart, ingenious and tough. Also, Nixon was intensely interested in the American political process and politics and he was a hard worker. As personalities though, they didn't blend well. Eisenhower would never have picked him as his favorite bridge companion. One thing dividing them was their age disparity as well as differences in experience and training. But their outlook on political matters was similar. It may surprise some that I would rate Eisenhower as basically more conservative than Nixon. Deep down Ike was a hard conservative as compared with most people, including Robert Taft.

**MR. THOMPSON:** Did Nixon resent the delay in Eisenhower's support prior to the Checkers speech?

**MR. HARLOW:** At that time I was campaigning out in the bush, doing political stoop labor and walking the manured fields. I was doing little booths at fairs in Oklahoma. I didn't know much about what the big people did. I took over the GOP booth at the Oklahoma State Fair, I remember, the day the Nixon bomb regarding his fund blew up. Here I was pleading for Republican support in a Democratic state trying to do right for Eisenhower. Believe me, I had a busy time at that booth once the fund news spread. But that crisis again manifested Nixon's extraordinary resourcefulness and confidence. Overnight he turned an extreme negative into a positive. How many people do you know who could have pulled it off? He was amazing. It was much more of a *tour de force* than people have appreciated. Actually, he has been vaporized by political nukes half a dozen times and resurrected by his own hand. He has breathed into his own mouth. I do not know of anybody else who could come close to doing what he's done to fend off disaster, nor do I expect to know anybody who could do it. He was shot down in the California governor's race in 1962, and left for dead (even he thought so at first). He retreated to New York and said he was through with politics. But he was the party's national nominee six years later, and he campaigned across America like a bantam rooster all during the intervening period. He was annihilated by Watergate and his enemies danced on his grave. Or was he really laid away? It doesn't look like it. He supposedly died in 1960 but was resurrected by 1962. He had to be put down all over again in 1962 (the missile crisis, carefully timed, did him in). The Democratic establishment tried the same stunt in 1968 with the bombing halt and missed defeating him by mistiming their announcement by about three days, or that too would have worked. So the confidence and recuperative powers of the man are phenomenal.

I'll make this statement: the intellectual competence of this man is probably the highest of any person ever to serve in the Oval office—the finest intelligence, the most disciplined at any rate. The universal talent that assures great accomplishment—a great intellect married to great force and dynamism—is combined with his competence. Put them together and you have a leader. There is no apparent way to stop Nixon. He is a cork—push him down and he pops right back up because of his uncommon gifts. He verges being on indestructible.

Hugh Sidey went to interview him in California at San Clemente shortly after his resignation. Sidey was to visit with him for about fifteen minutes. This was soon after Nixon's resignation and while he was trying to recover his health. Sidey spent over an hour with him, came out shaking his head and saying, "My God, what a pity that intellect is still not in full harness for the United States." The man is just that way with a superior intellect and force. It is invariably stimulating and often exciting to talk with him on matters of importance to our country and the world because of his encyclopedic information. He seems to remember everything. He is an ambulatory computer. He retains it all, correlates it all. So he tells you about precincts, districts, politicians, and movements in America, almost precinct by precinct. He can tell you about countless people, who they are, what they are, what they should be and whether or not you can depend on them, what they stand for and don't, how you deal with them. His knowledge of world affairs is conceded by his worst enemies.

He used to go to the auxiliary oval office across from the White House, over to the Executive Office Building on the second floor where this marvelous old-style, roomy office is located. Nixon was the first President to use it. He found it a great place to escape from the White House Oval Office, which he didn't care for, and once in this beautiful office firm instructions not to bother him would go out. He would take out a big yellow pad and analyze a major concern of the presidency at that point. He would bring along memoranda, studies and reports and lean back on a kind of lounge and, half-supine, would read, study, make notes, and prepare an outline of it all on his pad. When through, he would throw away his notes. He wouldn't need them anymore. He was now master of that issue; it was engraved on his mind. That's Nixon. That gift enables him to achieve more than less gifted people can.

I remember a speech we did together for the nation's editor's in 1967. They come *en masse* to Washington every year, as you know, to be fawned upon by all the politicians.

Nixon asked me to help prepare his talk. We went over it at the Statler Hotel. We kept on—wrote it, edited it, rewrote it, re-edited it, played around with it, and edited some more. Finally it was in shape and it was time for him to leave. He started out of the door and I said, "Wait a minute. Here's the draft." He said, "Oh, I don't need that." Well, frankly, it irritated me. I mean, you work like that, then have that happen; you think, "Well, good Lord, why did you have me over to do all this? I have other things to do." But I went downstairs and stood in the back of the hall to listen to him deliver his talk without notes. It was the draft virtually verbatim. He had passages such as, "And on this I have seven specific suggestions: Number one," and so on. All that was in the draft, of course, but he spilled it all out by memory, with subheadings as well. I watched and thought, "Great guns, what an incredible ability."

Well, then you may say, "All right, Harlow, you are enraptured with this fellow. Why, then, did he get into so much trouble if he is so brilliant?" I remember one of Lyndon Johnson's closest friends telling me not to work for Johnson when he was trying to hire me. He said, "Bryce, he cuts his corners too close. You wouldn't stay with him over six months." Was this a Nixon flaw as well?

What about so many people disliking him most of his life? There must be a reason. In the case of Dick Nixon, I have a view that is sheer speculation. For many years, those of us working closely with him had a difficult and puzzling problem to deal with. People were saying, "I just don't like him." We would ask why and they would say, "I don't know. I just don't like the guy." It used to drive us to distraction. Someone tells you he doesn't like your friend, but can't explain or justify it. I finally came to an opinion which I toss out here for whatever it's worth. It is that people didn't like him for the simple reason that he didn't like people. Life tends to do that. If you like people, they will like you. That's why people liked Ike. Ronald Reagan, sharing the same public affection, likes a charwoman as much as a queen and it shows, so the public likes him. In the case of Richard Nixon, I suspect that my gifted friend somewhere in his youth, maybe when he was very young or in his teens, got badly hurt by someone he cared for very deeply or trusted totally—a parent, a relative, a dear friend, a lover, a confidante. Somewhere I figure somebody hurt him badly, and from that experience and from then on he could not trust people. I've never talked about this with Nixon, it being none of my business. I would welcome the opportunity though. I would like to know why he has had to carry that awful burden of so many people saying they don't like him but don't know why.

Part of the reason some people have not liked him is because they have had a certain fear of him. Another reason goes back to the press and certain elements of the Democratic Party. He is charged with questioning their loyalty in 1954. House Speaker Sam Rayburn and Senate Majority Leader Lyndon Johnson displayed professional anger, in all ways, toward Nixon. Underscore the word professional, but realize it was also personal because they often attacked Nixon on this loyalty issue and meant it. He didn't impugn their loyalty, he swears, but they thought so and tried to destroy him for it.

In the spring of 1960, I was sent with Nixon by Eisenhower to "Leslie Arends Day" in Illinois. I was to carry a personal message from the President. Nixon was the featured speaker. Arends was the long-time GOP whip of the House and one of the most senior members of Congress. I flew there with the vice president, Pat Nixon, Herbert Klein, and Rose Woods. We went to Arends' home in the little town of Melvin of some 900 people. I don't know how they kept the population at 900, but that figure was on a sign outside town so somehow they did. At this point, on this festive day, they had some 15,000 people there to salute this extremely popular Congressman. It all began with a press conference at Arends' home. The conference was behind the house around a little patio. The press consisted mainly of the Washington reporters traveling with Nixon. By this time he was being viewed as the likely Republican presidential candidate in 1960, so the press was all tightly up around him. There were scores of the White House press corps there. Nixon stepped forward and opened the conference. It was the first time I had watched him in a press conference. Snuggled up behind a potted palm, I watched and listened to see how my principal would do. I could hardly believe what I heard and saw. I kid you not;

it was frightening. Nixon was in a snake pit, not in a press conference. The reporters were trying to wipe him out. He would respond to a question, and they would climb all over him, shout at him, snarl at him, interrupt and insult him. You wouldn't believe it. I couldn't imagine such behavior. I was aghast over the viciousness of it, the malice, the open hatred. Saliva was running. Fangs were bared. They were hot after him. It was scary. Like him or not, he was vice president of the United States. His office, at least, was entitled to respect and yet here he was being reviled by a bunch of top journalists. I lurked on behind the palm and watched this process go on. Finally, it ended and Nixon said thanks, much to my surprise, and we went on to the rest of the program, including the appearances he had to make and the message I had to present from the President.

Now we have left the good people of Melvin and are en route to Washington. We are in the stateroom of the airplane, relaxing and surveying how the day had gone. Nixon says, "Well, Bryce, how do you think it went?" I said, "Mr. Vice President, it went beautifully, with the exception of that terrible press conference." He said, "What? What did I do wrong?" I said, "You didn't do anything wrong. The press' behavior was intolerable. What they were doing was unbelievable." He said, "Oh, that's right. You haven't been to a Nixon press conference before, right? I'm glad you were there because I think the President doesn't have the slightest idea of what I have to go through. You tell him what it's like, what I have had to deal with all this time." And then he said, "Let me tell you something else, Bryce. Herb, you listen, too, and speak out if I'm wrong. Bryce, this is the easiest and least contentious press conference I've had in a long time." Herb said, "That's entirely correct." I said, "That scares the hell out of me. I can't believe it."

You could see the bile, the poison. The press was hooked on an anti-Nixon drug and could never break the addiction. It was a terrible drag throughout Nixon's political career. He couldn't get on with this crowd. He had to discontinue press conferences entirely in the 1960 campaign because each conference went like the one at Melvin. They were trying to destroy him, not interrogate him. He finally stopped having them. I remember that in Nashville I was standing by the aircraft at an airport rally, and Nixon was giving the rally speech to the crowd. I stepped out from under the airplane's wing to get a little stretch before we had to get aboard for the next stop. I'm standing there and here comes the noted political columnist, Bill Lawrence, of the *New York Times* swinging out of the hangar where the press phones were. He said, "Hey, Harlow, you know what story I just filed?" I answered, "No, Bill, what did you just file?" He said, "You know I looked out here and I saw this big crowd, and I said to the chief of police, 'How many people are out here?' and he said, 'Oh, about fifteen thousand.' So I asked the sheriff. He said about ten thousand. And I said, "Well, how many came when Kennedy was here?" The sheriff said, "About five thousand." Lawrence said, "So I wrote that Nixon had only ten and Kennedy had fifteen. How do you like that?" He walked off and got on the plane. I just watched him. That was par for the course. There was nothing we could do. That's how it was all the way in 1960.

Nixon lived with that all his political life. He was never able to stop or even ease it. I asked him to explain that. He said, "I've tried everything anyone can do." He told me that the night we flew back from Melvin. I asked him why he was being pilloried by the press. He said, "I don't know. I've tried everything to correct it. I've given interviews one on one, lots of them. I've had small, intimate interviews. I've have parties at my home. I've made myself accessible to them. I've given them news and information. I've played their game. It has never changed a thing. I don't know what can be done about it."

One day in the 1968 campaign we were in Hartford, Connecticut. The late John Osborne of the *New Republic*, a close friend of mine wanted to have lunch with me and I agreed. At that time I thought he was the best political reporter in Washington. We lunched somewhere in our hotel there in Hartford. John was draining me, as a good reporter should, and I was responding the best I could, and then suddenly I interrupted him and said, "Hold it a second. Let me ask you a question. Just why do you hate my guy so much?" He said, "Well, I don't really know, but . . ." conceding in effect that he loathed Nixon. Then, after a moment's silence, he said, "Bryce, I wish you hadn't done that. That was a dirty trick. I am ashamed of my attitude toward Richard Nixon. I don't have a right to that as a reporter, but I don't like him and I can't help it. I have no real basis to dislike him. He has done nothing to me." He reflected for a moment, and said, "I"ll tell you one reason a reporter has trouble liking Nixon. Bryce, we've never really met him. None of us have. Do you know what we call him in the press corps—the cardboard man." I said, "The cardboard man? Why that?" He replied, "Well, because we have never seen the real Nixon. He conceals himself somewhere behind a cardboard image of himself. He never comes out. I've talked to him in all kinds of ways. But I've never seen nor met the real man. I keep trying. Now, Bryce, you can't trust a man, you can't like a man whom you don't meet, who hides himself from you. You suspect him." I said, "John, now I understand. You have finally revealed yourself and your comrades. The real reason you don't like Richard Nixon is that he is smarter than you are. That's the problem. At last I know. You sit here, John, and you use me like putty because you are so much smarter than I am. And you say, 'I want some information on this or that subject.' I say all right, go after it, and you get all you want because I can't stop you, you being smarter than I am. But Nixon, oh no, he gives you just what he wants to give you, and no more. And you get all bent out of shape because you can't control it. He controls it. I see now why you and your cronies resent him." Well, there was a pause, and he looked at me, and he said, "You know, you may have something there. I had never thought of that, and it's quite possible."

Another side of this unusual man is that he has great sensitivity and compassion, to the surprise, I am sure, of many people, certainly to the surprise of those who for years have contended that he likes to cheat, lie, and marinate in evility. For instance, when I first retired for health reasons eight years ago, I went, in crisis condition, into the Arlington Hospital in northern Virginia. Shortly there was a call that President Nixon wanted to come and see me. A former president coming to see me at the hospital? I took the phone, and I said, "Mr. President, don't do that. You've got things to do that amount to something. You don't have to come over here. I know you like me but go do something memorable. Don't waste your time over here; that's ridiculous." He said, "I will be there in forty-five minutes." He came and spent an hour and a half with me, cheering me up. He brought a gift, something to read, and wanted to help pay my medical bills. Now that is empathetic and sensitive. It is a very warm, thoughtful person who would do that. Where does he keep that caring personality, where does he keep that warm part of Nixon hidden? I don't know. He doesn't advertise it, but it is there. There are other examples of it I could cite. That is the way he is. It is not known because he is such a private person. Maybe his Quaker indoctrination keeps it hidden.

**MR. THOMPSON:** Could I ask you to supplement all of this? Hugh Sidey spent a day with us, and he is an admirer, as your quote would indicate, but he did say one thing, and I wondered what your reaction would be to this. He said he once asked Nixon, "How is it that you can deal with evil forces, an evil empire like the Soviet Union?" And Nixon answered him and said, "Because I'm evil." Over the years Hugh Sidey has referred several times to Nixon as 'that scoundrel'.

I testified in 1952 before the Republican platform committee, and Senator Millikan was the chairman. I was either an instructor or an assistant professor at Northwestern, and I stayed up all night. The title of my presentation was "Negotiation vs. Confrontation." Nixon wanted fifty copies, and he said this was the best analysis he had heard. All the rest of the members of the committee slept. Senator Millikan said, "Just give us the paper. We've been up all night." Dulles, as you remember, came back from Duck Island with the foreign policy plank so it was an exercise. But Nixon asked questions, and I would have been floating on the ceiling as a young instructor getting this kind of treatment. But I came early, and he said much the same thing to Merwin K. Hart. I stayed late and Clark Eichelberger talked about world government, and Nixon said the same thing to him. Only Senators Ives and Nixon stayed awake, and only Nixon said anything to the three of us. The reference to his evilness, the tendency to exaggerate his praise to three utterly different people, the fact that Kissinger once said, "Think what kind of a statesman he would have been if one person had loved him in his whole life" suggests something about him which may have had some impact on the hostile press who were so brutal and so cruel. Don't you think so?

**MR. HARLOW:** You mean that there was something in him that forced all that? Well, obviously there was. It happened, and not by design; it was brought about. Again, I refer to what I said initially I thought the problem was. He had been hurt down deep inside. I think there is truth in that. But it goes beyond that. He doesn't, perhaps as a result, trust people, and if you don't trust people, you don't think highly of people in general. If you regard them as slobs or boobs, you're in a bad fix. The grouping that shaped up in the 1970s—Nixon, Haldeman, Ehrlichman, Colson, Magruder, and so forth—took on an eerie quality, like the man with wax wings who flew so close to the sun that he and his son fell to the earth; these people did that. They started vying for favor on Nixon's dark side. Colson started talking about trampling his grandmother's grave for Nixon and showing he was as mean as they come. The same with Haldeman and Ehrlichman. Everybody went *macho.* It was the "in thing" to swagger and threaten. I went to a White House meeting on campaign strategy in the spring of 1972. This was an inside group that held semi-monthly meetings. The President had asked me to attend them. Once, the summary firing of two men in the Agriculture Department came up during a meeting. I said, "Oh? What for?" I was told, "Because they've got to be fired." I said, "Well, what did they do?" "Nothing." These were to be a couple of innocent victims publicized for political gain. I looked up and said, "Well, I'll tell you what. You go ahead with that idea, and I'm going to let the President know about it. I want you to know that. Don't stop. I'm sure you will do it anyway, and I'm sure he will approve your program because I'm not in the administration anymore. I'm just a kibitzer. But I'm going to go in there and I'm going to tell him that I think this is terrible and wrong and he mustn't do it if you persist." They dropped it, to my great surprise.

You see, an orgy had begun and had started building. One morning, while having breakfast with Henry Kissinger at the Metropolitan Club, I told him, "Henry, we are lucky it was Watergate, because if it hadn't been that, it would have been something much worse, the way things were going." I believe that. It had gotten that bad, and it was getting worse rapidly. The President went through, and it is probably still in him, a process of some kind that made him disrespect people. I don't know whom he respects even now—really, really respects.

**MR. THOMPSON:** Ray Price or a few people like him?

**MR. HARLOW:** There are a very few people. There's one crowd close to him—those like Ray Price, Pat Buchanan, Bill Safire, Haldeman, Ehrlichman and such. But in the President's coterie, and the people he most nearly fully trusts, his web of true friends, I would first name Bebe Rebozo of Key Biscayne, Florida. I don't know why Nixon has such a close relationship with Rebozo. I would name probably Bob Alplanalp next although I have never seen the two together, so I don't know what there is in that relationship, but I think he should be there. I would put Julie Eisenhower in there. I don't know anyone else.

**MR. THOMPSON:** That's another question some have raised. Is there any president whose children have turned out better than Richard Nixon's children?

**MR. HARLOW:** I don't think so. I will tell you another thing. I would ask historians to look back over the years of history of the United States of America and tell me if any administration back to Washington's could have stood a two-year orgy of total recrimination and investigation with not a shred of major corruption being found. What other administration could do that? I don't think there has been one. The only item of corrupt behavior I recollect being found in Nixon's time was John Dean taking five grand to go have a honeymoon. I seem to recollect it was some kind of political contribution that he made off with, and I don't know if he replaced it or not, but he took the money. Aside from Ted Agnew, that was the only thing they ever found of any kind that was off-color or for material gain. The Agnew incident took place, really, before he was vice president.

Actually, Watergate should have been Lyndongate. The GOP tried for it. The Party trailed Billy Sol Estes, Bobby Baker, the Austin television station and so on into the Johnson Oval Office and White House. But what could be done about it? Nothing. The GOP leaders tried, but Chairman Sam Irwin saw his own President a bit differently than he saw Nixon. His committee voted several times not to investigate Lyndon Johnson. Eagerly, though, they went after Richard Nixon later. Lyndon told the Speaker of the House at one point, "You are going to have to put us all in jail if you don't stop this stuff," referring to efforts to probe the administration. So they dropped the curtain. They were able to because they controlled the Congress and, of great importance, the press was predisposed toward them in contrast to Nixon. Nixon was ordained for destruction by the only force in our political process outweighing our President—a journalistic-congressional complex. That can and will do a president in.

**MR. THOMPSON:** What about his relations with Congress, first as vice president and then as President?

**MR. HARLOW:** As vice president, he did many of the President's chores with Congress. General Persons, Gerald Morgan, Jack Martin and myself would meet with him very often. He would help us and work with us, and take on assignments important to the President. He would hold dinners and lunches. He took on chores for the Cabinet as well and also many GOP chores. These activities were in addition to the foreign travel, speech assignments, diplomatic chores and so on that he did right along for the President. As far as the Hill was concerned at that time, the crowd up there liked Nixon. Party members who worked with him actively respected him as a powerful, loyal Republican. And he was highly regarded, not necessarily liked, as a very able, solid, political, hard-working campaign leader. His relationships with the Democratic side weren't all that good because there was a professional desire on the part of the Speaker and the Senate Majority Leader to neutralize him. They saw in him a successor to Eisenhower and a danger to the Democrats, and they didn't want him to be Eisenhower's successor even if it took the election of Jack Kennedy to prevent it. They despised Kennedy almost worse than Nixon. That is how the Nixon vice presidency went. He looked good and did well in the political process as vice president. Maybe somebody else would see it differently for that period, but I think my picture is accurate. I believe Nixon was the first vice president really to pull hard in harness, with responsible chores, for his President. His precedent changed the office permanently.

In his own presidency, he started out, as most new presidents do, loving the world and reaching out for the whole world to love him. Filled with the sweetness of victory, they yearn to serve everyone well and faithfully and they are determined to be reasonable and get along with everybody. They are going to do great things for America, arm-in-arm with everyone. That's the way it starts. I remember, we came back from Key Biscayne after the election with a skeleton White House staff filled out and the President-elect said, "Bryce, get me a list of the congressional leaders and all the committee chairmen and ranking minority members, and I will telephone each one of them." He added, "We are going to get along and get things done together." He was quite sincerely counting on them to cooperate. Now, we're talking about some thirty-one committees, two members apiece to be called—sixty-two calls by a man who hardly had time to go to the john, plus a score of other leaders. He had to make some eighty calls to do this project. Each call would take at least five minutes, that is four hundred minutes, which is about seven hours. He did exactly that. He called them all. They all were flattered to have the President call and promised to cooperate as best they could in enacting his programs for America.

So he sailed joyously off with that beginning, so characteristic of a new president. He had to work hard at starting that way, which explains why I was with him. I was there to set up the same kind of Congressional process Eisenhower had used. I told him I would stay just long enough to do that and then would leave.

His congressional relations were as good as a president's relations can be within the constraints the founding fathers and 200 years of precedent have set up. You have your ups and downs in this activity, your struggles, and your irritations. I had to go up to the Senate in the late spring of 1969, for instance, and meet with all the Republican Senators and their administrative assistants in the Caucus Room. They could hardly wait to boil me in oil because they hadn't gotten their political appointments. They were irate. The situation was normal for a new administration because congressmen can never get all their appointments or get them in time. They're always apoplectic over it. I had been through this bath of acid before in Ike's time, so I was relaxed about it. I helped Larry O'Brien with his agony with the same problem in Kennedy's time. He almost jumped ship since they got so furious at him. I told him to forget it, that things were only going normally.

So Gordon Allott, Senator from Colorado and Republican Policy chairman, called me and said, "Bryce come up here and talk to the boys." I agreed to do so. So there I was, late spring of 1969, eyeball-to-eyeball with all these red-eyed Republican senators and administrative assistants. Allott threw me out to them like a piece of raw meat to hyenas. He said, "Boys, you all have known Harlow for all these years. Bryce, they're mad about personnel. What have you got to say?" I got up and said, "Thanks, Gordon, for that eloquent introduction," and then lit into them. The relevance of all this was the impact on the President's relations with Congress. My relations weren't in trouble—his relations were. I said, "All right, fellows, you are as mad as you can get; I know that. That's understandable. You are not getting the appointments you really want, and the ones you do get you don't want very much. Moreover, they are all long overdue—you just can't get timely action. You are frustrated and furious. That's why you have me here now. Now, let me be totally candid. You are not as unhappy yet as you are going to be. Understand that, because we don't have as many jobs to parcel out as collectively you want. Some of you, therefore, won't get the jobs you're after, and you will be outraged and will flog us with it the rest of the time we are in office.

Understand that I know that and would fix it if it were fixable. But it is not fixable. You should know that your feelings right now in this room toward me, toward the President, are simply natural, normal, and ordinary. I know it because I have been through all this before and so have various old-time Senators here. You have to feel this way if you are worth your keep as a politician, otherwise you ought to get out. So take it easy. You can do whatever you wish about me, I couldn't care less about it. I think you know I would help you more if I could. Let me add this. As soon as we finally get this personnel orgy settled down here it will be about the first of October. You will know by then how bad your hurt is, which promises we have broken, which of your best guys didn't get the jobs, and so on, and with all that over, will we have sweetness and light? Oh no, my friends. We are ordained to fight over something else. You will get equally made over issues and policies as on personnel. That will go on until the close of the first term, certainly for two and a half years more. Ultimately, in about three and a half years, the end of the first term, we'll have honed ourselves into a team and then we can have a happy dinner together."

Well, that's how it is for all presidents. That's the way it was for John F. Kennedy. By the time of his death he couldn't pass a mother's love resolution. The House of Representatives was locked against him. I have never seen our government as badly immobilized as it was in August of 1963. It was mostly because of the Kennedy emphasis on civil rights. It alienated the southern Democrats who, when added to the Republicans, gave House control to the President's opposition. At the end of his service he was congressionally impotent.

Nixon was a veteran legislator, knew both Houses of Congress inside out and knew politics. So until Watergate he was competent to deal with these people and problems. Watergate blew it all. In no time at all the Hill people were running from him, as they always do in such circumstances.

**MR. THOMPSON:** Could you have helped him if you had still been there?

**MR. HARLOW:** Well, I suppose I should give in to the temptation to say I would have saved the whole thing, but of course not. For one reason, he wouldn't have used me in a way that I could have helped much. You may recall, he got Melvin Laird and me to come back to the White House. Mel returned in the middle of June 1973, I returned the first of July. Both of us resisted going back, but concluded we had to because of the dire condition of things. We knew nothing about the Watergate mess but accepted the challenge of helping Nixon keep the presidency going.

By January, as far as we were concerned, Nixon was almost *incommunicado.* He dealt with General Haig, Ron Zeigler, Rose Wood, his counsel, St. Clair, and Fred Buzhardt. He stopped seeing anyone else. I left in April. Mel left in January or February because there was no point in our staying. We had gone back, reluctantly, on the insistence of the President and Al Haig that he wanted us to help him. On that basis alone we went back. If he wouldn't let us help, it was time to go. So we did.

**MR. THOMPSON:** Mr. Harlow, there is one issue that has come up continuously, and it has to do with the functioning of the Nixon administration. A number of people have said that things would have gone much better if he had a chief of staff. That kind of an issue is raised about various administrations. Also, several people who know you well and know the President have argued that you would have made the ideal chief of staff, and that you could have dealt with some of the problems that came up fairly early on. I wonder if you would comment from your perspective.

**MR. HARLOW:** People who say Haldeman was not a chief of staff need to go out and look up the words. The first chief of staff I knew intimately was Sherman Adams. He was chief under Eisenhower and to characterize him as secretary of the general staff would have been the right term under Eisenhower. The President was used to that in the military. John Foster Dulles made it very clear that foreign policy would be his alone, Adams had the rest of it, except defense, in his side pocket. He kept the trash away from the President so he could concentrate on the crucial matters, and made sure it was all properly coordinated and staffed out before it reached the President. He was very good, an incredible worker, tough as nails, and extremely capable.

John F. Kennedy didn't have a staff chief, at least not one I could ever identify. They ran the place like a country store. Lyndon Johnson was his own chief of staff and his own everything else. Nixon brought in Robert Haldeman and John Ehrlichman. Together they were a "Sherman Adams chief of staff." Neither one by himself was an Adams because Adams had it all, except foreign policy, but the two of them together had virtually all of it. For some reason, they did not want to confirm that publicly, maybe because they felt Eisenhower's military image was still around and unpopular. But together they ran a taut ship. Haldeman played it tough, which was exactly what the President wanted him to do. Now, could I have done that? No. It's not my background or instinct or training or disposition. I could have counseled about it more than I did perhaps, and George Shultz, for one, argued that I should stay there for that purpose. I told him no. I had been there over ten years, so now it was his turn.

Well, the simple fact is, I'm not trained as a chief of staff. I don't think I would have been good at it. I would have tried but probably blown it.

**MR. THOMPSON:** People would have trusted you, wouldn't they?

**MR. HARLOW:** Yes. They would have trusted me until I blew it. They might well have trusted me beyond that point. But what I wanted to do was to put in Melvin Laird, and I tried to do that. When they started sinking into their deepest troubles, members of the Cabinet were coming over to see me in my business office asking me to intervene with the President to save the deteriorating situation. That wasn't easy to do from my out-of-government location. The Cabinet was in a state of near mutiny against Bob and John. You mention the need for a chief; well, they were about to revolt. They said they wouldn't stand for any more arrogant behavior by Haldeman and Ehrlichman and being kept away from the President. As a matter of fact, George Bush, then party chairman, and I had a quiet meeting with them at the Alibi Club on Pennsylvania Avenue to pour cool water on them. Plainly they were breaking up and the administration was in critical trouble. At the White House, they were going through the "I can be tougher than you" syndrome. Plainly something was seriously wrong. This was a heady period after Nixon's landslide victory in 1972.

I thought the President could fix it all by putting someone in the top staff position who was big because he was big, not because he was in the job, someone who everybody in town liked and respected. Bob and John had accumulated a lot of Washington dislike. They were having a very hard time. Some of that is inevitable with jobs like that. I wanted to get the President to turn to Melvin Laird, not to do Bob and John in, but to let Mel run the place. Laird had great standing in Washington, great ability and forcefulness, and would have been a winner in that special situation. I couldn't suggest that to Nixon, however, without giving him, Haldeman and Ehrlichman the notion that I was trying to undercut Haldeman and Ehrlichman, which was not my objective at all. As a matter of fact, I was trying to save them from the inferno that was building against them. I just couldn't figure out a way to avoid that suspicion. I finally decided to talk with Tom Dewey, knowing the President thought the world of Dewey. I thought Dewey might agree to tell the President. The President would listen and know he was not trying to grind an axe. So I arranged to see Tom Dewey. He thereupon went to Florida and died. Right then. That knocked out my scheme, so I dropped it. But that was the kind of staff solution the President needed.

**MR. THOMPSON:** I sat behind Mel Laird's table the evening the American Enterprise Institute honored you, or you honored them. I couldn't help thinking about previous speakers' presentations on the Ford presidency and on how Ford was picked over Laird as minority leader in the Congress. As you look back, is there any chance that you overestimated Mel Laird and underestimated yourself?

**MR. HARLOW:** I honestly don't think so. I'm not trying to be professionally, deceptively modest; I'm trying to be dispassionately accurate. Melvin Laird is very talented at managing people. He is clever and a good leader of men. He's a strong influencer, a strong persuader, and tough. He's a hard worker. And he is smart as hell.

**MR. THOMPSON:** But he has more enemies than you do.

**MR. HARLOW:** Well, if you're a doer, you always have enemies. You can make yourself everyone's sweetheart by doing nothing forceful or controversial, and everybody will think you are at least acceptable. But if you push people around, which Mel would have done and a chief of staff has to do, you are not going to be universally loved. Mel has never minded the resentment of the right people. No, it should have been a Melvin Laird type, not a Bryce Harlow type. I'm too accommodating by nature, too responsive to people's desires, needs and feelings, too disposed to pay them too much attention and thereby waste time. For instance, I was ordered by the Nixon White House, the President and the apparatus, to be the one to dump Louis Hershey. He was one of my most admired friends. I had known him many years in the Army. I had to go to the distinguished old gentleman and tell him he was going to be forced out. I was expected to tell him that—that he was going to have to get out, and right now. I went over and said, "Lou, it wipes me out to tell you this, and you know it does, so don't feel sorry for yourself. Feel sorry for me for having to tell you. I feel worse than you do. Now, what are we going to do with you? What would you like to do? We've got to do something. I've got some suggestions." And I took care of his tomorrow. Well, that really fussed Haldeman. To him it showed an indecisiveness and lack of requisite toughness. Maybe he was right.

It was the same way with Murray Chotiner. He was supposed to be dumped as deputy chairman of the Republican National Committee. The head of the National Committee was to be a Maryland congressman, Rogers Morton, whom everybody loved. Rogers was to be chairman of the committee and our friend Murray told us confidentially that he would be number two. Well, he couldn't contain his enthusiasm and started acting like number one even before he was number two. He wore out his welcome before he had one. So by virtue of a mistake in judgment suddenly he was not suitable at all. John Mitchell telephoned me and told me to get somebody to fire him, get him out of the way and send him back to California to do something else. And I said, "What's he going to do?" He said, "Just tell him to get out." That's the way things were. Well, I went to Murray and we sat down and talked, and I did all kinds of things to take care of his future. He did fine. That didn't cost us anything but time. As a chief of staff, I wouldn't have had that time. Again Haldeman disapproved. So did Nixon and Mitchell.

It went the same way with about half a dozen others. I did the same thing. They came out in good shape and didn't feel so bad over their harsh treatment. Party chairman Ray Bliss was another one. I had to tell him to get out. I was very close to Bliss. That is why they picked me to plunge the sword. The news almost broke his heart. I suffered with him. I virtually forced the President to see him. I had Ray come to New York to the President's office. We sat him down and had Ray talk with the President for an hour. The President was as considerate as he could be. He offered Ray a choice of two ambassadorships, the Netherlands and Australia. He wouldn't take either one but he felt a lot better. The President explained why he was replacing him. He said, "Ray, it is not because of you, you know that. We have spent our lives together in politics. It is because we've got to get someone now who is a hardhitting partisan speaker, because we have the White House now. I can't do it. Someone's going to have to do it, and it is going to have to be the chairman of the National Committee, and that's not your way of doing business. You are not that kind of a chairman. You do nuts and bolts, put it together, and make it work. You've been great at that, but we now have to get someone who can drive home the issues, attack the Democrats, fight the problems, and that is not how you do business." I wasted the President's personal time being nice to Bliss. Or did I?

**MR. THOMPSON:** Lincoln wasted time that way too. May we ask just one last question. Do you think history will be kinder to Nixon than some writers are at the moment?

**MR. HARLOW:** Oh, sure they will be. One reason is because he is nothing nearly as bad as the conventional thought says he is. Another reason is that the country went through an orgy. It was a political orgy partly because it involved Republican Nixon, and partly because of White House history since 1932. It had to happen to a president in the 1960s or 1970s. The sins of the fathers visiting upon their sons is what did in the Nixon generation. The whole mess fell on Nixon, but the White House excesses started with Roosevelt. It had been endlessly building up until the White House was distorted and deformed. There had to be a reckoning. The White House had proven too powerful, too irresponsible, too independent, too self-satisfied and arrogant. It felt too big, it acted too big. It was dangerous. It had to be restrained and reformed. It should have happened earlier, and with a much more vulnerable administration like LBJ's. They escaped through political protection. Nixon couldn't escape because they had him surrounded by the combination of Congress and the press. One very important thing they did was to straighten up the White House, clear back to where the trouble started with Roosevelt. He spurned the imperial White House attitude and behavior in the 1930s but in the 1970s they put it on Nixon. That sort of thing, plus the Watergate incident, constituted the orgy. History will filter it out and return a perspective.

There's one interesting sideline to what happened. A luncheon meeting was held in Washington in 1972 at the Sans Souci Restaurant. At least two of the schemers are still in Washington, maybe all five. I used to know who the five were. Two of them, good friends of mine, are still there. They agreed they would destroy Richard Nixon and embarked upon a carefully considered program to do it. And, sure enough, they did it. It was butchery, beautifully done. I was told not to go back in the White House in 1973 by one of them. He asked me to dinner one evening, so we went to Duke Zeibert's, the Democratic hangout. Then my friend said, "Bryce, I wanted to tell you not to go back in the White House. I know you and Laird are under heavy pressure to go back. I know the President is after you; Haig is after you; everybody on Capitol Hill is after you. Everybody is trying to force you and Mel back there.

But, my friend, don't do it. I say that to you because I like you. Don't get in the way. We are going to destroy Nixon." Well, that's part of the history of all this. Historians someday will winnow it all out.

**MR. THOMPSON:** Is it too simple to say that whatever else, foreign policy will be Nixon's lasting memorial?

**MR. HARLOW:** I think probably it will be. But don't undersell him. He's got this enormous capability and talent. He could turn around and make his old position look like ethical behavior in the government. He is almost adroit enough to do it.

**MR. THOMPSON:** Thank you ever so much. We've stayed much longer than we should. We appreciate what you have done for the Miller Center.

# A BALANCE SHEET

## Maurice Stans

**NARRATOR:** Maurice Stans was educated at Northwestern and Columbia; he holds honorary degrees from Northwestern, Pomona College, De Paul, and other distinguished institutions. He was from the beginning a leader among certified public accountants; he has held offices in and received honors from the American Institute of Certified Public Accountants, the American Accounting Association, and the national organization of government accountants. He has received awards from the Tax Foundation and the U.S. Chamber of Commerce's Great Living Americans Award. He was twice chairman of the Republican National Finance Committee, and chairman of the Finance Committee to elect Richard Nixon and then to re-elect him. He then served as secretary of commerce in the Nixon administration. We are happy that Maurice Stans is with us this morning and that his gracious wife, Kathleen, is also with us. Welcome to the Miller Center.

**SECRETARY STANS:** Thank you very much, Ken. I think at the outset I should state very clearly the platform from which I'm speaking today. Although I met Richard Nixon when he was vice president and I was in the Post Office Department, I didn't know him very well then. But in 1962, when we were both living in California, I was finance chairman for his disastrous run at the governorship of California. From 1965 to 1968, however, when we had both moved to New York City, I saw him more frequently. When he had decided to run again for the presidency in 1968, I became, first, the chairman of his campaign committee and, later, the full-time finance chairman. In 1969 he named me secretary of commerce in his Cabinet, where I served for three years. In 1972 I resigned from that post, with some degree of unwillingness because I was enjoying the work, to become finance chairman for his re-election campaign. Because of that position, I soon became very closely entangled with all the aftermath of Watergate. In time I was fully absolved of any complicity in Watergate. After three years of being investigated on campaign finances, I was found not guilty of a single willful violation of any law. I was, however, held accountable for some technical, non-intentional infractions and I paid a personal fine for them, but the court specifically held that they were unwillful.

Those stressful experiences of that time did not color or alter my feelings toward Richard Nixon. My appraisal of him today is as objective as I can phrase it, and I will start with a summary of what I'm going to say about him:

—Richard Nixon was a man from a modest, near-poverty background, endowed with extraordinary ambition and energy and drive.

—He was an inherently timid man, uncomfortable in social settings yet dominant in political gatherings, and one of the most eloquent public speakers of his time.

—He was an introvert in a profession of extroverts, but learned to use that to his advantage. He was a warm and religious person under a cold-appearing shell.

—He was a person of broad vision seeking to innovate in major national and international events rather than merely respond to them.

—He was a man with a brilliant mind; a keen student in evaluating the pros and cons of a problem; decisive when he was satisfied with the facts before him; working at his job all the waking hours, probably the most hardworking President of this century.

—He was extraordinarily sensitive to criticism; impatient with opposition; profane under frustration; often bitter in defeat; and he was frantic over leaks.

—He was intolerant of mediocre performance in subordinates, but lacked the courage to exercise discipline over them; he was not given to frequent praise.

—He was highly disciplined in his personal life as evidenced by his very limited drinking, nonsmoking, regular exercise, and exemplary personal and family behavior.

—He was a pragmatist in politics and government; tenacious but not willing to fight windmills and did not feel himself bound by precedent in the presidency.

—He was an outstanding President in foreign affairs; constructive in domestic affairs but often blocked by political forces; and he had an overall record that would have rated him as one of the great Presidents had he finished his second term.

—His tragic downfall through Watergate was the result of excesses of loyalty, first, by his campaign staff who wanted him to win an overwhelming mandate in the 1972 election through a petty burglary unknown to him, and, second, by his endorsement of a cover-up to protect his staff and through them his re-election and his program for the nation—an excess of loyalty in two respects.

It may have been inevitable that in the early days of disclosure and recrimination for Watergate the public would lose sight of anything good about Richard Nixon. One cannot condone Watergate as a whole, but to be fair there are many things in the life and works of Richard Nixon that need to be brought back into the equation of judgment and evaluated carefully.

Let's look first at an overview of his career: his meteoric rise from his modest background; his perseverance in unveiling the treachery of Alger Hiss; his excellent and unflawed record as vice president for eight years under Eisenhower; his courage and perspicacity in fighting back after two election defeats; and above all his leadership as an international peace-maker. His success in opening long-closed barriers to understanding among the world's peoples may in the long run have saved millions of lives from the devastations of confrontation in war.

His foreign policy was imaginative and successful, and his work for world peace was historic. He ended the twenty-year Cold War by his personal initiatives. His breaking down of the curtains between the United States and the Communist nations of China and the Soviet Union set the stage for an ultimate understanding, even though postponed by intervening events. His mark on the domestic scene was less spectacular, but nevertheless worthy and notable. His first five years restored quiet to our cities and to campuses after a decade of violence and turmoil.

On the economic front he had only limited and uncertain accomplishments in his first term, and he found no way to cope with the worldwide inflation that followed the unprecedented rise in the prices of international commodities, especially oil, at the beginning of his second term.

He did succeed in many other domestic initiatives, and he achieved progress in reducing racial bias and improving the nation's health and stability. He kept up a steady flow of innovative proposals to Congress but unfortunately some of his ideas scarcely got off the ground in his first term. Had he served for eight years they might have fared much better.

Government reorganization, from the standpoint of reducing the burdens on the occupant of the White House by reducing the number of persons reporting to him, has a lot of merit. His plans may not have been the best conceivable but they offered a change that would have been worth trying. Reducing the size of the federal establishment and localizing government decisions is another goal that he urged; they got only a token start through partial adoption of his revenue sharing and grant-combining proposals.

He ended the military draft in favor of an all volunteer force, increased the proportion of the budget going to human resources, and removed the post office from political control for the first time in its history. He also gave support to federal mass transit financing, instituted a drive against organized crime, sponsored a tax reform bill that was enacted in 1969 with most of his proposals intact, and induced Congress to protect senior citizens against inflation by providing for automatic increases through indexing of social security benefits. Furthermore, he expanded unemployment insurance coverage, got Congress to enact a new Manpower Training Act, provided greatly enlarged funding for control of air pollution and water pollution, and sponsored a new Foreign Aid Act. Nixon made many proposals for consumer protection and occupational safety and created the Environmental Protection Agency. Not all of these were enacted on his terms, but the range of his initiatives is clearly evident.

A *Fortune* editorial in September 1970, only two years after he took office, conceded that: "Nixon has already presided over a massive reordering of national priorities. It has been a vigorous political leadership of which the President and the public have a right to be proud." That appraisal by *Fortune* does not stand alone because when his record was submitted to the American people at the end of four years, they not only re-elected him but did so by a one-sided vote that gave him sixty-one percent of the vote and forty-nine states.

Despite the fact that there were intimations of Watergate improprieties before the election, the public clearly wanted him to carry on his programs for the nation. They liked what he had done and approved what he proposed to do. Regrettably for history, fate blocked him from finishing the job.

Richard Nixon had all the attributes for a successful presidency, especially broad experiences, keen analytical ability, decisiveness, courage, and stamina. He was a man of ambition, high energy, clear goals, and dedication. He was one of the most adept and persuasive political speakers of his day. He could have been one of the great Presidents of this century.

Now, with all that generalization, let's look at him more closely, beginning with his response to two potential crises before he became President.

When Eisenhower was incapacitated twice by serious illnesses, Nixon conducted himself well and discreetly as acting head of the government, with dignity and without appearing either timid or presumptuous; he came out of both extremely well.

In the second case, he put the interests of the country ahead of his own ambitions and future when, after he lost the 1960 election by a hair-thin margin, he rejected the advice of many of his partisans to contest the ballot-counting in several close states that were notorious for vote frauds and where there was pretty good evidence that they occurred then. He knew that the leadership of the country would be handicapped and presidential actions would be in legal doubt while that kind of a controversy went on in the courts. He did not want to subject the nation and its orderly processes to that kind of turmoil—a highly creditable action by a man who could have fought the battle through at that time.

Now to the man himself. I don't believe any man could have been more determined to do the best possible job as President than Richard Nixon. He was trained for it through many years of service in the House of Representatives, in the Senate, and as vice president. He won his second attempt to gain the White House by a very close margin in 1968 without carrying either wing of the Congress for his party. Thus he was destined at the outset to be a minority President, with all the difficulties that can mean under our constitutional system of the separation of powers.

Nixon's dedication to his job made him probably the most disciplined man ever to head the government of the United States. He drank sparingly; he didn't smoke or gamble; he exercised daily; he displayed no interest in extramarital sex, something of a feat in itself among our Presidents; he stuck to a strict diet to control his weight; and above all he managed his work load better than most Presidents. He regulated the monstrous demands on his time so that he could keep his head above the grindstone and be able to find quiet to contemplate and develop major initiatives of national and international policy. Nixon did not want merely to respond to events, he wanted to anticipate them, to influence their direction and outcome, and in the process to create means that would reduce future problems.

He had some drawbacks. His early political struggles had given him an image of ruthlessness. He sometimes appeared ill at ease in formal situations. Because of that or because of an inherent social diffidence, he was considered a cold personality. President John Kennedy referred critically to his stodgy, graceless exterior. To me, he was an introvert doing his best to act like an extrovert, which was what his career demanded.

He had another disadvantage: without doubt his long history of contentious relations with the press contributed to the venom with which some of them attacked him. Liberals among them still resented his cornering of Alger Hiss. His 1962 "last press conference," as he called it, in California has never been forgiven because to the media it represented his inner feelings of disdain for them. Most of all there was a carry-over of negative media feelings from the trying period of the Vietnam War, of distrust that originated with Lyndon Johnson's presidency that carried over into Nixon's. In retrospect, it's likely that at no time in his career did Nixon really trust the media and they knew it and didn't trust him. All of this came back with a vengeance when he allowed himself to get off-base in Watergate and it pursued him relentlessly to the end. His failure to find the formula for an amicable working relationship sometime in his political life may have made impossible any hope of balanced reporting when he was finally caught in retreat.

The Nixon presidency was an intense one: hardworking, determined, wide-ranging, organized and creative. He was a man of action, knowing what he wanted to do in his job and certain he could override the obstacles he had to face. At the same time he was a modest man seeming to be somewhat awed by the circumstances of position and power that he had reached. This may account for the care and attention he generally gave to consideration of the details of his new ideas before he adopted them. He wanted to know in writing, fully thought-out by those who were knowledgeable, the various options on a new proposal and the pros and cons of each option, and he studied them carefully before deciding.

Like many brilliant minds, Nixon was not very tolerant of mediocrity. He was not demanding in an unreasonable way, as Lyndon Johnson was of his subordinates, but he did expect quality performance from those around him. He could be caustic about those who didn't deliver. Like Eisenhower, he did not often praise people face to face but he often remarked to others on a man's good performance. He searched out opportunities to increase the responsibilities and recognition of those he thought capable. He put a high value on loyalty and responded in kind to those who demonstrated loyalty to him. That was a key element in his actions in Watergate.

Like other Presidents before him, he was irate about leaks that inhibited the careful management of the government by premature disclosure of matters under consideration or under correction, or that disclosed information that he believed best served the nation by being kept confidential. The leaks that came out were accountable for his distrust of the bureaucracy, which he once said was "ninety-nine percent against us," and for much of his occasional profanity. He wanted interdepartmental differences of opinion worked out quietly, not in the press. Many times he expressed the belief that the press was strongly antagonistic to him and his administration. At times his words evidenced a kind of underdog mentality, a sketch of a man fighting to do the right thing as he saw it against odds unreasonably imposed to impede his progress.

He had an unlimited capacity for hard work, and was all business at all times with an average workday of sixteen hours if protocol events are included. He was competitive to a high degree, taking the challenges of the Congress or the media as calls to battle, demanding strategy that planned the game many moves ahead. He didn't like to lose and sometimes was bitter about losing.

Nixon did not react well to criticism although he usually tried to shrug it off. Like most strong-minded men who were confident of their goals, he perceived most criticism of his actions or proposals to reflect ignorance of his long-term aims and unreasonable distrust of his motives. Yet when differences of opinion were more softly phrased to him as suggestions to consider, he was quite willing to listen.

Despite his all-business attitude, Nixon could be mild-mannered and considerate of others. He spent time on phone calls and messages to friends on occasions of their birthdays and weddings or greetings in times of illness or hospitalization. He was generous in dividing his perquisites as President with his Cabinet officers and others associated with him in the administration. He allowed them to use the presidential facilities at Camp David, the Sequoia on the Potomac, the Western White House, and his box seats at the Kennedy Center.

When it came to subordinates who did not perform to his standards he was chickenhearted. He disliked firing or criticizing anybody as was demonstrated on a number of occasions, notably his confrontation with Interior Secretary Walter J. Hickle. He agonized over that.

He is a very religious man at heart. There is no other way to account for his active associations with top churchmen like Norman Vincent Peale or Billy Graham, or his holding regular Sunday religious services in the East Room of the White House whenever he was in Washington. Each service was conducted by a clergyman of high reputation, selected from among many different religions, accompanied by a choir from churches around the country. It would be hard to believe that Nixon had any motive other than spiritual in presiding over these events. It would stretch the imagination to believe that he was hypocritical in presenting them for any other purpose, considering the demands on his time.

In his campaigns, Nixon was especially diffident about contributions and contributors, then or later. He did not want to be present when solicitations were made, and he did not want to handle contributions. He did not like to speak at fundraising parties in his own behalf. He resented people who would thrust envelopes or hand checks to him during public or private affairs. During a campaign, he did not want to know who had given money to help and only after it was over would he briefly peruse and discuss the lists of contributors with me. He did not want contributions taken from anyone who felt he was entitled to something in return. He specifically named certain people in advance from whom I was not to accept any money because he suspected their motives. He was willing to consider later, after the election, the appointment of contributors to government services on the basis of qualifications but not as a matter of commitment. As finance chairman, I was not allowed to make any commitments.

There is one more thing that I think expresses his character and feeling. In the 1968 campaign Nixon had promised to help black capitalism, and right after he took office he named me chairman of a Cabinet committee to develop a plan. Within a month the committee had approved my proposals to create in the Department of Commerce an Office of Minority Business Enterprise, and he signed an executive order giving authority to create that office and initiate a program. There was urgency in his command and at the same time a sense of reality. "Both morally and economically," he said publicly, "we will not realize the full potential of our nation until neither race nor nationality is any longer an obstacle to full participation in the American marketplace." Privately he said this to me: "Maury, this is something long overdue and I want you to give it a high priority. Politically there aren't any votes in it for us, but we'll do it because it's right." To me, that signifies a man of deep compassion and consideration for which he has never been given proper credit.

How then do I account for his Watergate? Here's my analysis after a great deal of thought and living on the fringes of it. Richard Nixon came from a family of limited means. He is a shy person and even in his greatest moments never overcame that inherent shyness. It is entirely usual that he would have determined from youth to try to make a mark of some kind in life. That picture of a young man struggling up from poverty all the way to the presidency is an uncomplex one and does not require the psychological analyses to which he has been subjected by some writers. He was an ambitious, capable American living the great dream, working hard all the way. When Nixon ran for the presidency in 1968 he was the best trained man the country had ever found for the job with his two terms as vice president, and his "acting" presidency during Eisenhower's serious illnesses; and he had been in the tough world of business for eight years with an opportunity realized by very few high-level politicians and only a few previous Presidents to see firsthand how the nation's productive wheels turn.

There can be no doubt that in all those experiences a man of his analytical capacity would have been accumulating ideas as to what the country needed for the long-term future and what the world of nations needed. These ideas could easily be translated into what he would do if he were President, something he could have been thinking about all along, perhaps not as a program in numbered paragraphs but certainly as a partly conscious, partly subconscious catalog of plans that he would draw upon. There is no doubt in my mind that on January 20, 1969 as he took the oath of office, Richard Nixon had such a concept of his forthcoming job, and that he wanted, through the powers of his office, to improve life in the country and in the world. He knew it would be difficult. His Republican party was in the minority in both houses of Congress, which meant that he could expect an item by item struggle to get legislation enacted, and that's exactly what happened. Some of his proposals were badly abused, some not enacted at all, some twisted into shapes he couldn't accept. There was a running fight and he lost many bitter encounters on partisan grounds.

Frustrated by some of those developments in his first few years in the White House, including the defeat of his proposals for welfare reform, government reorganization, and blocked grants for welfare and education, it was inevitable that he contemplated a new election coming up in 1972 with some hope of relief. If he could win big, his position would be different. His entire organization caught that mood of the necessity of winning big, so big that he would have a mandate for the next four years that the Congress could not ignore. With a smashing victory would come more Republicans into both houses of the Congress to give power to his plans. It was not a question of just winning, it had to be a matter of winning by the biggest margin in history. That goal was to corral every conceivable vote, every conceivable percentage point, and that's the way the election campaign of 1972 was run. As its finance chairman, I saw it in the overkill, the overkill of repeated television, radio, direct mail, telephone, and person-to-person appeals. Under the circumstances, no expense was considered by his aides to be too great. Even if the incremental return from spending another million dollars was only a possible 100,000 unneeded votes, the money was spent. That's why the 1972 campaign cost fifty-six million dollars, a massive increase over the previous high of about thirty-five million.

Within that environment of eagerness, his campaign staff decided, without his knowledge, that some benefit might be gained if the moves of the opposition could be anticipated, perhaps by bugging their phones or reading their files or putting informers into their organization. Similar tactics had been used before by both parties. That was the genesis of Watergate.

Nixon was not a party to the Watergate break-in; he didn't know about it in advance. That has been established. There is no evidence to the contrary. Why then did he allow himself to be involved, first passively and then actively, in the cover-up? Why did he not insist on immediate disclosure in June 1972? I can't be sure how carefully he made that decision, or what his calculations were. It seems to have been hasty and without much initial thought. In the first instance there was the matter of protecting his loyal people. I think the case can be made for his believing that in preventing the facts of Watergate from being known (and with that the plumbers' operation), he was trying to insure not only his re-election but that his programs for the nation would have the greatest possible chance for success, which would not have been likely if the mandate he hoped to obtain and did obtain on November 7 was severely marred or even lost by these disclosures of impropriety in his organization. In that manner he could reason that since he was not covering up acts of his own, the national benefits of the cover-up far outweighed the normal objections of conscience. To him, on the political battlefield, the end justified the means.

That line of thought would not be unlikely in a man so totally dedicated to the mission and so sure of his course. Then when the propped-up structure began to collapse and the culprits, one by one, began to walk out, the frustration at the top was unbearable. The thrashing around for something to grab on to for survival generated the brusque profanity on the inside and equivocation and mistruth on the outside. The oppressive struggle with a problem that wouldn't be solved drove him to desperation and his greatest mistakes. Suddenly it was a hopeless cover-up that stumbled on erratically until it eventually fell apart in all directions. Desperate firings and hirings, speeches, press conferences, and counterposed leaks served little purpose to stem the tide once the dam was broken. Confronted with a long impeachment trial that would seriously divide and injure the nation, he chose to resign.

None of this excuses the actions but it does rationalize them in a way one can understand. It seems true now that Nixon did no worse than two or three of his predecessors in using power in his own way to safeguard his administration and harass his enemies. While the precedents set by others in office before him may not excuse some of Nixon's actions, they certainly do make his actions easier to comprehend and they do raise the question of whether he was not grossly overmaligned and grossly overpunished for them.

What about the tapes which seemed to indict him in his own words? The expletives, I think, can be dismissed, not because they are in any sense proper, but because they can be condoned under the pressures of the office and the situation. Dwight Eisenhower could be just as caustically profane as Richard Nixon. I heard him many times. Lyndon Johnson was noted for vulgar expressions and I doubt that Harry Truman or John Kennedy were any more pious under the stress of tough decisions and unnerving frustrations. But this is important, I believe: only a tiny fraction of the tapes, one percent, has been made public. Who knows what genius, what generosity by Nixon may be contained in those that have not been made public? Again, time and events may bring about a much more favorable balance of the evidence.

In conclusion, it's easy now to forget the political and social climate that Nixon inherited and which he significantly turned around in his first term. It has become commonplace for observers to write off this whole web of Watergate as proof of Lord Acton's famous axiom that power tends to corrupt and absolute power corrupts absolutely. Anyone who challenges the application of that rule here may be in the minority, as I am, but I don't see it as appropriate.

Watergate happened at the top because Richard Nixon was an ambitious man who wanted power, not to accumulate personal gain or wealth, but to serve his country better. It happened in the concentric circles near him because those persons who were loyal to his mission, in their overeagerness to help attain it, went too far across the line. No one sought to gain wealth for himself—not a Magruder or a Mitchell or any of the others. They were evidencing their dedication to a cause and the intensity of that dedication led them astray. It had happened in earlier administrations, sometimes with similar motives, sometimes with more mercenary objectives. But then the standards of integrity were less strictly enforced and the powers of the media were less developed. Nixon was a generation too late. In an earlier decade he would have escaped his fate.

It may take quite a few additional decades for the historians to bring together the total record of Richard Nixon and evaluate without bias the pluses and the minuses among the elements of his career. When that's done it is likely that he will stand out on balance as one of the most farseeing and capable Presidents of this century. That trend is already becoming evident.

**QUESTION:** In the book by Alexander Haig it said that he often assumed the duties of President when Kissinger was out of town and when Nixon was drunk. That isn't compatible with what you said about him. Is there any truth in that?

**SECRETARY STANS:** I can't believe that. I've seen Nixon on a number of informal social occasions where it would have been very easy for him, as for other Presidents, to take three or four drinks, but his habit was almost universal to take one and carry it around all evening or as long as other people were drinking. I don't believe that he drank in office despite all the pressures on him. I've never seen any sign of it and many of my friends who were in the administration say the same thing. Haig may have seen him on one occasion or another when for some reason he seemed not responsive, but I didn't.

**QUESTION:** It has been said that one of the curses of our current civilization is a double standard of morality in which it is all right to cheat government but not to cheat one's friends, that a person who would never cheat at poker doesn't hesitate to cut corners on his income tax or at customs. Do you think that that double standard of morality affected Mr. Nixon's position when he placed loyalty to his friends over other considerations?

**SECRETARY STANS:** I don't believe that is quite the way I would put it. Nixon believed that he had a right to follow precedent in his job and he knew about many of the things that had been done under the Kennedy administration and under other presidents who used taping and the Internal Revenue Service and the FBI to investigate friends and enemies. He had a pretty good knowledge of how the game was played and he just assumed that he could play the game the same way. So far as I know he used the Internal Revenue Service very little compared with some of the other Presidents. But it was commonly understood that this is the way the presidency is conducted.

**QUESTION:** I wonder if you've thought at all about a Nixon presidency without Watergate. What might have happened in the second term with relations between the President and Congress, the plans that he had and so forth?

**SECRETARY STANS:** That's very interesting to contemplate. I've thought about my own situation and his and a lot of others. I've thought a number of times that someone ought to write a book on Nixon without Watergate. It would be fascinating. Think of what could have been accomplished with the Soviets and the Chinese without a mid-term change in the presidency. As you know, Khrushchev tried to treat Kennedy as a schoolboy and abused him at Vienna. Other Presidents have tried to move into the relationships that Nixon established but they never succeeded as he did, at least not so far.

Nixon's book, *The Real Peace*, concisely expresses the philosophy of how we have to operate to live in the world with the Soviet philosophy. I don't think there has been at any time since his day a person who was as knowledgeable on foreign affairs, who was as realistic about it, and who had a concept of how we could deal with the problems and live in today's world.

I'm sure there would have been some changes in the form of the government in his second term. Nixon believed that there were just too many people reporting to the President, and that if the government were run as a business organization it would follow the principle that the man at the top has no more than five, six or seven people reporting to him and all others going through them and that decisions have to be thrashed out within the organization, quietly, without coming to the top man except in major cases. I think his plan for solving the welfare problem probably would have been enacted. His plans for creating a greater degree of financial independence within the states would have been a very attractive means of reducing the size of the bureaucracy in Washington. All of those things were part of the great dreams that he never got to carry out. One can very easily visualize the country operating on a different scale and much more successfully than it is operated now with the massive budget deficits and the other problems that are so demanding of the President's time.

**QUESTION:** Would you evaluate the Agnew situation because that was not a part of Watergate?

**SECRETARY STANS:** The Agnew situation was again a case of his living according to the standards of the time and the place. Maryland was a state in which a degree of free handling of money existed in politics, and the contributions made by contractors and others were almost automatic. They went into the coffers of the party. They really weren't considered by the people who participated to be bribes or anything like that; they were considered to be contributions to maintain positions for everybody, and Agnew was caught in that system.

With Agnew in that position, there was no way Nixon could defend him. It's pretty clear to me from the circumstances that existed at the time that when Agnew resigned, John Connally would have been named vice president. They worked very closely; Nixon had high respect for Connally and his ability, his political acumen and so forth. But John Connally had a little problem also. He was under criticism, under investigation, for having received an illegal contribution from the Milk Producers Association—ten thousand dollars. Because of that circumstance Nixon had to look elsewhere because there was no way of knowing, of course, exactly how the Connally matter was going to come out.

If you want an education in politics go through the Freedom of Information Act and get the papers of the Watergate special prosecutor's staff people on the John Connally prosecution because they will show you how far afield their conclusions went in trying to get a basis for "hanging" John Connally. Their report says in perfectly clear words that "we are going to have trouble with this case because we only have one witness of substance and he's under indictment in Texas on eight counts of stealing money from a Savings and Loan Association. It's going to be hard to convince a jury that a man of John Connally's wealth and background would be found taking a bribe of $10,000. Besides the guy that paid it to Connally went and got $15,000 to give to him and can't account for the other five." A number of things like that made it such a specious situation that it's one of the tragedies of Watergate. He was one of the innocent victims and he might have been President if that Milk Producers matter hadn't been raised.

**QUESTION:** I've often heard it said that the efforts of Mr. Nixon to cover up was really the basic cause of why the country turned against him. Would you comment or speculate on what might have occurred had utter candor been applied rather than a cover-up? Would this have been a palliative or was the hostility of the fourth estate, the press, such that they would have continued their campaign to get him?

**SECRETARY STANS:** It can only be speculation, of course. The antagonism of the press was so great, particularly in the one that led the fight against Nixon, the *Washington Post*, that once there was any kind of a breakthrough or even any minor indication that this was a significant matter for the public, there would have been no way of holding it down. The degree of candor that he would have had to use in telling the story would have had to involve—not necessarily himself because he had no part in the break-in—exposing a number of people. It's inconceivable that those people would not have been heavily investigated, or that the matter would not have been pursued to a very deep degree. I find it rather hard to believe that there was anything he could have done or said at that time that would have quieted the whole situation.

**QUESTION:** Mr. Secretary, do you have any thoughts about how more use can be made of the former Presidents in the foreign policy field? A lot of people feel now that we don't have any long-term body developing foreign policy and that there is a big dispute always going on between the National Security Council and the administration and the State Department. Some people say maybe some body, despite all the political difficulties, could be set up to make more use of these people and their valuable experience and also give us perhaps a more consistent long-term foreign policy. Ours tends to vacillate whereas Mr. Gromyko was responsible for Soviet foreign policy for many years.

**SECRETARY STANS:** That's one of the great weaknesses of the democratic process of the United States. Gromyko has been in office through, I would guess, eight or ten secretaries of state and probably an almost equal number of presidential advisers on foreign policy, and a similar number of our representatives to the United Nations. He has a consistent policy and he is backed up by his government on anything he says. We vacillate from one President to another.

I had an interesting experience on my trip to Moscow in November, 1971. I went over there six months ahead of Nixon to work on the economic issues with the Soviets, including the settlement of the Lend Lease debt. It was a very successful mission. One of the principal men I dealt with was the minister of foreign trade, Nicolai Patolichev, and at one of our meetings he said, "I don't see how you can run the government in the United States the way you do with all that turnover. I've been minister of foreign trade for ten years; in that period of time you've had six secretaries of commerce," and he said, "They don't sing off the same sheet of music at all." The irony of that is that in the eleven years since then Patolichev still holds the job and we've had another six secretaries of commerce in the United States. That's a parade of twelve men on our side against one on the other side. Now that's one of the elements of strength in the Soviet government: they are consistent. They are a unity, and they are long-lasting.

**QUESTION:** Mr. Secretary, you made a rather interesting statement when you referred to President Nixon's business background. It possibly had to come between the vice presidential role and his presidential role. Could you expand on that background?

**SECRETARY STANS:** After he lost the election in 1960 by 100,000 votes or so to Kennedy, he did go into the business world. He was on various boards of directors and was consultant to a number of them, the most notable of which was Pepsico. He traveled the world for Pepsico and other interests. In his law practice he got to know a number of corporations in the country, saw how the game was played, what the problems of business were and understood the relationship of business to government perhaps better than any President. Certainly better than Roosevelt, better than Truman, whose business relationship ended with a haberdashery shop in Kansas City, Jack Kennedy and Lyndon Johnson. You can go down the list, and you'll have to go all the way back to Herbert Hoover to find a businessman in government. It gave Nixon a perception of what to expect from business when he proposed something and how to deal with business when there were differences of opinion, and I think that was very valuable to him and to the country.

**QUESTION:** Mr. Secretary, do you think that President Nixon should have been pardoned and do you think that there was any deal cut between President Nixon and President Ford?

**SECRETARY STANS:** That's a subject, of course, that will be considered and debated for a long time. Certainly it was one way of restoring government to the United States because any kind of an impeachment proceeding would have had blaring headlines for another year or longer and would have tied the hands of the Congress and the presidency in accomplishing anything. It would have overwhelmed the processes of government. The pardon was a perfectly logical and proper thing.

As for the second part of your questions, I don't think that there was any kind of a deal. I don't believe it; I don't think Jerry Ford is that kind of a man. I'm sure he knew from the day he was sworn in that he had that as an option and considered it, but I don't believe that he lied when he said there was no conversation or understanding and that it was just a selection of one of the options that he had to make his job easier and quiet the country.

**QUESTION:** Do you see any irony in the fact that President Nixon made a professional career of being anti-communist and then made such a tremendous turn? Do you see a tie-in between the recognition of the People's Republic of China and the huge grain deal to Russia as an attempt to end the war in Vietnam?

**SECRETARY STANS:** Of course. Nixon, being a rational man, realized that the world couldn't go on forever with the constant threat of war between the United States and the communist powers and that the conflict had to be dealt with in some way.

His concept was a détente, as he calls it, a hardheaded détente where we dealt from strength, where we did not unilaterally give ground but nevertheless worked upon the necessities of the other nations to take care of their standard of living and their people and their unwillingness to engage in warfare, and find a way to develop common ground that would allow communism to exist where people wanted it, not where it was imposed, and allow our type of democracy to exist in the world without interference from communism. So he shifted from being a total antagonist of the communist nations to one who sought an accommodation in the best interest of all sides and bring about an uneasy but peaceful understanding that could grow into a time in history when the peoples of the world would get along with each other.

**NARRATOR:** One of the things that is said about all Presidents is that they have their mafia and Nixon is always said to have had Haldeman and Ehrlichman. But the quality of some of his appointments and the known independence of people came up when he said the other night that he knew somebody would leak the episode of the prayer in the Lincoln Room. So he picked Kissinger, not because he knew Kissinger would defend him; he picked him because of his ability. There were a number of Cabinet appointments of other strong people. But what did he think of his subordinates? Did he expect absolute loyalty? Did he prefer people he had known or did he go far afield to get as much talent as he could?

**SECRETARY STANS:** He went far afield to get all the talent he could and he sought advice from a lot of people as to who might work in his government. He had two standards: one was the quality of the man, including ability and all the other characteristics; the other was loyalty. He couldn't see running a government unless he had total loyalty of everybody—to him and to his programs. That didn't mean that he would throttle anyone with another point of view but he wanted it presented through channels for consideration, and in that sense he had an organization that I think was of very high quality. Haldeman and Ehrlichman have been maligned. They were, of course, found guilty in Watergate so it's hard for people to understand how well they did their jobs, but they were excellent, religious people and the thought of knowingly doing anything illegal was anathema to them. They were the kind of people that we could all respect.

When you look at the broad sweep of the Nixon government there is one statement I think I can make with impunity and that is that there was not in the Nixon administration up to Watergate the measure of scandal that had existed in previous or subsequent administrations. Go back and think of the Billy Sol Estes and Harry Vaughan and other situations; there was none of that in the Nixon administration. You have to go pretty far down the line to find any evidence of impropriety; what there was was very small in scope. He did have people of integrity, by and large, throughout the whole government, people of ability and people who were loyal to him.

**NARRATOR:** I'm sure I speak for all of you in thanking Secretary Stans. He's come here at his own expense to share thoughts and ideas with us. He has had, as a private citizen, a continuing interest in civic efforts and in the field of public affairs. He has supported a museum to the south of us and assisted other centers of culture and civic affairs. He continues to play a role in American society that does him credit and we thank him for his contribution to our inquiry.

# THE PARADOX

## Elliot L. Richardson

**NARRATOR:** Perhaps a one sentence introduction is to say that Elliot Richardson, over recent decades, has continued the great tradition of Robert Lovett, Henry Stimson, Clark Clifford and that handful of Americans who contributed selflessly and with imagination to the tasks of American government in critical periods in our history. He has been secretary of defense, secretary of HEW, secretary of commerce, and undersecretary of state. He was lieutenant governor and attorney general of the State of Massachusetts. He served as law clerk to Learned Hand and Supreme Court Justice Felix Frankfurter. His military career was one of honor and distinction with several combat awards. He has published in the fields of law and government. He has been concerned in a long-term and effective way with the law of the seas. He is a member of one of the nation's most respected law firms and must indeed feel some division of responsibility between his duties and tasks in that firm and the responsibilities he has assumed in the field of public affairs. It's a great privilege to have Elliot Richardson with us and to continue our series of portraits of presidents with a discussion of the Nixon presidency.

**MR. RICHARDSON:** Thank you very much, Professor Thompson. I appreciate those very generous and flattering words of introduction, particularly your bracketing me with individuals whom I so much respect. But I must, with appropriate self-awareness, disclaim the use of the word "selflessly." I so much enjoyed public service that, had I the resources, I would have been quite willing to pay for the opportunity to hold some of the jobs I've had.

At any rate, since I'm now practicing law and trying to get myself reaccustomed to thinking in terms of legal procedures, it occurs to me that an appropriate first step is to qualify myself as a witness on the subject on which I have been asked to testify this morning. I first came to know Richard Nixon, although then only superficially and tangentially, during his vice presidency in the Eisenhower second term. At that time I was assistant secretary of health, education and welfare for legislation, and in that capacity attended a number of legislative leaders, meetings with the President and vice president. I was acting secretary of HEW from time to time and saw Nixon at Cabinet meetings. Then, when he was running in 1960 for the presidency against Jack Kennedy, he enlisted me as a member of his so-called "Kitchen Cabinet," which began to meet from time to time in the spring and summer of 1960. But at that time I was United States attorney for the district of Massachusetts and I discovered after a while that United States attorneys were under the Hatch Act. Since I didn't want to resign as U.S. attorney, I had to get off the Nixon committee. I came into his administration in 1969 and served under him in four jobs: deputy secretary of state, secretary of HEW, secretary of defense, and attorney general. I turned in my resignation as attorney general in October 1973—not quite ten years ago.

Having said all that in qualification of myself as a witness, I'll now have to say something in qualification of the qualification. I have read nothing about the Nixon administration to speak of, none of the Watergate books, for example, and I have a very bad memory. I not only have a bad memory in the sense that I forget things but a fallible memory in the sense that I often remember them wrong. So, whatever I say needs to be understood both from the perspective that I have at least occupied vantage points that should have given me useful insights into the Nixon presidency, but with the awareness that what I remember about it 'ain't' necessarily so.

The most comprehensive single statement to which I could attest with conviction is that Nixon had within his reach to be the most successful postwar President, at least up through the period for which he was elected. I think it's fair to say—having had glimpses of his successors up through and including the present—he had it within his reach, because to a greater degree than the other Presidents in that period he had what I would call a strategic sense toward the opportunities of the office. He saw very clearly that the United States was at a stage when the most significant contribution by a President would be adaptation to the then current and prospectively foreseeable realities. He saw that we had emerged from a period in which domestic politics were dominated by conflict over the revolutionary, or at least massive, changes brought about by the New Deal, and that we were at a stage of broad-based national consensus with respect to the general obligations of government toward the welfare of the American people. There were, or seemed to be at the time, no significant fundamental issues on that score. The only remaining problems were problems of means and process, but not of the basic proposition that the government has a responsibility toward people in those situations where they cannot meet or deal with their own problems.

Globally, Nixon saw with equal clarity that the United States needed to adapt itself, and quite rapidly, to the end of the era in which our margin of military and economic superiority was so great that we could afford to neglect the careful delineation of U.S. interests, the farsighted shaping of contingency plans, and the husbanding of U.S. resources for the advancement and protection of U.S. interests. To a degree that I think has not yet adequately been perceived, Nixon moved in the first four years of his presidency a long way toward bringing about that adaptation. Foreign policy was, of course, his paramount and almost obsessive interest.

Perhaps a second general point to be made about his presidency is that he was driven by the perception that it was within his grasp to achieve greatness. Nixon, in my view, never ceased to be the boy brought up in a genteel but pinching poverty, whose family, at least as I visualize it, strove to keep up appearances despite illnesses and other drains on family resources. I think that Nixon's life was in large measure the product of a determination not so much to get even as to establish some margin of superiority over the kinds of contemporaries who looked down on him somewhat because of that period in his life.

I think this accounted for the fact that his ambitions as President were in the end brought to a tragic demise as the result of the same tragic flaw that grew out of this early experience. He somehow could not bring himself to overcome the perception of opponents as enemies. I had never had a really close personal relationship with him, but when he asked me to become attorney general there was a moment when I thought that his need for me had created a bond of a kind that had never existed between us before then. In a conversation at Camp David on April 1, 1973, after agreeing to do it, I said, "Mr. President, there's one thing I've been wanting to say to you for a long time, and it is that I wish somehow deep down inside yourself you could come to believe that you have really won. You won not only the election of 1968 but reelection in 1972 by an overwhelming margin. The American people are rooting for you to succeed. Even your former opponents have a deeper feeling toward the well-being of the United States than a sense of resentment or enmity arising out of past political conflict. If you could only bring yourself to reach out with magnanimity toward your former opponents, you would thereby establish a foundation of support that nothing could overcome." He looked at me, but he said nothing, nothing that I can remember. I don't think he really got it.

I didn't know until later, when the revelations of Watergate emerged and when some of the tapes were made public, the depth of his cynicism or the degree to which suspicion and vindictiveness were deep-rooted elements of his character. I didn't know, as many others who associated with him didn't, partly because I didn't want to know; we tended to rationalize away the glimpses we saw of this ugly side of his character. But it was also that he was on his good behavior with us. He was certainly always on his good behavior with me. So it's a little like—this is a somewhat clumsy image, but it's the only one I can think of to convey what I'm trying to say—picking up a stone with a streak of quartz in it. You can't tell from looking at the surface of the stone whether that streak narrows down below the surface or widens out. The unpleasant side of Nixon was visible in the sense that the streak of quartz is visible. What those of us associated with him didn't know then was that it widened out below the surface. In any case, it's hard to imagine a presidency that so nearly fits the elements of the classic Greek tragedy, the hero brought down by his *hamartia,* his tragic flaw. Of course the tragedy is greater to the extent that the hero's potential for achievement and leadership is great.

My first job in the Nixon administration was deputy secretary of state. In that job I attended all National Security Council meetings and, of course, some Cabinet meetings as acting secretary of state. I can attest, without any equivocation at all, that Nixon was *the* architect of the Nixon foreign policy. I said earlier that he had a sense of strategy, and by that I mean that he kept steadily in view a large-scale map of the terrain in which he was operating. He could see individual moves and their relationship to his overall objectives. I was enormously impressed early on by his decision—and it was his own idea—to go to Bucharest on his European trip. He could thereby signal to the Soviet Union and the Eastern bloc that the United States was going to take advantage of opportunities to reestablish a degree of normalcy in East-West relations. He could recognize through his visit the relative independence of Ceausescu and Romania in the conduct of its external relations—it was by far the most independent of the Eastern bloc states from Soviet foreign policy dictation—and, at the same time, lay a foundation that could later be used in moving toward his opening to China. I have personal evidence in the same period that he was interested in moving toward China because, as a result of discussions with my own staff, I sent him a memorandum suggesting four things that could be done if we wanted to send a signal to China that we were serious about normalizing our relationship. I got back the original memorandum with Nixon's handwriting on it and his initials saying, in effect, go ahead on this and this, take tentative steps toward the third suggestion and hold back on the fourth. This was in March or April of 1969. Nixon was a very astute political tactician and I think it's important to stress the fact that you can't be a good strategist in foreign policy without being a good politician.

I think I probably ought to close with this thought to allow maximum opportunity for questions and discussion. One of the ironies of the Nixon adminstration was the fate of John Mitchell. John Mitchell, as you recall, was a law partner of Nixon's in New York, and Nixon drafted him as the chairman of his national campaign in 1968. I can't prove this, but my version is that he wanted Mitchell because Mitchell was a sensible, respectable man and because there would be no question of Mitchell's asserting his own independent judgment on any important aspects of the campaign; it would be clear between Mitchell and himself and indeed other key people that Nixon was the real campaign manager.

It took very cool judgment, the kind of judgment that Nixon, for better or worse, made later on in connection with some of the critical stages of the disengagement from Vietnam, and in not trying to capitalize in the short term after the Democratic convention in Chicago in 1968 with the reaction against Democrats generated by the demonstrations. There was a sharp surge, if any of you recall the polls, away from Humphrey at that moment and a corresponding temptation, therefore, for the Nixon campaign to move to the left and try to consolidate that potential support. The Nixon campaign did not do that. Many people were critical of its failure to do so. But as it turned out, of course, that reaction ebbed, and the election became a very close one with the vote dividing more or less along traditional Republican-Democratic lines and with the independents splitting. But the refusal to move to the left made it possible for Nixon to win a combination of basically conservative southern border and mountain states, which were critical to the electoral vote majority and which he could well have lost had the temptation to move to the left been seized in August and September. I don't know it for a fact, but I'm certain that this was a Nixon judgment. It's characteristic of him.

The irony that I alluded to was that Mitchell then took office as attorney general of the United States with a reputation as a political mastermind. My own view is that he was a political ignoramus whose only recourse in the circumstances was either to confess that he was no mastermind or to do what he did do, which was to keep his mouth shut, puff on his pipe, listen to the argument until the last possible moment, and then deliver himself of some sententious and pithy observation and get out of the room. I saw him do this many times.

All of this, I'm convinced, explains what happened when those characters from the CIA who had been from time to time employed by Chuck Colson on various nefarious errands came to see Colson in the 1972 campaign and said, "Chuck, old buddy, you know we've had a lot of intelligence gathering experience, and we're sure that your campaign needs capable intelligence operatives. Why don't you pick up the phone and call your friend John Mitchell and tell him he ought to hire us?" So Colson, lacking any good reason to the contrary right off the bat, picked up the phone and said, "John, I've got these great guys here, Hunt, Liddy, and so on. You'd better talk to them because they could be very useful to you." So they go over and see Mitchell and present a $700,000 plan for intelligence gathering. Mitchell doesn't know whether or not national campaigns normally spend that kind of money on intelligence gathering, and his only immediate recourse is to say, "Well, um, that sounds a little rich, $700,000, I mean, couldn't you maybe go back and see if you could scale that down some?" So they say, "Ok, we'll bring you a scaled down proposal." They send in the scaled down proposal a little while later, but nobody calls back, and so they go to Colson and they say, "Chuck, we're being stonewalled across the street. CREEP won't give us the time of day. Mitchell asked for a scaled down plan, we gave it to him, but he won't return our calls." Colson picks up the phone again and said, "John, you've got to see these guys. What are you trying to do?" So they come in the second time. The plan now costs $250,000 or something like that, and Mitchell can't think of any good reason to stall any more. He says, "Well, why don't you go ahead and just stay in touch with Jeb Magruder here. Anything that comes up, just talk to Jeb."

I'm not sure if that's the way it happened, but that's the way I think it happened. I think it happened that way because Nixon was his own political strategist in 1968 and thereby contributed to creating an inflated political reputation for Mitchell which, in turn, led to the creation of the monster that brought him down.

Well, that's perhaps as good a place to stop as any. I'd be glad to react to any questions or comments any of you have.

**QUESTION:** One of Mr. Nixon's biographers is rather hard on him for his foreign policy and particularly in his allegation that in the early seventies the Nixon administration failed to play its European card. I wonder if, in fact, there was an opportunity to play the European card and I would appreciate your comments on that.

**MR. RICHARDSON:** Well, I can't really comment because I'm not sure what he means by "playing the European card."

**COMMENT:** I got the impression that he thought that somehow the Nixon administration could have encouraged the Atlantic Alliance partners to assume a greater share of the defense management and perhaps even to move closer to a form of European cooperation, almost on the Gaullist conception of a middle level partnership.

**MR. RICHARDSON:** The Nixon administration never wavered in the consistency with which it advocated greater European unity and increased initiative. This had been a consistent U.S. position from the era of Schuman and the Coal and Steel Community down through the Treaty of Rome. I'm not aware of any flagging in this, nor am I aware of any missed opportunity to have promoted a greater degree of unity or autonomy. But it was explicitly understood within the Nixon administration and by Nixon himself that the initiative, unity and autonomy that we were encouraging would have as a corollary and price the creation of a Europe that would be in significant respects harder for the U.S. to handle than a more fragmented Europe and that a consequence would be the risk, as in the case of de Gaulle, that there would arise situations of friction or strain.

**QUESTION:** How would you explain the fact, to go back to the core of this character analysis, that someone who seemingly was as anxious as Nixon did what anxious people often are unable to do, namely pick strong people like yourself, Kissinger, and others?

**MR. RICHARDSON:** I don't think we want to get diverted into a discussion of the implications of the term "anxious." I don't think I would have used that word. I think he was, in significant respects, insecure and tense. This insecurity in turn created an insatiable need to impress himself on the world and to receive the feedback that goes with power, prestige and so on. But he was intellectually self-confident enough to be sure that he could learn enough about any substantive issue, hold his own on it and do so effectively, and that he could manipulate people and situations to his own ends even though the actors were people of some independent strength. I don't see any real contradiction between the drives that derived from his insecurity on the one side and his manifestation of those drives in the creation of as effective a combination of people as he could put together.

His manipulative characteristics are things that historians will have to recreate. I have a lot of data that isn't accessible now. I was a victim of his manipulative tendencies in the week leading up to the so-called "Saturday Night Massacre" to a degree that I didn't even realize until months after it was all over. But it was clear, after reconstructing what had happened, that his and Haig's objective had, from the beginning of their first contact with me about the verification of the tapes, been to precipitate a situation that would get rid of Archibald Cox on terms that I would then rationalize to the public. I played the game from the beginning of the week on the simpleminded assumption that they really wanted a compromise with Cox that would, on the one side, make the relevant portions of the tapes available and, on the other, protect any genuine concerns with national security. He certainly was manipulative.

It's hard, I might add as a parenthetical observation, to be successfully manipulative in a situation where you are dealing with a whole lot of people who talk with each other and take notes. The result, in turn, is that there is a lot less intrigue and a lot less scheming in Washington than most observers, particularly press observers, believe.

Do you mind a further aside on this? I was riding on a plane in November, 1980 (I think it was the shuttle from

New York) and I found myself sitting next to a political reporter from one of the networks. We were talking about power in Washington. I said, "You know, you really ought to take a second look sometime at the assumption that Washington is a city in which there are a lot of scheming and intriguing people with a ruthless compulsion to get ahead of each other. Think for a minute. Suppose you were determined by any possible means to get yourself appointed to a subcabinet job in the Reagan administration. And let's assume, however unfairly, that you are totally amoral about the pursuit of this objective. You really don't worry about the means because you think the end is so important. What would you do beyond trying to identify people you know who may know somebody who knows somebody else who could help, and then try to see them or call them?" He couldn't think of anything else, and the fact is there isn't much of anything else.

Suppose you adopt a really Machiavellian approach, one that seeks to determine who your competitors are for a given job so that you can embark on a character assassination effort. It's not likely to work. For one thing, subcabinet people tend to get picked from a pool of eligibles rather than to be viewed from the outset as qualified only for a given slot. For another, you can't possibly know enough about the personal connections of anyone with whom you talk about one of these rivals. You run the risk, therefore, that whatever you say about them may get back to them and lead them to conclude that they'd better get even.

The result is that while the level of virtue in Washington may not be higher than most places, the morality of the conduct of most officeholders is quite high. They cannot successfully practice intrigue. The qualities that most contribute to success tend to be qualities of common sense, gregariousness, friendliness, diligence, and loyalty, all of which are linked to the desire to be respected and to enjoy the perks and publicity associated with public office. Washington is a city of cocker spaniels—people who have a far greater desire to be petted, admired and loved than to wield power. Nixon and a handful of others over the last thirty years really have had an overriding desire to exercise power, but that is not a common characteristic in Washington.

**QUESTION:** Richard Nixon seems to be the most resilient public figure, certainly in my time. He's lost elections, even said you won't have him to kick around any more, and he comes back. He comes back strong. What is it about him? You don't hear anything like this from Jimmy Carter or anybody else. What makes him that way?

**MR. RICHARDSON:** I think he is strong in the sense of vitality, energy, drive, and ambition. One has the feeling that he's thinking all the time. His mind is turning over. Of course there's a radical difference between the loss of a gubernatorial election in California and his eventual nomination in 1968 and the situation that followed his resignation in 1974 and its consequences in the 1980s. He's alive as a public figure, and inevitably so for a whole lot of reasons, including the uniqueness of his downfall and the fact that he can still speak provocatively and trenchantly on current issues. But I wouldn't look for any comeback like a return to major office.

**QUESTION:** Since you said that Mr. Nixon was *the* architect of his own foreign policy and Mr. Kissinger has given some of us another impression, how did you see Mr. Kissinger's role in the construction of the Nixon foreign policy? Question two, did Nixon have a sense of humor?

**MR. RICHARDSON:** Yes. Yes, he did. He didn't have the quality of humor of a person who is genuinely relaxed and comfortable with himself. I was being interviewed yesterday by a reporter about Bill Ruckelshaus. Bill Ruckelshaus is really funny. I once said about him that I never knew a person who was so comfortable in his own skin. I think that sense of knowing who you are and being comfortable with yourself can create a capacity for instant humorous reaction to a situation, whether or not at one's own expense. Nixon doesn't have that quality by any means. He couldn't have had and still be the person he is. But he has a sense of humor in the sense that he recognizes when things are funny and can tell or laugh at a joke. He has a sense of wit. His version of humor is sometimes cutting, but I wouldn't call him humorless.

By the way, I haven't seen or talked to him since 1973. For a long time I dreaded the prospect that I might run into him. I didn't want to have to talk to him. I don't think I would find it particularly unpleasant if it were to occur tomorrow, but I won't go out of my way either.

**QUESTION:** Do you care to comment on the Kissinger question or pass?

**MR. RICHARDSON:** No, I didn't mean to overlook it. Nixon loved to develop his ideas about foreign policy in colloquy with somebody, at least from time to time. He enjoyed very much in the early days of his presidency—I don't mean to say he didn't enjoy it later on—the opportunity to talk with Kissinger about all his foreign policy ideas and to explore the implications of various possible approaches to dealing with the problems of Vietnam, arms control, and so on. Kissinger's intellect, background, knowledge, and conceptual capacity were ideally adapted to his serving as an interlocutor with Nixon. But I think it's also clear that the perception of the role of the United States and the need for its adaptation to the processes of change that have been occurring from the fifties through the sixties and would continue foreseeably to evolve in the future, and its corollaries, e.g., the so-called Nixon doctrine, were essentially Nixonian. Indeed, in those days I had frequent contact, several times a week, with Kissinger, and the impression I've described came at least as much from talking with Kissinger as from my own observations.

**QUESTION:** I'm curious about your depiction of Nixon as being very smart, rational and essentially sound, I guess. Looking back over the decades, back to World War II when, incidentally, I was a near neighbor of Mr. Nixon's in Fairfax, we had repeated illustrations of his behavior which I would say were pretty good predictions of Watergate. We had repeated statements about a new Nixon, meaning he had gotten over these things. Back in the early postwar years Nixon's name was very close to McCarthy's name. He got into Congress by destroying a congressman. My impression was that he has been a liar for years. Was there ever a new Nixon?

**MR. RICHARDSON:** No, I don't think so. The extraordinary thing about the American press is that they're willing to report in a matter of fact way that so-and-so is changing his or her image and to report it in such a manner as to lead one to believe that the change is not just a public relations exercise but is accompanied by some form of inner transformation. Why that has ever been supposed to be true, I don't know. I'm thinking of the nexus between the advertising process and the candidate's behavior. Just today, for example, David Broder of all people, as sophisticated a political observer as you could have, credited John Glenn with having lived down his reputation for dull and humorless speeches on the basis of the speech he gave as a representative of the Democrats at the Gridiron dinner. Any boob asked to give the Democratic speech at the Gridiron dinner goes out and hires the best team of comic writers he can find. Then all he's got to do is stand up and deliver the stuff. That proves absolutely nothing about John Glenn's sense of humor. Even I could read the copy as well as he did.

No, I don't think Nixon has changed. I think there were probably many of us partisans who wanted to think the best of our candidate. I think many Republicans, including me, were quite willing to believe that Nixon had grown, matured, and was a better person than he had been in the early stages. Although we may have thought that for a while, the Watergate revelations confirmed that we had the same old Nixon with us all along. But that is not a denigration of his capabilities at all. Not at all. I have never, not even in the week following my resignation, said one word in derogation of what I believe to be Nixon's capacities, his actual achievements, or his potential achievements. You could well say he never would have been President if he hadn't had that basic core of insecurity. You could easily say that, except by chance, no totally healthy human being is likely to become President of the United States under the present circumstances. You could make a pretty good case for that proposition because of the character of the drive required to achieve the office. Only by chance could you get a Ford. But Ford is quintessentially an individual who never would have been a candidate for President in the ordinary course of events.

**QUESTION:** What do you think was achieved by your resignation as attorney general in 1973 and do you, in retrospect, see any need for a change in the institutional relationship between the office of the presidency and that of the attorney general to make similar resignations unnecessary in the future?

**MR. RICHARDSON:** I think my resignation has to be seen as part of a closely linked series of events which in turn then triggered what Haig called "the fire storm" following the resignations from the Department of Justice on Saturday, October 20, 1973. Taking the episode as a whole, we at least achieved a demonstration of the fact that the American people really are watching. Despite what often seems to be a cynical, relaxed and not very deep concern about the political process, nevertheless, when its vital essence is threatened, the public can, and in that instance did, react in a manner that demonstrates the depth of their emotional commitment to the integrity of our system. That was a very reassuring manifestation in itself. That in turn led, along with other aspects of the whole Watergate episode, to a demonstration of the strength and resilience of the American constitutional structure, including the checks and balances. The checks and balances worked in an absolutely textbook fashion in that situation. I won't pause to demonstrate that. I'm sure you're all aware that it's quite clear.

As to the Department of Justice, I had earlier sought to articulate lines of propriety in the relationship between Justice and the presidency. The management of the Cox-White House relationship from where I sat was a difficult exercise in this respect, but I don't think very significantly generalizable. There are, however, problems pointed up by that period that warrant a good deal of further thought. Dan Meador here at the University of Virginia has done more and better work on this set of questions than anybody else I know, and I believe that his report on this subject could and should get a lot more attention than it's had. I wish I were myself more deeply versed in all the pros and cons of his recommendations, but I was very impressed with them.

I hope that renewed thought will be given to the question of how to better define the relationship between the president and the attorney general who, as head of the Department of Justice relates to the president in the same manner as other Cabinet department heads, but whose department includes responsibilities for the conduct of litigation in situations where it is clearly inappropriate for political interference to occur. You have difficult lines to observe as, for example, in the anti-trust field where the White House may feel that a legitimate political judgment toward the conduct of anti-trust policy is not being properly reflected in an individual case. I guess it's sufficient for the moment to say that hard problems are hard problems, and the fact that one could have difficulty in deciding which of several competing considerations ought to govern in such a case doesn't detract from the vitality of those generalizations as they apply to the easier situations on both sides of the line.

**QUESTION:** I would like to ask you the European question about Nixon if I may. There is a general view among people who are interested in foreign policy in Western Europe that not only was Nixon's foreign policy the most impressive that the United States has conducted since World War II, but also that this was the period when Europe and the world were safest and when the risks of nuclear conflict were reduced to the lowest level. There is a belief in Western Europe among many people who are concerned with foreign policy that there is some sort of a taboo, which began to be observed by Mr. Ford and has been observed since, in preventing politics from following the lines which Nixon followed and which in the European view were so productive of good results both for America and for Western Europe. Of course there were differences of opinion about minor things, but broadly speaking there is disappointment that the Nixon policies are not followed. Would you care to comment?

**MR. RICHARDSON:** I share, on the whole, the European attitude in this respect or, to put it another way, starting from a different personal perspective, I come out at about the same place. But I think the taboo you refer to is a consequence partly of supervening events, for one thing the destruction of South Vietnam by the invasion of the North. This had a significant discrediting impact on the policies that created that peace. I think that had Nixon been able to serve out his second term without the weakening impact of Watergate, if you could wipe Watergate out of the picture, it's quite possible that he and Kissinger would have been able to manage the situation in a manner that successfully deterred the northern invasion. In any case, subsequent events, Angola and the involvement of Soviet proxies, Ethiopia, the Horn of Africa, Afghanistan, and Poland—particularly the latter two—have made it far harder politically to sustain the atmosperhics of détente and the rhetoric associated with it.

Talking to Russians is a curious experience. I was in Moscow about a month ago with a United Nations Association group to talk about arms control with a Russian group led by Arbatov. In such situations they try to deal with Afghanistan and Poland as if they were non-problems. Insofar as in their own eyes they are so regarded, or insofar as they are successful in getting others to think of them that way, then of course any justifiable reason why the U.S. relationship with them or the attitude of U.S. Presidents toward them should be different than they were in the Nixon era automatically disappears. Conversely, however, from the American perspective, to deal with them as if those situations didn't exist is politically impossible. The problem, therefore, is how to bridge these differences.

The distinction fundamentally between Nixon, Carter, and Reagan in this context is that Nixon was capable, in my view, of a much greater degree of subtlety. One of the things that makes Europeans nervous, apart from their feeling about Nixon versus his successors, is that we don't recognize that as the leader of the free world and in most respects still the world's most powerful country—in any event the only superpower counterpart of the Soviet Union—how we say things, our declaratory policy, is critically important. The President's speech the other night in which he floated the idea of a anti-ballistic missile defense, whatever there is to be said for it, was made with total disregard for the reverberations of declaratory policy on the whole strategic weapons context. It's fair to say, to put it another way, that the Reagan administration came into office in somewhat the way an individual trained to fly a fixed-wing airplane might try to take over the controls of a helicopter. I don't know whether the analogy is clear to all of you, but what it amounts to is that you can handle the stick of a fixed-wing plane a whole lot more clumsily without any bad results than you can handle the very sensitive thing that controls the helicopter. To use another image that may be more familiar to some of you, it's like the difference between having been used to rowing an ordinary row boat and then getting into a single shell. They simply haven't understood the repercussions of the rhetoric they are using.

My own view is that in dealing with our European colleagues it goes a long way to be able to talk with them on the same level of sophistication regarding the difficulties, ambiguities, complexities, and intractabilities of the problem. If instead we talk with them as if it were all simpler than it is, as if we thought the rediscovery of the wheel was indeed a brand new invention, and as if we expected to be congratulated on a flourish of rhetoric which to them sounds, if not hackneyed or tired, inflammatory or crude, we make them uneasy about the steadiness and wisdom of our leadership. That difference in approach to the East-West dialogue, I think, accounts for a considerable part of the problem and contributed significantly, for example, to Schmidt's impatience with us.

**QUESTION:** In my twenty-five years in government, which ended before the Nixon administration, I dealt mostly with diplomats, but I never knew an American official to tell a deliberate lie. My question is simply has that reputation of American officials suffered in the last fifteen years or do we still have the reputation that we did have in those days?

**MR. RICHARDSON:** I don't really know. I haven't heard any comments from foreign friends or colleagues lately that would suggest that this is a significant problem. I don't have any reason to think that the situation has deteriorated. I think there are other problems with the quality of our representation. I'm currently engaged in steps toward the creation of a new organization to be known as the American Academy of Diplomacy, one of whose functions will be to recognize distinguished diplomatic service through election to the academy, but once the academy is in existence another of its functions could be to appraise the qualifications of ambassadorial nominees. I think it could create a pretty impressive committee for that purpose. Incidentally, Nixon, to his credit, increased the ratio of foreign service diplomatic appointments from the very beginning of his administration. As far as I know it was unprecedented. His administration treated incumbent ambassadors around the world with a degree of courtesy that has not since been emulated. The Carter administration was absolutely brutal in this respect, and Reagan's almost as bad.

**QUESTION:** Mr. Richardson, near the end of his term or maybe just a year or two earlier, President Nixon seemed to take a great deal of pride in equating himself with Prime Minister Disraeli. He may have been that way on the international scene but he certainly wasn't on the domestic. Could you make any comment on that?

**MR. RICHARDSON:** I may give you a comment which is not directly responsive, but I can't resist. You're quite right that Nixon got very interested in Disraeli and undoubtedly saw a certain parallel between his own character and career and that of Disraeli. It was the consummate courtier, Pat Moynihan, who first had the bright idea of introducing Nixon to Robert Blake's biography of Disraeli, which appeared in the mid-sixties. I have derived from that fact what I consider to be the definitive explanation for Nixon's resignation from office. It goes like this.

Blake's biography of Disraeli may well be, and probably is, the best biography of Disraeli that is ever going to be written. But the reader puts it down with the sense that this extraordinary, exotic, even bizarre creature remains elusive. How the dandy, the satirist, the Jew, ever an alien, could have become leader of the Conservative party,

Chancellor of the Exchequer, prime minister and favorite of Queen Victoria still remains, to a significant extent, a mystery. It seems reasonable to assume that Nixon put down the Disraeli volume with the same thought. When the time came, therefore, when it was the obvious move in self-preservation to destroy the tapes, he couldn't do it. The tapes were going to be the indispensable tool whereby *his* biographers would gain the insights denied to Blake in accounting for the career of Disraeli. I put this to Lord Blake at a British academy dinner. "Lord Blake," I said, "do you realize that you're probably responsible for the resignation of Richard Nixon?" He looked at me blankly. I said, "No, I'm quite serious," and then I gave him an only slightly expanded version of this hypothesis. By the time I got through he looked quite shaken.

Now, as to the analogies. There were some insofar as the major achievement of Disraeli both domestically and in foreign policy in bringing the leadership and the policies of the Conservative party abreast of the realities of British domestic industrial society and the British global role. He made enormous contributions in ridding the Conservative party of many of the attitudes that had tied it to an aristocracy unable to recognize the legitimacy of the pressures for some response to the conditions generated by a wage-dependent industrial society. He saw that foreign policy problems are never solved; they're managed. He saw that if you can cope with the Balkans and turn the situation over to your successors without there having occurred a breakdown of peace or a general war, you may have done all that anyone could accomplish. What Nixon was trying to do both domestically and abroad was to match existing realities to American capacities. The less that is achievable by the direct exercise of muscle, the more has to be accomplished through the skillful management of marginal resources applied at critical points for the preservation of a stable balance. I think that these were things that both Disraeli and Nixon understood very clearly. For the reasons I stated at the outset, greatness was nearly enough within Nixon's grasp so that even his career, as it stands, deserves to be taken very seriously as a demonstration of the potential for the wise, prudent, and skillful exercise of presidential powers, as well as their abuse.

**NARRATOR:** It may be fortunate that along with the complexities, ambiguities, contradictions and strengths and weaknesses in the Nixon presidency there are a few clear truths that are not ambiguous. One of them is the Republic's good fortune that Secretary Richardson, in addition to carrying out fully his private responsibilities for Millbank, Tweed, Hadley and McCloy, continues to enlighten the nation on crucial public issues. There are many other questions on other themes that we hope we might explore with him at the Miller Center, including the mandate and agenda of a center such as this. As we proceed with further examination of the Nixon presidency, we're deeply grateful for one of the first shafts of light in interpreting this important presidency. We thank you very much.

# II.

# THREE VIEWS OF THE NIXON WHITE HOUSE

# THE NIXON WHITE HOUSE AND PRESIDENCY

## H. R. Haldeman

**NARRATOR:** The Miller Center has had a very heavy demand for the Eisenhower volume, which begins with Milton Eisenhower and ends with Sherman Adams and others. That volume is typical of what we have tried to do in the Portraits of American Presidents series, namely, to enlist those people who had the closest and most intimate relationship with a particular President and to draw on their knowledge and experience in coming to a fuller understanding of that presidency. Naturally, one purpose is to help provide the materials which can be of value and benefit to future scholars who will, in the years ahead, be writing about particular presidents. Another contribution will be to fortify columnists who are writing on the basis of what John Seigenthaler has called "somewhat brash revisionism" without having the benefit of the considered evaluations of the people who have worked most closely with a given President.

We have especially wanted Bob Haldeman to be with us to pursue our inquiry into the Nixon presidency. The Nixon presidency operated on the basis of a chief of staff system, and Haldeman was that chief of staff. He was born in Los Angeles and was a student at several California institutions: Redlands, the University of Southern California and UCLA from which he received his Bachelor of Business Administration degree. He served in the Navy in World War II. He returned to become an account executive with J. Walter Thompson, covering both Los Angeles and New York from 1949 to 1959. He became vice president and general manager of the Los Angeles office of J. Walter Thompson and worked in that capacity until he became chief of staff of the Nixon presidential campaign in 1968. During those years he was also a member of the Board of Regents of the University of California and a board member and chairman of the executive committee of the California Institute of the Arts. He then went to Washington and was chief of staff from 1969 to 1973 in the Nixon presidency.

He was chairman of the Nixon Foundation and a member of the White House Fellows Commission and the executive committee of the board of the Kennedy Center in Washington. Since 1979 he has been senior vice president of the Murdock Development Corporation and president of Murdock Hotels Corporation. He moves back and forth, as I understand it, from the East to West coast with intermediate stops in China, from which he has just returned. We look forward to his discussion of the Nixon presidency.

**MR. HALDEMAN:** Thank you very much. That was a remarkable summary without any notes. You did a better recap than I could have done, I think. I'm delighted to have the opportunity to spend this time with you, hopefully in a productive exploration of whatever is of valid interest in looking back into the Nixon presidency. I think that each presidency is almost completely unique because it is, under our Constitution, an office held by one man, and that's all there is to the Office of President, that one man. The rest of it is structured to accomplish for him whatever he needs in order to carry out the constitutional, legislative, and other dictated responsibilities of that office, including the demands of the public and our relations with other countries.

The Nixon presidency is particularly unique because of its unfortunate early demise. From my viewpoint it was unfortunate, both personally and substantively. The trauma of the collapse of the second term of the Nixon presidency, in its broadest aspects, dropped a heavy, black curtain and left a lot of what had taken place in the preceding four years unexplored, unrecollected, and of no particular interest for some time. Hopefully the time, now ten or eleven years later, has come when at least some interest is rekindled as well as some desire to explore that particular presidency in the same manner as the others. The Miller Center is methodically exploring recent presidencies on an overall basis. The worlds of academics and journalism now also seem to be developing an interest. The Nixon exploration was totally overshadowed by obsession with Watergate and all of its lurid aspects. It ignored the substance of the presidency that lay before and behind Watergate.

Rather than trying to guess or inflict upon you what I think is important enough to be covered, I felt it would be much more productive to respond as candidly and, hopefully, validly as I can to any questions, comments, or areas of exploration that you'd like to pursue. On that basis and given the pretty thorough background you have to begin with, you know where I fit in. Let me say that I think, without danger of challenge from a knowledgeable source, that I can explore with you the Nixon presidency, particularly the first term let's say, in a way that probably nobody else can. There is no question I was the closest person to the President during the first term. Physically, I spent, by a wide margin, many more hours with him than anyone else did, both alone and with other people. I worked with him on the total range of duties of the President as contrasted with everybody else who worked with him in one area or another but not in overlapping areas.

I think that the conventional wisdom that has come out of the Nixon presidency has been badly distorted. The journalists tend to feed off each other and what is initially printed becomes conventional wisdom and fact, whether or not it has been challenged and whether or not it's true. Consequently, a mythology develops that has some basis in fact but isn't totally accurate. Hopefully some of that can be cleared up by an exploration of this sort. I think that is enough of a prologue. I'd like to turn to whatever areas you want to explore, and I'll try to answer succinctly so that we have time to explore a number of areas.

**NARRATOR:** Could I ask the first question? Could you tell us a little about the role of the chief of staff in the White House and why Nixon preferred to have a chief of staff?

**MR. HALDEMAN:** Like everything else, most of what happens happens in a evolutionary way, not in a consciously predetermined way, and I think that was true in the establishment of the post of chief of staff. That was not an official title. It was an informal title that was picked up. My official title was assistant to the President, and my commission was an assistant to the President.

When I came into the presidential campaign in 1968, John Mitchell was the campaign manager. Nixon had an idea of what he wanted me to do in the campaign, but it clearly conflicted with the role of the campaign manager in some respects, and I was determined not to have conflict with the manager. Consequently, my designation during the campaign was chief of staff for Mr. Nixon. My role in the campaign was that of managing the candidate, the candidate's operation, his staff, his travel, and everything the candidate did, as contrasted to John Mitchell's role of running the campaign which included the relations with the party and political organizations, the volunteer structure, fund-raising structure, everything other than the candidate himself.

When we went into the transition period after the election and started the process of setting up the White House staff structure I had the chief of staff label from the campaign, and it stuck, but not really intentionally. Our intention was to go in with five equal assistants to the President, all of whom would range across the board, and would be flexible and available to the President on whatever was needed at any given time or in any given direction. As Bryce Harlow very wisely and sagely said at the time, based on his many years of experience in working in the Oval Office and its precincts, "There is no such thing as five equal assistants to the President. There will be one who will be more equal than the others," and that proved to be the case with my role. The chief of staff title stuck on that basis.

As the transition continued, President-elect Nixon brought General Andy Goodpaster back to Washington from his post at NATO to spend some time with us on structuring the White House staff because of his earlier function as staff secretary to President Eisenhower. Nixon was very familiar with his role, having been vice president under Eisenhower. We worked with Andy on developing a modification of some of the Eisenhower staff structure approaches and most particularly the concept of a staff secretariat. Out of that it became clear that someone had to be the broker within the operation, both for external Cabinet-level type interrelationships and the internal White House staff relationships. My role evolved out of that and the chief of staff title, which was unofficial, simply came along as a result of the aftermath of the campaign.

**QUESTION:** My question goes to the area of staff. In 1969, what problems did you foresee that you had to solve in building a staff in the White House? How did you go about solving them? How did you move out from a core group? What kinds of considerations were involved in constructing your staff?

**MR. HALDEMAN:** To a degree we intentionally let it evolve. We started with the five equal assistants concept and honestly intended to pursue that route but the evolutionary process, once we were in place, moved us away from that fairly rapidly. John Ehrlichman, who was one of the five, evolved into having the responsibility for domestic policy development and implementation. Henry Kissinger was clearly identified in a general sense in the foreign policy and national security area and from the outset was designated as national security adviser. Bryce Harlow evolved into congressional relations and liaison as his primary area of responsibility but also worked a lot on policy development because that's interrelated with congressional relations. Pat Moynihan was brought in as an urban affairs counselor from the outset but became more so officially as things shook down. Moynihan was also the house Democrat and the inside gadfly to poke at us in a political sense. He tried to bring us some recognition of the arguments from the other side and introduced his interesting and intriguing concepts of urban policy into our thinking, so that we would not fall into completely ingrown concepts.

Nixon believed in and wanted to set up within the staff (and I think we succeeded in a lot of areas) a concept of adversarial relationships on a constructive and friendly basis. The model in microcosm might be the speech writing staff where there was no chief speech writer but there were several speech writers, and they were intentionally ideologically quite different: Pat Buchanan on the far right, if that's a proper nomenclature; Ray Price in the middle; and Bill Safire on the more liberal side of our spectrum. The three of them had very different views on policy, how to articulate it, and how to appeal to the various constituencies that the President must deal with. The adversarial relationship was established intentionally to provide that.

The same thing took place in urban policy development with Moynihan. At the outset it was Moynihan *versus* Arthur Burns, which is an interesting contest. People forget that Arthur Burns came into the Nixon administration as domestic policy adviser on the White House staff. It's no secret that he was slated to move to the Federal Reserve as soon as William McChesney Martin moved out. He nevertheless spent some time working on domestic policy planning. There was an intentional conflict set up and a play of forces within the operation. We worked out that process within all aspects of policy and operational development with my role being that of an honest broker. The objective people who served with me at the time will tell you that we did achieve that objective of an honest broker relationship, getting both sides or all sides of adversarial positions presented, weighed, and considered properly, and a decision made on the basis of consideration of all aspects and varying views rather than the development of a policy intentionally starting from a preconceived viewpoint to arrive at a preconceived destination. Is that responsive at all?

**QUESTION:** Yes. Let me complicate it a little bit more. When the President came in, the Congress was Democratic. There were intentions to do some things to the bureaucracy that didn't necessarily make it friendly, and the media relationship with Richard Nixon has never been that friendly. I guess what I'm interested in is whether there were any efforts within the staff organization to cope with that situation, or was it more of a matter of attitude?

**MR. HALDEMAN:** No, there were efforts. Bryce Harlow had the responsibility to counsel and work with the development of a congressional relations approach that would deal with the Democratic majority as well as the Republican minority. He had a remarkable background in Washington, both on the presidential staff under Eisenhower and as a lobbyist in the intervening years dealing with Congress on both sides of the aisle. There was a clear mission assigned to Bryce—dealing with the Democratic majority and working out the ways of dealing with the majority. There was a strong concern on the President's part that we appoint some key Democrats to major posts and the attempt to do that wasn't altogether successful. Scoop Jackson was expected to be secretary of defense as was John Connally, who was at that time a Democrat. Hubert Humphrey was offered the United Nations post on a very straightforward basis in a desire to put him into a meaningful slot.

On the press side, where there also were historically bad relations, Herb Klein was brought in for a unique role as communications director, not press secretary. Ron Ziegler, a relatively inexperienced young fellow, was brought in as press secretary with the clear understanding that he was solely a mouthpiece. He was not a Jim Hagerty, and Nixon did not want a Jim Hagerty who made press policy. He wanted a press secretary who articulated the President's policy to the press precisely as it was to be articulated. He had no leeway of his own to deal with issues. Klein, on the other hand, had a strong substantive relationship with the President, going back many years, and also had a strong relationship with the press, both the antagonistic press and what little there was of a favorable press. So Klein's mission was to deal with that perceived problem.

Moynihan was brought into the White House, again, to deal with the domestic relations areas that we knew we were going to have problems with as Nixon tried to move into his committed areas of welfare reform and some areas of economic reform. But the one factor that none of us has mentioned, which totally overrode all of those factors at the start, middle, and finish of that first term, was Vietnam and its effects. The effect was not only militarily enormous and awful, but the effect fiscally was also enormous and awful. It was an immense strain on the budget, and we kept dreaming of the peace dividend, if we could just get the war ended, and what could be done with all the money that was going down the drain every day.

The most important factor, however, was the effect within the country and with our allies and antagonists in the world that arose out of our participation in the war, the lack of sympathetic understanding within the country for the war itself and Nixon's efforts to wind down the war.

All were factors that were clearly recognized. President Nixon's primary focus, his personal attention in the early part of the first term, was almost totally devoted to ending the war in Vietnam, which he thought and expected he could do by the fall of 1969. That didn't work out because what he had been led to believe in as the possibility of fruitful negotiations turned out to be a false hope. So that remained an overriding factor throughout the first term and until we finally negotiated the cease-fire and the end of the war, if you want to call it that.

All of those things worked together and they were all recognized. The staffing structure, the approach to policy-making and the operational policy were developed with all these things in mind and with a recognition of a strong need to be flexible because we had to be able to respond on a day-to-day basis to events which were beyond our control.

**NARRATOR:** Nixon is always described as somebody who never forgot a rebuff, never forgot somebody who had done him wrong. During the transition to the second term, some people tell stories about his ticking off the names of people who were suggested for positions and ruling them out if they had challenged him anytime in the past. Yet there is the fact that he picked Kissinger and Moynihan and considered Humphrey. How do you reconcile Nixon's alleged vindictiveness with his breadth of outreach on personnel? How would you contrast it, for instance, with a later concept that it wasn't enough to be for Reagan; you had to be for Reagan before Iowa? How do you explain his proceeding in the way you have just described?

**MR. HALDEMAN:** I don't quarrel with either aspect of the premise you've outlined because, with some modifications, it is essentially true. I'm sure he must have forgotten some of the people who did him wrong because there were so many of them, and he couldn't possibly remember all of them. He did have a remarkable ability though to keep most of them pretty well catalogued, and they were clear in his mind. But, in Nixon's view, one wasn't necessarily against Nixon simply because one wasn't for him. I guess maybe that's the key to the dichotomy. He did not view someone who was not for him as being an enemy; he only viewed someone who overtly and actively carried out the role of an enemy as being an enemy. The fact that he had campaigned against Hubert Humphrey did not decrease his regard for Hubert Humphrey. He had a strong personal regard for Humphrey, first of all, and he had, in certain areas, substantial respect for Humphrey's ability. In other areas he had very limited respect for Humphrey's ability. It was a rational view of the man, and he was rational in his approach to it.

The same with Senator Henry Jackson; he never saw Scoop Jackson as an enemy, although he always saw him as a Democrat. He always totally opposed him on domestic policy matters, but was in very strong accord on national defense and security policy matters. He saw Jackson as a valuable ally in the national security area, and, recognizing the Vietnam problem, he felt that we needed bipartisan help that Jackson could have provided in winding down the war.

The other people, and there were lots of them—it's so far back now I'm not good at instantly recalling all of them—but there were a lot of people who one might have supposed would not be considered for posts but were. Henry Kissinger was the prime example among them. Henry Kissinger was a Rockefeller ally. There was nobody on the Republican side of the aisle that ranked higher than Nelson on Nixon's adversary list, except maybe his brother David. Nonetheless, even though Henry had been advising Rockefeller in his efforts to defeat Nixon's candidacy for the Republican nomination, Nixon saw Kissinger as a valuable adjunct to his own foreign policy development process and brought him in on that basis. He brought

Moynihan in on the same basis. He brought others in, both Republican and Democrat, who would not normally have been perceived as "Nixon people," and had a record of not being so. That didn't bother him. What bothered him were the people who had, in his view, unjustifiably gone out of their way to do something that wasn't, in his mind, a proper move in opposition to him or who were responsible for what he regarded as inaccurate and unfair slices by the press and by other politicians.

But generally, as most professional politicians do, he had a respect for the professional politician. He knew how the game of politics was played. He got along extremely well with Lyndon Johnson. That transition has to have been one of the most smoothly conducted transitions from one party to another that anybody can recall. First of all, President Johnson did a superb job of cooperation and insisted that all of his people do the same. Some of them didn't, but he insisted that they cooperate and most of them did. President-elect Nixon was committed to working with President Johnson in that transition. Had President Kennedy survived and had that transition been from Kennedy to Nixon, I suspect that because of the relationship between the two men and the personalities of the two men, it would not have been the model transition that the Johnson-Nixon one was. Johnson was a professional politician, respected and in some ways liked by Nixon. Kennedy was neither respected nor liked by him, so it was a different kind of relationship. Each one is an individual case, and that, I think, is the answer to your question.

**QUESTION:** May I ask you about Vietnam and the "madman" theory? You mention in your book that you first heard this from Nixon during the campaign on his famous walk on the beach. Do you remember when that was? How early or late in 1968 was it?

**MR. HALDEMAN:** It was probably late summer.

**QUESTION:** The analogy of course is with the end of the Korean War and Eisenhower scaling down the war very quickly with his major threat. Did Nixon talk about that a lot?

**MR. HALDEMAN:** No, and it was not a constantly recurring thing, but it was clearly one of the tools in his kit. He believed conceptually that it was important that the enemy and those counseling or controlling the enemy, as then perceived in Vietnam, have, if not a conviction, at least a concern that he might be pushed to a point where he might do something totally irrational. That was a strategic concept, not a planned intent, and there was never any consideration given to doing anything to carry out the "madman" theory. It was a concept that he wanted to be, at the least, a concern to the other side.

**QUESTION:** Was it a bluff in order to get Vietnam's attention?

**MR. HALDEMAN:** Yes, it was a bluff.

**QUESTION:** In looking back to 1953 there were a number of things that Eisenhower frequently pointed to besides the threat. One was that the Chinese were basically exhausted from the war. Another was the fact that almost exactly at that time Stalin died, and it was shortly after Stalin's death that things suddenly started to move. Did Nixon ever talk about those other two possible explanations? What he was trying to do was apply a lesson in history, wasn't he?

**MR. HALDEMAN:** He was to a degree, but he wasn't as committed as that implies to the lessons of history. That was one factor, but there was a recognition of something else. The one thing I hope can be accepted about Nixon by those who find it hard to accept anything good about him is that the man has an incredibly astute grasp of the complexity of the geopolitical situation in the world and how the factors fit together. He's not limited to an historical appreciation of it. On that basis, we were faced with several different problems and he clearly recognized them in Vietnam versus the problems that Eisenhower faced in Korea. The concept or execution of the war was obviously totally different. But also the relationship of the combatant enemy with its clients or with those of whom it was a client was different. The relations of Vietnam with the Soviets and the Chinese were totally different from the relations of the North Koreans with the Chinese and the Soviets. Consequently, he was dealing with a totally different kind of situation and that was part of what didn't materialize that he thought might materialize. There was less control by the dominating powers than he had hoped there would be. That turned out not to be there.

Also, the whole China initiative was evolving conceptually at that time on the basis that Vietnam was a very troubling factor, not just because of Vietnam but also because of the wedge that it drove into any question of a U.S.-China dialogue. Beyond that, there was what turned out to be the lack of control and probably intransigence of the government of South Vietnam. There was President Nixon's determination not to abandon South Vietnam. It was the peace-with-honor concept that he was working for and which has been ridiculed in some circles. As a nonforeign policy expert and a nonpolitical scholar, I still believe that we ultimately achieved peace with honor. I think that peace could have been sustained on the basis of the continuing strength of the presidency had the Nixon administration not collapsed immediately thereafter.

**QUESTION:** Just one thing. Do you think he felt that the threats had been adequately communicated to the right people?

**MR. HALDEMAN:** He was never sure. That was another real problem: to know what was getting through and know it was getting through, and Henry Kissinger never could quite figure that out. He drove the President up the wall with his constant interpretation of nuances: what color was the tablecloth when he met with them this time at the Paris talks? How many times did his opposite number smile when they took the first lap around the garden? I'm not sure Henry's Teutonic mind was properly reading the Oriental minds.

**QUESTION:** When you were setting up the White House staff initially, what thought did you give to the issue of deciding how many people should have direct and independent access to the President *versus* how many people should have to come through the chief of staff? Did your ideas on that change as you moved through the Nixon presidency, and have they changed since?

**MR. HALDEMAN:** The mythology is somewhat different from the facts in that a lot more people had direct access to President Nixon than is popularly believed. The question is not so much how many had access but by what means did they have access? You have to structure each President's staff to fit that President's method of working. You cannot institutionalize on any permanent basis the Office of the President. You must build a new Office of the President for each president, and it must evolve as that president evolves in office. If you look at the recent Presidents, everyone of them has evolved up or down, some of them in both directions, during his term of office. He becomes a substantially different man with different methods of working than he was the day he came in. President Nixon was not any different in that respect.

At the outset, he gave lip service to the concept that all Cabinet officers would have direct access to the President any time they wanted it. He told them so at the Cabinet meetings. In fact, he told their wives that they would too. That was a historic first. You can imagine what might happen if Adele Rogers called to discuss something with him or, even worse, Martha Mitchell. Martha always figured that she did have direct access and used it.

He didn't really mean that any more than he meant that the vice president was going to have a very strong policy role and would be sitting in the office at the end of the corridor right down from the hall from the President. The vice president decorated that office and got it all set to move and I moved into it. The vice president moved over to the Executive Office Building and was hardly heard from again. Unfortunately, he was eventually heard from in the wrong way.

In my opinion, the accessibility of a president in modern times has to be controlled in some way if he is an orderly-minded president. He may be the kind of president or politician who works on the basis of disorder, which is my impression of Lyndon Johnson, and I don't say that derogatorily because I'm not so sure that's not a better technique. But it is only a good technique for the man who can work that way. Nixon couldn't work that way. Johnson apparently not only could but had to and loved it. In our situation, the control of access was not a question of deciding who could see the President but of deciding how to time and work out the seeing of the President by people in a way that suited the President. My responsibility was always, as the insiders know but a lot of other people don't want to recognize, the carrying out of the President's decisions in that regard. They were not my decisions. There was not a delegation of power to me or anybody else as to who could and who couldn't see the President or when they could see him.

My job was that of a traffic manager on the "who sees the President" question, not that of a doorkeeper in the sense of "who will I let in and who will I not let in?" It was, how do I get in the people the President wants to see today? We went through a lot of very skillful and careful planning of the President's time in order to make it possible for him to see and deal directly with the maximum number of people that he chose to deal with. Those were not necessarily people who would tell him what he wanted to hear and that kind of thing. He very strongly wanted to hear what the people who didn't agree with him felt, but he didn't want to hear it from unknowledgeable people.

We went through a thing that was interesting in this regard. Franklin Murphy, who was at that time chancellor of UCLA and a good friend of mine, had been offered a very substantial post in the administration. President Nixon had a high regard for Murphy. He was appointed to the Foreign Intelligence Advisory Board, which caused him to come to Washington once a month for three-day seminars and meetings on national security and intelligence gathering, and afterwards they would always meet with the President for an hour or so. Murphy, out of his academic wisdom, came up with the thought that the President should set up a regular procedure whereby he met once a week, every two weeks, or once a month with a small group of Franklin Murphy-type people to discuss general things where they could tell the President things that he probably wasn't hearing because he didn't stand in checkout lines at supermarkets anymore and was missing what was going on. We tried that a couple of times, and the problem we had with that is that the knowledge level of such people is so far behind the knowledge level of the President on the matters of real concern that it takes too long to get them up to steam, and you don't accomplish anything.

So, there was a screening of who saw the President, but the President himself did the screening. I just carried it out. It worked out well because I took the blame for those decisions, and this was better than the President taking the blame, especially when a congressman or a senator or some other self-important individual did not get to see him. It was better for him to go away thinking that that S.O.B. at the door kept him out instead of that that S.O.B. on the other side of the door didn't want to see him. We handled it that way intentionally.

Cabinet officers, with the exception of a few who became total bores and time-wasters, could always see the President anytime they thought they needed to. They couldn't always come to the door and walk in at a given moment, but they could always tell me, "I've got to see the President. I'd like to see him today, or tomorrow is o.k., or I've got to see him before noon today, or I've got to see him immediately," whatever their priority was, and it invariably worked out. There are some who will tell you that that wasn't the case (those are the ones I was referring to), and they can identify themselves by telling you it didn't happen.

**QUESTION:** I'd like to ask a somewhat broader question that deals with the presidency itself. The office has evolved into something that was not predictable forty years ago. One thinks of nineteenth-century Presidents walking rather freely around Washington. Even Harry Truman sometimes would simply walk out of the White House and up the streets and people followed along with him asking questions.

**MR. HALDEMAN:** President Nixon got loose once, too.

**COMMENT:** But coming into the Nixon presidency, those of us on the outside thought of you and Mr. Ehrlichman as being fairly potent barriers between the public and the President. Now we move on into the Reagan presidency, and we have Mr. Reagan shown on television every evening. At a certain point Larry Speakes stands in front of him and tells him he is finished, and away he goes. I can't imagine anybody getting in front of either Franklin D. Roosevelt or Harry Truman and telling him, "Mr. President, you are finished. Now you leave."

**MR. HALDEMAN:** I never did that to President Nixon, either.

**QUESTION:** No, I am not talking about him. I am talking about evolution here. The question I am raising is whether or not you see an evolution that is going in some direction that may be damaging to the Office of the President and not necessarily serving the best interest of the nation?

**MR. HALDEMAN:** I think to a degree there is some evolution going that way, but I also think it is dangerous to assume an evolution on as small a sample as we have when we are dealing with twentieth-century Presidents or post-World War II Presidents. There haven't been many Presidents in that time and the individuals who have been Presidents have been quite different. I think the phenomenon that you referred to as the Larry Speakes-Reagan phenomenon is much more a reflection of Reagan as President than it is of an evolution of the office of the presidency.

I worked with Reagan some; he appointed me to the Board of Regents in California when he became governor. I worked with him on university-related matters, and I found somewhat the same *modus operandi* in his governorship entourage and operation as you are now describing in his presidency. I'm not at all familiar with the operation of the Reagan White House, so I'm not a qualified commentator. But looking at it from the outside I think there is a problem. But what you've got to recognize, I believe, is that the President has a very strong responsibility to communicate his policies, decisions, challenges and hopes to the American people and to the world, and he's got to do that in the way that he feels he can best do it. That's what you see as the Speakes-Reagan phenomenon, and you saw it differently in the Nixon administration. When we got to important stuff Nixon charged into the press room, sometimes to the dismay of whomever it might have been and depending on whose area it was, Ehrlichman or Kissinger or Bill Rogers or whomever. He articulated what he wanted to say the way he wanted to say it.

Nixon felt strongly that he was the best communicator of his policies and that he as President was best able to move the country in the directions that he was trying to move it. He was partly right and partly wrong in that feeling but that was his feeling, and therefore, it was the way he worked. President Eisenhower, I believe, felt that he was not, except on broad policy and high level things, the best spokesman, and he used Hagerty as a spokesman and almost a developer as well as articulator of policy. Lyndon Johnson went both ways because he got terribly frustrated in both directions. Jack Kennedy clearly was his own best articulator and did it himself. I don't know how to evaluate Carter, but I think he tried both directions and Ford really was the same way.

I don't think there is an overall evolution. I don't think that you are ever going to see the President of the United States conducting the kind of office that Abraham Lincoln did where he had afternoons when anybody could line up outside the White House and come in and chat with the President about whatever he had in mind. That is not logistically, physically, or in any other way possible today. But I'm not sure that's very necessary or even desirable because letting anybody come in means that the most aggressive people are going to be heard, and the most aggressive ones are not necessarily the most representative of public opinion on any particular issue.

I think there is a danger. You asked if there is a danger of the President becoming too isolated, and I think that there definitely is. I think there always has been, but that's the President's decision. If the President decides he is going to be isolated and wants to be, he can and will be. Our remedy for that, as the people of the United States, is almost exclusively that of getting another President because it is pretty hard to change one President's view on the degree of accessibility except as he evolves in office and decides that he is successful or unsuccessful at being accessible. I think that the pendulum is going to swing back and forth. I don't think we are on an inevitable course at all.

Reagan fancies himself, and is generally reputed to be, a great communicator, but his great communication is clearly prepared communication and not off-the-cuff communication. I don't know if that is necessarily bad. You don't have to go very far back to remember that FDR's communication was totally controlled. It appeared to be off-the-cuff but there was a very high degree of control with the press and everybody else. Prior to FDR and televised press conferences, these off-the-cuff things were never even considered by a President. We are moving toward a much more open approach, but we are also zigzagging back and forth and will continue to do so. Part of that zigging and zagging is going to depend on the President himself.

**QUESTION:** To what extent on the whole would you say that Nixon was an original thinker and generator of ideas, or was he a shrewd adapter of other people's ideas?

**MR. HALDEMAN:** A good question. In the foreign policy area I think he was very much an original thinker. In my prejudiced view, he is almost without peer in that area. There is no question that Kissinger was an incredibly valuable ally in the process, but most of the creative evolution of foreign policy concepts was initiated from Nixon's mind and then became the result of give and take between Nixon and Kissinger, and in some cases others. Kissinger was an incredibly good foil for Nixon; he had a deeper knowledge of history than Nixon did. But Nixon was an avid scholar. He used Henry, and he read the things that Henry told him to read. He was constantly pushing Henry to provide him with background to substantiate something that Henry drew on from his own knowledge.

In terms of domestic policy, because it was an area of less interest although not necessarily less concern, I would say that he was not a great original thinker but was a good catalyst at drawing out original thinking. He was always seeking original thinking. Some day we've got to go back and study our welfare reform program and the whole welfare concept that evolved from the Family Assistance Plan and that sort of thing. Most of it was probably the result of the original thinking of Pat Moynihan but molded and pushed by a lot of other people and by the President to a strong degree. There were some basic philosophical concepts that the President insisted upon that Moynihan worked into the structure that he was putting together.

In other areas Nixon just basically had little or no interest, and in those areas he didn't waste, as one would have thought, much time in trying to develop original thinking. Instead, he turned to better minds in the field to present concepts of original thinking from which he would pick and choose.

**QUESTION:** In the area of domestic policy there is a revisionist school of history which holds that the record of the Nixon presidency was liberal. Do you think that is because anything looks liberal by comparison with the present administration? I think that Attorney General Mitchell said, "Don't look at what we say, look at what we do." People argue this way and talk about the indexing of social security and certain health care measures. If that is true, do you think this was the result of a real conviction on President Nixon's part to help people who are less fortunate or was it more of a cynical strategy?

**MR. HALDEMAN:** Unfortunately there isn't a simple or unequivocal answer to the question because the true answer is a complex one that is yes to almost all of the above in the sense that I don't know how you define liberal and illiberal in terms of domestic policy, first of all, so I don't know where you come out.

As for the welfare state concept, the Nixon administration moved strongly in some directions that were tempered by some very strong, what I would call conservative, assumptions that Nixon held. He believed philosophically, deeply and personally, that people who, through no fault of their own, could not take care of themselves should be cared for properly. But he also believed, equally deeply and strongly, that those who could take care of themselves but were not doing so, for whatever reason, should not be cared for and rather should be, by appropriate incentives or disincentives, required to provide for themselves at least some of the care that they could provide. That was the conceptual basis for the Family Assistance Plan and the Welfare Program. It was not to abandon those who had to be helped, but to require those who could provide for themselves to do so. It also aimed at eliminating the disincentive of welfare in the sense that there were people who could make more money by not working than they could by working. To deal with the problem he perceived in the welfare system—this was Moynihan's theory incidentally—he concluded that we needed a service welfare system rather than a benefit welfare system. You eliminated the cost of service which, with due apologies if any of you are represented here, in effect eliminates the intermediary social worker and sets up a welfare system that provides money directly to the welfare recipient. Then he can spend it for his own needs rather than be guided and counseled by social workers who are siphoning off a substantial percentage of the monies that are allocated to welfare. There was a strong feeling that too much money was being earmarked for welfare, and there was a desire to reduce that particular budget allocation.

We also moved, and he pushed very strongly, for direct grants to cities, building on the concept that the federal government was better than local or state government in collecting taxes but much worse in expending tax revenues. It was better to move the expenditure of tax funds down to the lowest possible level rather than handling it all at the federal level. His desire was to get the grant process down to the local and state governments and get it out of the hands of the federal bureaucracy. He was not a strong proponent of the federal bureaucracy in any respect, and the bureaucracy sensed that. One of my theories is that it was a strong contributing factor to his downfall.

**QUESTION:** I wonder if you could tell us a little bit how he developed his thinking on economic policy and especially the control of inflation, price controls, and related matters.

**MR. HALDEMAN:** I wish I could in a scholarly way, and I hope you will have someone here who can because that is a field in which I consider myself even more ignorant than several of the other fields we have been discussing. I don't feel competent to give you a very good answer.

He was groping in the area of economic policy. I think it is fairly evident when you look at the record. The Camp David August Summit that resulted in the major shifts in the whole gold standard was a part of that. At one point he announced that he was a Keynesian, which astonished most everybody who had read anything from him prior to that date. My sense is that he never found what he believed to be a sound foundation for economic policy and therefore was never able to develop, within his own thinking, any degree of confidence in what he believed to be a sound economic policy.

He relied on a number of people, but principally Arthur Burns. To some degree Moynihan had some influence but not really very much. Burns had strong influence; Herb Stein had a very strong influence; Paul McCracken did to a degree but not as much as Stein did. In the latter part of the first term Connally came in with some politically oriented economic approaches which had some appeal to the President and were a factor in the August Camp David moves. In my opinion, no real base was ever developed to the President's satisfaction as an approach to economic policy.

**QUESTION:** This is a question in the area of national security and defense. We all know that every administration, every presidency in modern times has been plagued by rivalries within the military. I wondered if you have read what President Eisenhower said in his farewell comment, "Beware of the military industrial complex and that relationship." Did Mr. Nixon ever express any views on that to you before or during his presidency?

**MR. HALDEMAN:** Yes. I think he shared the Eisenhower view and as you look at some of the efforts that were made, despite the fact that we were engaged in an active war through the entire first term, they were in the direction of trying to deal with that problem. Nixon wanted to get rid of unjustifiable defense expenditures without weakening our real defense posture. The problem that has to be dealt with is real *versus* perceived defense posture. I think we have let ourselves be led into and locked into a trap which measures our defense capability by our defense expenditures. The only way we can say we've allocated adequate funds and the only way we can say we have adequate defense is to prove we are spending more money than we did at some previous time. That, in my view, is a totally fallacious assumption. I think we can build a much stronger defense and I think we need to. I think we do have serious problems in our defense capability. But it isn't met simply by throwing money at it, and it can be met in a lot of other ways much more effectively.

The other point I would like to make is that the second term would have shown a number of changes. The Nixon presidency didn't end the way it should or would have ended had we not fallen into the Watergate mess. I think on the foreign policy side that peace in Vietnam would have become a sustained peace in Asia. Under strong leadership in the second term, I think we would have built up our position in the world very substantially over those four years. We would have because we had already started it, and we had every intent of pursuing it. We would have totally reorganized the executive branch and particularly the office of the presidency along the lines of the reorganization plan that was presented after the second inaugural. The defense posture and the whole approach to it would have been radically changed. The one area in which I can't say that I feel convinced we would have gotten the things done that we set out to do is the economy, because I'm not sure we knew where we were going to try to go.

**NARRATOR:** Perhaps I should be the one to ask the tactless question to wind things up. One of your predecessors in the series, Elliot Richardson, talked about going back to consider Mr. Nixon's childhood and the insecurity that he felt was manifest all through Nixon's political career. He said that he thought that Watergate could largely be explained in those terms, that the President went into that election and everybody told him that it was going to be something on the order of a landslide and that only his sense of insecurity led him down the Watergate track. It seems to me it would be a real omission if we didn't at least get your views, however briefly, on this subject.

**MR. HALDEMAN:** Elliot, incidentally, was not close either personally or operationally to the President, despite the many posts he held under him. However, I think there is some basis for his feeling. There is no question that Richard Nixon as a young man, congressman, senator, vice president and to some degree as President, did have that sense of insecurity and concern that caused him to move into overkill in dealing with perceived and sometimes actual problems. That was a problem that I had in dealing with him. Another area where some people give me some credit was—and I think it was a valid function I performed—in not doing some of the things that the President wanted done. But sometimes when I didn't do what he wanted done, he found a way to get around me, just like a lot of the Cabinet people when they wanted to get to him. He did get around me on some things, and I'm not absolving myself of blame in the Watergate thing. I clearly share blame with everybody else who got caught up in it. I blame my part on stupidity and a failure to perceive a problem at a time when the problem could have been readily dealt with. I didn't perceive it as a problem of the nature and magnitude that it became. I honestly believed it was a third-rate burglary, as Ron Ziegler said, and that it was a stupid thing.

The interesting challenge on Watergate is that none of us here today, nor anybody else that I can identify knows who ordered the break-in at the Watergate or why it was ordered. It is fascinating that despite the most intensive investigation ever conducted of any crime in American history, and despite Judge Sirica's constant protestation that all he was out for was the truth and that he was going to find out who did it and why, the one thing we never found out was who did it. We know who broke in, but we don't know who told them to break in. We know the men who carried out the act, but we don't know who issued the order to do it, and we don't know why they issued the order. Somebody knows it because somebody issued the order. I don't know whether that somebody is still alive or not, and maybe someday someone is going to tell us, but the fascinating thing is that despite all that, we still don't know the answer to that one question.

That has become an insignificant question because it really doesn't matter why or who ordered the Watergate break-in. What really matters is how we dealt with it after it happened, and that's where we made our fatal mistakes. I agree with Nixon's statement to David Frost that, "I gave them a sword and they stuck it in me," and that's exactly what happened. They—and there were a lot of theys—were waiting to undo Nixon, especially after the incredible landslide and presumed mandate with which he came into the second term. That was terrifying to the people who didn't want to see Nixon do what Nixon declared he was going to try and do. All of those factors were mobilized, and some of them stemmed from his insecurity, some of them were the dislike of a substantial part of the press, some of them were a fear in the bureaucracy of the reorganization and the kinds of things that we were planning to do that would have broken up a lot of cozy relationships between the Hill and the executive. Some of them were things I've alluded to in my book. I don't recommend my book. I'm not proud of it because it dealt in a superficially popularized way with what I don't think should have been either superficially or popularly dealt with.

I think the intelligence community was very concerned about a lot of things. I think we've got very serious problems with our intelligence situation and community. I don't think we have even an adequate, let alone a good, security and intelligence apparatus. Compared with Israel, China, Germany, and probably still Britain, I don't think we have the foggiest notion what's going on, and I think that's terrifying.

That community was concerned about what the President was going to do; the bureaucracy was concerned; a lot of the Congress was concerned; the press was concerned. I think he did give them the sword and unfortunately some of us unintentionally helped him hand it to them, and they stuck it to him. I personally feel that was a great tragedy because whether or not you are in full accord with Nixon policies, I think the second term and the ultimate result of the eight-year Nixon presidency would have been a remarkable, landmark presidency for the United States and would have had overwhelmingly strong accomplishments on the international scene and the defense scene and quite probably some substantial progress on the domestic scene.

**NARRATOR:** We've learned a lot about the Nixon presidency, and we've learned something about Bob Haldeman that was not in the popular press.

**MR. HALDEMAN:** I greatly enjoyed being with you. It's fascinating. I don't do this any more. I'm busily engaged in building and operating hotels and office buildings. It's fascinating to think back over those years. There is no question in my mind that the opportunity I had was the greatest thing that anyone could hope for. The office of the president is fascinating, and I still think it's a superbly conceived office and that normally we select at least good and sometimes superb men to fill it. Sometimes we make some mistakes, but I think the system is uniquely devised to survive all of our stupidities and errors and that it is going to go on doing so.

It is wonderful that you are studying the office because it needs to be studied, not only for guidance for the journalists who are going to be writing about it and the historians who are writing the history of it, but also for the guidance of those who are going to be filling those slots in the years to come. There wasn't a lot for us to read when we went in. There is much more today than there was in 1969, and hopefully there is going to be much more in the years ahead because the one thing that you really need is guidance and feel, and it is such a rarified atmosphere that it is hard to get that kind of guidance. Thank you.

**NARRATOR:** We thank you.

# OBJECTIVES AND PEOPLE

## Leonard Garment

**NARRATOR:** Leonard Garment did his undergraduate work at Brooklyn College and obtained his law degree at Brooklyn Law School. He then joined the law firm of Mudge, Stern, Williams and Tucker. One member of that law firm was named Richard M. Nixon; that part of the history is fairly clear. It is striking how often Leonard Garment was called on to tackle some of the most difficult and crucial tasks in the Nixon Presidency. Today he is respected across the political spectrum by moderates, conservatives, and liberals alike. We are fortunate that there are men like Leonard Garment who move in and out of government and bring their enormous professional competence and judgment to the task. We are delighted to have him with us.

**MR. GARMENT:** I'm delighted to be here. I have read some of the published work of the Miller Center. It is not simply courtesy on my part when I say that it is truly outstanding historical material. I approach this invitation with a certain amount of anxiety in view of its splendid tradition.

I'll start by giving you a very brief run down on myself in relation to politics and then a little bit about the Nixon administration as I saw it. Then I'll take any questions you may want to ask.

For the sake of order in the presentation, I think it is fair, if a little oversimplified, to say that my life in politics has been divided into more or less three phases. From 1963-1969, I was quite active in what came to be known as the Nixon Law Firm but which was actually Mudge, Stern, Williams and Tucker before Mr. Nixon joined the firm in

1963. I became close to Mr. Nixon at that time for two reasons. First, it seemed that somebody had to perform the task of interpreting Wall Street to Richard Nixon and help him work his way through the legal jargon and other such problems. Secondly, I felt a real desire to know more about him. At that time I was not active in politics. I was a birthright Democrat. But during this active phase, I was associated with his work in his so-called comeback into national politics in the years from 1963-1969. I did recruiting for him. I tried to bring in people that had not been ordinarily associated with Mr. Nixon. I found him to be a man full of surprises. He was a man of truly large intelligence. He was a tremendous worker. He had an interesting variety of private attitudes toward politics and politicians and toward life in general.

During that period I gradually came to be associated with his planning in some of the more important areas of his political life. He sent me here and there to meet a variety of people over the first few years. Ultimately, they came together at one convention or another and became the main cadre of his campaign for the presidency. I think he knew where he wanted to come out right from the beginning. He organized his campaign brilliantly. He planned to take advantage of all possibilities. He allowed enough time to train and fit people into particular roles in the campaign.

The second phase of my life in politics after Mr. Nixon was elected was a considerably more quiet one. I came to Washington, at his suggestion, to run the Washington office of the law firm. I was to be part of the traditional so-called "kitchen cabinet" or outside advisory group. I did various kinds of housekeeping errands that presidents like to have friends perform for them, while at the same time maintaining my professional responsibilities at the law firm. That didn't work because I really didn't know anything about Washington-style politics; I couldn't play the inside-outside role because I didn't know what either role amounted to.

So after a couple of months I told the President that I would either go into the government or go back to New York. I went into the government in the role of—it's been described various ways—utility infielder, or free safety, or as the President put it: "Do whatever you want; just don't get into trouble." Initially, I had certain delineated areas. I was responsible for minority issues, which included civil rights. Later this was reversed, and minority questions were subsumed under larger legal questions of civil rights policy and civil rights enforcement.

The culture area was also assigned to me, as was the role of foreign policy "messenger." I think the Nixon foreign policy organization depended upon different levels of communication. The formal level, of course, would be the traditional State Department, National Security Council, White House apparatus. The second would be the informal relationship between the President and his White House foreign policy advisers. Then there were other people who performed informal activities and who were outside the organizational structure. I served in that capacity. I also had *ad hoc* assignments in the domestic policy area.

The last and probably most active phase was after the news of Watergate broke out. I became acting counsel to the President in the spring of 1973 replacing John Dean. I continued in that capacity while theoretically holding these other responsibilities, but there really wasn't much time for anything else except survival efforts through the last couple of years. That was more or less the role I had until the President's resignation in August 1974.

Since that time, I have returned to private life as a lawyer, doing a stint as U.S. representative to the UN Human Rights Commission and practicing in New York with my old firm, then returning to Washington to join a smaller firm.

Now I will address, very generally, the objectives of the Nixon administration as I saw them, the organization of the government for the development of policy and the machinery put in place to carry out those objectives. It is a little daring to make sweeping statements about the objectives of the Nixon administration. There are different views. But I am prepared at this point to identify what I think the people were doing then and why they were doing it. I have a little better sense now than I did then of the relationships. I've read most of the books the others have written, and I've had a chance to reflect on them.

*Leonard Garment*

Mr. Nixon's over-arching concept of his presidency, particularly when he took office, was that foreign policy was the preeminent responsibility of the chief of state. He believed domestic policy was governed by the corollary proposition that one should do whatever is necessary in order to undergird a strong U.S. foreign policy.

If I don't get much more complicated at this point and if my thesis is correct, you will see that many aspects of the Nixon administration are harmonized by that simple statement of objectives. President Nixon frequently said that it would take a genius to wreck the American economic system, but it wouldn't take much to cause serious problems in foreign policy. There are people who say he didn't care much about domestic policy; this is an incorrect way of putting the proposition. One of the great English parliamentarians and prime ministers also felt that there was a natural primacy to foreign policy and that a national leader must do whatever is necessary in the domestic arena to carry out that foreign policy. That does not diminish the importance of domestic policy; it is simply a matter of proportion.

I think the structure of the Nixon administration, the selection of people, and the ways in which policy was formed were based on this premise that one would do what was needed domestically to ensure that one could handle complex and slowly evolving foreign policy problems without eroding the domestic base necessary to the effective conduct of foreign policy. Given that central idea, it follows that Mr. Nixon focused his personal attention during the transition period on the selection of his foreign policy team. That, of course, involved the selection of Henry Kissinger and then an appropriate collaborator at State, Mr. Rogers. I think Bill Rogers—an old political friend from the Eisenhower administration—was seen as an effective, intelligent person, experienced in politics although not particularly so in foreign policy, and one who would be a reliable spokesman for the policies to be developed by Mr. Nixon and Mr. Kissinger. I think President Nixon did have in mind very clear strategic ideas, having to do principally with China and the Soviet Union, together with the winding down of the Vietnam War, all as aspects of the establishment of a new relationship with the Soviet Union.

The development of these policies would take time and would involve a large amount of domestic stress that would have to be dealt with by an appropriate domestic political policy.

One of the earlier issues was whether or not our commitment in Vietnam should be continued or rapidly terminated. My own sense of what transpired is that, although President Nixon intended to bring the Vietnam War to an end as soon as feasible, he concluded that he could not withdraw abruptly from Vietnam without jeopardizing the effort to normalize relations with China. Normalization was the key to the development of a new relationship with the Soviet Union. Right at the beginning that was President Nixon's main mission. I think everything else was subordinated to that.

Coming back, then, to the formation of the government, beyond the selection of the national security establishment—that would include Mr. Laird, in addition to Mr. Kissinger and Secretary Rogers—the other Cabinet member whose selection was a matter of a significance to President Nixon was the secretary of treasury, Dave Kennedy, again because of the foreign policy implications of that post. Beyond this group, most of the scouting and analysis of possible candidates was left to John Mitchell since the dominant considerations with respect to the other Cabinet members was political. Obviously they had to meet a decent standard of competence, but they were basically selected in light of the kind of constituencies they had and whether their political reach would make them effective in those areas.

For the White House staff itself, I think the emphasis was upon an efficient White House structure. Bob Haldeman and John Erlichman were the managers of the White House. Both were relatively non-ideological. The President trusted them to carry out their missions of organizing the activities of government and reporting accurately to him without trying to affect policy or carry out some private political position of their own.

Pat Moynihan came into the government as part of an effort to have some fresh, intelligent, experienced thinking in the area of domestic policy. He was originally thought of as the secretary to HUD, but that post had been committed. The President quickly saw the possibility of bringing Moynihan on as his adviser. Arthur Burns and Bryce Harlow were the other two principal counselors. Herb Stein was associated with the Council of Economic Advisors. That is the group that sticks in my mind as the "control group" in the White House. They were a very intelligent, effective and loyal group of White House officials.

The President's domestic policy objectives were carried out successfully in the first term. During these years, a great deal of ground was freely given on the domestic side because it was a matter of secondary importance to the President. It was not possible to affect major reductions in the budget. It was not possible to move too quickly towards reduction of the size of government or to carry out some of the other so-called "Republican" or "conservative" ideas. As a matter of fact, I think those who look back on the activities and the policy developments of the first four years of the Nixon administration are frequently surprised to see the extent to which major social programs were not only kept alive but increased. In the civil rights area the expenditures for civil rights enforcement rose during that period from approximately one billion to over three billion dollars. This is an example of the record of domestic activities which was in fact contrary to the general perception of the administration as a very conservative Republican administration. But remember, the basic Nixon need was to keep the home front tranquil while large foreign policy strategies evolved.

The second term started with a strong sense of the Nixon administration's intention to carry out major domestic reforms as well as to continue the big initiatives in foreign policy. That momentum quickly dried up with Watergate. In a sense, some of the Watergate momentum was refueled by the fact that after four years of relatively benign social policy there was a clear indication at the beginning of the second term that substantial changes were going to be made. Truly basic reforms were contemplated and announced with respect to the budget, the organization of government, and the fundamental prerogatives of the executive branch and the Congress. I think these changes together with the strong political and cultural tensions generated by the Nixon administration in its continuing conflict with the liberal establishment were among the most important factors in generating so much Congressional heat and drive in the Watergate investigation.

Now that is a very general outline of some of the things that interested me about the administration, and I will be very happy to answer questions about any of those subjects.

**QUESTION:** We have heard other speakers comment on the secret negotiations in Warsaw that led to open discussions in China. Were you involved in that as part of your errand-running in the foreign policy field? How well was this known in the administration? Was this a broad or a very narrow policy?

**MR. GARMENT:** It was very narrow. I should have added that, with the exception of one or two domestic social issues during the first few years, I was not part of the central group on the big questions. I was given the task of organizing policy in connection with school desegregation which occupied me for the better part of two years. I knew there was much going on, but it was held very closely. I did not have anything to do with China. I didn't know of it. Even the secretary of state didn't know. The inside group included the President, Kissinger, Haldeman and, I suppose, Erlichman. It was really held closely. I think Richard Nixon always felt that the ability to keep the China initiative secret was crucial. It gave him great credibility with the Chinese.

As a matter of fact, the administration's creation of "the plumbers" and its concern about leaks arose because they were considered so threatening to secret foreign policy initiatives like the opening to China. Just as an orderly withdrawal from Vietnam was considered vital to the credibility of the United States in its dealings with the Soviet Union, the maintenance of secrets was considered vital in the negotiations with China because if it came out prematurely the initiative would be aborted. It is amazing that security was maintained. But the secret was kept and the deed was done.

**QUESTION:** I would like to know your thoughts on the changing role of a President's wife. For instance, if Robert Dole were to become President—Mr. Donald Regan's comments and apology notwithstanding—how do you see the role of the President's wife in the future?

**MR. GARMENT:** Well, it obviously varies from wife to wife. It's made known to all presidential wives in some fashion that it would be desirable for them to take some role in the life of the presidential community. They have the opportunity to find an activity that is congenial to their personality and private interests. Mrs. Nixon was a very private person. Her interests generally focused on the children and their problems. So she had some activities organized in a formal way for them in that area.

Mrs. Johnson was an immensely active lady as was Mrs. Carter. Mrs. Reagan has moved from being associated with matters of high fashion to more substantive activities such as combatting drug abuse.

**QUESTION:** I've watched several presidencies; I've never understood why they thought they could maintain secrecy in Washington, D.C. What mind-set did you observe in the Nixon administration that made them think that they could domesticate secrets in that town?

**MR. GARMENT:** It's just about impossible now. It was difficult then, but some secrets were kept. Among other things, the president wasn't that interesting to the press. Before Watergate, investigative press activity was nothing like it was during and since. Huge amounts of junk are published now disguised as significant "source" information. In fact, there are very few secrets that are truly important. Most matters are secret solely by reasons of timing—not what's going to happen, but when. Many leaks are misleading because they are only a small part of the story.

It is extremely difficult to maintain secrecy now. Doing anything important that requires more than two people is very dangerous because leaking a so-called "secret" has become the way in which many young and not so young people involved in a swollen bureaucracy and really don't have much to do can achieve a feeling of power. They breach their responsibilities for the sheer joy of getting on the telephone and telling a reporter from the *Washington Post* or the *New York Times* that they know something nobody else knows. Of course, they rationalize this by saying they're doing something useful.

I feel very strongly about this kind of abuse. We go through pendulum swings in everything. I have a sense that people are getting a little sick of investigative journalists who overdramatize accounts of government activities or injure people in government at the request of a rival by leaking phoney information or through the untimely release of some sensitive information. I think responsible journalists are also reacting against this kind of reporting.

**QUESTION:** If you had to guess on the leak of the Weinberger letter opposing the first Reagan-Gorbachev summit conference, what would you guess?

**MR. GARMENT:** My guess is that was leaked by someone at the White House. People always say "White House" as if there are three or four people living there; there are 3,000 people "in the White House." People who had access to that document number in the dozens or scores because copies are made of everything.

My guess is that it came to the *Washington Post* and the *New York Times* from a senior member of the White House staff who wanted to capitalize on what was not a particularly astute covering document for the transmission of a report on the Soviet arms treaty negotiations. It could, on the other hand, be that the Defense Department leaked it to the press to make Weinberger's case public. It's a fairly complicated business.

**QUESTION:** Can you tell me what role Alexander Haig played in the Nixon administration? Did he make important decisions?

**MR. GARMENT:** He did. I know Haig quite well. I worked with him even before he was Colonel Haig. He was then on Henry Kissinger's NSC staff. Before that, he was in McNamara's group over in the Pentagon and at the White House; he knew the place pretty well. I think he was back at West Point when Henry Kissinger was staffing the NSC, and Kissinger's old professor at Harvard, William Yandel Elliott, knew Haig's work and recommended him highly to Henry. If you ever needed to find out what time it was, you could go to Al Haig's office and ask him what time it was, because he was there day and night.

Later on, when he was vice chief of staff, he was summoned from there to his new battle station, Watergate; his job was to run the White House staff during that chaotic period. He came over in April 1973. During those years the President was still functioning effectively in foreign policy, but Haig was there day and night working away, making a lot of the big decisions in the domestic areas. He also worked on the Watergate case itself. But it is not correct, as people have said, that he served as a surrogate President. He certainly didn't take over for Richard Nixon in the foreign policy area. Right to the end, Nixon functioned effectively there.

This raises a point about the presidency that has always interested me. A president must have a special capacity for compartmentalization, the ability to move from meeting A, in which he has heard something really terrible, to meeting B in which he is receiving the credentials of the ambassador from a newly-created country, then to a luncheon, a political speech, and so on. A president has to have immense self-discipline, a special capacity for abstracting himself from one event and moving to the altered atmosphere of another event. During Watergate there were some things that happened to Richard Nixon that were not his fault, that should never have happened, that were the result of staff stupidity or accidents or worse. They were such that it was clear to him at that particular moment he was in danger of losing his presidency and losing it under circumstances of the most painful disgrace. Yet after hearing those things he would have to go to another meeting and talk about housing policy. He did it without skipping a beat. If it had happened to me, I would have gone home to cry a lot and drink a lot. Maybe that's why he is still so much with us.

**QUESTION:** Let me follow up on Haig. Three of your predecessors have said that no one knows who issued the order for Watergate. One of them hinted that Haig might have had a role in the disclosure of what happened at Watergate, that he might have been "Deep Throat."

**MR. GARMENT:** I don't really think there is a "Deep Throat." I think Woodward and Bernstein in *All the President's Men* needed an organizing device, a Greek chorus, someone or something to hold together the flow of events, to give them focus. I'm sure there was a large number of sources. I really don't believe there were a lot of those meetings taking place in a garage. I don't believe all that flower pot stuff. There are specific reasons why I say this. But in the end, what difference does it make? Who cares if there was a "Deep Throat" or ten sources or a whole Westminster choir? It has nothing to do with anything. It's just hype. Serious things happened during that time; but that's another story. It may take years before people can look at Nixon and Watergate with some degree of detachment.

**QUESTION:** Do you think someone did issue the order on Watergate?

**MR. GARMENT:** Which order are we talking about?

**QUESTION:** To the plumbers.

**MR. GARMENT:** To the plumbers? It is not altogether clear to me what they did, but we'll leave that aside for the moment and accept the common perception that they did a specific thing because they went into the Watergate to get certain secrets. My belief is that there were general instructions. I think some people connected with the administration knew they were going to do this but at a much lower level than anybody is talking about.

**COMMENT:** Both Haldeman and Erlichman said that no one to this day knows. One of them said privately that they thought Mitchell issued the order.

**MR. GARMENT:** That I don't believe. I know John Mitchell very well. Some would say it's an act of loyalty on my part; I wouldn't be ashamed of that, but that's not really why I'm saying it. John Mitchell was my law partner. I made a suggestion to Nixon that he look at Mitchell as the overall campaign manager. We were friends in the law firm. We were good friends in the government and still are. He did not want to go into the government. He knew he had a problem with Mrs. Mitchell. He was quite content to practice law. He went into the government because Richard Nixon insisted that he become attorney general.

John Mitchell was anything but a fool. He was a very shrewd man. He was chief adviser to Nelson Rockefeller for years. He was the preeminent adviser to governors in this country in relation to their state business and bond financings for over twenty years. He may have been tired towards the end of the Nixon years; he may have been distracted; he may have been badly served by that laconic manner of his when it came to people pushing for authority to do something. But I don't believe he gave a specific order that specifically authorized an illegal entry. That's something I would bet on.

**QUESTION:** Could you clarify the role of counsel to the President?

**MR. GARMENT:** It varies. Most of the jobs in the White House vary from president to president. The president makes the White House what he wants to make of it.

There are certain things that are always part of the job; it depends on who he is and what the President wants to make of him. Judge Rosenman was President Roosevelt's lawyer and was his White House lawyer. He was also a speechwriter and he had a lot of other responsibilities. Ted Sorenson was special counsel to John Kennedy so he did policy and wrote speeches. He didn't do too much lawyering. Dave Ginsburg was also in that administration. He did the more traditional White House lawyering.

Lloyd Cutler was very much a White House counsel in the large sense. He created and ran a traditional type of law firm in the White House. He also took care of clearances, the disclosure issues, and helped Cabinet members who had to be confirmed. He was brought in as a fireman when there was a scandal or some problem on the

Hill. In addition, he had the larger portfolio of advising the President on a whole range of foreign policy matters and working on speeches and statements. He ultimately became a special emissary, dealing with the Congress on arms control issues.

In our administration, we started with John Erlichman as counsel to the President. He had a number of deputy counsels who did the routine legal work, any kind of legal problem that White House people would have thought related to their official responsibilities. But John Erlichman's larger duties were in the policy area. He became much more interested in the flow of memoranda, documents and option papers to the President. That eventually led to the creation of the Domestic Council. He worked with different presidential task forces or Cabinet committees—interagency groups that would be organized *ad hoc* to deal with new initiatives. I think he saw that that didn't work too well, so he organized the Domestic Council. That became his interest rather than being counsel to the President.

John Ehrlichman told me the President wanted me to take on his counsel job in 1970. As a matter of fact, the President had announced that he'd decided to appoint Hobart Taylor, a friend and former government official. Somewhere, overnight, the decision was changed, and John Dean was made counsel. I have never been able to find out how that happened, but I want to thank whoever was responsible.

**QUESTION:** Most people have said exactly what you said. Herb Stein, for instance, had some doubts and then he met Nixon and watched him. He was impressed with his intelligence, the range of his interests and his ability to articulate. Three or four speakers in this series have said that the thing they can't understand is the language of the tapes. They never heard the President speak in this way. He slurred his words. There were expletives to be sure, but the general language wasn't any language they had ever heard him use in their relationships.

**MR. GARMENT:** I'm about to make myself unpopular. I think the general attitude toward the language on the tapes is one of the most distasteful exercises in piety that I've ever encountered. I'm talking about the casting of eyes to heaven, "God, isn't it awful that a President would use that dreadful language." People use dreadful language. People say all kinds of things under strain. I think there was an understandable amount of strain during those conversations.

The basic question is why were those tape machines rolling and how could it be that the taping process was so totally ignored by the President? Of course, that was the problem created by a highly successful technique. The idea was to have a record that would be withheld from public hearing until the President chose to weed out the junk and get rid of everything that was personal and irrelevant and to preserve the historical materials with the aid of archivists and historians for use at some later date. Then Mr. Nixon would have a true and accurate record without any posturing for posterity. So he simply forgot that the tape was running. It was, as it was supposed to be, a completely automatic process.

When I saw the transcripts I had the feeling—there were a few others who did too—that the language was going to turn out to be the big problem, more than any substantive admissions or statements. There was the sense that to have this presented to the country, even though it was never intended that anybody would hear it, was a terrible thing because children would read or hear about a President talking in these terms. That again goes back to the process, which was itself a mistake, rather than to the fact that Nixon used bad language. If I had a spontaneous record of my own conversations with my own staff in my law firm, I would be very embarassed to have my twenty-five old son hear it, much less a bunch of ten-year olds.

**QUESTION:** You had heard President Nixon use language like that yourself?

**MR. GARMENT:** Occasionally. He had a public posture and a private one. On the tapes we hear a private man under stress.

**QUESTION:** Some other things that happened in the Nixon

adminstration suggest that he was suffering from a disabling nervous breakdown.

**MR. GARMENT:** I don't think he was suffering anything like a nervous breakdown. He was under great strain. He had the sense of a situation that was out of control. He did not know where to turn because almost everybody he ordinarily relied on for guidance and assistance had an opposing interest. It was incredibly complicated. But the idea of his having a nervous breakdown or being incapable of performing his duties is simply wrong.

In fact, the surprising thing is how good his performance was right to the end. It's a curious thing; very close to the end he signed legislation establishing the legal services corporation. He signed it despite the fact that his self-interest lay in vetoing that legislation because the pro-Nixon stalwarts on the Hill, the very conservative Republicans, wanted that legislation vetoed. Some of them said that their residual support depended upon his vetoing that legislation, but he didn't.

**QUESTION:** Would you say a little about how President Nixon dealt with the Cabinet and the White House? One of the comments that Haldeman and Erlichman made is that the President didn't deal one-on-one with anybody and that on some important issues they had to pull him out from under the desk when somebody came in to talk with him.

**MR. GARMENT:** I didn't spend enough time with him to know. That was the latent phase of my political development. I had my own activities. I really think it was a mark of our good relationship that he asked me to work on matters about which he knew I had strong feelings: civil rights, minority economic development, the development of the cultural endowments. These activities tended to introduce some helpful ambiguity about the administration during a time when one of the main crisis areas was domestic unrest. The war protests, the civil rights protests, the development of the women's rights movement—this was a time when Washington was feeling the consequences of the cultural revolution of the sixties. I think Nixon felt that the crucial domestic issue that his administration confronted successfully was the desegregation of the southern school system.

During the first four years, he supported my work. He gave me the necessary money and the necessary support from the Office of Management and the Budget for these programs. He picked the right people to work on these problems. George Shultz was a close collaborator with the President in the work of the Cabinet committee on school desegregation. I generally met with the two of them in larger group sessions. I was rarely one-on-one with the President during that period, mainly because there was no need. I don't believe it's necessary to go in and sit on your mentor's lap all the time. There are many people in government who feel their work is not worthwhile unless they get a daily dose of high level appreciation. Fortunately, that's one problem I've never had.

**QUESTION:** Did you have allies on civil rights?

**MR. GARMENT:** Yes, Pat Moynihan, George Shultz and John Ehrlichman. A lot of the things I've gotten credit for in the books owe at least fifty percent of the outcome to Ehrlichman. He was right there with the President all the time; he put the papers before him and asked him to sign or discuss things; and the gatekeeper is a crucial ally. John Ehrlichman was one of the two key men. Haldeman was the other but I think Haldeman considered his job to be that of a value-free assistant, a conduit of data. He didn't try to slant the outcome. When the President began to have an excessive reaction to something or to propose doing things that shouldn't be done, it was Haldeman's job, which he performed with diligence, to find ways to say no, to let the paper slide, or to make sure it didn't happen. He was very good at that.

I think Ehrlichman would sometimes try to put his weight on the seesaw to affect the outcome. To that extent he helped the civil rights program. The Republican Nixon constituencies in the South and Southwest and other places, business executives as well as the parents of children being bussed around to schools, were not very keen about a large dose of civil rights enforcement. So it took some doing to maintain some balance and to do the right thing.

Let me tell an anecdote. In 1969, a lot of civil rights problems were generated. There was an effort to have the federal courts reconsider the premises of the case law on desegregation and busing. The players in the government were trying to determine what to do and how to find a position that would become the administration position. Bob Finch, the administration liberal at HEW, and his staff were very *gung ho* on civil rights enforcement. That's the nature of the HEW constituency. There was a time when the constituency came in and tied up all the phone booths and sat in the hall, but they didn't get anywhere. Things have changed a little bit.

On the other side, there was the Justice Department, which had a different institutional view, and then there were the people in the White House who represented the Southern point of view. There was no real administration policy during that year. The administration would take one position and the courts would knock it down; they would take another position and the courts would knock it down, too. The press was howling about our retrogressive behavior. It may have been objectively retrogressive, but it wasn't consciously so. The policy was all reactive; there was simply no strategy.

Things were rapidly getting out of control. In the early spring of 1970, there were a number of legislative initiatives: anti-busing amendments to bills, anti-busing constitutional amendments and a lot of other things that could really cause damage. This was especially true of the constitutional amendments; they were pointless, divisive and destructive. Everybody knew that they were a bad idea which would serve no purpose save to stir people up. There was also a lot of press talk that we were heading for a bloody confrontation. At the beginning of the school term in the fall of 1970, the courts had ordered instant desegregation everywhere. It was to be done instantly, and no longer with "deliberate speed."

Vice President Agnew was given the assignment of making a tough speech in Atlanta. One of his staff people described it as something to "rip the scab off and let it all come out." Pat Buchanan was assigned to write the speech, and I assure you Pat can write a very tough speech. Ehrlichman said to me, "Now you get in there and work with Pat. Don't leave his office. Keep some balance to this thing."

Buchanan and I had been friends through the whole campaign. He had been up in my law office during the years before the election and we knew each other well. So we had a day-and-night-long wrestling match. He had a draft; I had a counterdraft. He had a sentence; I had a balancing sentence. Of course, he couldn't write that way. The point was to make sure he had an unsatisfactory text. He knew what was going on. He was himself a bit uncertain about whether this Agnew speech was a good idea.

While this was going on, I wrote a memorandum for the President saying this speech was too important, too delicate, too complicated to be given by the vice president. It was the kind of thing presidents do. Even of you are going to say the same thing, it just shouldn't be done by number two. The speech was to be given the following night. During the day, there was a kind of hold on it. That night, there was a White House state party of some kind. I saw Haldeman there. He was always writing little notes; he held up a little note that said, "You win!" A decision had been made to cancel the speech and start a project, which then took three months, of research on the whole school desegregation business. Haldeman and Ehrlichman played a constructive role in that decision. I was then put in charge of coming up with an analysis of the problem, of the cases and options and a recommended way of dealing with things. A speech was drafted by Ray Price. Ultimately that produced a presidential paper, rather than a speech, as a more formal and calmer way of discussing this complex issue. The statement was issued on March 10, 1970.

Out of that message came a Cabinet committee on school desegregation and the creation of bi-racial committees with conservative white leaders, civil rights leaders and black community leaders organized to work together under the general theme of "obey the law without regard to what your feeling is; get the schools open and let us proceed with our children's education. We should fight out battles in the Congress, not on the streets." Shultz ran that effort and the President became deeply involved in meeting with parents and community leaders. We did television and radio commercials. Billy Graham and many other prominent people donated their voices and time to the effort to get schools open and functioning peacefully.

Then the Emergency School Aid legislation was enacted to provide funds to ease the way for desegregating schools. It was altogether a rational and constructive process.

**QUESTION:** What in the world did Mr. Agnew say in Atlanta?

**MR. GARMENT:** He didn't. You can find a copy of that speech in Bill Safire's book, *Before the Fall*, which is a very good biography of the administration before Watergate. The whole incident is laid out.

**QUESTION:** We always ask as the final question how will history evaluate the President?

**MR. GARMENT:** Very well, I think. To put it in a light way first, history has a way of separating the men from the boys. More seriously, I think that as time passes and the partisan feeling about Richard Nixon and his administration diminishes and the problems of the time domestically and abroad are seen more dispassionately, the Nixon administration will emerge as the good and strong administration that it was.

President Nixon's leadership meant a number of important things to this country and others. The opening to China was put in place largely by Mr. Nixon. There was the beginning of a new relationship with the Soviet Union based on a number of tough decisions during the Nixon administration, particularly in relation to Vietnam. SALT I laid the groundwork for future negotiations, even if only in small areas, between ourselves and the Soviet Union. The major peace steps in the Middle East owe a great deal to the work of the President and Henry Kissinger after the Yom Kippur War.

I could go on at book length, but I think that is essentially the way history will come to judge Richard Nixon, the way history is in the process of judging Richard

Nixon right now. There's a long line of pundits and savants who were among the sharpest, most passionate critics of Richard Nixon, now waiting to see him in New York and at his home in Saddle River. He is greeted with respect abroad and at home by virtually everyone who has anything to do with foreign policy, whether Republicans or Democrats. He's recognized as a man with special wisdom, the insights that comes from a long career and a durable character. So he continues to have a central role.

How will people come to view his presidency? I made a list, it's not exhaustive, of the people who are leaders in government today who were brought into political prominence by Richard Nixon fifteen or twenty years ago. It tends to suggest that we are still in a kind of Nixon era: George Bush, Caspar Weinberger, George Shultz, Jim Baker, Pat Moynihan, Arthur Burns, Henry Kissinger, Anne Armstrong, Bill Ruckelshaus, Russell Train, Paul Volcker, Herb Stein, Al Haig, Bud McFarlane, Dick Lyng, Don Rumsfield, Bill Simon. They are people who were trained to lead a government in an intelligent and moderate way in the Nixon administration. They are still basically at their old stands. Diane Sawyer was a press helper; she's a "60 Minutes" principal now. The four speech writers: Bill Safire, *New York Times;* Pat Buchanan, White House; Ray Price, syndicated widely; Ken Khachigian, Ronald Reagan's assistant on his big speeches. I rest my case, and I thank you for inviting me.

**NARRATOR:** I think I speak for everyone in saying that you've given us new insights in areas which no one else has discussed—civil rights, for instance—and in the connection between domestic and foreign policy as well. We thank you.

# THE WHITE HOUSE AND POLICY-MAKING

## John Ehrlichman

**NARRATOR:** Our Forum speaker today was a key figure in the Nixon administration. He is a native of Seattle, Washington. He had a distinguished war record being decorated with the Air Medal with Clusters and the Distinguished Flying Cross. After the war he graduated from UCLA with a Bachelor of Arts degree and then from Stanford Law School in 1951. He became a partner in a Seattle firm, Hullin, Ehrlichman, Roberts & Hodge and continued in that capacity until 1968. He became director of Nixon's convention activities for the 1968 Republican convention, tour director in the Nixon for President campaign, White House Counsel, and Assistant to the President for Domestic Affairs from 1969 to 1973. He has since been an author and a TV and radio commentator. He has authored the much discussed *Witness to Power* and also *The Company* and *The Whole Truth.* He is now a resident of New Mexico, where he continues to write.

As we explore the Nixon presidency nothing could be more appropriate than to talk with John Ehrlichman who, as someone said the other day, "didn't just make the appointments" but had considerable influence on policy, especially domestic policy, through the Domestic Council and through his other activities. He was a member of the Federal Property Review Board, the President's International Economic Policy Committee, and so on. But it was in the domestic area that he made his major contribution. It is a pleasure to have you with us.

**MR. EHRLICHMAN:** Mr. Thompson has provided me with nine questions which I am going to use as the text of my sermon. We can spend the bulk of the morning on your questions. I invite you to interrupt me as we go along.

The first question was: How did your association with Richard Nixon begin? I suppose it is kind of a typical campaign story. I had a college friend, H. R. Haldeman, who remained a social acquaintance although he and his wife had moved to Connecticut. One time when I was practicing law I happened to be in New York and went up there for Sunday breakfast. He was about to go off to the New Hampshire primary—this was in 1959—and he wanted to know what I thought about coming up and being an advance man. At that time my practice was reasonably prosperous and fairly dull, and this all sounded quite exciting. So I signed on as an advance man in the early stages. My first advance trip was to a Lincoln Day dinner in Milwaukee, Wisconsin. That was my first exposure to real politics.

I was not a passionate Nixon person going in. Probably if some college friend had invited me to go advance for John Kennedy I might have done it. My family had been Republican since the early days but I had stayed out of politics because my law practice involved problems of land use. Problems of land use involved the courthouse, and the courthouse in our town was predominantly Democratic. So it was to my clients' interest that I stay out of things partisan. I managed to operate on two levels from 1960 on. I had this national political connection, but the Democrats in the courthouse didn't penalize me for that hobby. I managed to get along with them and the land use practice thrived.

I went through that campaign as an advance man and came out at the end with a number of impressions of Richard Nixon, largely favorable. Nixon was a politician was a with enormous ability, a very good mind, and almost infallible political instincts—up to a point. In the last week of the campaign he had involved himself in the minutiae of the political campaign to a fault, and he scheduled himself in the last week of the campaign to redeem a promise that he would go to all fifty states. There is just no point in it. I live in a state that nobody ever visits, New Mexico, because it has only four electoral votes. You send the vice president into New Mexico to have a photo opportunity at the airport. It shouldn't take more than twenty minutes and then he's on his way. But in 1960 Richard Nixon said, "I will go to all fifty states." They got down to the last week of the campaign and realized he hadn't been to Alaska, South Dakota, and I forget what the other two were, but there were four of them that he hadn't been to. So he said, "I'm a man of my word; we're going to go to those places." Nobody could talk him out of it. So he dashed off to four nothing states in the last week of the campaign. It was a very ridiculous thing to do. Obviously he should have been in the ten battleground states trying to get the electoral votes.

I came away from that experience and watched more-or-less from a distance, not being involved in the advances of any of those states, with a feeling that maybe this guy's instincts weren't all that wonderful. I was asked to come and help him out in California in 1962 when he ran for governor and I couldn't do it. I did a little part-time scheduling for them when their scheduler got sick, and I happened to be there at the moment of "you're not going to have Nixon to kick around anymore" when he read the press off after a night of drinking, sleeplessness, remorse, and lots of other emotions. I came off of 1962 thinking this fellow may be his own worst enemy.

At the 1964 convention, after his rather remarkable speech of reconciliation, he had a party in his suite. He got pie-eyed, which cut across the grain as far as I was concerned, and I came away from that thinking well, that's the end of my relationship with Richard Nixon.

About 1967, Haldeman asked me to come back because Nixon was getting cranked up to run for President again. I said I didn't think I was interested. He more or less urged me to come to New York and have a talk with Nixon, which I did. I leveled with him. I said, "I really don't think I'm interested in getting involved in another one of your campaigns. I have a feeling that you are highly susceptible to alcohol. I'm not interested in coming away from my practice and my family and going out and beating my brains out if this is going to be a problem." He got very serious with me; he said he thought I was right. He made me a very solemn pledge that it would not be a problem. He asked me to come and help him and I was persuaded.

**QUESTION:** Were you speaking of Nixon or Haldeman?

**MR. EHRLICHMAN:** Nixon. We met in Nixon's New York office and had this conversation. As a footnote I'll say as far as I'm concerned he kept that promise all through that campaign. He was fit; drinking was not a problem. Physiologically, this fellow has a disability. One drink can knock him galley-west if he is tired. Even if he is not tired about two and a half drinks will do it. He is much more susceptible than a lot of people; he simply has to watch it.

Anyway, I became sort of the resident Nixon manager in Miami Beach getting ready for the 1968 convention. We had Rockefeller opposing him and it was quite a lively convention, particularly the maneuvering before the convention started. I managed that with a fellow named Bill Timmons, who turned out to be the manager of the most recent Republican convention.

After election day, we all sat up till three o'clock in the morning to find out how Illinois was going to go. Finally, Nixon was declared the winner by the networks. That made it official and he took seven of us with him to Florida to organize the government: Mitchell, Finch, Bryce Harlow, Kissinger, Haldeman, Zeigler, and me.

There is a lot of newspaper copy about Richard Nixon in Key Biscayne, Florida, with bulging briefcases and doing a lot of work. All baloney! What generally happened in Key Biscayne was that he went over to his house, which was on the west side of the island, and we went to a hotel on the east side of the island and never the twain did meet. We did have a couple of meetings but basically we were left on our own to compose the government.

At that time I fully intended to go back to Seattle and practice law. I had no intention of entering the government at all. Somebody passed that word to Nixon so he took me along on a ride to the airport where he held a reconciliation meeting with Hubert Humphrey. Humphrey was on his way to the Virgin Islands and landed in a Convair. He was still vice president for another couple of months. He and Nixon went into the operations building to make up. Humphrey cried and was very emotional about the whole thing.

On the way back, we were talking about Hubert and Nixon turned the conversation to me and asked me what I wanted to do in the government. I said "nothing" and that I intended to go home. Maybe some day when he was in a weak moment he could make me a federal judge or something along that line. I really didn't want to get involved. He tried a couple of things on me that were pretty ridiculous. At that time John Mitchell had told him he didn't want to be attorney general. So he wanted to know if I wanted to be attorney general and I said, "No, thank you." Finally he said, "Well, why don't you come into the White House for a year and be counsel? Then you can go back and get rich practicing law because everybody will want to hire you because you are the President's friend. It will be good for your career." I was sort of intrigued with the idea of seeing how the White House operated from the inside and that seemed like a pretty good position from which to do it. So I talked to my wife, who was not crazy about the idea, but we decided to give it a whirl for a year. So that was what I started out doing with a couple of young lawyers from the campaign staff. We were set up in the Pierre Hotel with our transition group and our job was to screen the incoming Cabinet officers and make sure there were no conflicts of interest and that kind of thing. Eventually I moved into the White House to do legal chores.

In fact, I didn't do one single legal chore. From the first day I got to the White House, they had me doing everything else but that. I advanced the first trip to Europe—eight countries—and found myself hobnobbing with the King of Belgium, the Pope, and all those folks. It got to be very heady very fast. Then almost at once the domestic side of the White House became a serious problem for the President. He had hired two fellows, one from the campaign and one from Harvard: Daniel Patrick Moynihan from Harvard, and Arthur Burns, an old associate from the Eisenhower days who had been very helpful in the campaign. They were somehow or another to divide up domestic chores. There was something called the Urban Affairs Council set up with Moynihan and a bunch of young Turks, and there was Arthur Burns and a bunch of conservative young fellows doing domestic policy. There were very ill-defined lines between them, and the two young staff groups were oil and water. Very quickly an animosity developed, an ideological animosity.

Both Burns and Moynihan had been around Washington long enough to know how to play the game extremely well and it got to be the game of who talked to the President last. Nixon quickly became disenchanted because both were pounding on him all the time. As quickly as Burns walked out, Moynihan would come in and undo everything that Burns had done. There were battlegrounds involving urban renewal, welfare reform, and immigration—subjects across the whole domestic landscape. Burns and Moynihan were fighting it out on liberal and conservative terms.

Along about the fourth month, Nixon turned to Roy Ash and his Citizen's Commission that consisted of John Connally and others, a very prestigious group. He said to them, "Why do I have to put up with this on the domestic side? There's got to be a more orderly way of going about the development of domestic policy than this. Henry never bothers me like this. Henry always brings me nice, neat papers on national security problems and I can check the box. Nobody badgers me and picks on me. But these two wild men on the domestic side are beating me up all the time." So they went off and devised the Domestic Council and the Office of Management and Budget.

There was another problem. David Kennedy, the secretary of the treasury, had brought with him a fellow named Robert Mayo, who was installed as director of the budget. Almost immediately Richard Nixon decided that he didn't like Robert Mayo. So I was recruited as a buffer between Richard Nixon and his Burns-Moynihan problem, number one, but also as a buffer between him and his budget director, whom he didn't like. That became almost a full-time job for me to somehow or another talk these two strong, experienced guys, Burns and Moynihan, into submitting their views through me to the President rather than directly, and explaining to this budget director why it was he could never have an appointment with the President. As we got closer and closer to the date that the budget had to go to the printer, that became more and more awkward.

Mayo was a guy who was not at all stupid; he knew what was going on. He had a forced jocularity that was embarrassing and Nixon hated it.

Eventually the Citizens Commission came up with a proposal to institutionalize the Office of Management and Budget and set up a sort of rationalized domestic policy apparatus akin to the National Security Council. Nixon's solution to all his problems was to bring in an outsider to take Burns' and Moynihan's places. He looked around and I happened to be walking by the window at the time and he said, "I'll take him."

He made Moynihan a member of the Cabinet and he sent Burns to the Federal Reserve. The symbiosis between Richard Nixon and Arthur Burns as chairman of the Fed was a wonderful thing to see, not always easy, but very productive. I became a firm believer in the necessity of there being a close tie between the President and the chairman of the Fed. I am concerned about what we see now: Ronald Reagan and Paul Volcker do not let their hair down together. I think it is very important to have coordination of the monetary and the fiscal policies of the government.

I inherited the two absolutely diverse staffs—Moynihan's liberals and Burns' conservatives—and it was impossible to make it work or at least impossible for me to make it work. One by one I put people out to pasture. That's a nice thing about the federal government; there are always wonderful things that you can find for people that you don't want to have working for you. Some of them went abroad and others found secretaryships and assistant secretaryships and gradually we got everybody out of there except one guy whom Nixon had an attachment to and who continued to be a problem. This was Martin Anderson.

Martin Anderson eventually popped up in my old job for Ronald Reagan, which I thought was poetic justice. I could never make it work because Martin is an ideologue of strong convictions. My theory of the job is that the domestic assistant should bring to the President every conceivable point of view and every option on the questions that were being presented to him. When I gave Martin an assignment he gave me a range of options that were always over on the right-hand ten degrees of the range, and it was predictable. I would have to find somebody else to do the other ninety.

But Richard Nixon asked continually, "What have you got Martin Anderson doing?" and that was a problem. So he stayed and he did things like the all-volunteer army that he was passionately interested in, and that was fine. Eventually he went back to Stanford and then had a rebirth when Ronald Reagan came along. He became Reagan's domestic assistant for the first year of that administration.

How did Nixon organize the White House? Our White House was ever changing, very fluid. Anybody that takes a cross section of the Nixon administration White House and says it is this kind of creature will be right for a certain moment in time. But things changed, and as we got into trouble, things changed very rapidly.

The general function on the domestic side was to do a certain amount of planning and forecasting of what our problems would be. A man named Ed Harper, a Ph.D., came to us with a broad background in one of the management companies and local government. He not only did our forecasting but was also our liaison to the Office of Management and Budget. He participated in the early budget deliberations each year so that he could come back and say, "Well, in the negotiations with HEW it looks like next year our problems are going to be these." Of course there are action-forcing events: bills that expire and have to be renewed, Congressmen forcing an agenda of one kind or another the *Washington Post* forcing an agenda on an almost daily basis.

I might say, by way of footnote, that we got out a news summary every day. You may be familiar with the President's news summary; that was an innovation in our administration. We had a staff of four people working all night canvassing all the networks, the news magazines, and fifty of the newspapers in order to summarize the news. A copy of the summary would be in my car every morning at six o'clock, and I would read it as I went to work. It would enable me to predict at my morning staff meetings what the President was going to be concerned about when he got is copy of the news summary and began to make marginal notations. Sure enough, by about ten thirty in the morning my copy of his news summary would come up with his marginal notations. There would be work assignments, and there would be circles drawn around things, notes like "Fire this guy," and things of that sort. You had to be flexible because what turned up in the news summary in the morning could very often be your agenda for the day regardless of what was on your calendar and particularly if the President thought it was important.

Anyway, in short-term predictions and in long-term predictions, we tried to figure out what our problems were going to be. Then it was my function to make assignments to working groups consisting of a person from my staff, a person from the Office of Management and Budget assigned by Shultz, people from the departments and agencies who were expert in the subject matter, and folks from the outside that we could pull in from the private sector, from academia, wherever we could find them. These working groups, chaired by one of my people, would meet and attempt to draft either a position paper or an option paper depending on what the President was going to be called upon to do. Once they got it in some kind of form, it would be sent to the Cabinet members involved. It would be passed around the White House if there were people in the White House who had areas of responsibility involved. Eventually it would come to me as a final product and I would hand it to the President for his weekend reading. He might carry two or three of these away on a weekend, fairly thick documents with a covering memo of anywhere from half a page to ten pages. The covering memo always ended with a summary of what we thought his options were.

Kissinger always claimed that he selected option number two of three options. He said, "You people are very foolish to give him more than three options. You must always arrange it so that the one you favor is the second one." I liked to give the President as broad and as long a list of options as I could. It was a game between him and me to see if he could figure out some options that I hadn't thought of and then he would pencil them in. He preferred that mode. He didn't want meetings around the Cabinet table with passionate advocates pounding away at each other and at him and he cross-examining them. He was not comfortable with face-to-face contact.

If he gave you an assignment it was either one of two kinds. It was either pure rhetoric and he really didn't intend it, an "off with their heads" kind of an assignment that he expected you not to do, or it was a real assignment which he expected you to do and which he would then ask you about later, without any notes or ticklers. About three days later he'd say "What did you do about that?" The other thing he wanted to know about a real assignment was "Who is in charge? I want one man in charge of this that I can talk to, and frequently."

I had a fellow named Ed Morgan on my staff. He had been one of our advance men. Busing was one of our continual problems during those days. He wanted a guy responsible for busing, and he would call Morgan in because Ed was the fellow designated. He would call him in and they would sit and talk by the hour about this busing problem: who the players were, state by state; the Charlotte-Mecklenburg decisions, what did they mean? Who were the judges? Why did they think that way? He would chew the subject over and over and over. I was delighted to have someone like Ed designated because if Nixon didn't chew on him he was going to chew on me. Richard Nixon was like a cow. He would chew his cud over and over on a subject and turn it over and chew it some more, and turn it over and chew it some more. So if you could enlist some junior staff man for that process, it was a whole lot better than to have your whole day soaked up with those long monologues.

There are, I understand, seven or eight thousand hours of tapes that no one has heard. A very high percentage of those will be chewing the cud, I think, and people will come away saying, "My God, this man is indecisive and redundant. How in the world could he be called an executive?" Yet this is the way he operated. He would turn the same rock over a dozen times and then leave it and then come back to it two weeks later and turn it over another dozen times.

Haldeman went off on holiday a couple of times and I was dragooned into taking his place. I discovered that he did that on the political side and on the housekeeping side even more than Kissinger and I did on the substantive sides. He would sit in there by the hour. A campaign would be coming up and Nixon would want to talk about buttons and bumper stickers, about what color the bumper stickers should be, where they should be on the car, and how you made sure that they were put in the right place; endless chewing.

On the Alice in Wonderland side, there were the instructions which made him feel good—"I am the President" kind of instructions where he would say, "I want all federal money cut off to MIT. Do it now, do it today, there is no appeal. I don't want to hear any conversation about it; just go do it." So you would make a note of that and go out and do nothing. Two or three days later he might say, "What have you done about cutting off all the federal money to MIT?" and I'd say, "Well, I haven't done anything about it." "Well, I've been thinking about it; it's probably just as well," he would say.

One place the Nixon administration got into difficulty was that there were people around who didn't know the difference (such as the Marine Corps types). They saluted and went out and did whatever they were told. Colson in the early days was one of those. You have heard about the fire bombing of the Brookings Institution as one of the Watergate episodes. I had no doubt that somewhere back in the origins of that was one of these rhetorical instructions by Richard Nixon. He was given to these kinds of excesses and you just simply had to know the difference. I wouldn't be at all surprised to learn that Colson saluted, did an about-face, and went out to collect fire bombs. It's very logical to me, knowing the players.

How harmonious were relations between the White House and Cabinet-level departments? Richard Nixon originally ran on the promise that he would have a strong Cabinet full of preeminent leaders. I don't know if you remember, but we did a very grandiose television introduction, the one and only time that I know of a President actually staging a prime time television show to introduce his Cabinet to the nation; that took a bit of doing. We had to pull all those people in and it was supposed to be a big secret, so the press couldn't see any of them. We brought them in through the basement of the hotel and he sprang them on a grateful nation.

All of these fellows were hired on the representation that they were going to run their departments and be more or less autonomous. We were going to have a weak White House staff that was going to be small, lean, not advisory but assistant to the President, and the Cabinet officers were going to be advisory. That lasted until the middle of the first year. Then he became very unhappy with some decisions that were being made, particularly at HEW on civil rights. He thought Secretary Finch had been captured by his bureaucracy and that the civil rights lawyers were leading him around by the nose. Didn't they understand that he was the President and that he was going to have to run for reelection? The policies in this government had to be his; they couldn't be Finch's. That began also to manifest itself at HUD where Governor Romney was off saving the world, and Secretary Volpe at the Department of Transportation was saying some funny things about air bags and other things.

We began to get these long soliloquies about how tough it was to be President surrounded by idiots. You began to get instructions from him: "You are to call Mitchell and tell him that I will not have these kinds of statements being made by the Office of Civil Rights and the Justice Department, or "Get rid of that fellow Allen over at HEW." "Call Finch today and fire him. He is going around saying that we favor busing; we don't favor busing. Don't they understand?" More and more as we proceeded through the first year he began taking back all of those delegations of absolute authority that had been rather frivolously handed out in transition time. Well, that caused a good deal of heartburn out in the Cabinet, as you can imagine.

Cabinet meetings were never substantive. They were always show and tell. As we got farther and farther into the administration they got more and more perfunctory. He would call Henry in and say, "Henry, I want you to take twenty-five minutes with these fellows and explain to them about starvation in Africa." He'd call me in and say, "Haven't you got something you can tell them about welfare reform?" You know, pull something right out of the air. So we would have charts prepared or slides or overhead projections and the Cabinet would sit there and these things would be put up. Romney would raise his hand and begin to discuss, and Nixon would say, "George, I'm terribly sorry but I've got an NSC meeting that I've got to get ready for. I wish I could extend this meeting. Why don't you write me a memo on this?" He'd then get up and run out of the room as fast as he could go. There was very little deliberation. It got so bad that in about the third year we learned of a rump session of the Cabinet. They actually held a meeting over at Romney's conference room to discuss economic problems because they couldn't get any discussions at the Cabinet table when the Cabinet met.

Nixon sent me over to break up that meeting. I was not a invited guest but I was there. Talk about a skunk at a garden party; I was it. They didn't want to see me. But I sat through their meeting. Red Blount, the postmaster, Romney, Volpe, and Paul McCracken, the chairman of the Council of Economic Advisers were there. They had, I would guess, a quorum of the Cabinet. They tried to carry on a discussion that would have been a good deal more revolutionary, I'm sure, if I hadn't been there. But since I was there it became quite moderate and sort of perfunctory. But Nixon was terribly upset that they would call such a meeting behind his back. He called Arthur Burns and told him under no circumstances could he attend. He called McCracken with the same instructions, but McCracken went anyway. It was a mini-revolt.

**QUESTION:** How did you get wind of it if there were no invitations?

**MR. EHRLICHMAN:** Oh, we had our sources. The first day I was ever in the White House was to visit Harry McPherson, who was counsel on the Johnson staff. Harry said, "If you're going to survive around here you need your sources at the middle levels." You've got to know what's going on in the departments and agencies. You can't wait until it's printed in the *Washington Post*." So my administrative assistant came in one day and said, "Do you know about the rump Cabinet meeting?" I said, "No, tell me more." It came from a friend of our's in HUD whom we had cultivated.

I had six assistant directors of the Domestic Council staff and they were responsible for six subject matter areas: one fellow had all the environmental and interior problems; one had labor, commerce, and the business community. Within those areas they got to know colleagues in the bureaucracy rather well. OMB was a valuable source of information. They had their own contacts at the lower levels. Such sources are absolutely vital because nobody is going to send you an engraved invitation to the things that are problems.

What problems arose between the White House and the Cabinet? A lot of problems arose. It got very bad after awhile because Nixon personally did not want to see most of the Cabinet. I would come in and say, "Secretary Romney has developed his plan for the reurbanization of Detroit. It is going to involve a fair amount of money, and you are going to have to talk to him about it." "Well, you talk to him about it." I said, "I have talked to him about it." "Well, what do you think?" "I think you ought to listen to him." "I don't want to listen to him. He comes in here and he bends my ear and wastes my time, and he whines a lot because I don't see him enough. I don't want to hear all that." We've got the reputation—some terrible books have been written about this—of building a wall around the President. The fact is that he was down under his desk saying, "I don't want to see those fellows," and we were trying to pull him out.

He was simply not fond of some of the people he had picked earlier. Relationships deteriorated. Just before the 1972 convention it got very bad with George Romney. There was a very bad flood in Wilkes Barre, Pennsylvania. HUD sent people up there to troubleshoot and we were being killed in the newspapers. Milton Shapp, governor of Pennsylvania, was bashing us every day about how we weren't doing enough and were getting in the way. According to the press, people were unhappy and old ladies were sleeping in the mud. So Nixon said, "I want Romney sent up there. I want him to go up there today. I want him to get this straightened out. There is no excuse for this. Get him up there." So, I called his administrative assistant and said, "Use one of our airplanes or helicopters and get him up there. The President wants him there on the scene. He's got to straighten it out and talk to the press. Let's neutralize this problem. Pennsylvania is a big battleground state, a very important political state, and we're coming into a critical time." Romney evidently had other plans which he had to rearrange and it caused him to be extremely unhappy at the summary way in which he was dispatched. I got a note from his wife saying, "You people at the White House are mistreating my husband." It was a poignant little note. Lenore Romney is an activist sort of lady and very much her husband's partner in things, and she thought I was picking on him.

Romney came in and wanted to resign. He managed to get an appointment with the President to tell him that. In his heart nothing would have pleased Nixon more, but he knew he couldn't have a resignation of that kind just before the convention so he persuaded Romney to stay until after the election. We had a big love feast and a lot of things out front so that the press would write that everything was o.k.

Then Nixon decided that he was going to get rid of all these people after the election and he was going to have a nice, shiny new Cabinet. He was going to get a bunch of people in who cared about him and looked after his interests instead of their own interests.

Relations with the Congress were also strained. We were the first administration in I don't know how many years—I guess since Eisenhower—to have both Houses of Congress against us. It was tough, very tough. We had a brilliant man named Bryce Harlow, very experienced in Washington, as our congressional relations man. When he left Bill Timmons, another first-rate man, took over. Again, we ran into the problem that Richard Nixon simply didn't want to spend the kind of time that was required to cultivate these folks. But he spent more time doing that than he did with his Cabinet, fortunately. He was able to forge a number of working coalitions—conservative coalitions and moderate coalitions—on various issues. We got a remarkable amount of legislation enacted and we managed to head off some terrible legislation. On balance, his legislative record was pretty decent considering what we had stacked up against us. He was very activist in the area of legislation. We moved packages of legislation on the domestic side on an average of every nine or ten days. We had stuff up there all across the board: pension reform, environment, economic studies, welfare reform, government reorganization. The list is as long as your arm and some of it was very good.

**QUESTION:** Where did that originate? Did it originate in the departments? These packages?

**MR. EHRLICHMAN:** No, it would usually come out of the working groups that I told you about. Some of it was strictly one department's. But the executive branch is so badly organized these days that you can't conceive of much legislation that is strictly within one department or agency. Almost all of it touches several departments and agencies, so you have to bring them together and get everybody's input on the thing. One of the big packages we sent up there that never went anywhere was governmental reorganization, the reorganization of the executive branch. We wanted to reorganize it along functional lines; it's organized along constituency lines now: labor, commerce, and so on. We proposed four general departments—natural resources, human resources, and so on. The functions of the existing departments and agencies were to be folded under each new department. That cut across the alignments of the Congress and the lobbyists and the other interests in Washington. We couldn't get any committee hearings on it and nothing happened.

**QUESTION:** Was that to be a replacement of the old Bureau of the Budget and management function and apart from the Bureau of the Budget?

**MR. EHRLICHMAN:** No, no. The Office of Management and Budget was very much a part of that.

**QUESTION:** So you folded it into the existing function of the Bureau of the Budget.

**MR. EHRLICHMAN:** The Bureau of the Budget was broadened by the late 1969 change to embrace management and they developed quite a management capacity.

**QUESTION:** So it was superimposed?

**MR. EHRLICHMAN:** No, side by side with it.

**QUESTION:** Was it a parallel function?

**MR. EHRLICHMAN:** Yes. Functionally it worked this way.

How did Nixon pick the White House and other personnel? The answer to that question is not very well. The personnel process during our transition from Johnson was a shambles. Somebody had the brilliant idea of writing a letter to everybody listed in *Who's Who* to ask them who ought to work in the Nixon administration. They sent forms out to everybody and, as was predictable, all of the forms came back in. Here was a room full of these things and somebody had to read them and try and make some sense out of them. It was ridiculous.

What happens immediately when somebody is elected President is that every congressman and every senator telephones to suggest people, including their office and committee staffs, to be appointed to various important positions. So the congressional liaison person has mountains of pink phone slips from everybody in the Congress proposing people to be appointed. You have to sift through all of this stuff and rationalize it and try to make some decent appointments. In those days it was a very imperfect process. I would guess that with data retrieval it might go better today. But it is one of the more difficult things to do.

We had Office of Management types, McKinsey and Booz Allen-type guys who, when you had a vacancy coming up, would send resumes of people that they had scouted out around the country. Actually we got some very good folks that way.

You remember Nixon asked for everybody's resignation after the 1972 election? He went off to Camp David and began restaffing the executive branch. He had some guiding principles. The Catholics had been enormously good to him in the election and he was going to have some Catholics in this administration. He didn't have any Catholics in the Cabinet except Peter Brennan from New York. So the personnel office cranked out a bunch of names and there were Italians and so on. One of them cranked out was a man named Brinegar who was an executive of Union Oil and highly recommended by Fred Hartley, who had been a partner in a national accounting firm. Nixon mulled that over and said, "Brinegar. At last we are going to have some ethnic breakthroughs in this Cabinet and we're going to get a good Irish Catholic." So he decided that Claude Brinegar was going to be the secretary of transportation and take Volpe's place. This was duly announced. He interviewed him and then had Brinegar come back up to Camp David for one more conversation and to have their picture taken. He began asking Brinegar about the cardinals and Brinegar explained that the Steelers were really his ball club. Nixon said, "No, no, you know like Kroll and those cardinals," and Brinegar said, "Well, I don't know any of those cardinals. I'm an Episcopalian." So we had a big housecleaning in the personnel office. But Brinegar went on and was a pretty good secretary of transportation as it turned out.

**QUESTION:** May we ask about Watergate strategy?

**MR. EHRLICHMAN:** Nixon and I were at San Clemente shortly after the break-in at the Democratic headquarters. At that time I felt that it was possible for him totally to insulate himself from that problem. There were some people at the Committee to Reelect involved and as far as we knew nobody at the White House was involved. We talked about making sure that the problems did not infect the White House. We had one hundred and some days until the 1972 election. If we could keep it out of the White House for that length of time he'd be home free. Intellectually, he agreed with that and I thought we had an understanding that that's the way it was going to work.

Much later, when I was in deep trouble and the prosecutor had to make the tapes available, I listened to them and discovered that within hours of the break-in Richard Nixon was in the thing up to his ears: plotting and counter-plotting and discussing, chewing and conspiring and very much involved in it. It was a little like the tar baby—once you touched it you were stuck—and he was stuck within six days of the break-in itself. All our conversation and his pious undertakings and everything after the fact were really too late.

**MR. EHRLICHMAN:** The break-in itself made no sense to me; it never has. There was no reason for them to go over there but they did, and Nixon got himself involved. Those were the seeds of his undoing. Beyond that he is a person who, having been in politics for thirty years, is simply emotionally and constitutionally unable to deliver himself to his enemies to any degree. He will fight, bleed, and die before he will admit to Jack Anderson that he's wrong or that he's made a mistake. I learned eventually that the best way to handle a mistake in Washington is to step out and say you've made a mistake, and on occasion I did that. I proposed that to him, though probably too late. He couldn't bring himself even to consider the possibility of stepping out and saying to the American people, "Look, we have a very serious problem here and I've fired eighteen guys and I'm going to put this behind me," very much like Jerry Ford did with Bo Callaway. Do you remember when Callaway showed up as potentially having a conflict of interest in the national forest leases out in Colorado? They immediately fired him as chairman of Ford's reelection committee and put a lot of distance between the President and the problem.

The other way to go is the way Carter did with Bert Lance, and say "I have great confidence in Bert," in effect clutching him to your bosom. That hurt Carter badly. It sounds sterile and heartless but actually a President must put distance between himself and a problem. I don't care whether it's a substantive problem or a political problem or a scandal or whatever it is. He's got to distance himself. If somebody else gets hurt in the process then they get hurt, but the presidency must go on.

Nixon couldn't bring himself to distance himself, not so much because of affection for any individual involved but because he just could not leave intrigue alone. He loved it; he loved politics; he loved the intrigue side of politics, and when this came down the pike he was drawn to it like a magnet. I think that's the root of the crisis. The farther we got into it the more difficult it was for him. No one was able to persuade him that the course was fatal.

I guess I'm the first one who uttered the word "impeachment" in his presence. He never took it seriously. I guess he did take it seriously briefly but then he managed to paper it over as not a possibility, as just my alarmist view of things. I left at the end of April of 1973 and he was there for another year and some months. But before I left I began to feel that he didn't know what the truth was. He didn't know what he had said, didn't know what he had done, and the fact was whatever he was saying was truth at that particular moment.

In the very last conversation I had with him we talked about the break-in in California—the Ellsberg psychiatrist break-in—and at that time a couple of our people were in some difficulty on that. There was an investigation going on and he said, "I didn't know about that, did I?" I had to indicate to him that he did know about it. "Well, if somebody told me about it, I paid no attention to it. I didn't know there was a taping system in the room at the time." Since then it has occurred to me that he was talking for the record, among other things. But at the same time I am convinced that he really didn't know the difference between what was true and what wasn't true at any given moment. He could persuade himself of almost anything, which is too bad.

What about other crisis areas? We had a lot of them. We took over when there had been riots. One of the first visits I had was from Warren Christopher who later became famous in the Iranian hostage negotiations. He had been deputy attorney general and was an old law school friend of mine. He arrived in my office with a big package of documents and suggested that we keep them on hand all the time. They were proclamations to be filled in. You could put in the name of the city and the date and the President would sign it and declare martial law. Lyndon Johnson had these things on hand all the time because he had riots in Detroit, Washington, and all over the country. Fortunately, we never had to use those things but we did call out the troops. We had enormous demonstrations in Washington and New Haven and other places revolving around the Vietnam War. There was an extra barricade around the White House; there was the whiff of tear gas from time to time; we had mobilization day on the first of May when they tried to shut Washington down; and we had a lot of troops out that day. So we had crises of different kinds. The inflation rate was down around five or six percent; unemployment was down around five or six percent; interest rates were down around four or five percent in the good old days. It wasn't all bad, but we had our ups and downs.

What were Richard Nixon's main strengths and weaknesses? I'd say his strengths lay in his intellect primarily. He has a brilliant mind in the areas in which he is interested. He is a hybrid, as I've written. He is like a race horse specially trained to run a particular race and no good for pulling wagons or riding kids around the block. He's for running the race to be President and that's what he lived for. The result is that he's not the sort of fellow that you'd find fascinating as a next door neighbor. He wouldn't come over and play Scrabble or talk to you about a new record that he just bought. He saw the same movies over and over again, which was kind of indicative. He has a very narrow range of interests. If you are willing to talk to him about the things that he's interested in, he's fascinating. But if the conversation at the party turned to something that he wasn't interested in, he might go home or go upstairs and take a nap or go for a walk around the block because he is simply not able to get involved in things that he's not interested in.

I would say that his major weakness was in interpersonal relationships. He was a fellow who at the time I knew him—bear in mind I haven't laid eyes on him since 1973—was very weak in family relationships and in friendships. He had no strong friendships based on an exchange of interests and views and mutual confidence. His personal relationships, as with Bebe Rebozo and one or two others, were almost unilateral, not reciprocal.

Some of the worst times I ever spent with him was when he tried to fire somebody. He knew he had to do it, but couldn't do it. It was a little bit like killing the Thanksgiving turkey with a dull axe, hack away and back off and ask somebody else to do it. He was terrible at that kind of thing.

He tended to avoid controversy by presenting an aspect of himself which he probably subconsciously calculated would be acceptable to the person that he was dealing with. He could switch around and present the opposite aspect to another person. There were people on the staff with whom he was very profane because he thought that was where he made contact with them. There were other people with whom he would never use a swear word. He was very complex and anybody who writes a biography of Richard Nixon and tries to explain his personality has a real job cut out for him. These psycho-histories that are on the market now are dreadful: Fawn Brodie's and the others. They miss the mark so badly that they are not worth the price.

There is yet to be a good explanation of Richard Nixon and I think the reason is that when the authors come to people like me, they get the five blind men and the elephant. I tell them it's a rope and somebody else tells them it is a tree trunk and we are both right. To me it was a rope and to the other guy it was a tree trunk. I doubt seriously that there are many people that have seen the complete Richard Nixon. So that's a problem of definition that people are going to have. Maybe the true explanation will be an anthology with twenty contributors. Maybe you will be able to triangulate from that.

How will future historians judge the Nixon presidency? Well, I think "mixed" is probably it. It is becoming the age of the historians. More and more historians are beginning to tackle this job. I'm beginning to see some of those who come by and want to talk about specific things. Somebody has just done the definitive work on the postal reorganization and somebody else has done a very thick book on the Alaskan Native Claims Act. They are beginning to pick away at pieces. Stephen Ambrose, who has done the two-volume book on Eisenhower, is about to start on a Nixon biography. Unfortunately the archives are locked up and you can't get into them. The tapes are not yet available so some of the conventional source material for historians is still unavailable. But a little perspective is beginning to creep into the subject and I think as we get farther away from the taste of the scandal, more perspective will come into it. People will begin to make a more balanced judgment of the accomplishments and failures of the administration.

**QUESTION:** Tell us a little bit more about what this chewing the cud did for him. It isn't clear to me what function it performed.

**MR. EHRLICHMAN:** It is the way his mind worked. He did a lot with personnel as an example. He'd see that he was going to have a vacancy coming up or he decided to fire somebody and then one of his favorite pastimes was to say, "Well, let's see, if I moved Bill Rogers to the Supreme Court and I moved Kissinger to the State Department, and I brought Richardson into the White House and moved Weinberger over to HEW, how would that work?" "I don't think Weinberger would be too good at HEW." "Maybe not. Let's see. If I moved Weinberger over to the State Department and I moved . . . ." We'd go on like that for hours.

**QUESTION:** It wasn't necessarily an exchange.

**MR. EHRLICHMAN:** It was unilateral. Probably you'd grunt at the right times or make some comment or other.

One of the last conversations I had with Henry Kissinger was a couple of years ago, and Henry said, "You know, you and I are going to look like perfect fools when those tapes come out. We are going to sit there and he is going to say the most outrageous stuff and we will not protest. And we will be seen by historians as acquiescing." Well, I reassured him and said, "Certainly someone is going to understand that far from acquiescing our minds were probably drifting off to other things," but maybe not.

**QUESTION:** Why do you think he taped it all?

**MR. EHRLICHMAN:** One, I don't know, and that's the bottom line answer. I didn't know there was a taping system as long as I was there. Nobody told me, but in talking with Bob Haldeman and John Connally since, I get the impression that Nixon was very concerned that there be an uncontestable record of his conversations with and assignments to Henry Kissinger so that in future years there would be no question as to whose mind the ideas sprang from. It was partly a matter of credit, partly a matter of being able to go back and make clear to Henry what his instructions were within certain limits or in a certain direction. I would have to say that Nixon didn't entirely trust Henry and I can vouch for that. But why he did it, why he didn't burn them, why they were as they were, is something that I just can't help you on. I don't know.

**QUESTION:** I hear talk of a great deal of loyalty, though, in the staff to Mr. Nixon. I suppose it is confidence. Is that loyalty to him or to the presidency?

**MR. EHRLICHMAN:** Both. When I say both, I think a mixture. There were very few illusions about Richard Nixon, I think, among the senior staff, particularly as we got into things. There was a good deal of wry humor about his mannerisms, his foibles and his prejudices and a lot of anguish on our part about not being able to work out a better relationship between him and his Cabinet, and things of that kind. Nevertheless, we worked for the President of the United States. He is the only President around; we all worked for him and it was up to us to make it work.

I've just been to a collection of old White House staff people: Jack Watson from Carter, George Reedy from the Johnson and Kennedy years, and Jack Marsh from Ford, and so on. The commonalities of attitudes toward the Presidents is very interesting: tolerance, some affection, very few illusions, a willingness to be very forthcoming (on the part of everybody but the Kennedy people) about the shortcomings of their guy. People like Sorensen are still building the shrine, but that is sort of unique to the Kennedy people, I think. The rest were pretty matter-of-fact about it. It is loyalty as much to the presidency as to the man, I think.

**QUESTION:** I was wondering if you'd say a few words about the President's relationship with Vice President Agnew and then subsequent relationships with John Connally and President Ford.

**MR. EHRLICHMAN:** I can't say anything about Ford as the

vice president because I wasn't around, but we can talk about Ford as minority leader.

I suspect that Spiro Agnew was a mistake in the sense that Nixon thought he was getting a liberal. Agnew was an early and vociferous supporter of Nelson Rockefeller for President and I would be very surprised if anybody had made clear to Nixon in advance of Agnew's selection that he was really very conservative. But that is something I cannot answer. I just have that suspicion.

Generically, presidents and vice presidents are different. One of the reasons that they are on the ticket together is because they are not from the same part of the country, don't have the same philosophies or same styles and appeal to different groups. Once you get them there they are expected somehow to work together. When it works it's probably pretty close to a miracle. It didn't work in the case of Nixon and Agnew. As I've indicated, Nixon was not crazy about meeting with people. Any vice president depends on an appearance of access for whatever little clout he has and Nixon was not interested in giving Agnew a lot of access. He was continually saying to us things like "Find him something to do," and we'd say, "Like what?" He'd say, "Well, give him health, put him in charge of the health reforms." We'd put Ted Agnew in charge of something like health and it got to be a terrible disaster because he wouldn't do his homework. He wasn't good at chairing a meeting, had rigid, narrow and unacceptable ideas, unacceptable in the sense that if you brought the President a recommendation that Agnew stood behind, you knew that ninety-nine times out of a hundred Nixon would reject it because they had such different approaches to things. It was very tough to get Agnew involved in substance.

The vice president was very prickly and concerned about his prerogatives. He had, by genetic selection, ended up with a Secret Service detail that was the biggest bunch of thugs you ever saw. The whole Agnew operation was unattractive to all of us, including Nixon. Nixon sent Agnew overseas. As an example, he sent him on a trip to Africa. While Agnew was gone, Nixon announced that he was going to China. The CIA then reported back that Agnew was bad-mouthing the China opening to every leader he encountered in Africa. This, of course, landed on Nixon's desk and he said, "What's he doing over there? Why is he doing this to me?" It further strained the situation.

Finally, the time came that Nixon had to decide what he was going to do for the second term. Was he going to take Agnew or somebody else? That was easy; he was not going to take Agnew. But the thing you have to understand about Richard Nixon is that he was very sensitive about his right flank. He didn't want to antagonize the conservatives in the Republican party. So he was marching around the White House saying "I'm going to get rid of this guy." John Mitchell drops in and says, "What's all this talk I hear about you dumping Agnew?" Nixon said, "Well, it's impossible. I can't work with this guy; he's terrible. He wants to come in here all the time and bother me and it's a very unhappy relationship." Mitchell said, "You can't dump Agnew. Barry Goldwater, George Murphy and the conservatives of this country would be outraged if you dumped Agnew. Whom do you want?" Nixon said, "I want John Connally," and Mitchell said, "My God, Connally is a Democrat. You will never get him through the Republican convention." So Nixon chewed on that for two weeks and decided that Mitchell was right and that he would have to keep Agnew on.

Then he said to me one day, "You know what we might do? We might put Agnew on the Supreme Court. That would then make a vacancy and under the Twenty-fifth Amendment I can appoint Connally and then he could run with me for reelection." I said, "How are you going to get Agnew confirmed by the Senate?" He said, "That's right. Well, it won't work." So that's as close as Spiro Agnew ever got to the Supreme Court.

John Connally was Nixon's only begotten choice for President and he wanted in the worst way for John Connally to succeed him. He thought he was the finest presidential material on the landscape and I daresay he may be right about that. If there is an American who is by temperament, training, and experience suited to sit down and be President of the United States, I think it is probably John Connally. But getting nominated and getting elected are two problems that lie in between and were insurmountable, I guess.

Nixon thought a lot about it. Connally was quite realistic about it and finally said," It's not in the cards and thanks just the same" and went home and began making money. Then he got enmeshed in that milk fund problem and that was the end of his presidential chances.

Jerry Ford was kind of an interesting guy. When I first started working with Jerry Ford, he was minority leader in the House. I would have to go up and sit down with Hugh Scott, who was minority leader in the Senate, and Jerry Ford and talk about our legislation. It was quite a conversion process because these fellows had been the minority and they had been the opposition all through the Kennedy and the Johnson years and they weren't used to having to carry a President's bills. They didn't really like the idea too well. Ford was very effective as minority leader of the House and was just about right for that job. By the time I left I had very high regard for him. I would say he was limited. By comparison with, say, Nixon's intellect, Ford was less sharp. But he was a good fellow and about right for the Congress. You can't be too flashy in the Congress or people resent you. It's not a lowest common denominator phenomenon but it is a matter of coloration, I think. You don't get too far ahead of your colleagues or else they don't go along with you. Ford was the right guy in the right spot for that. He would have made a brilliant vice president for that reason. I think that as President he may have been a little bit beyond his level of competence.

**NARRATOR:** We can't recall many Forums where there was more outspoken candor and critical interpretation to help us understand what a particular presidency was all about. So we are grateful and thank you.

# III.

# NIXON AND THE ECONOMY

# NIXON AND THE ECONOMY

## Arthur Burns

**NARRATOR:** Ambassador Burns was born in Stanislaw, Austria. He was educated from the bachelor's through the Ph.D. degree at Columbia University. Throughout, one notes a recurrent pattern in his academic career. At Rutgers, he began as an instructor and ended as a full professor of economics. He was first a visiting professor at Columbia and then John Bates Clark Professor. He was initially a research associate at the National Bureau and ultimately chairman of the Bureau. That was one stage in his life when I had a very modest contact with Ambassador Burns. The Rockefeller Foundation gave support to the National Bureau of Economic Research, largely because of the immense confidence they had in Professor Burns and in the work that he and others were doing there. Many would say the golden age of the National Bureau was when Arthur Burns was chairman. In the Eisenhower administration, Ambassador Burns served as chairman of the Council of Economic Advisers from 1953 to 1956. From 1969 to 1970 he was counselor to President Nixon. From 1970 to 1978 he was chairman of the Board of Governors of the Federal Reserve System. Only recently, he returned to Washington from his position as ambassador to the Federal Republic of Germany in the Reagan administration.

Among many other awards, he is the recipient of the Alexander Hamilton Award from the Department of the Treasury and the Jefferson Award from the Institute of Public Service. Next to Father Hesburgh, he must have the largest number of honorary degrees of any living American. I counted thirty before I stopped counting. In every way it's a great honor to have Arthur Burns with us. We thought we would conduct our session essentially on a question and answer basis. Perhaps I might ask the first question.

When did you first meet and come to know President Nixon? Several speakers in the Miller Center presidential series have said that President Nixon had great faith and trust in Arthur Burns, so it would be interesting to know when that relationship began and how it evolved.

**AMBASSADOR BURNS:** Thank you for your kind words of introduction, Mr. Thompson. When you spoke of my career, I realized I haven't been able to hold on to a job. My first job was that of a house painter. I learned something about practical life at an early age. I've been lucky through the years. I've done work I thoroughly enjoyed and I'm still lucky.

Now to turn to your question, Mr. Thompson, I first met Mr. Nixon in 1953 when I was with the Council of Economic Advisers to President Eisenhower. I attended Cabinet meetings regularly and was tremendously impressed with Mr. Nixon's utterances at those meetings. He spoke clearly and effectively. It was obvious he was a man who had a very fine analytical mind. In fact, watching him at those Cabinet meetings, I arrived at the conclusion early in that period that Mr. Nixon could have held down a chair in political science or law in any of our major universities and would have served with great distinction.

President Eisenhower called on me frequently during Cabinet meetings to discuss the condition of the economy, where we were going, where we should be going, and how we might get there. Mr. Nixon would speak to me after those Cabinet meetings and comment on the economic discussion we had. I was impressed not only by his intellectual vigor, but by the courage that he showed in expressing views that were hardly associated with practicing politicians at that time. We became not personal but professional friends. I left Mr. Eisenhower at the end of his first administration, but I was to see Mr. Nixon with some frequency after that.

I think it must have been 1958 or 1959 when Mr. Nixon was appointed to a committee dealing with economic growth and I helped him establish that committee. Knowing that Mr. Nixon would be a candidate for the presidency in 1960 and, feeling as I did towards the end of 1959 that our country might well be moving into a recession in the early months of 1960, I made up my mind—but didn't communicate this to anyone—that I would wait as long as I thought prudent before informing Vice President Nixon that I felt a recession was about to occur, and that some government measures might be useful in preventing or delaying its onset or, if not that, minimizing its impact.

Being a conservative in financial matters, I did not want the government to rush in too quickly. In fact, I would have preferred to have the government stay out of it entirely. Yet I thought Mr. Nixon would make a good President and I wanted to help him. So, I delayed until I decided that it was unwise to delay any longer. Then I telephoned him and was told that he was presiding over a session of the Senate. I asked that he call me back as soon as he could, because it was urgent. He did within an hour and then I gave him my prediction on the course of the economy. He took my advice, but President Eisenhower didn't take Mr. Nixon's advice and, of course, he lost that election.

I gave him some political advice, but it was poor advice. He struggled with the question of debates; should he or should he not debate Mr. Kennedy, who was putting pressure on him? If yes, how many debates should he agree to ? I advised him to debate Kennedy just once, and thus finish off that nice young man from Harvard. Well, I couldn't have given him poorer advice, and fortunately, he didn't take it. He debated Kennedy three times and his first debate was a disaster. He improved in the second and third debates, but he never recovered fully from his disastrous performance in the first debate.

It took me years, really, to diagnose what happened. In his first eight minute pronouncement, what Mr. Kennedy said in substance was this: we have a wonderful country, a beautiful country, a great tradition, and our task is to make our country more beautiful, more wonderful still. That was his message and he said it eloquently. How do you respond to a speech like that? When Mr. Nixon responded by tackling specific issues such as agriculture and citing statistics, I knew he was on the wrong track, but I didn't know what the right track might be. I knew he had lost the debate then and there. It took me years to decide how Mr. Nixon should have answered. His answer should have been a repetition of Mr. Kennedy's speech in slightly different language. There was no other answer that could have made political sense at that time.

You know the story of what happened in Mr. Nixon's candidacy for the governorship of California and the rather brutal treatment of him by the press in that campaign. But he recovered. I remember most vividly a conversation I had with him at his apartment in New York City at a luncheon meeting which, I think, occurred in June, 1968. The Republican convention had not yet been held. The polls, in the sense of delegate counts, indicated very clearly that he would be overwhelmingly nominated by the convention. They also indicated that he would probably be elected. Mr. Nixon was very confident at the time and he outlined what he intended to do as President. He devoted himself entirely, in that luncheon meeting, to a statement of what he would do in the field of foreign affairs. That was clearly the most important thing to him if and when he became President. He told me that he would seek a rapprochement with the Soviet Union; he'd go at it vigorously and establish a détente. He told me he would build a bridge to communist China and that would be his basic objective in the presidency. Third, he would bring about an early end to the war in Vietnam.

Well, as you know, he carried out the first and second objectives. I should add that Henry Kissinger has been a close friend of mine for many years. The last thing I would want to do is to take anything away from Mr. Kissinger's reputation. In fact I've often described him as the one man I've known in Washington who was in the most literal sense a genius. But as far as our policy with regard to the Soviet Union and the People's Republic of China is concerned, the credit belongs to Mr. Nixon. There were Mr. Nixon's ideas. In fact, I believe that Mr. Nixon had never met Mr. Kissinger until after the election of 1968. Of course, he was unable to achieve his plan with regard to Vietnam.

One thing more happened during that luncheon which I'll never forget. I don't recall in what connection but he told me that he would be a one-term President and he wanted me to know that. I was astonished to hear him say that. "Why?" I asked him. His answer was, "As President, I will have to do so many unpopular things that I almost certainly could never be reelected. Second, these will be difficult years and I will be thoroughly exhausted at the end of those years and probably could not carry on physically." I was pleased to hear him say that, but I took it with a grain of salt.

After the election Mr. Nixon asked me to prepare a transition report for him. I went to work on it. I prepared a rather sizeable volume dealing with legislation and executive orders that he would probably have to deal with in the first six months of the administration. The objective was to help him get started constructively. Having prepared that report, I was ready to submit it to him. I did so on January 21, 1969. In fact, I had the first appointment with him.

A number of things happened during my meeting with him on that day. I may speak of them later on. His whole manner during that meeting was such that I arrived at the conclusion that he was already running for the second term. When I came home I told my wife, "You know, Mr. Nixon is running for the presidency once again. He has started his campaign for the presidency in 1972." My wife asked, "Did he tell you that?" I said, "No, he didn't say that." "Did he intimate that directly?" "No, not a word," I said, "but I'm still absolutely sure."

Perhaps I'll stop with this. I've given you a lengthy discursive answer to your question about how I got to know Mr. Nixon.

**QUESTION:** I would like to first recall one exposure I had with you in Washington when you asked a few of us to come down as a task force on small business. At the first meeting you came in and listened to our deliberations. When we were going to leave for lunch I asked, "Arthur, do you have any departing words of wisdom to guide us through our deliberations on improving the prospects for small business?" You turned and paused, held your pipe for a second and said, "Yes Wilson, I think you fellows should leave something for Congress to do."

Arthur, you've been chairman of the Council of Economic Advisers and, of course, chairman of the National Bureau of Economic Research. There's another person who's held those two positions and in each of them has left an impression somewhat different from the traditional posture which you always projected. Will you comment on the contrast of the incumbency of each of you in that office? In studying the office of the presidency and Mr. Feldstein's relations to his chief, anything that you say would be of enormous interest.

**AMBASSADOR BURNS:** Martin Feldstein and I brought different philosophies to the conduct of the Council of Economic Advisers. When I became chairman of the Council under President Eisenhower, the first thing I did was to study, as closely as I could, the legislative history of the Employment Act under which the Council was set up. I arrived at the conclusion that the Congress wanted an Economic Report prepared by the President. To be sure, the President would get professional assistance in preparing it. To be sure, the report would be written by others, chiefly the Council of Economic Advisers, but it would still be the President's report, bearing his signature.

My predecessors at the Council had arrived at a different conclusion. They put out a report containing an introductory essay of some five to ten pages signed by the President and then a lengthy substantive report signed by the Council of Economic Advisers. When I studied the legislative history of the Employment Act, I concluded that that was wrong. The Congress wanted a report by the President. To the extent that it wanted a report by the Council, it simply wanted a housekeeping report and nothing beyond that. Having concluded that the earlier Council had arrogated a certain power to itself that Congress never intended it to have, I broke with that tradition. During my tenure, the Economic Report of the President became the President's report in its entirety, in the sense that he signed the whole report.

Perhaps I should add that my decision to function that way might have been based to some degree not only on my reading of the legislative history of the Employment Act, but also on my personal temperament. In any event, I thought that was the right way to proceed. Why have two reports and give journalists and others the opportunity to look for minor differences and perhaps exaggerate them? My successor (I had something to do with having him appointed), Mr. Saulnier, proceeded with my plan during the second Eisenhower administration. When Mr. Kennedy was elected President, Walter Heller became chairman. He reverted to the earlier practice and that has been the practice of the Council of Economic Advisers ever since.

You may recall Mr. Feldstein's last report of the Council of Economic Advisers. It was characterized by Mr. Regan, then secretary of the treasury, as a document that could be thrown into the wastepaper basket. That could not have happened if my plan had been followed. Mr. Feldstein, whom I love dearly and respect as one of the very ablest economists that we have in our country, gave the President excellent advice. However, he now and then diverged in his public pronouncements from the administration's position. I think that put him and the Council, and for that matter the White House and the President, in a difficult position. The President lost confidence in the Council and was ready a year ago to recommend to the Congress that the Council be abolished. Learning that, I went to see President Reagan, and I think I had something to do with persuading him that the Council should be retained. After all, he could instruct the new chairman to be the President's adviser and not play an independent, public role. That, I think, is the route that the present chairman is observing.

Feldstein is one of the ablest economists in the country. His advice to the President on economic issues was consistently sound, but he made the fatal mistake of pursuing a quasi-independent role. If you are the President's adviser you can't quarrel, or even appear to be quarreling with the President in public. You can quarrel and fight, yes, but you must do it privately.

**QUESTION:** A subject that has been discussed and debated over the years is the relationship between the chairman of the Federal Reserve Board of Governors and the President. I wonder if you could describe your relationship during those years, and the extent to which the President may have wished or tried to influence the actions that were taken by the Federal Reserve.

**AMBASSADOR BURNS:** As chairman of the Federal Reserve, I had the opportunity to work with Presidents Nixon, Ford, and Carter. I also had the opportunity to observe the relationship between the President and the chairman of the Council of Economic Advisers. Confining my remarks for the moment to these three Presidents with whom I worked as chairman of the Federal Reserve Board, I would say that, from the viewpoint of the Federal Reserve, Mr. Nixon's record was by far the worst. Mr. Ford's record was by far the best. Mr. Nixon tried to interfere with the Federal Reserve both in ways that were fair and in ways that were, by almost any standard, unfair.

Mr. Ford, on the other hand, was truly angelic. I met with President Ford frequently, alone in the privacy of his office. He never inquired about what the Federal Reserve was doing. He never even remotely intimated what the Federal Reserve should be doing. The closest he ever came to it was during a conversation which began on his part with the statement, "Arthur, I'm going to ask you a banking question and the question may be improper. If it is please attribute it to my ignorance, my innocence, and don't hold it against me. Just ignore it. Don't answer it if it's even remotely improper." I said, "Well, I'd like to hear your question, Mr. President." Around that time a series of articles had appeared in the *Washington Post* on problems in the banking world. These articles gave some emphasis to problem banks. They were somewhat sensational articles. The *New York Times* couldn't be far behind and began publishing articles of a similar nature. Mr. Ford said, "I've been reading articles about problem banks; is this something that I should be interested in?" That's as close as he ever came to asking a question that the Federal Reserve was at all involved in.

President Ford's record, to repeat, was perfect. Mr. Carter had a good record but not a perfect one. Mr. Eisenhower had a good record, but again, not perfect.

I recall President Ford announcing one day that he was coming over to the Fed. Some of my colleagues were disturbed. I wasn't disturbed, but I was curious. Why would he want to visit the Federal Reserve? I began making some discreet inquiries and the only item of information that I thought might be useful was that it was his birthday. I had some fun introducing him to the Fed staff, telling him the awful thoughts that had crossed my mind about his purpose in coming to the Fed, and how I dismissed one awful thought after another, finally deciding that he couldn't think of a better place to celebrate his birthday. Actually, he came there to tell us what he thought of the Federal Reserve and how he valued the Federal Reserve's independence. Every President I've known has made remarks to that effect. Gerald Ford believed it and practiced it. It's almost hard to believe that a President could act so judiciously and show much self-restraint about matters that were obviously significant to him.

**QUESTION:** I was wondering if perhaps the explanation of Ford's very unique relationship with the Federal Reserve might stem in part from his congressional background. Unlike Nixon, who believed that he had a right to give orders to anybody, including the chairman of an independent agency like the Federal Reserve, Ford was a man who believed in compromise and listening and working out arrangements. So, while he valued the independence of the Fed, he may also have been the kind of person who was interested in behind the scenes compromise, behind the scenes advising. While he supported strongly the legal independence of the Federal Reserve, what he was interested in was a close and informal working relationship that may very well have been unique in the history of the Fed. I was wondering if you might subscribe to that?

**AMBASSADOR BURNS:** I was informally a member of President Ford's economic team. If there was a name for it, I don't recall. I attended meetings, expressed my views, but, perhaps a little unfairly, it was a one way street. I did not indicate to any of the Presidents I worked with, or their secretaries, what the Federal Reserve was all about and what it was planning. In fact, I would inform the Treasury, the White House and the Council of Economic Advisers about two to five minutes before the press was informed. My intentions were never disclosed. The reason for reticence was that I feared leaks and their effect on financial markets. Thus, I learned what the administration was doing and gave my advice, but I never disclosed what the Federal Reserve planned to do except in the most general terms. We aim at stability. We aim at full employment. We aim to drive out the monster of inflation. I did not disclose to anyone in the administration or to anyone else how we would proceed and what actions we might take. This, of course, was resented by some who might perhaps criticize me for conducting the Federal Reserve System as I did. But if I were doing it again, I would do it the same way. Right or wrong, it's my way. But I am profoundly convinced it's the right way. The Fed must not play favorites or run the risk of rocking markets.

**QUESTION:** In the early meetings with President Nixon was there any sign of any weaknesses? You mentioned his foreign policy strengths, his brilliant mind, and his ability to take hold of things. But I wondered whether in view of the ultimate tragedy, the final tragedy of Watergate, whether you had any indication that something might go wrong later in the administration. You hinted at it with the reference to the election.

**AMBASSADOR BURNS:** I arrived at the conclusion during the late 1950s that Mr. Nixon was a poor administrator. The basis for that conclusion was very simple. As the vice president, he had a small staff, but like everything else in Washington, that has mushroomed. I think he had a staff of eight or ten at the time, and he could not handle them efficiently. His office was inefficient. I would write him a letter and might get two replies to the same letter, sometimes no reply and sometimes a reply that had nothing to do with me or what I had written about. Friends of mine who corresponded with Nixon had similar experiences. I had a very different experience with Eisenhower during the second administration. We would correspond frequently, and I would get a pertinent response immediately. I kept wondering, if Nixon couldn't manage an office of eight or ten properly, how could he possibly manage our enormous government where the President needs to have superb managerial skills? Eisenhower, by contrast, was an extraordinary manager. I was worried about that, and the only solace I was able to derive was that Mr. Kennedy in 1960 also failed to show any special administrative skill. One way or another we would have a poor manager. It was a weakness I detected early and a conclusion I never had reason to change.

When I was counselor to Mr. Nixon in early 1969 there were many indications of weakness on his part. By that I don't mean that I anticipated the Watergate tragedy, or that I anticipated what the tapes would reveal. I did not.

**QUESTION:** Earlier you spoke of your meeting with him on January 21, 1969, in which you deduced that he might run for reelection. You mentioned at that time that there was a good bit of conversation, some of which you might refer to later. Would you?

**AMBASSADOR BURNS:** I don't believe it was in that context that I referred to the conversation, but I don't remember the context in which I did speak. On the twenty-first of January, Mr. Nixon and I were negotiating. He wanted me to be chief of staff of the White House. It was a position that I simply refused to take. I told him that if I accepted any position in his administration, it would be a financial position, an economic position where I had some ability. Running the White House staff was a task for a young man with different interests.

On January 21, when I arrived there, I still refused to take any position in the Nixon administration. I should say that we did talk about the Federal Reserve position, but at that time the position was not open. After I handed Mr. Nixon my transition report, he took me into the Cabinet room and showed me a chair. He said, "This is your Cabinet chair." It had my name on it, "Counselor to the President." He didn't give me a chance to speak. He showed me the splendor of the White House. I still tried to tell Mr. Nixon that I had a university position and could not accept the position in the White House at this time. He paid no attention. He asked if I would come to a Cabinet meeting the next day and present my transition report to the Cabinet. I said of course I would. I came the next day, but could not present everything in my lengthy report. I talked about its general character, and picked out a few specific items of emphasis. In connection with the specific items, Mr. Nixon said, now you meet with this Cabinet member, and you see that one, and so on and so forth. He kept setting up meetings for me with individual Cabinet members while I still refused to accept any position. I should say he handled me then and there with extraordinary skill, but he wasn't always that skillful.

When he was inaugurated on the twentieth, I watched him closely as he walked down the steps of the Capitol. I could not detect a touch of humility in his demeanor or in his facial expression. That troubled me very much. That, combined with his attitude when he took me through the White House and talked about its splendor, led me to conclude that he was already running for the second term.

**QUESTION:** Dr. Burns, in view of your close relationship with the Federal Republic of Germany in recent years, would you please comment on recent German economic success?

**AMBASSADOR BURNS:** I remember a lengthy conversation with Chancellor Schmidt in June of 1978. He was then preparing for a summit meeting. He wanted my views, and he told me what he expected to do. There was pressure on him at that time to have his government adopt monetary and fiscal measures that would energize the Germany economy. You may recall the phrase that Germany was to become the locomotive economic force in Europe. He said he intended to comply. I said to him, "Now you're making a serious blunder if you comply with pressure from the Americans to become a European economic locomotive. Germany's economy isn't strong enough for that, so you're not going to succeed. Moreover you have an island of stability in your country. Keep it that way, protect and preserve it for your own people and as an example to others in the world including my country." But he had his reasons for proceeding. He told me he expected some things from President Carter particularly in the field of energy. I told him President Carter couldn't deliver anything in the field of energy. Congress was not going to support him. Then he told me something else which was rather moving. He said, "Well, in view of the record of Germany during the Nazi era, it's very difficult for me, as chancellor, to turn down an urgent request by an American President." How do you answer that? I stopped arguing.

The record of Germany and Switzerland on the inflation problem is, by and large, a good record; better than ours. They are among the best in the world, but the corruptive influence of inflation has already spread even to those countries to a degree.

**QUESTION:** In view of some of the actions of President Nixon at election time or prior to election time, is there anything you care to say about the economic advice that President Nixon had and his capacity to make use of it and his grasp of economics? Everybody always refers to economics as the dismal science and takes pride in not knowing much about it. I wondered how Nixon would come out in your estimate, in terms of his knowledge and practice in the field of economics and economic policy.

**AMBASSADOR BURNS:** I think his knowledge was better than his practice. As a former professor I'd give him a B on his knowledge and a C- on his practice.

**QUESTION:** Would you want to add any final word about how you think history will judge the Nixon presidency?

**AMBASSADOR BURNS:** If we have peace over the next fifty years, I think Nixon will go down in the history books as one of our truly great Presidents. The Watergate episode will then receive a mere footnote in the history books.

**NARRATOR:** That's a good note on which to end our discussion. We thank Ambassador Burns very much. It's been a long trek for him which he has generously made in our behalf. We hope this will not be his last visit to help us to try to understand American presidents. Thank you very much.

# THE ORGANIZATION OF ECONOMIC POLICY-MAKING

## Herbert Stein

NARRATOR: We are pleased to welcome a good friend of the Miller Center, Herbert Stein. Mr. Stein received his B.A. from Williams College and Ph.D. from the University of Chicago. He has had and continues to have a distinguished career as an economist. He served as a member of the President's Council of Economic Advisers from 1969, and as chairman from 1972 to 1974. From 1974 to 1984 he was A. Willis Robertson Professor of Economics at the University of Virginia. He is the author of many important books: *U.S. Government Price Policy During the World War, Jobs and Markets, The Fiscal Revolution in America, Economic Planning and the Improvement of Public Policy, The Economic System in an Age of Discontinuity, On the Brink, Money Power, and Presidential Economics.* Mr. Stein is currently a senior fellow at the American Enterprise Institute. Today he conducts a Forum on "Nixon and the Organization of Economic Policy-making."

MR. STEIN: Ken has provided me with eleven questions on the subject of the Nixon presidency. I will go through them, maybe not answering all of them. They provide a good outline and I wish I knew the answers to all the questions.

He asked me when my association with Richard Nixon began and the answer to that is very simple. I first met him on the day he appointed me to the Council of Economic

Advisers. I had never met him before that day. I guess I had seen him in person only once, when he spoke to the Committee for Economic Development. I was not a long-time Nixonite. I had lived in Washington for thirty years at that point and had been reading the *Washington Post* throughout those years and so I had a certain impression of him. I considered myself an independent in politics during most of this time. But I began to think in 1968 that I would like to have some involvement so I offered my services to Nelson Rockefeller, who did not do much to avail himself of them, which was probably a good thing. But after Mr. Nixon had been nominated, two friends of mine, Milton Friedman and Arthur Burns, called me from his planning center out in California and asked if I would be willing to be involved in task forces preparing policies that Nixon might consider if he were elected. I said that I would work on one having to do with the budget.

There is an interesting observation about that which you might take into your general studies of the presidency. These days almost all candidates who are not incumbents set up task forces of experts to prepare papers on issues that they will presumably encounter if they become elected. But my impression, not only from our own experience but from the experience of others, is that these task forces and their reports have absolutely no influence on the subsequent policy of the administration. The task force is set up merely to demonstrate to the public that this particular candidate does have a certain amount of support from a certain number of intellectuals. That's for the benefit of a small fraction of the voting public that cares about that. They set up these task forces, but the task forces are quite insulated from the candidate and the candidate is insulated from them during the campaign, and afterwards the reports that they have written are generally lost. I can't even find a copy of the one that I wrote.

After the election I thought I might do something in this administration; I didn't have any idea what. Mr. Nixon appointed me to the Council of Economic Advisers. I'm sure he named me because Paul McCracken, whom he had named as chairman, asked to have me as a member.

How did the President pick people for the Council of Economic Advisers? The Council consists of a chairman and two members. The two members are selected on the recommendation of the chairman. Of course, it is essential that the chairman should have members working with him that he can rely on. The President, at least in my experience, has relied on the advice of the chairman. While I was chairman we had to select four new members and the only advice I ever had from the President about that was that on one of these occasions he would like to have a woman member. So I then went through the director of the American Economic Association, which at that time must have had about fifteen thousand members, looking for a woman. Most of them turned out to be Catholic sisters teaching at Catholic schools, but we did find a very good one. In fact we could have found her without going through the directory. It was Marina Whitman, who had formerly been a staff member of the Council.

How does the President find the chairman? I think in our case Mr. Nixon found Paul McCracken because Paul McCracken had been a member of the Council of Economic Advisers in the Eisenhower administration when Richard Nixon was the vice president. As Paul McCracken said at the time we were first introduced to the press, the President wanted to have three Republican economists, and there weren't that many to choose from. I think there are more now but in my mind many of them are ineligible for one reason or another.

I have been asked my initial impression of Mr. Nixon as a leader. When I first met him—this was in the transition period between the election and the inauguration—he had a floor at the Hotel Pierre in New York where his people who subsequently became famous, like Haldeman and Ehrlichman, were presiding over the flow of activity. I was brought up to meet Mr. Nixon and he was very genial and cordial. I was impressed by that, but I was not very impressed with him as a leader, a President, or a thinker. I came with a certain feeling that I was almost as old as Mr. Nixon. I had been around this track of economic policies so much longer than he had, and that was what he was going to discuss with me, so I was like a professor with him. Also, I had a certain illusion as a result of having spent about twenty-two years working with a committee of businessmen. I knew all these eminent people and thought he was just another one of them.

It reminds me of a story. When I was at the Committee for Economic Development we arranged to have an exchange with the Soviet Union, the first exchange of economists with the Soviet Union. The arrangement was that they would send some economists here and we would send some economists there. Then we would have an exchange of principals. The exchange of economists worked out perfectly well. Then the question came as to who would be the principals. Our chairman at that time was a man named Donald K. David who had been the dean of Harvard business school and director of many corporations, including Pan American Airlines. The Russians wanted to send a man named Kosygin who was the head of their planning agency. Our trustees said, "Kosygin, Kosygin, who is he? He's not the equivalent of Donald K. David." So they didn't do the exchange. They thought that Mr. Kosygin was not at a sufficiently elevated level. So I guess there was something of that in my first look at Mr. Nixon.

But my perception of him did change very soon and very fundamentally. I guess my perception of relative ability has changed. I remember when I was first a member of the Council and we had the first Cabinet meetings, I sat back against the wall and observed them. I began to think that this group of people, many of them not very well known, were really quite able and compared quite favorably with all these chief executive officers with whom I had been spending the previous twenty-two years. They knew what they were doing; they were articulate; they had mastered their departments in a very short time. They were a much better group of people than the impression the public got of them.

But coming back to Mr. Nixon, the general point is that anybody who has been appointed by a President and is accepted by the President as a member of his team comes to feel a very great admiration for him. That's a psychological fact which I observed with respect to nearly everyone I ever knew who worked for a president.

I saw him first at meetings discussing economic policy and was impressed by his ability to absorb the arguments that went on among a lot of people over subjects, many of which were new to him, and his ability to synthesize the arguments in his mind and come to some conclusion. He was a very well organized thinker, very retentive of information. We used to send him daily memoranda about the economic statistics of the day and what they meant. Weeks later he would remember better than I did what the CPI did last month or what the unemployment figures did. But I think more than that he had a very great capacity for retaining and organizing this information. He also had a very good capacity to lead a small discussion. I thought that he was very much more convincing in a discussion with a small group than he was in speaking to a big audience or speaking over television. He got wooden in those appearances, but in small groups he had a good deal of charm and persuasiveness.

What impressed me most within a few weeks after we were there were the meetings of the Cabinet Committee on Economic Policy. It was a group of twelve or fourteen people, mostly Cabinet secretaries and the heads of all the departments that had anything to do with economics. Hendrik Houthakker and I were the lowest ranking people around this table, but he always wanted to know what we thought. He always called on us and gave us a chance to express our views. Of course that endeared him to me though it may not have endeared him to the other members who were there. But I thought that showed a certain respect for the people who were on his team.

Another thing I might point out is the political role of the Council. Mr. Nixon said right off that he did not expect us to participate in political events; he did not expect us to speak at political meetings; he did not expect us to do much speaking. In general, he thought we would speak to groups of professional people and economists. I think he was trying to protect us against all that corruption. Also, he probably thought we would be of no great interest to anybody else. In any event, he showed a good understanding for our position, and not only in that kind of personal respect. I think he had some understanding of what economists do and do not know. He did not hold us responsible for errors in forecasting or other kinds of mistakes which became obvious. He realized that this is a very difficult and uncertain business. I did think he had more respect for economics than for other so-called social sciences.

He used to kid Pat Moynihan about sociology being a soft subject. Once when he was rewarding the medals of science to a group of biochemists and astrophysicists and so on, he got up on the podium and said, "I notice there are no political scientists receiving medals. Maybe there is no political science."

To go back more generally to his role as a leader, I think that he led his administration. There was relatively little uncertainty about what his administration was for or what the policy of his administration was. As I look at the Reagan administration or the Carter administration, there always is uncertainty about what the President is for. You hear somebody is for this and somebody is for that and the secretary of state is for this and the secretary of defense is for that. Only in the last round do you discover what the President is for.

I think we had a fairly well coordinated administration. Some people criticized that. They used to talk about our Prussian guard in the White House, Haldeman and Ehrlichman, who were maintaining coordination. But I think that coordination is a necessary condition of an administration. So my view is that he was an effective leader.

How did he organize the White House and what was our role? I can't speak about that in its totality. There are a lot of aspects of the White House with which we had very little to do. We had very little to do with the National Security Council, for example. For one thing he inherited an already organized White House. The organization of the White House has developed since the time that Roosevelt introduced and asked for those six anonymous assistants and established an executive office. A certain organization then is passed down from one administration to another; it is not organized anew every time.

The Nixon administration did bring at least one new element into the White House organization and that is the establishment of the Domestic Policy Council, which at first was chaired by Pat Moynihan. Its exact charter was a little unclear but at least he had a staff of people who were to look after the making of domestic policy in the administration in a way that the National Security Council presumably did with respect to security policy. It was not supposed to be concerned with economic policy because presumably the Council of Economic Advisers would look after that. Of course, the line between domestic policy and economic policy was rather unclear. I remember one time we had some argument about whether unemployment was an economic problem or not. But I think we persuaded them that it was. It wasn't any great boon to have that piece of turf, but nevertheless we had it.

I really can't compare his organization of the White House in detail with others. I was greatly impressed from the very beginning with how thoroughly it was organized. Whether all of this was inherited from earlier administrations or not, I don't know. But the flow of paperwork was very well regulated; that is, there were printed forms. You would get some paper from the White House staff with a printed form on top of it telling who has seen it, who is to see it, what are you supposed to do about it, by what time are you supposed to do it—not just March 15, but two o'clock on March 15. Somebody was checking whether you delivered all these things. This was part of a mechanism for making sure that when a problem came into the White House the competent or relevant people all got a chance to express their views about it.

I'm asked whether the White House staff was too large or too small. I don't feel that it was too large; I think it was an adequate size. There were a number of people around whose qualifications were rather unclear but an awful lot of them had been advance men during the campaign. You know what they do. They go and arrange for the school children to be along the line of march when the President comes. They are then entitled to have some position in the government, and many of them came into the White House. But a lot of these young people turned out to be very energetic and able doing the things that they were supposed to do, mainly organizational things, making contacts with others and so on.

I would say something more particularly about the organization of economic policy-making. There was an existing organization which we inherited, which I think really developed in the Kennedy administration. That was the Troika consisting of the secretary of the treasury, the director of the budget, subsequently the director of the Office of Management and Budget, and the chairman of the Council of Economic Advisers. The Troika had three levels: T1 which was those three people; T2 which consisted of a member of the Council of Economic Advisers, an assistant secretary of the treasury, an assistant director of the OMB; and T3 which was the staff level of working economists from each of these three organizations. By the time we came in, a system had developed for managing this organization which had mainly to do with macro-economic policy, which was essentially budget fiscal policy. It was a useful core for forming any other kind of group for dealing with economic policy.

It was unclear at the time we came in, and I don't think it has ever been specified, who was the head of the Troika. In the early stages after we came in, Paul McCracken, as the chairman of the Council of Economic Advisers, took a certain amount of leadership in organizing the meetings of the Troika and setting its agenda because he was the only one of the three who really knew what the whole operation was about, for he had served in the White House previously. Secretary of the Treasury David Kennedy, and the director of the budget, Bob Mayo, were new to all this and, moreover, were rather mild and retiring characters. This all changed when we got a new secretary of the treasury, John Connally. Before John Connally came, the Troika commonly met for breakfast in the Cosmos Club, as Paul McCracken was a member of the Cosmos Club and he was more or less the host. After Mr. Connally came in we met in the secretary's dining room at the Treasury and he was the host and the leader. There was no question about that. This Troika remained a central body for the discussion of economic policy.

But the President, to our surprise, after we got there brought in a counselor with Cabinet rank, Arthur Burns. He was by profession an economist and that created a certain question about what he would do, what his role would be relative to the Council of Economic Advisers. But that worked out pretty well. He had been formerly chairman of the Council of Economic Advisers, so he was concerned about its function. We did not have any particular trouble with him and then he moved on rather soon to the Federal Reserve so we were free of that.

But a more difficult problem arose because at least one of the members that the President appointed to the Cabinet had been with Nixon for a long time. He had been in the Eisenhower administration and felt that he ought to have a role in the making of economic policy. He wanted to be a member of the Troika, but nobody in the Troika wanted him to be a member. A place had to be found for him, and, partly for that reason, but not exclusively for that reason, the Cabinet Committee on Economic Policy was set up which included the secretaries of the treasury, labor, commerce, agriculture, the director of the budget, the assistant to the attorney general for antitrust, the under secretary of state for economic affairs, the counselor to the President, and probably a few other people.

The Council of Economic Advisers served as the secretariat of this group, prepared its agenda, organized the papers, and Chairman McCracken briefed the President before the meetings. It became clear, certainly before the first year was over, that this was not the kind of thing that the President liked to deal with. There were too many people talking on subjects that they didn't know anything about. He found it a waste of time, but he didn't want to abolish it. He made the vice president chairman of the Cabinet Committee on Economic Policy, and once he made the vice president the chairman, the Cabinet members began sending their under secretaries. The thing then disappeared.

Then he introduced another body called the Committee on International Economic Policy (CIEP) to handle the perennial problem that international economic policy was not well coordinated. The secretary of commerce thought he should have something to do with it, as did the secretary of state, the secretary of the treasury, the National Security Council and so on. The CIEP was set up and served a useful function. Peter Peterson was its first director followed by Peter Flanigan after Peter Peterson moved to Commerce.

The whole tone of the organization of economic policy changed when we went into price and wage controls. The price and wage control became a kind of dominant factor in economic policy. We were launching a grand new economic policy in which everything was now going to be brought to bear in the fight against inflation. This Cost of Living Council was set up with John Connally as its chairman and Paul McCracken, the chairman of the Council of Economic Advisers, as the vice chairman. I soon became the vice chairman. All the relevant economic agencies were on it, including the consumer representative. For a while this became the scene of all of the large-scale discussion of economic policy. There was enormous public attention, as some of you may remember. When it would hold a meeting it met in the Roosevelt Room in the White House. The television cameras would be there, which of course assured that everybody was present. I discovered that if you sat next to Virginia Knauer you were sure to get in the picture because the television crews liked to have the woman in the picture.

I thought the Cost of Living Council was quite effective for a while. During the early period there was this feeling of having launched some grand new venture. We would meet very frequently and discuss things quite efficiently. John Connally was a very good chairman; he was a wonderful public spokesman. After a while that kind of dwindled also and things changed. Contrary to some impressions of John Connally, he was not a domineering person with respect to the making of economic policy. He was eager to reach a decision but he was not eager to steamroll a decision over the objections of other people.

But as I've said many times, the ideal way to organize economic policy in the government is to have George Shultz in charge of it. When George Shultz became secretary of the treasury we developed the Shultz style of organization. He became the assistant to the President for economic affairs and chairman of a new committee on economic policy in which the President did not personally participate. Essentially the President delegated the leadership of economic policy to George Shultz. Shultz had an enormous capacity for bringing everybody into the picture, making everybody feel that he was contributing, getting the results that he wanted, and moving the process along.

The process was quite informal. Although there was this committee, it didn't meet very often. But every morning at 7:30 a group of us would meet in Shultz's small White House office in the attic of the White House and there would be the director of the Cost of Living Council, the under secretary of the treasury, the associate director of the budget, somebody from the National Security Council, and somebody from CIEP. In a half hour meeting every morning we would decide what was going on. We would exchange our views, decide who was going to do what next, and what the line was for the day. After that there was a meeting of the White House senior staff which at first Haldeman chaired and later Haig. It included not only some of the economic people but the press secretary, the legislative liaison people, and so on. That went on for another thirty or forty-five minutes. By the time you got back to your office at nine o'clock in the morning you had done most of your day's work and knew what was on the agenda. Of course, we always had a lot of things that were not so action-oriented that we were working on. But still it gave a good deal of focus to the whole operation.

The ability to be effective depends very much on a person whose leadership will be accepted by the others. Of course Shultz was this person. When Shultz left, the problem became who would be the leader of this general group? Who would be the leader of the committee? Who would be the leader of this informal morning group? There was competition for this role between the new secretary of the treasury, Bill Simon, and the director of OMB, Roy Ash. The President resolved that by bringing in his old law professor, Kenneth Rush, to be the chairman. The organization didn't operate in the same way under his leadership because he was then in competition with these two other people, Simon and Ash, and because he didn't have the standing in this field. I think that organization was a good one but depended on a certain person. I sometimes wonder whether Mr. Regan, now that he is in the White House, will take on a similar role.

In our relations between the White House and the Cabinet, I would say that there was certainly a feeling of "us" and "them." There was the perception that there are the inside people, which was the White House, the executive office, and the treasury, and then everybody else out there who was not necessarily kept informed but who would be consulted and brought in on matters relating to their own area of competence. If you are going to do something about unemployment compensation, the secretary of labor would be involved; or if you were going to do something about agriculture, the secretary of agriculture would be involved. But they would not be regarded as the last word or as necessarily the most competent people. Many of them have expressed the feeling that they were not treated as being at the center of affairs. But I guess since I was at a certain position it seemed to me a perfectly satisfactory arrangement. I don't really know that problems arose about it.

What problems arose and how were they handled? Well, some Cabinet members left or it was suggested that they should leave. After the 1972 election the President had a reorganization plan, which would have created four big Cabinet groups with people in charge of each group who would be both inside the White House and secretaries of a Cabinet department. This was an attempt to bring about a closer-knit organization which never worked out. Congress and others were not very happy with it, so it never really worked. But I don't think that there was any great problem. One thing that Shultz did, which I don't think anybody else has ever done, was to bring the State Department actively into the picture with respect to the making of international economic policy. He even had the secretary of state involved in the discussion of international monetary matters, which I think surprised him, but that worked quite well.

What were the main crisis problems which arose and how were they handled? I'm not quite sure whether we had crisis problems or whether we created the crises sometimes. But the thing you'd naturally think of is the imposition of price and wage controls. It was such a dramatic, unexpected gesture, but it didn't seem to have been in response to a crisis. It was a response to a situation in which we had four and one-half percent inflation and six percent unemployment, which now looks like the ideal combination but at that time looked like something totally unacceptable. We had a dollar problem then, too. We were running a deficit in our balance of payments of about seven billion dollars a year compared with the present one hundred billion. Of course, we made today's hundred billion not a crisis by closing the gold window. Once we closed the gold window the deficit may be a problem but it is not a crisis.

The most dramatic things we did in economic policy were the imposition of the price and wage controls and the closing of the gold window. Those decisions were made in tandem and outside the usual channels. This was discussed between the President and John Connally, one-on-one, for some time. They had decided that they would do this if the circumstances arose. If it looked as if something radical needed to be done then this was what they would do. Perhaps I'm incorrect to characterize this as having been decided one-on-one. There was a group working in the Treasury, the Volcker group, that was in charge of international financial problems. It was in this connection that the idea arose that if the international financial problem persisted and especially if somebody came in and asked for his gold that we would close the gold window. That might be an occasion also for imposing price and wage controls to demonstrate that by closing the gold window we were not about to embark on an upsurge in inflation. Everybody in the country wanted us to impose price and wage controls, except a few people outside like Milton Friedman. So there was this committee, the Volcker Committee, which was working on this possibility, but I think on another track Nixon and Connally were working on the possibility and agreed that this is what they would do.

Meanwhile, the rest of the government was totally in the dark about all this. Various interagency committee meetings were going on about what we should do about our great balance of payments deficit with the Japanese. The option of devaluing the dollar was generally ruled out by everybody. The Department of Commerce and the Department of State were trying to develop plans to deal with the Japanese problem. We would put quotas on them or we would go and talk to them or we would do this or that.

When we went to Camp David August thirteenth to fifteenth to work on this plan, nobody was there from the Department of State, which they subsequently remembered with considerable annoyance. But anyway the problem was handled in this rather close knit way and the decision reflected the President and Connally more than anything else. Most other people around either thought we shouldn't do it or couldn't do it. The final decision reflected, I think, a combination of the President's love for the dramatic gesture and a desire to get away from a "policy of three yards in a cloud of dust," as he used to say, while they throw the long bomb. He finally had a man on his team, John Connally, who also believed in throwing a long bomb. That's how that came about.

I'll mention one other crisis. It was handled in a different way and I think was the one really very bad decision we made. We had gone through the last part of 1971 and all of 1972 with a very low rate of inflation; the price controls looked as if they were working. But then in 1973 they began to come unraveled. Food prices were rising; we couldn't help that. Oil prices were rising and we couldn't help that. Since those prices were rising, workers wanted wage increases, and we couldn't really withstand that very much. So the whole thing was coming unraveled and there was a great furor in the country.

Everything seems like a much greater furor in the country if you are sitting there in the Executive Office Building than if you are in Charlottesville. In 1971 when we were going into the price and wage controls, we had the feeling that the country was just ablaze with determination to have controls because of the anxiety about the inflation that was going on. However, in the small-town Virginia newspapers those things were hardly mentioned. There were people out there who were concerned with the apple crop whereas we sat there reading *Time* and *Newsweek* and watching CBS news and thought that the whole world out there was demanding that we do this. That is the misconception that you have when you are sitting in the White House. But anyway, this time we felt that things were really heating up again.

The President at that time was feeling the heat of the Watergate business. I remember when the President and Mrs. Nixon gave a breakfast in March of 1973 for the members of the Council and their spouses because one of them was leaving. He raised the question of going back into the freeze, which he had regarded as a great success.

I said to him, "You cannot step into the same river twice," and he said, "Yes you can, if it's frozen." It was the best joke I ever heard him make. He does have a very good sense of humor.

So this economic problem was bubbling up and his political problems were bubbling up and there was a desire for some other grand successful gesture with respect to the economy. So we started a series of intensive meetings about what we could do. He brought John Connally back to advise us because John Connally had been his dramatic coach before. But John Connally had run out of dramatic ideas. He suggested that we should call in all the green currency and issue yellow currency, or gold colored currency.

But the President persisted with the idea that he would like to try another freeze, and he kept getting unanimous advice from his advisers that that was not a good idea. Then he'd say, "Well, let's go over this again. Write me some more memos." Several of us went on an overnight trip to a meeting in Paris thinking that we had persuaded him. On our way back we received a message that he was unpersuaded and asking for more memos. But eventually he found somebody who advised him to do it and he did it. I've observed that Presidents do not like to leap off into the dark without being able to have some kind of respectable advice in support of what they want to do. So that was the crisis where a bad decision was made under terrible political pressures.

I'll just comment on one more question. How do you think future historians will judge the Nixon presidency? When I saw that it suddenly occurred to me to ask, how would people have judged the Franklin Roosevelt presidency if he had left in 1938? Suppose he had died or for some other reason had left, and we had just had the 1937 recession, which was the deepest recession we've ever had? He had made his unsuccessful attempt to pack the Supreme Court. He had made an unsuccessful attempt to purge the Senate. Many of his early actions had been found to be unconstitutional, and in economic terms he seemed to be floundering. I think we'd have a rather different picture of him. That doesn't say anything about Nixon except that he left under circumstances which make it difficult to evaluate the results of the presidency. Of course the evaluation of Nixon will be mainly in terms of Vietnam, Watergate, the opening of China, and détente, and not very much about economics, I imagine. In terms of economics what will be said will depend on who writes it.

I think he will deserve credit for moving towards the deregulation of freeing up of the economy. We did free up the currency after we got rid of exchange controls and control of international capital movements. We got rid of the draft, which was viewed at the time, and I think properly, as a move towards freedom in many directions. We began a movement towards deregulation of the transportation industry. He resisted demands for protectionism and initiated another round of trade negotiations which did lead to further reductions of tariffs. He initiated the movement towards the deregulation of the financial industry.

I think the price and wage controls will be regarded probably as a mistake. There are still people who regard price and wage controls as a good thing. The only mistake in their mind is that it was done by people who didn't really believe in them. I think the price and wage controls will be recognized as a mistake but as it turned out, not an irreparable one.

I think we will be regarded in some way as kind of the tail end of an era which began in the great depression when the overriding obsession was unemployment. The first thing President Nixon asked me when I met him in the Pierre Hotel was what were the problems. When I said that the problem was inflation, he said, "But remember, we must not have any increase of unemployment." Unemployment was Mr. Nixon's overriding obsession. So I think that we suffered from that in many respects.

In economics there was a kind of transitional phase. I think he personally, as a manager of economic policy, and given all the other difficulties that he faced, including the Congress, which was constantly opposed to him, deserves credit. Aside from the decision for the controls, he had a good record.

**NARRATOR:** Somebody should send Mr. Nixon the message

that we found a political scientist. Who would like to ask the first question?

**QUESTION:** Mr. Stein, which came first, the unraveling of the price controls or the increase in money supply in the fall of 1972? Were they related?

**MR. STEIN:** We were beginning to get the expansion of the money supply in the fall of 1972. I think that had some effect on it, but I think that the unraveling would not have come so quickly if we did not have the big food price increase, which was connected with the crop failures in the Soviet Union and the sale of grain to the Soviet Union. I don't think we were yet feeling very strong demand pressure, but I think your general point is correct—that not only the Federal Reserve but the administration was misled by the early success of price and wage controls into thinking that we could push expansion policies further than, in retrospect, was correct. This was an error which we said all previous price controllers had made, and we would not make, but we made it too.

**QUESTION:** When Mr. Nixon put on the second wage and price control against your advice, was that when you realized what a mistake it had been?

**MR. STEIN:** Oh, no, we realized much earlier it was a mistake. I mean some of us have been in the business of being against price control for a billion years. So it was from our standpoint a mistake. I think the public realized it was a mistake during the second freeze. The second freeze was even more rigid than the first one because it was an attempt to control farm prices. It was then that you began to have pictures on TV of the little baby chicks being drowned and the cattlemen slaughtering their calves because they couldn't afford to feed them under the price control system as it then existed. That made it clear to people that price control interferes with production, which they didn't realize up to that point. They thought you could have all the same products but just at a lower price.

**QUESTION:** As I look at Nixon's economic policies it seems to me that we are still feeling the effects of closing the gold window. You mentioned that people at that time said that he couldn't do that. What made it possible to do that, despite the fact that it appeared that people wouldn't accept that change?

**MR. STEIN:** People thought that the other countries would not allow us to devalue, that is, that even if we closed the gold window and said we would not support the dollar, they would support the dollar because they would not want the dollar to decline in relation to them. When we closed the gold window we put on the ten percent import surcharge with the understanding that when we arrived at new value of the currency we would eliminate the import surcharge. So we then entered a round of negotiations and the other countries agreed to the devaluation of the dollar by an agreed amount and we removed the import surcharge. I think the people who said we couldn't do it were just wrong. Others were not going to go on buying dollars if we didn't offer some final support for it.

**QUESTION:** Could you expand on your view of the politics and economics of Nixon's decision on wage and price controls? The cynical interpretation is that he knew this wasn't doing anything; it was strictly a political move to gain popularity. Or is it your sense that he did think that this would have beneficial or economic results?

**MR. STEIN:** He didn't have much confidence in it, but I don't think he would have done it if there had not been some people whose views he respected who had said it was a good thing and workable thing to do. There was Arthur Burns saying, "Well, the old methods don't work. For controlling inflation you need something directly against the rise of wages and prices."

But the political situation was partly that the Democrats were exploiting the fact that we had this combination of inflation and unemployment—which by subsequent standards did not look very severe—but they were constantly saying we had the worst of both worlds. In 1970 they had passed a piece of legislation giving the President authority to impose price and wage controls. They did that with the expectation that he would not do it but they would be able to say from then on, "Well, look, we gave him the authority to stop this inflation and he didn't do it." Then when that thing was about to expire, the question of opposing its renewal came up. By that time John Connally was the secretary of the treasury and his view was, "Why rock this boat and get into a fight about this? Let it go on."

But even the Republicans in the Congress were petitioning the President for some strong action in this field. Business organizations were saying we needed something. Pressure was very widespread, at least in establishment circles.

The President was faced with a choice between a more moderate thing, wage price review boards, nominally voluntary and applying only to a few large corporations and unions, or this across-the-board mandatory thing. A few weeks before he did it he asked us to write up options on those two proposals. But I think it was clear that he had decided he was going to do the whole thing. When he left the Oval Office after he asked us to write these options he said, "Well, if I do it, I'm going to leapfrog them all. I'm going to get out there so far that nobody will ever be able to say I didn't do enough." He thought if he took some moderate step, he would continue to bear the responsibility.

What we didn't know was how long this thing was going to go on. We thought we'd have this ninety day freeze, and then go back to the free market, having knocked inflation and inflationary expectations in the head.

When we came down from Camp David after the decision to impose the ninety day freeze, there was only a vague idea of what would come next. But he knew we didn't like it and he knew that it was very inconsistent for him to be doing this because he had been talking against it all his life. He had worked as a young lawyer in the OPA during the early part of the war and came out with the view that this was a terrible mess.

I was in charge of the committee to plan Phase II. George Shultz and I went to him with a proposal of what should follow the ninety day freeze. He said, "It's a good thing it is we who are doing this because if this baby seems to be getting too strong we can strangle it in the cradle." But of course we couldn't. You could only turn it off very slowly because it was very popular.

**MR. MALONE:** I was interested in your comment about Nixon's place in history. I thought at the time that Nixon was at his best in foreign affairs. I thought that Nixon knew more about foreign affairs than most of his successors, any of them really. But the fame of any President is so dependent on what happens afterwards. We thought at the time, at least I did, that what Nixon did about China and Russia was very fine. But so far as the Soviet Union is concerned it has gone very sour and so far as China is concerned it is now going very well. The final judgment on whether those things are wise or not is going to be almost entirely dependent on what happens.

Now this budgetary process of ours seems to be very cumbersome. People have said that Margaret Thatcher is not having trouble getting her budget but just look at Reagan. This business of the control of the purse by the legislative department goes back to the very foundations of American history when the colonial legislatures used the control of the budget to make the royal governors behave. I just don't think you are ever going to get Congress to give up its control. So we've got a dilemma. Now how do we get out of this dilemma?

**MR. STEIN:** Maybe this is because I'm not a political scientist, but I don't think you can devise processes in a democratic system that will make the system work well if there is not some general understanding in the public of what the requirements are for it to work well. I don't think our problem with the budget is a matter of procedure. I think we are getting the budgets that the American people want. When they decide that they don't want this, or if they decide they don't want that, we will get something different. There have been some changes, but I think that what they want is influenced a good deal by experience and intellectual movements. There is a theory that people always want more expenditures and less taxes, and therefore we are always going to have big deficits. But we went for one hundred and fifty years without big deficits. The public was just as greedy then as it is now. I think that experience of a depression and certain changes, first in economics and then in popular understanding of economics, led people to accept big deficits. We had the deficits and nothing happened. We still have the big deficits and people have not yet been convinced that anything is going to happen. Either something will have to happen or something will have to convince them that something is going to happen. Then I think Congress will respond. We haven't reached that point yet. I don't think a constitutional amendment is our solution to that problem and I don't think the fault is in the procedures.

**NARRATOR:** We have been greatly enriched this morning. Thank you for coming back to the Miller Center.

# IV.

# THE PRESS
# AND
# THE CONGRESS

# THE PRESS AND THE NIXON PRESIDENCY

## Lou Cannon

**NARRATOR:** One of the things about the Nixon presidency that nobody has quite answered but various people have raised, is the question whether the atmosphere in the White House promoted the actions that were taken. On the one hand, somebody like Leonard Garment says that these "plumbers" were a bunch of wild men. To this day nobody quite knows who gave the order for the break-in. The question that arises is whether somehow people thought the President would be happy, whether he issued an order or not, with the actions that were taken. One thing that we've noticed is that with Eisenhower and with Ford just about every person that has come here has been delighted to come. Many of them have talked about loving the president. Nobody has talked about loving Nixon. Many people have talked about admiring him and about his brilliance, especially in foreign policy, but was there kind of a conspiratorial attitude that fed on Nixon's psychological make up? That leads to the first question, "What were your impressions of Nixon as a man and leader?" "When did you first meet him?" "Did your impressions change over time?"

**MR. CANNON:** The first question is valuable when you are asked to talk on anybody. My relationships with Nixon are much more episodic than they are with Gerald Ford, let alone Ronald Reagan.

I grew up in a Nevada/California political environment. I was seventeen years old when the Helen Gahagan Douglas campaign was waged. My own politics were left of center at the time and I had this peculiarly California view of Nixon, which was exaggerated. Many of the things that Nixon did had been done by others. The milieu was one which not only permitted smears but encouraged them for lots of reasons that probably we shouldn't waste our time on.

When the Nixon term started I was still in California covering Reagan. I came to Washington for Rider Publications soon after that. I was covering Congress and seeing Nixon from the other end of the telescope. Also, I was doing a book on Congressman McCloskey, who challenged Nixon on Vietnam. So in a sense I suppose I had a view of Nixon that tended to reinforce my earlier, more political views. I covered every day of the Ford administration except for three months when I was off writing a book. I had known Ford a long time. I didn't have that kind of closeness with Nixon. I went over to the *Post* and ended up covering the fall of Richard Nixon. The *Post* had not conceived of it that way, but that's really what I did. Nobody knew it was going to be the fall. After the Watergate revelation and Nixon's reelection and before John Dean and everybody started spilling their guts, the view at the *Post* was that someday history would justify us. No one that I knew from the top editors on down, including Bob Woodward, had any idea that we were going to get such a rapid unraveling.

I think we have to be very careful about Nixon. His presidency is more difficult to analyze than any of the others. It is more difficult because there is a tendency to ratify our own prejudices, to see something inevitable, even to see this thing all playing out as psycho-history. Every history of Nixon seems to be a psycho-history. Psychiatrists will probably start suing historians. I'm a little skeptical of psycho-history anyway. There is a great temptation to view the Nixon administration, not as a presidency that had strengths and weaknesses, but as a morality play in which the bad guys lost. I have trouble with that.

This question of whether or not Nixon was really liked by his staff is an interesting one. I think there were plenty of people who had affection for Nixon. I think Ron Zeigler had genuine affection for Nixon, and I know that

Ken Clausen did. I suspect Steve Hess did but I think that would be a good question to ask him.

As for the incident Elliot Richardson has recounted, I'm not sure it says anything other than that Nixon often was uncomfortable with people. I spent a lot of time researching his character. I talked with the people who knew his parents and tried to compensate for any prejudices I might have had. I didn't come out of it as a Nixon admirer, but I did come out if it realizing that it was more complicated than I had originally thought. Nixon had this total inability to make any kind of small talk. There has probably been no figure as successful as he was up until Watergate who was as lacking in the social graces which we tend to think of as political prerequisites. There is a story that David Broder recounts in one of his books. They were introducing some flight attendants to Nixon. They were great fans of his and they had a party the last night of the campaign. To these people who were crazy about him, Nixon says, "Oh, the 'B-Girls'." They were in Billings, and he tried to recover by saying "B for Billings" and it just got worse and worse.

I have my own story. I had come back to Washington in 1969 and in 1970. Walter Ridder, who was the head of Ridder Publications which is now part of Knight/Ridder, had the happy custom of taking the newest member of the bureau as his guest at the Gridiron. Walter was being made president that year, too. They had a nice cocktail party beforehand in the suite and Reagan, who was then completing his first term as governor, was present. Nixon came in. There was a receiving line, and I happened to be standing next to Reagan, who is much the same now as he was then—except that his hearing was very good then and he heard everything. He doesn't now. Nixon came up and Reagan said, "Hello, Mr. President; this is Lou Cannon. He has written a book about me." Nixon sort of stared at both of us because he and his people were always worried that Reagan was going to run. Anyway, Nixon stared and then he said, "Well, I'll skim it." With that, he walked down to the next person. As soon as he got out of earshot Reagan turned to me and said, "Well, Lou, he just took care of you and me."

I don't know how many would-be athletes there are in this room or people who, like me, went out for the high school football team and played every day and were terrible. There is the Thurber notion that every grown man falls asleep dreaming of striking out the Yankees. Nixon had this to an extraordinary degree. He was an extraordinarily uncoordinated and physically clumsy person throughout his life who yet wanted to be an athletic hero. That's why he called in plays to the Redskins coach. There was one incident during the Watergate ordeal when Nixon went to an airbase. The story came out that Nixon slapped this airman, which of course made no sense. What he had done was hit him in the face while trying to shake his hand. Here was a person who was on stage a lot. He was conscious of his lack of grace and clumsiness, and I think those sorts of things bothered him a great deal. I don't think he was truly happy being out there on stage. We have a President now who delights in it. He feels natural there, but that's because he is a very secure person. I don't think it's because of his acting past. I think Kennedy delighted in it, too. I think it's because some people like to be center stage. Nixon recognized that he had to be center stage. He understood the precedents intellectually, but never really liked it.

Nixon didn't like clamor. He didn't like to have a bunch of people around. It was much worse than that he couldn't fire anybody in the White House. He couldn't stand a lot of disagreement in his presence. He liked briefing papers and to work *through* people. In short, he liked to work by himself. You could wander freely as a reporter in those days through the Executive Office Building but the security in Washington is now much tighter, and it's oppressive and gets worse with every presidency and with every terrorist attack. I don't think Reagan has ever gone over to the Executive Office Building except to give a briefing. However, Nixon had a hide-away office there. He liked to go and work there. He was a loner.

Woodrow Wilson was a loner, too. I'm not a Wilson scholar, but I don't think he was actually a successful president. I think there was some way in which Nixon needed an instrumentality. He needed staff people in whom he could put zealous trust because he needed that kind of buffer.

I wonder what we would be saying about the Nixon presidency now, and I wonder who would be coming here to talk about it if they hadn't kept those tapes. Maybe it was inevitable though. I have argued, written, and I guess I believe that Nixon kept those tapes because he didn't trust anyone's version of history except his own. Still, you have accidents. I'm very uncomfortable with the notion that it was inevitable he should bring himself down, though I think that the things that brought Nixon down were within himself.

**QUESTION:** Looking back, Watergate causes us to look at Nixon through eyes conditioned by this remarkable episode. Independent of that, his was an extraordinarily successful political career involving a dramatic rise in California, his defeat of Helen Gahagan Douglas, being vice president, then recovery from a defeat for governor of California and also a defeat for the presidency. How did he last? How was he able to come back? What did he have that made for such an extraordinary career?

**MR. CANNON:** I think there were two reasons and one you still see in him. That is, he has an extraordinary analytical ability in terms of seeing what the hour is ripe for. Now at its most elemental, that may be some fairly cheap demagoguery through red-baiting, but in its grandest, it's seeing that this is the time to forge a new relationship with the People's Republic of China. Curiously, I don't think he is always given even ungrudging credit for that. He's given credit in the way that liberals and others who don't agree with him give him credit where they don't really want to give it by saying that only Nixon, a President from the right, could have done this. But it still took somebody to see that it had to be done and to go about doing it. It wasn't an inevitable thing. If you look at our relationships in the world now, the consequences of that action have been tremendous. We could have had a succession of conservative presidents and not gotten the same results. There was just an inertia there. It took a creative act. I think that happened also in arms control negotiations with the Soviet Union, the results which I am personally less pleased with because I think that SALT I has some negative consequences for this country. But on every issue he had a globalist vision in the best sense of the word.

Even on the Vietnam thing, which he inherited and from my own view let drag on too long, he had a view which was totally different from Johnson's. He saw the war as a drain on American resources. For political reasons, he didn't liquidate it in a way that he probably should have. But he had an over-arching view of what was in America's interest and what wasn't. The Russians realized that. Arthur Burns realized that. Nixon's personality is so unpleasant, and Watergate casts a long shadow. But if we really believe, as Theodore White and other people have written, the world is shaped by ideas, then Nixon shaped the world. He was a man of ideas. He asked where this country would be at the end of the century, not just where the country would be at the end of the next election. I think that was his strength as President.

The other personal characteristic which you still see is his enormous drive. He's trying to redeem himself now, but in a sense he was always trying to redeem himself. He was trying to stay on the Eisenhower ticket, which he did with the infamous "Checkers speech." He was trying to stay in the public eye after Howard K. Smith and others had done the obituary on him after the disastrous race in California. He was always trying to prove himself. In those days the only times he seemed successful to me, a completely obscure and unknown journalist, was when he was trying to show that he could deal with the press. Jules Witcover, in what I still think is by far the best book on Nixon, *The Resurrection of Richard Nixon*, says that Nixon figured that the press would feel that they owed him something because they supposedly had done him in in California. In those days no journalist was too obscure or unknown for Nixon to hunt him or her out, spend time with or give an interview. It was very calculated and very smart. I think now you see he's still trying to secure and polish up his place in history with the same kind of single-minded determination.

I don't think that mere personal ambition would have worked if he hadn't had that broad vision. Nixon's critics, of whom I'm obviously one, dismissed his attempts to revamp the welfare system. A book, *Nixon's Good Deed*, was written on it. But the truth is that Nixon saw that the welfare system had to be reformed. If whatever task force Reagan has appointed comes in with serious recommendations at the end of this year, which I personally think they will, I wouldn't be surprised to see them talking about a welfare system that looks something like what Richard Nixon was talking about in 1970. One of the reasons he was defeated twice on this issue in the Congress by a liberal-conservative opposition and the reason he didn't stay with it was essentially Ronald Reagan. He was worried about Ronald Reagan's stand on the right side of the issue.

**QUESTION:** Is the gap too wide? Is the gulf between the ideas and the cynicism and the opportunism one reason people worry about him?

**MR. CANNON:** After admitting that Nixon had this command of ideas and his persistence, the next question was what were his values? From my own experience, the work and reading I've done and the people I've interviewed who know him much more intimately, I've always thought that Nixon was amoral. He did not have enough of an idea of himself or who he was to have an idea of how others should behave. I have a friend who worked in the Ford White House and knew Nixon pretty well, and he was an academic. He said that Nixon would do something like hold prayer breakfasts. This is an example, not a specific incident necessarily. Anyway, he felt Nixon did things like that, not because he wanted to pray or project that element, so much as he saw that other people did it. That is, politicians did it and people liked it. Nixon did have this moral sense that came from his perceptions of various social or religious norms. He would see that people liked something like a prayer breakfast or this or that and would do it. But somehow those actions didn't come from conviction or from the heart.

I always come back to the fact that Nixon lied very frequently. Weinstein's wonderful book on Chambers and Hiss shows, of course, that Hiss was a liar, something I think most of us knew. But it is interesting that the reviews of that book don't often discuss the point that the only person that it is almost as hard on as Hiss is Nixon. Nixon just regularly and relentlessly lies. He lies through fulsome praise. He just has no inner sense of what the truth is.

The *Post* was very scornful when he finally resigned and couldn't be honest about it. But he told the truth and people didn't recognize it. What he said was, he lost his political base when they went to him to get him to step down. That was true. That is how Nixon saw what had happened. It was also literally true, but I think it shows an absence of values as a basis for moral judgment. That gets me into all kinds of problems, though, with people who try to see that tendency in every Nixon policy or decision. I simply don't see it that way. There were some very able people working for Richard Nixon. Some of them were a lot more able than the people who worked for Gerald Ford or Jimmy Carter or Ronald Reagan. There were a lot of good things that the Nixon presidency did. But I think that the thing you talk about is a gap. I think there was some point at which people perceived that amorality.

Nixon could obviously have helped himself. The reason I think that is Nixon's resurrection would have been accomplished more easily if he were just a person who was self-serving and always took—I'll use the phrase he always used—"the easy way out." The easy way out for him would have been for him to have apologized for this and to have searched his soul. There is no question that the American people would have forgiven him. People *want* to forgive former presidents. Carter has gained twenty points simply because he's out of office. The same is true with Ford. Of course, Ford wasn't quite as unpopular, but he has gained also. If you go out of office you rise in popularity, dead or alive—particularly alive. Nixon can't do this because he doesn't find it necessary to do it. He thinks he's done it when he talked about mistakes.

**QUESTION:** Who were the ablest people around him and did they share some of these characteristics? Hans Morgenthau used to say of Kissinger, to whom he was close, that Kissinger doesn't lie, he simply compartmentalizes. He tells the whole truth but only within a certain compartment.

**MR. CANNON:** I think that's true for a lot of people. I think that complaint against Nixon is a special case. Henry's compartmentalizations may be more monumental because he's got a more monumental brain and ego to go with it. I think Kissinger is a phenomenon in himself. He seems to dwarf every president he's associated with.

I always say that the wrong people get the credit and the blame. When I was a kid I was on the left, and we used to talk about the men around Stalin, men whom we now know lived in literal fear that some whim of the dictator would wipe their families off the earth. Then we used to talk about the men around Nixon. It isn't the men around those people, it's the person. Sure Kissinger had some of this, but Kissinger was also the guy that Nixon chose for this opening to China, and Kissinger deserves some credit. Of course, he is associated with the administration and the failure to liquidate the war quickly, but he is also associated with its greatest foreign policy successes. I would not be prepared to make the leap that Kissinger is an expression of Nixon.

Nixon hired able people: Pat Moynihan, Arthur Burns, Kissinger, and Steve Hess. I think Pat Buchanan is quite capable too. I don't think he should be where he is in this administration because I don't think that President Reagan needs to have his ideological backbone straightened. I think if you look at the Nixon administration and if you look at the most able and accomplished people in this Cabinet, you'll find some correlation. The ablest people in this Cabinet are Shultz and Weinberger—though I have my differences with Cap—and they are graduates of the Nixon administration. You've had three presidents since then and still the two most prominent Cabinet members in this administration are people who came out of the Nixon White House. Nixon did attract good people, and I don't know how he did that. I think he wanted good people. In that way I think Nixon is probably more like Kennedy and FDR than any of the other modern presidents, including Carter and Reagan.

**QUESTION:** Could you say a little more about his relationship with the press?

**MR. CANNON:** Nixon hated us. It was reciprocated in some ways, but not as much as he thought. I think relations with the press are important, but I think they are only important at the margins. If they recognize China or commit a burglary we are going to cover it pretty much the same way. On the margins it helps, I suppose. It's helped Kennedy; it's helped Reagan. They are people whom journalists like as human beings.

In my articles on Nixon and to some degree in a very valuable and neglected book on him by Bela Kornitzer, which appeared some twenty years ago, Nixon's distaste for the press is traced to his father. At one point Nixon had some press people at his house interviewing him after one of his victories. It was not an adversarial situation, but his father was there and wanted Nixon to throw the reporters out of the house. His father hated the press, and I think Nixon grew up with that.

He took a lot of heat for his campaigns against Voorhis and Douglas, and yet it has always been strange to me a little bit because as I'm sure most of you know, the thing that made Nixon as much as anything else was his investigation of Alger Hiss. He was advised and helped in that by Bert Andrews, a very good reporter for the *New York Herald Tribune*. Nixon, unlike some politicians, wasn't so distrustful of the press that he wasn't willing to associate, make friendships and make use of them. In a sense, he knew better. In 1962 in that "You-won't-have-Nixon-to-kick-around-anymore" speech, he was praising television for its supposedly objective coverage. Carl Greenberg was the *Los Angeles Times* reporter who was also singled out for praise. Carl told me afterwards that he went and called up the editor and offered to resign. They said "No, Carl, you're doing a fine job," and this was true.

I don't think there was anything that special in his attitude toward the media. The media became his adversary because the media, particularly the *Washington Post*, had so much to do with his downfall. I was told that Nixon was so upset about those press conferences that he would throw-up beforehand. Part of it was that he prepared so hard: he over-prepared. His factual command was stunning. He had an absolutely brilliant command of facts, important and trivial. But the thought of going out there and being questioned really scared him.

Some of my colleagues will tell you how much he hated and loathed us. I think he couldn't face people very well and that we were a manifestation of that. He wasn't inimical to the first amendment in any theoretical sense. I think that some of us in the media may be oversensitive. After all, why should we be different? Who did Nixon love? Maybe we were hated, but mostly we were just there and we forced him into personal experiences that he didn't like.

**QUESTION:** When you watched the Nixon press conferences there was a sense that many in the press corps, not you personally, knew that they could bait him and challenge him and that he was threatened. Were the Nixon press conferences, for that reason, different than other presidents' press conferences?

**MR. CANNON:** I think at the end they might have been. There was a feeling in the White House press corps, which I had just joined and didn't share so much, of how we had been betrayed and lied to. If you are looking at that, Watergate did change everything. One of the first times I covered Nixon as a regular for the *Post* we went down to Key Biscayne. We were coming back, and I had written this article. I actually had a few sources in the Nixon administration because people in the administration had begun to question how deep this Watergate thing went. In March or April of 1973, Diane Sawyer, who was then working for Richard Nixon, was talking to Richard Valariani and me. She was saying that nobody inside questioned it. I was very polite because I like Diane, and I hadn't been on the beat long enough to argue with anybody. I just said that I did find some people who didn't feel that way. I think the article was coming out the next day, and she said, "They are not true loyalists. They are not true Nixon people," or something to that effect. The inside notion, and it was very pervasive, was that the president was impregnable. Once the truth came out, a lot of people felt a sense of betrayal, and I think that showed up in those press conferences. I think the reporters were angered. I don't think they were angry at Nixon, though of course some of them were. It wasn't so much Nixon personally but that they were angry at having been lied to and, in some cases, having been a part of that lie.

Watergate was not a story people fell all over. I heard Ben Bradlee explain that he wished television had picked that story up in September and October. But it was really hard to get the Watergate story picked up. People didn't want to look like they were hounding a President who was going to win big and besides, they had no evidence. I remember one 1973 press conference in a parking lot in San Clemente that was very ugly. I thought the feelings were very bad on both sides. Dave Broder saw that and said he thought the American people watching probably were very uncomfortable. The people would have been uncomfortable with Nixon, uncomfortable that the President was put in that position, and uncomfortable with the behavior of the press in allowing such a situation to develop. Nixon went way down because of that thing. The media too, but not anywhere near as much as he did. The people were just not comfortable with things like that.

**NARRATOR:** We thank you very much.

# NIXON, THE PRESS AND THE WHITE HOUSE

## James Keogh

**MR. THOMPSON:** James Keogh is the executive director of Business Roundtable, an organization that has played a determining but largely unpublicized role in some of the crucial episodes in American public life. It is a leading business organization with some very distinguished members.

Mr. James Keogh is from Platte County, Nebraska. He graduated with a Ph.B. degree from Creighton University. He was reporter and city editor of the *Omaha World-Herald* from 1938 to 1951; he joined the staff of *Time* magazine in 1951, and in the period from 1951 to 1968 served as contributing editor, associate editor, assistant managing editor, senior editor, and executive editor of *Time* magazine. He was a special assistant to President Nixon from 1969 to 1970. He was a freelance writer from 1971 to 1972 and then director of USIA from 1973 to 1977. He assumed his present duties as executive director of the Business Roundtable in 1977. He is the author of *This is Nixon* and *President Nixon and the Press*, among other books. He has received various awards, including the Distinguished Nebraskan award.

**MR. KEOGH:** Thank you very much.

I recall my first encounter with Richard Nixon. It was at the Republican national convention of 1952. I was a writer at *Time* in those days and we closed the magazine on Monday night and our weekend was Tuesday and Wednesday. I remember that on that occasion we closed the pre-convention issue on Monday night. Together with some writers and editors, I flew out to Chicago to get some of the sights, sounds, and smells of politics firsthand. We usually had to depend on our correspondents for that type of information.

In the gallery at the convention that year, *Time* and *Life* had a rather large section in the magazine area, and we had a number of floor passes for the use of the writing and editing staff. We would take our turn to go down and wander around the floor to pick up what we used to call "color, quote and anecdote." I took my turn one morning going around the floor and when I came back to our section of the gallery, Harry Luce was there. He wanted to know if I had picked up any information. I told him that the most interesting thing I had heard was that if Eisenhower got the nomination, Senator Nixon of California was the most likely candidate for vice president. I remember that we sat there and chatted about the subject a while. At the time, there was still a contest in the convention between Bob Taft and Eisenhower although a good many of us thought that it was pretty clear that Eisenhower would be the nominee.

Later on, I got up in the front of our gallery place, picked up the binoculars and looked around the floor until I came to the California delegation. At that moment, Senator Joe McCarthy of Wisconsin was speaking to the convention. During those years, tremendous division of feeling about Joe McCarthy prevailed. A certain percentage of the delegates was rising, applauding and cheering as he made his points, and others were sitting on their hands. As I looked at the California delegation I saw Bill Knowland, who was one of the California leaders, showing his enthusiasm at something that McCarthy had just said. When I ran my glasses down to the end of the line of the first row of the California delegation, there was Richard Nixon, arms folded, staring dead ahead at the podium not demonstrating any type of support for Joe McCarthy. I remember the moment very well because it was important to me as to how I felt. I found out later on that Richard Nixon, who had a reputation as a fighter of subversion and an investigator of subversive activities, had distanced himself quite thoroughly from Joe McCarthy.

Early in 1954, when the question about what to do about McCarthy was very sensitive and difficult for both the Republican party and the Eisenhower administration, Nixon made a speech about subversion. He made the point about the need of routing out subversion, but when doing so, those involved in that kind of work had to act in a proper and fair way. I recall the following line which he used in the speech, and I later used in a story: "When you go out to shoot rats, you've got to shoot straight." Throughout that speech he did not mention McCarthy, but it was one of those speeches that had a clear implication: the vice president of the United States was attacking the senator from Wisconsin.

I wrote a good deal about Richard Nixon for *Time* in those years and at the end of 1955 and early in 1956 I wrote *This is Nixon.* It was not a typical biography, but more a book about what he had said and done. I drew heavily on his statements about various issues. Since Eisenhower had been ill during 1955, there was great interest in Nixon. There was speculation that the President would not run again, and rumors about his lack of health circulated. The interest all this created was the impetus for *This is Nixon.*

Just recently, I pulled out the book, and I looked at the last page. This was the message of the last few sentences in the book: "This is Nixon. In just ten years of public life he has done and said a great deal. At the time of the political convention of 1956 he will be forty-three years old. He is going to be around a long time in public life in the United States and that's a prospect that dismays his foes and heartens his friends." After thirty years, I think that foresight was pretty good.

Sometime in late 1958 or early 1959, Vice President Nixon asked me to come to Washington. I went there and had lunch with him in the vice president's office in the Capitol. When we got to the point of the meeting he said, "Well, it's fairly obvious I'm going to run for President in 1960, and I haven't done a thing about it yet, but it's time now that I begin to build my staff. The reason I asked you to come here is that I would like to have you come aboard as my 'principal issues' man." Those were his words, "principal issues" man. He continued, "And then from there, as we go down through the weeks and months ahead, we'll build a campaign staff." I turned him down with some regret because it was a fascinating possibility. I did so because my career at *Time* was on a rising curve. I didn't want to be in politics and government; I wanted to write about politics and government. I had a large house and two children in college. If I accepted, I would have earned far less money than I was making at *Time.* That wasn't the main reason, although it was a consideration. The principal factor was that I just didn't want to do it.

Ten years after that, in the 1968 presidential campaign, he came to me again and said, "I have very talented people in my research group." He called it his research group. He continued, "They are big talent but they are not producing what I need. There is a certain amount of bickering among them, but in the main I'm not getting what I need and I no longer have the time to manage this operation. Would you come in as a kind of managing editor and see if you can make that group produce what would really be useful for me?" By then I was in a different situation at *Time.* I was on a nice plateau and I could foresee that what I would be doing over the next several years was very similar to what I had been doing for several years earlier. I was at the stage in my life where I was looking for a new challenge. I had finished paying for my house and the children were out of college. I decided to agree. I took a leave of absence from *Time* and joined the campaign.

Many well-known figures were in that talented group. Alan Greenspan, who later became chairman of the Council of Economic Advisers and is now one of the most noted economists in the United States, was the economic adviser. The adviser on foreign affairs was Richard Allen, who for a short time was the director of the National Security Council in the Reagan administration. Martin Anderson was in charge of research. The writing group included Bill Safire, now a columnist for the *New York Times*, Patrick Buchanan, the current communications director for the White House, Raymond K. Price, who was the best writer of all of us and worked with Richard Nixon for many years, both before and after his presidency, and Bill Gavin, who is now principal staff member for Robert Michel, the minority leader in the House. Some time later, I brought in a young man named

Lee Huebner to the group. He is now the editor and publisher of the *International Herald Tribune* based in Paris. It was quite a group.

After I joined up I spent most of my time on the campaign plane with some of the members of the group while the rest of them were back at the headquarters. I needed a deputy to "mind the store" while I was not back at our little campaign office in New York. The deputy that we signed was a fellow named William Casey. He is now director of the CIA.

Early in that period Richard Nixon asked me to get Bryce Harlow involved in the group. I was surprised that he had assigned me that task, because they had a working relationship in the past. Harlow was in the Eisenhower White House. But I got hold of Bryce and invited him to join the campaign. He accepted and of course he immediately had his own role as a political adviser.

On another occasion, Richard Nixon said to me, "Let's get this fellow Kissinger involved." I had met Henry Kissinger when we had him up for lunch at *Time* but I didn't know him. So I went to Kissinger through an intermediary. I've forgotten who played that role, but someone else approached him. The word came back that he had declined to join in the campaign because he had been involved with Nelson Rockefeller's campaign in the contest for the nomination. He didn't want to be seen as an opportunist by jumping to another ship. But he added that he would be pleased to be involved later if that opportunity should arise.

When the campaign ended I was assigned the duty of finding out if the members of our group wanted to participate in the administration. I was asked first, and my answer was, "I never really wanted to be in government. That's not my thing; however, if I were to go into the government there is one thing I think I'd like to do. I'd like to be director of the United States Information Agency because that's what a fellow with my background ought to do in the government." And that suggestion was greeted with some amusement. There was surprise at my desire to run an agency that had subcabinet status, when a position in the White House was being suggested. So I succumbed. I went into the White House to do what I had done in the campaign. I served as a kind of manager and editor for all of the President's statements.

When I asked the others in the staff group what they wanted to do, I recall that Safire, Price and Buchanan wanted to join the White House staff, and they did. Alan Greenspan wanted a position as secretary of the treasury or chairman of the Council of Economic Advisers. But at that point he got neither one of those positions nor did he join the administration. Richard Allen wanted to be director of the National Security Council. But Richard Nixon appointed Henry Kissinger to that position at a very early stage. This deeply disappointed Dick Allen. Pat Moynihan, who became a key domestic policy adviser, was another one of the first appointees.

At that time, both Kissinger's and Moynihan's appointments sent some shock waves through Nixon's supporters, especially those whom I'd define as the Nixon loyalists. I think that this kind of action was very characteristic of Richard Nixon. He was not an ideologue although some people thought he was. He was a moderate and a pragmatist. Therefore, he wanted to try to get those people whom he thought would do the best that could be done. The incorporation of Kissinger and Moynihan onto his staff exemplified this aspect of his personality.

Henry Kissinger and Richard Nixon always had a very interesting relationship. I'm sure that each was fascinated by the talents of the other. The arrival of Kissinger on the team brings to my mind a point that I think should be mentioned. There has been some argument over the years as to the genesis of two of the main thrusts of Nixon's foreign policy: détente with the Soviet Union and the opening of China. I heard and saw the indications of those two thrusts in the campaign of 1968. Both were implicit in Richard Nixon's speeches during the campaign. Any discussion of the genesis of those two fundamental thrusts has to take into account that they definitely came from Richard Nixon himself.

Despite the seriousness of the substance they were dealing with, there was often a touch of humor in the Nixon-Kissinger relationship. I recall that at an early stage of the administration, during a meeting, Kissinger came in as director of the National Security Council to brief the

Cabinet on a very sensitive subject. I don't remember what it was but it probably had something to do with the ABM controversy at that time. He briefed the Cabinet on the sensitive information involved in the issue. After he finished, he began to gather his papers to leave the room. While that was going on the President said to the Cabinet, "Gentlemen, I want to advise you and to caution you not to say anything about this to anyone outside this room because there are leaks and these leaks are troublesome and difficult and I don't want anything leaked about this because it will cause us great trouble." He had just finished that admonition as Henry reached the door to exit, and the President said in quite a loud voice, loud enough for Kissinger to hear, "And there goes Henry, out to call the *Washington Post*." This was a classic piece of Nixon humor. He was thought of as a very serious man and he was, but he did have that kind of sense of humor, and it very often had a bit of a needle in it.

Kissinger was very important from the beginning of the administration but I remember an interesting place of background. In the first weeks or perhaps months of the administration, Henry was not allowed to be seen or heard in public. It was a strict rule and the reason for it was the "Doctor Strangelove syndrome." (As you recall, during those years Dr. Strangelove was a prominent character in the film world.) Here was this man, a key figure in foreign policy and the administration who had a heavy accent and wore thick glasses. The concern was that such was the wrong image to project, so he was very much under wraps early in the game. Gradually those restrictions were released and he was allowed to come out and have his voice recorded, and ultimately, to appear on camera. Of course, the irony is that he ultimately overcame all of that and became the most visible of all.

Richard Nixon was a man who cared very much about and took a great deal of pains with anything that he was to read or say. For a written speech he would project what he wanted to say to the writer. He would then take a draft and work on it intensely—changing, editing, rewriting. His speeches had to be typed up in a very unique way, in the style that he wanted them to be so he could follow them exactly as he wished. And he paid a great deal of attention to that kind of thing.

However, the little mini speech without a text was his most remarkable talent. He was a master of these. For example, just imagine him at a State dinner with a head of state where he had a toast to make. Of course, he would get a briefing paper from the departments involved: State, Defense, or whoever it was. Our routine was to send a page and a half, double-spaced, of what we called "suggested remarks." Most of these were peripheral because it was assumed that experience, knowledge and the briefing papers gave him the basic substance. So, what he wanted or needed from us was something that would add what he might not have. We tried to give him some lines, possibly some humor, possibly some analogy, possibly a bit of history. He had a remarkable talent for taking all of those things—from his own mind, his memory, his experience, the briefing papers, and these pieces that we gave him—and weaving them into the most complete mini speeches with a beginning, a middle, and an end, all with sentences and paragraphs. All of that came right out of his head. His mind—I've never encountered a mind of that kind—had the capacity to store all this, organize it, and then spin it out. I used to go to some of these things and sit there and listen to him, marveling how he did it. I was often disappointed when he used so little of our material as we had given it to him, but always quite pleased when something was used.

I stayed on the White House staff for two years. I left at the end of 1970. Three of us left at the same time: Bryce Harlow, Pat Moynihan and myself. I left because I didn't like it. I was somewhat frustrated, somewhat uncomfortable, and not pleased with what I was able to do there. I felt that we as a group and I personally did not have adequate access to the President and that there was too much distance. This was a problem. Now one has to recognize that everybody wants access to the top man. But I felt uncomfortable with the Haldeman-Ehrlichman screen, and I had recommended a number of changes in the structure with the thought of improving the situation. However, I just wasn't comfortable and didn't like it, but I wasn't angry. I had no premonition that anything was going wrong, but I didn't like the way it was and felt that I wasn't doing the best that I could for the President under those circumstances in that structure, so I left. And as I say, I wasn't angry when I left. I decided that if that was the way the President wanted it, it was fine, but it was not the way I wanted it.

After I left, I wrote *President Nixon and the Press*, which was a gentle book. I saw it as the work of a journalist who had crossed the river and watched his profession from the other side and did not like some of the things he encountered. My fundamental point was that there was too much advocacy rather than information in the news columns. There was too much concentration by the media on what made an interesting story as contrasted to what was really happening. And very often those two concepts are quite different.

Then I went back to the Nixon administration. Right after the 1972 election I got the call from the White House. The call was "O.K., now how about USIA?" I rather liked that. Four years earlier that was my interest, and somebody remembered. Almost on the spot I accepted. In early December of 1972, I had made my analysis of the situation: Nixon has just been elected by this enormous margin; he is vindicated, he will now be the leading statesman of the world for the next four years; he is the senior statesman of the world. We are looking at four years of real progress in international affairs. What better time to be director of USIA? We all know how wrong that analysis was, but it seemed pretty good at the time.

I went down to Washington to see Nixon a few days after the phone call and I expected to find a man magnanimous in victory, relaxed, looking forward to the same situation that I envisioned. But in the Oval Office in that December of 1972 I saw a very troubled man. I spent about an hour with him that day, along with Frank Shakespeare, who had been my predecessor as director of USIA, and Bob Haldeman. We talked about many things. I left the office concerned because I could see that he was troubled. I sensed in December of 1972 he, as a perceptive man, already knew how serious the road ahead was for him.

I found that President Nixon was very interested in the work of USIA. It was a time of detente and of course one of the things that he wanted to do and that we actually did was to pour into the Soviet Union all of the information we could about the United States in every way possible. Among our best efforts was the series of exhibits we sent to the Soviet Union.

My first visit to the Soviet Union was in September 1973 and shortly before I went there, I decided that I should meet with Ambassador Dobrynin. I contacted him to explore the possibility of having lunch together. He said that he wanted me to come over to the embassy and have lunch with him. The advice from my people was not to go because it implied going over to his territory; it was preferable to have him come to me. And he did. We had lunch at the International Club, at a time when the country had a meat shortage. He had to jibe at me a bit; he looked at the menu and he said, "Aha, we have roast beef, maybe tomorrow no roast beef." Well, he had roast beef and we had a bottle of California Cabernet, and in the course of the conversation I said to him, "We are in a situation now where we are trying to improve our relations and communications with the Soviet Union. President Nixon wants us to do this. I don't understand why your country jams the Voice of America. It costs you a lot of money and people listen to it anyway; they put the radios under the pillows and they listen to it. Why do you do that? The main purpose of the Voice of America is to try to tell the rest of the world what is going on in the United States." And he said, "Well, what is news in one country is not news in another," or something of that sort. But we ended the conversation on good terms and I prepared to go to the Soviet Union.

Just a day or two before I was to depart, early one morning one of my officers came hurrying into my office. He said, "We've been monitoring and I think they've stopped jamming." And sure enough they had. They stopped jamming the Voice, and for the next several years into the early period of the Carter administration, they did not jam the Voice of America which, in my view, was a great plus for us because we could openly pour all the information about the United States into Soviet ears. Of course, I'd like to think it was that bottle of California Cabernet that created the breakthrough, but I won't make that claim.

The Watergate problem burst upon us in a big way in the spring of 1973, very early in the game when I was at USIA. I recall the day that we really had to decide that it was a very, very serious matter. It had been serious up to then but this was the day that President Nixon fired Haldeman and Ehrlichman. On that day I fired Gordon Strachan, a young lawyer who had been brought into the Nixon administration. When I arrived at USIA, I discovered that he had been sent over there ahead of me as general counsel, and the gossip around was that he had been planted there by the apparatus to watch me, and that irritated me, but I endured it. But he was one of those who was involved in the Watergate matter and was later indicted. On the day that the President fired Haldeman and Ehrlichman, I called Strachan in that morning and said, "Well, you will have to go." We had several meetings throughout the day and finally at the end of the day he came in with his lawyer, with whom I worked out the resignation statement.

Then this young man left my office sobbing. This is the kind of tragedy it was, of course. I remember him saying to me, "Well, this is like something out of Kafka," and it was. But I went home that night satisfied that I had done what I had to do, but nevertheless troubled.

It was about that time that we had to decide what we were going to tell the world about Watergate. I worked out a brief basic statement of policy as to what we would say. We decided to tell the world that people at very high places in the United States government had been charged with not only malfeasance but crime. "These charges are being investigated through our legislative process, through the congressional committees, through our judicial process, through the grand jury system, and all of it is being covered openly by our free press. This country has institutions that are strong enough to survive this. When the investigations are completed the matter will be resolved, whatever remedial steps are necessary will be taken, and the country will go on from there." Of course I had no idea how serious those remedial steps were going to be. This was the basic thrust of what we told the rest of the world throughout that period in which we openly reported about the Watergate investigation matter on the Voice of America and in our news service and other materials. And that worked very well. People ultimately understood that. But we had a great problem in many countries of the world trying to explain what the U.S. was so excited about. They could not understand why there was all of this criticism and excitement about what seemed to them to be a matter that was so ordinary and usual.

Watergate was deeply painful. A lot of us were wounded by it. Many of us had come into the Nixon administration thinking that a good deal of that kind of thing had gone on in previous administrations, and we didn't think it was going to go on in our administration. But if this sort of thing had gone on before, that didn't by any means excuse the fact that it went on again. It was a tragedy. One major point of consolation for me was that none of that group of writers and researchers I had in the White House was implicated in any way in what happened.

I stayed on then through the entire holocaust, through the resignation of the President, the new administration, and on until after the election of President Carter in 1976. In that whole period of time, certainly until the resignation of President Nixon, I had very little in the way of guidance from the White House about how to run the agency. Watergate consumed the White House. I was on my own. That was good in one way and very troublesome in another. It was good in that I could run it the way I wanted to. On the other hand, when I needed support on various matters I didn't have the support that one could use.

I have not seen much of Richard Nixon since he left the presidency, but I have had dinner with him a couple of times and I've seen him on various public occasions. I remember one particularly; it was one of the first speeches that he made when he emerged. He spoke to the New York Economic Club. There were two thousand people there, black tie dinner, mostly New York financial, legal, business people who at one time would have been very anti-Richard Nixon. It was classic Nixon performance. He came to the dinner and stepped up to the podium with one sheet of paper with a few lines, that's all. He spoke for forty-five minutes on international affairs, domestic affairs, and some politics for fun. It was a *tour d'horizon*; it was totally remarkable. He was interrupted several times by applause, received a standing ovation when he finished the speech, spent another forty-five answering questions, with frequent applause interruptions, and got another standing ovation when he finished his answers to questions.

The man is a stunning survivor when one considers what has happened to him. It would have destroyed a lesser person. He is lively; his mind is working well as I see it. He is a survivor almost beyond comparison. And, again, that makes me rather pleased with my projection thirty years ago that he would be around a long time.

**MR. THOMPSON:** We may now proceed with the questions.

**QUESTION:** Mr. Keogh, why didn't President Nixon choose Alan Greenspan?

**MR. KEOGH:** I don't know why. Alan Greenspan wanted to be secretary of the treasury and the President chose Mr. Kennedy, a Chicago banker for that post. For chairman of the Council of Economic Advisers, the President chose Paul McCracken. But I don't know how the decisions were reached in those choices.

**MR. THOMPSON:** One of the mysteries to some of us, even after hearing you speak is how Nixon had problems with the press despite his almost unbelievable ability with speeches. Bryce Harlow, for instance, spoke about this. James Schlesinger also emphasized his intellectual powers. Yet somehow or another, all these natural talents didn't come into play in meetings with the press. Did he just hate the press or did the pressures and stress affect him?

**MR. KEOGH:** Probably both. Surely stress was a factor. In a stressful press conference situation, he was not as good as he was in other speaking situations.

There is another side of another situation that I have never been able to quite understand. Why didn't he cut his losses in the Watergate situation? I must clarify that my question is not: Why didn't he destroy the tapes? There have been many questions about that, without a good answer. But when one reads the Watergate transcripts, one can see the day and the hour when he should have said,

"Hey, wait a minute, I'm going to fire everybody that's involved. I'm going to suspend everybody who might be involved; I'm going to call a press conference tomorrow and I'm going to tell them all about this and I'm going to launch our investigation immediately." Had he done so at the correct time, I think he would have been reelected by as large a margin, almost as large a margin as he was and all of the terrible trouble that happened after that would not have occurred. But he couldn't and/or obviously wouldn't do that. But there was a moment when he should have done that, a moment when a good manager would have done that.

**MR. THOMPSON:** Could we press you just a little more on your feeling of unease with White House people? In the Eisenhower Portrait that we did, almost every speaker said, "We loved Ike; we felt good around him; the atmosphere was good." People haven't quite said that there was a bad atmosphere during the Nixon years, but one of our very recent guests said that one problem with President Nixon was that he divided politics from governing. "Governance was what you did for the good of the country; it was high principled and he had vision in this area. Politics was the law of the jungle and he felt that however evil it had to be done. He was perfectly able to shift gears and talk with Haldeman and Ehrlichman in a language that people who dealt with him on governance had never heard." Is that going too far? Was there a bad atmosphere in contrast to the Eisenhower administrations? In the White House, were dirty politics and dirty tricks either tolerated or promoted, or is that going too far?

**MR. KEOGH:** I think that's going too far. I don't think that was my experience, although others might say so. There were contests among various people for authority, but I would not describe the atmosphere in the White House as bad while I was on the White House staff. That was not my problem; my problem was I just thought that both my group and I were not as close to Nixon as we needed to be. Therefore I felt that I was not able to deliver as much as I should, and I left the White House. But I wouldn't say that it was a bad atmosphere at that time. It is true that I used to wonder who was going to get into trouble and I didn't realize that so many would end up having problems. In every administration somebody gets into trouble, and I had a candidate: John Ehrlichman. I thought Ehrlichman was over his head and I thought probably he would get into trouble. I never thought that Bob Haldeman would get into trouble. I should point out, however, that my first-hand experience with what was going on in the White House ended at the close of 1970. So I am not a good witness as to how it was after that.

**MR. THOMPSON:** I would like to hear your reactions to the following comments. When Haldeman and Ehrlichman were here, they blamed Nixon for poor human relations. In a phrase, they said 'we had to drag him out from under the desk to get him to talk with people. He didn't like dealing face to face; he didn't like confrontation; he didn't like debate; he liked to deal with memos and work with people in that way. He was at his best in looking at a substantive paper and distilling the essence of it and then making up his mind what he thought about the issue. But he wasn't good with people.' Henry Kissinger is supposed to have said, 'think what a statesman he would have been if just one person, including his parents, particularly his father, had loved him. Nobody loved him so he didn't love anybody else and he didn't trust them.'

Again and again people have talked about this awkwardness, this sense of unease with people and in face-to-face relationships. Do you think that is exaggerated?

**MR. KEOGH:** I think it is exaggerated to a degree. I think he did not like to chastise anybody. He didn't want to criticize people to their face. I have seen that aspect. He was not very good in day-to-day, one-on-one contacts, particularly with people he was not comfortable with. But Nixon was excellent in small groups. He would sit in a small group and talk about policy and what was going to happen, and be quite impressive. I think that essentially it was one of those ironies: a public figure who got such prominence, but essentially was a shy man. And I think that shyness stayed with him all the time. Today, I guess he is less shy and more open than ever in his life.

**MR. THOMPSON:** We always ask at the end for a balance sheet, if the person is willing to give it. What were the strengths and weaknesses of Nixon as a political leader? Finally, how do you think history will judge President Nixon?

**MR. KEOGH:** First of all, I think that his greatest strength was to analyze, to conceptualize and to work out in his mind what the thrusts of a political campaign or policy should be. His greatest strength was his mind. It is an exceptional one, and that was certainly the greatest asset. One always hesitates with the greatest weaknesses, but I think it perhaps was a matter of personality. I wish that he had spent a couple of years working in New York as an advertising salesman or something of that sort. He'd always been a lawyer and a legislator. A position as a television reporter or something like that would have taken some of that edge off which people found unattractive. And I wish he had had more experience as a manager before he got to the White House. There was a lack there.

In terms of the way history will judge him, I think he will ultimately be regarded quite well. In the longer term, particularly in the area of foreign policy, I believe history will have a good judgment of his early concept about China and his early push in that direction. I happen to believe, and always did believe, that his approach to the Soviet Union was exceedingly wise policy, especially the aspect of his policy that came to be known as détente, which essentially called for tough negotiations but also communication in every possible way. I happen to believe that was, is and will be wise policy. And those were two very fundamental thrusts that came from him which I think are going to look very good in history.

**MR. THOMPSON:** I'm sure I speak for all of you in saying that the reputation that Jim Keogh has sustained the reputation he had in the Time-Life Building years ago when people would say, "There's a fellow who defines his problem, writes about it clearly and well, and sticks to his guns." It was a good reputation and it has been evident today. Thank you very much.

# NIXON, KENNEDY AND THE PRESS

## Clark Mollenhoff

**NARRATOR:** It is my pleasure to welcome Clark Mollenhoff to the Miller Center. He was special counsel to the President of the United States from 1969 to 1970. From 1970 to 1976 he was bureau chief in Washington of the *Des Moines Register and Tribune.* From 1976 to the present he has been professor of journalism at Washington and Lee University. His books include *Washington Cover-up, Strike Force, Organized Crime in the Government,* the Pulitzer prize winning *Tentacles of Power, Despoilers of Democracy, The Pentagon: Politics, Profits, Plunder, George Romney—Mormon in Politics, Game Plan for Disaster, The Man Who Pardoned Nixon, The President Who Failed: Carter Out of Control,* and *The Investigative Reporter.*

As a Nieman Fellow he was early on identified as a questioner of "unusual imperturbability and aggressiveness." His publications show an early "innate trait to probe, to examine, to draw forth as much of the truth as possible." It is a pleasure to have you with us.

**MR. MOLLENHOFF:** Well, thank you Kenneth. In talking about any of these matters, I'm reminded of the story of the business agent for the Teamster's Union who was appearing before the McClellan Committee. An old lawyer in the back of the room noticed he was nervous and went up and tapped him on the shoulder. "Young man, would you like to have me go forward with you?" The young man looked up and said, "No, this time I'm going to tell the truth."

The longer one is in the business, the more difficult it is to determine the precise truth. This has been true particularly as I've been preparing to present this Forum. We all have perceptions of people over the years and we forget what we thought of them at some earlier period of time. I tried to go back and review that and establish just exactly what the situation was in 1951 when I first met Jack Kennedy and Richard Nixon.

I must say that I had a very negative view of both Nixon and Kennedy. Some of it was justified but some of it was not. In any event, each appeared better than that original perception at later stages. Much of this can be explained by my background. As Ken said earlier, I'd been largely involved in nothing but local politics in Iowa. I wasn't concerned with what was happening in Washington. I'd probably followed events as well as most of the correspondents in Washington, but I didn't really know what was going on.

As a Nieman Fellow at Harvard, I was for the first time doing an in-depth study and meeting national politicians. There I met Archie Cox and Louis Lyons, both very deeply involved in Americans for Democratic Action. I was influenced to a large degree by Louis Lyons. At that time Joe McCarthy was the major villain on the national scene and almost every other thing in politics was viewed in relation to McCarthy.

Jack Kennedy was a genial, nice fellow to deal with. He had been a reporter himself and he fancied himself as being a friend to reporters; he was a jocular sort of a fellow and everybody got along with him. But he was also regarded, justifiably so apparently, as a woman chaser. He didn't spend much time at work; he was not the workhorse of the House.

Nixon, on the other hand, at that stage had come to the point where he was highly regarded among Republicans in the House. He had just won an election in California. I had a biased view against that particular race at that stage because of the influence of Louis Lyons and the ADA group where I was getting much of my information.

At that particular juncture I was interested in investigations, as I always have been and always will be. Nixon happened to be on the Senate Permanent Investigations Subcommittee. He had been put there to replace Margaret Chase Smith, who had been critical of

McCarthy. McCarthy was the ranking Republican on that committee and he got her bumped for Richard Nixon. Now Richard Nixon, in that particular context, was aware of the reactions against him for his campaign tactics, justified and unjustified. He was aware of the drawbacks of being too close to McCarthy. In fact he disagreed with many of McCarthy's tactics, but he didn't know how to separate himself politically. He put his emphasis on steering away from the anti-Communist crusade at that stage and emphasized investigations that were aimed at corruption and mismanagement in government. There was enough of both so that he was the center of attention in criticism of the Truman administration.

One of the tax administration scandals in that period involved Henry Grunwald, that mysterious figure whose clout came from fixing things for the Democrats. But he was "bipartisan" and so he had a few crooked Republicans. Senator Owen Brewster from Maine and Styles Bridges from New Hampshire were dominant friends of his. The fact emerged that Richard Nixon had received $5,000 from Henry Grunwald. Five thousand dollars was a big chunk of change then. I had an opportunity to question Richard Nixon about this. He gave me a reasonable and plausible explanation: he didn't know where this money came from. He was relying upon Brewster and Styles Bridges, who were in charge of gathering money for their Republican senatorial campaigns. He didn't even know who Henry "the Dutchman" Grunwald was. It seemed satisfactory then, and I haven't heard anything since then that would disprove that particular account. It was plausible and he seemed to be forthright so that I was properly impressed. He never held it against me that I had pressed him quite sharply in exploring that. He made this favorable impression not only upon me but also upon others in that period. He was on the committee and he was a very good questioner. We would be sitting there in a committee meeting for half the morning and he wouldn't be there. But he would come in and within a matter of a few minutes—and he had this timed as I found out later—he would be given the floor. He would ask a series of questions that had not been asked by others; he zeroed in on the precise point that everybody was thinking but was not saying. Then he would have a prepared statement which he would read which would suit the purposes of the press completely. It would be colorful; it would be critical, it would be just a little understated, if anything.

I was quite impressed with the fact that this fellow had a terribly bright mind. This aspect permitted him to be the focal point of the investigations of Alger Hiss. He didn't do the investigations. The FBI did the investigations. The FBI used him as their vehicle for taking care of Hiss and he was an effective vehicle to get those questions asked and to push that particular point.

Jack Kennedy, by contrast, was getting ready to run for the Senate in 1951. He was over in the House making no big splash, spending much of his time chasing Jackie and others, but also politicking up in Massachusetts to set the stage for his race against Cabot Lodge. My association with him in that period was through a friend of mine, Eddie Milne, who was with the *Providence Journal* in Massachusetts. I'm sure that my friendship with Eddie Milne was the only reason that Jack Kennedy knew my name. Eddie was a great fan of Jack Kennedy, but he thought he was a little lazy and didn't pay much attention to the House of Representatives chores. His staff did, of course, but he himself didn't involve himself in the chores. Eddie also looked down on him because he didn't take a tough enough stand against Joe McCarthy. If he had, it probably would have been political suicide in Massachusetts because Joe McCarthy had a great following among Irish Catholics in the United States. Whether he thought McCarthy was wrong or not, he didn't say since his father was a big supporter of Joe McCarthy.

Working with this permanent investigation subcommittee, I got to know Joe McCarthy well. In fact Eddie Milne and I wrote some of the first stories exposing Joe's involvement with those Lustron Corporation payments. This was all the subject of a special election subcommittee report. Senator Guy M. Gillette from Iowa was intimidated. Even though he had this staff report he wasn't going to let it out because he was afraid Joe McCarthy would get after him. Eddie Milne and I got our hands on that report and published it. It raised a stink. Senator Flanders didn't read that report; he didn't know anything about that although he was in the Senate. His discovery of that report in 1954 is what caused the censure of Joe McCarthy. That report would never have been published if we hadn't published the contents in 1952.

When Joe McCarthy got up on the floor and said—I've forgotten the exact terms—that Senator Ralph E. Flanders was a little addleheaded, he wasn't far from wrong. Nevertheless, that was McCarthy's big crime. The Senate did not censure him for all the bad things he did; they censured him because he said something bad about another Senator and held Senator Flanders up to public criticism. McCarthy was off on his tangents against the communists and, in his own inimitable fashion, was making a mountain out of a molehill, and making himself highly vulnerable in the process.

**QUESTION:** What were the sources of strength of Nixon and Kennedy that you hadn't seen in the beginning that later may have become apparent? How did one of them achieve a great landslide in his reelection, and the other become a folk hero of the American people as President?

**MR. MOLLENHOFF:** They were very much alike, really. Both had very quick minds. Jack Kennedy was not present through much of the labor racket hearings except to come in when Bobby wanted him to be there to support him. If Jack was there backing him up, nobody else would get involved because of senatorial courtesy, particularly since he was quite agile. None of them wanted to cross McClellan either. With Jack and McClellan you had a kind of impenetrable fortress as Joe McCarthy found. Joe McCarthy became the leading defender of the Teamster's Union. No surprise, he was always defending crooks.

But back to Jack Kennedy and Richard Nixon, I think that both were quick studies. Both also were rather pragmatic; they would do what works. I think both wanted to be great Presidents. I can't imagine anybody being president who didn't want to be a great president. Jack didn't really want to work at it too hard but he selected a lot of able people to operate pretty independently. He really didn't want to be bothered with it unless it was some big concept. Most of these big concepts he hadn't thought through. Look at the Peace Corps. He threw it out in a speech and that became the Peace Corps because it was seized on by the reporters. Jack didn't know what he was proposing. This is what happens too many times. They'll do something almost by accident and then it clicks with the public.

Nixon's strength was that he could come into those hearings and ask the questions that everyone all day had wanted to see asked. Then he would have prepared this nice colorful little statement where he drew the conclusions about the graft or corruption. He had a good analytical mind. Jack Kennedy was the same way when he put his mind to it. Occasionally they didn't. With Watergate, Nixon didn't.

**NARRATOR:** We thank Mr. Mollenhoff for this stimulating discussion. We wish him well as professor of journalism at Washington and Lee and as a continuing investigative reporter. Thank you very much.

# NIXON AND THE CONGRESS

## Kenneth BeLieu

**MR. THOMPSON:** There are a lot of people who make money and who are on the front page of newspapers every day. There are others who do the hard grubby work and keep the government running. Kenneth BeLieu certainly is in that latter category. As his biography indicates, he has served in many positions in government since in the early 1950s after completing a distinguished military career.

In the Nixon administration, he was first deputy assistant to the President from 1969 to 1971, and then undersecretary of the Department of the Army. In the Kennedy-Johnson administration he was assistant secretary and then undersecretary of the navy. In the 1950s he was a member of the staff of the Senate Armed Services Committee. He was chief of staff or staff director of the Senate Committee on Aero and Space Science.

He was born in Portland and is a graduate of the University of Oregon. He studied advanced management science at Harvard University. He is one of a small group, which included Bryce Harlow and Bill Timmons, that dealt with the Congress in the Nixon presidency. He may want to make comparisons with the Kennedy-Johnson administration and even perhaps the Eisenhower administration. We are delighted that he is with us and look forward to the discussion.

**MR. BELIEU:** My view of what happened in the Nixon administration is not nearly as broad as Bryce Harlow's, but at least I did see some facets of the stone. My early contacts with Nixon were probably like everybody else's. I knew we had a vice president but didn't pay much attention to him. I think it was Franklin who said that "vice presidents should be addressed as 'Your Superfluous Excellency.'" During the McCarthy-Army hearings, my boss, Secretary of the Army Robert Stevens, was called to a luncheon, in Nixon's office. I made a remark in a Washington columnist's house, which was full of press, one night that "I didn't think the vice president had much sense in doing that." Walter Winchell picked it up and said that the town wasn't big enough for a certain colonel in the army and the vice president. I had a few moments of misgiving about that.

On the Hill in 1955 when I went to work for the Armed Services Committee, I met the vice president because he was president of the Senate. I never really had much to do with him until the year of Khrushchev's visit. The Senate was in session; Johnson kept it in session long hours. On this night we had been in session all night and adjourned at 6:20 in the morning, *sine die*. There were two senators on the floor and Nixon was presiding. They were Dirksen, the Republican, and Johnson, the majority leader, and Johnson moved to adjourn *sine die*, and called for a vote. Johnson voted aye and Dirksen voted nay; we had a tie vote. Nixon, in the chair, said "I will cast my vote this one time for the Democratic majority leader," and he voted aye and they adjourned. Johnson said to me, "Have the cafeteria set up a steak breakfast and some Bloody Marys in my office for about sixteen or twenty people. We can sit down and discuss what has happened." Well, it was a privilege to be in there. Sixteen to eighteen people came in: Sam Rayburn, Jim Wright and others of the Texas delegation, Dirksen, Nixon and some others. Everybody there thought they were looking at the next president of the United States, one or the other, because elections were the next year. Kennedy was in the offing but nobody knew it. We were indeed looking at two future Presidents.

Nixon regaled everybody with his trip to Moscow and problems he'd had in South America. Johnson told stories about the hill country in Texas. Both of them were leaders of a different kind. I had no further early dealings with Nixon except when I served nominally as a consultant to various of his lieutenants during the campaign.

A friend of mine had been taking candidate Nixon around to various places. He called me in Washington and said, "I want to see you. I just got off the airplane with Mr. Nixon and he is talking about an exciting idea, a new voluntary armed force. I wanted to ask you, with your military background, if you think it is feasible." I said, "Oh, yes, it can be done; it has been done before." He said, "How would you do it?" I said, "You'd give every private $100,000 a year and you'd have a recruiting line from Foggy Bottom to Scappose, Oregon, but it won't work in combat." He asked, "Why?" and I said, "Even $100,000 doesn't encourage people to get shot at."

Well, there was a sequel to that. A few months later, there was a meeting in the White House on the voluntary army. Three people voted against it: Schlesinger, Haig and BeLieu. Haig got bawled out for voting against it. I don't think anybody dared bawl out Schlesinger. Nobody said a word to me.

My first indication of getting into the White House as a staff member—which I had no thoughts of doing because I was enjoying private business—was a call from Bryce Harlow. He wanted to know if I would come to New York and discuss something with him. Even though I had worked for Lyndon as a majority leader, I used to carry messages down to Ike and Bob Anderson and others because Lyndon and Ike were very close sometimes. Bryce and I worked a lot together so we had become well acquainted. He had been a staff man on the House side, I on the Senate side. We spoke the same language. I went to New York's Pierre Hotel, and Bryce said, "Would you consider coming back in government?" I said, "Yes, if I could pick my job." He said, "You can't." I said, "If I had my druthers . . ." and he said, "No, you don't have your druthers. However, if you don't want the job we have in mind for you, we'll see what we can do about your druthers." I said, "What's the job in mind?" He said, "In the White House with me in charge of the Senate." I said, "Well, I'd like to go home and talk to my wife about this." This was on a Monday. Could I let him know by Thursday? He said, "Yes, that would be fine." "I suppose this is in confidence." "Yes, it is." I didn't want anybody to know I was being offered it if I turned it down.

I got on the plane and went back. I hadn't told my wife anything yet. I went into my office and there was the chairman of the board of Ryan Aeronautical Company, a guy by the name of Bob Jackson. He said, "Congratulations, Ken." Then I realized he had just come from Congressman Bob Wilson's office, the congressman from California who was high in the Republican hierarchy. Obviously they had cleared my name with him before they offered me the job. Well, the cat was out and I needed some advice. I called Arleigh Burke who was former chief of naval operations and a dear friend. I said, "I'm over twenty-one, Arleigh, and I can make up my own mind but I want somebody to listen. See what you think." I told him I had been offered the job and I didn't know whether to take it or not. He said, "Well, Ken, if you don't take it, you will always wonder what would have happened, and if you do take it, even if you don't succeed, you'll know you tried." That was pretty good advice. So I went home and talked to my wife; we decided to take the job.

I called Bryce and said yes, but nothing happened for a while. Then Ziegler announced it one day. When he started to leave the room a reporter asked, "Is Mr. BeLieu a Republican?" Nobody had asked my race, creed, color or religion. Ziegler said, "Of course he is." I'd never met Ziegler. I was a Republican—I worked for Landon and worked for Wilkie before going in the Army—and here I had ended up the so-called chief of staff to Lyndon Johnson. Chief of staff was an inaccurate word, because with Lyndon if you were by the door when the garbage went out, you were a garbageman. If you were by the door when the secretary of state of Madagascar was in there, you were secretary of state. But I did handle a lot of work for him.

I want to talk some policy but I'd also like to discuss the practical things. The president-elect's staff was mostly assembled in Federal Office Building Number Seven, which is a rather plain brick building on the corner of Pennsylvania Avenue and Seventeenth Street across from the Executive Office Building. We had two or three floors. Paul Warnke was up on the floor above us with a defense task force. Mel Laird, who had been chosen for secretary of defense after Scoop Jackson turned it down, was hidden in the Carlton Hotel. Warnke was up there busily putting a defense staff together and Mel Laird was putting one together which was going to be the real one.

I had been used to the majority leader's office and my own office as undersecretary of the navy, and I walked into this bare place with partitions, a couple of raunchy desks, no secretaries, a few telephones, and I guess a wastebasket, and that was it. Bill Timmons came down from New York in his private car carrying with him four or five bags stuffed with mail. This was mail addressed to president-elect Nixon and weeks later still had not been answered. Bill Timmons arranged to get a secretary from the Hill and I called the Navy and said, "Give me a secretary." They sent one, a lovely lady. So the four of us started making sense of the mail. I went out to a drugstore and bought some office supplies and we started getting into those letters. We had two files: one called Hot Senate and one called Hot House. The letters in those bags should have been acknowledged, especially one from Senator Williams who was going to raise hell in financial policy, and one from Senator Margaret Smith who didn't like to be kept waiting. Both letters were at least six weeks old. I got on the phone and called them because there was no other way to handle that.

The president-elect doesn't have an organization or any real authority until he gets sworn in. Imagine being a presidential candidate and suddenly finding yourself elected—everybody sends you everything. They all like you now; I found that I had new lifelong friends who appeared as job applicants. If it hadn't been for Lyndon Johnson it would have been worse. When Lyndon found there was no money for the president-elect, he had money set aside so the next one could pay staff and so forth. I didn't take any salary because I didn't need it. We cleaned out the business that had accumulated and had several organizational meetings.

We went on to plan moving into the White House. Bryce Harlow, Bill Timmons and I knew most of Johnson's staff. We arranged through Harry McPherson to get in the White House the night before the inaugural. We looked over the office space and laid our claims. Bryce was assigned space that Bill Moyers had had; I was assigned the space that Ted Riordan had upstairs in the southwest corner of the West Wing. Bill Timmons was next to me. Juxtaposition to the president is everything. I didn't realize it at that time but if you are not next to the head of the White House, you're out.

We moved into the White House about noon on Inauguration Day. The best way I can describe it is from past experience. On the battlefield, I've gone into command posts vacated by the German army or the North Korean army, and this was like going into a vacant command post. Telephones were strewn around the floor and desk drawers were open. In my office there was a book called *Presidential Papers*, one of the volumes which contained prints of the president's papers. I opened this one to find my letter of resignation to Lyndon when I had resigned as the undersecretary of the navy. Well, we finally got established in the White House.

We had a congressional relations staff with Bryce Harlow as the leader. He had been with Ike for eight years and was exceptionally well known and highly respected in town. I was known in town as well because I'd been there a long time. Bill Timmons, a pro, had been with Bill Brock in the House. Responsibilities were divided between us. I had the Senate, the Armed Services Committees in both Houses, the Atomic Energy Committee and the Space Committee. Timmons had all the rest of the House. We had two other gentlemen in the office but they were, at that time, in specialized fields. Other than Harlow's office, there were really two people and two stenographers to start with. Lamar Alexander, now governor of Tennessee, was a young assistant to Bryce.

That small group handled contacts with over 500 congressmen and senators and their staff and the congressional liaison staff with all the departments. Bryce had said to me, "We are going to keep a low visibility staff, because we want quality." It is the only mistake I ever saw Bryce make in that business. He was used to the Eisenhower regime where things had been more chivalrous and gentlemenly. Now we were in the rapid flux of Vietnam. We were also stuck with the budget that the previous President had. It is like moving into a house and the payment for the electric bill and everything else depended on the budget of the people that were there before.

What were the problems? Initially our staff was too small. It would have to be expanded. Another interesting problem at that particular time was that there were secretaries and other people on the White House staff who had been borrowed from other government agencies. I asked one young lady where she was from and was told she was from the Department of Agriculture and carried on that department's books. She had been in the White House six years. There were lots of stories in the papers about White House staff. In fact, when I'd worked for Lyndon one of the jobs I had was staff director of the Preparedness Investigating Subcommittee, and he wanted me to investigate Ike's number of staff in the White House. Three times he told me to do it and three times I said no.

Well, Lyndon had a bad habit. He'd reach out and grab you and say, "Why?" You would almost lose your fine thoughts. He said why to me and I said "Because I don't want to see a future president try to investigate his own nest." He let go of me right away. But he had borrowed people. Now Nixon really was one of the honest ones. When he came in, he cleared the books of the borrowed people and counted the staff on the payroll accurately. A little later on he got criticized for having too many people, although he didn't really have as many as others.

We had some interesting housekeeping problems to start with. One of my first jobs was to get the Cabinet confirmed. But regardless of what we had to do, we were inundated with telephone calls. Bryce, Timmons and I were known, while the Cabinet wasn't known or confirmed yet. All the people who wanted to talk policy were searching for somebody they knew in the White House, so they would call. We might be outside doing some work or on the telephone and unable to answer them. It was not uncommon at eight o'clock at night for Timmons and me to sit in front of Bryce's desk with eighty to one hundred pink slips of unanswered phone calls spread all over the desk. We would each take part of them and we still had maybe thirty or forty of our own to answer, but his were more important. This went on for about six months.

Another problem was a routine one—establish rapport with the congressional liaison people within the various departments: State, Defense, Agriculture, etc. They had good civil servants and all they needed was policy direction. They were moving and all that was necessary was to contact them by name. But I had to go on the Hill and make contacts too. Dirksen gave me the freedom of his office. Mike Mansfield, a wonderful gentleman and sometimes an opponent of the President, said to me, "We've known each other since I was an assistant to Lyndon. It's not good for the President's man to be seen walking around the halls by himself or looking at loose ends. I know the executive does not have an office up here but we have space in my office you can use." Here was a Democratic majority leader giving a Republican President's man on the Hill an office of his own and an offer to "use my phone and come into my office any time you want." He was very gracious and very effective.

Nixon wanted to have all the Cabinet sworn in at once. It became clear that Hickel, the designated Secretary of the Interior, was going to have some problems. Bryce said to me, "You'd better get with Hickel and see what you can do." He'd been very outspoken as governor of Alaska and made some enemies, and Drew Pearson had written him up rather heavily. I made an appointment to see him. He was ensconced in a suite at the Shoreham in Washington. I got there at about six o'clock at night. They were having cocktails and Hickel was sitting behind a big desk in his suite. He was pontificating to the people who had been on his staff in Alaska about how he was going to conduct himself in the confirmation hearing and what he was going to tell the senators. They were all agreeing with him. When I walked in he said, "This is the man from the White House who is supposed to tell us what we are going to do." When he got through he said, "What do you think?" I said, "You are doing three things wrong." I guess the staff had never told him he did things wrong. There was a big silence. I said, "First, you are telling the senators all about the secretary of the interior and what you are going to do there; they've seen secretaries of the interior come and go so they won't be impressed. Two, you are answering every question with so much verbiage that you will make them ask ten more questions. Three, you are sounding arrogant and downgrading the senators and that's one thing they will not tolerate."

Well, his biography said he had been a prizefighter; I figured if he had been a prizefighter he would take coaching. He said, "All right, what should we do?" and he was excellent. It did take him a while to get confirmed. One time a senator asked him about something which Drew Pearson wrote that Hickel had said fifteen years earlier. Hickel said, "I don't remember but it sounds like me." All of us started laughing and he got through all right.

There were bigger problems, however, than that facing this new ship of state. There were icebergs in the way like there were with the Titanic. But the Titanic was sunk by a submerged iceberg and we faced anticipated icebergs. Vietnam was probably the biggest followed by foreign affairs with domestic policy always coming down the track, but there was an even bigger obstacle. Imagine the transformation from candidate to president and the gala inaugural. You dance with your lady and everybody is congratulating you. The next day you come down the parade ground, walk into the White House and the drawbridge goes down on the fortress. Nobody can come in or go out unless you agree or your staff lets them. You can't get personal phone calls, see your friends, go on a picnic, or go window shopping. You are a prisoner.

What is needed is an instant do-it-yourself kit to put a professional football team on the field and play them that day and win. You have some players who've never played the position, never worn a uniform before, don't have any game plan, don't have any signals, don't know each other, and don't even know the opposition. They start shooting at each other just like fresh infantry regiments do in combat if they see or hear firing. A chain of command must be established that runs information up and down, so decisions can be made and policy known, and one must do this with people who haven't any experience in government.

When Harlow participated in the Miller Center Eisenhower Portrait, he said Ike had the ability to bring in an experienced team; this is awfully important. We had a Cabinet where some were good, but some had no experience. So this was really the big problem. Bryce Harlow told me how angry Ike got an the end of his first four years when he found out that he didn't have control of the government. A general who can't talk to his troops, get a command to them, and make sure they do it, isn't in complete control and neither was the President.

Staffing is a difficult thing. The normal political campaign does not produce people that are necessarily the right ones for administering the government properly. I asked Bryce why Nixon put Ehrlichman and Haldeman in the jobs that he did and paid so much attention to them. It was clear they were bright young men, but they didn't understand government. They didn't know how to spell Defense Department. One of the things they did know was how to use a sun lamp to disguise heavy whiskers. Bryce said, "Because they helped Nixon get elected."

Foreign relations was probably the major concern because over everything hung the ominous lightening-filled cloud of Vietnam. It had been going on for four or five years. I guess Nixon had a plan in his own mind to stop it. But he was never able to prove that he had a plan, especially to the press. Vietnam went on and on and on, so it didn't look like he had one. I think he felt he had a plan to do something. He thought about it, he was going to do it, but he did not get down to the practical nuts and bolts like tightening the screw or opening the door to see how it is going to work.

He appointed Kissinger as his top man in foreign relations. I think one of his first mistakes was not that he did use Kissinger, but the way in which he used him. Kissinger and Vietnam, during the entire time I was there, were almost synonymous with foreign relations.

I asked one senator who had known Kissinger before, what he thought about him. I thought Kissinger was brilliant, articulate, and had a unique grasp of world affairs The senator said, "He is one of the most brilliant minds in Washington. He also has the greatest ego and every time his mind competes with his ego, it loses." Henry would have made a good broken field runner in football. He could look one way and drift another way. Before anyone knew it, if someone tried to tackle him, he was gone. He wanted to move power from State to his office in the NSC and he succeeded. Rogers was short-circuited completely.

Juxtaposition to the presidency was Henry's strength and he fought to keep it.

I'll give you two small examples. One night Bryce and I invited Senator Russell to the White House, at the President's request, to have a meeting on certain military aspects of foreign affairs. Kissinger was there too. Nixon, Kissinger, Harlow and BeLieu were all in the room. We had a couple highballs and something to nibble on. We discussed the subject with Senator Russell. When he had to leave, Bryce and I escorted him to the diplomatic door of the White House and let him out. The President said, "Ken, you and Bryce come back and we'll have a nightcap and discuss some of the things we have been talking about in here." Bryce and I took Russell to his car and came back. Kissinger met us at the door and said, "The President and I have something to talk about. Good night." He blocked anybody who got close to the President and the President let him do it.

Later on, when I was undersecretary of the army, Kissinger sent Haig over to my office. Haig asked, "Would you come over to the White House and talk with Henry if he asked you?" Mel Laird had a prohibition against dealing with the White House unless you went through him. I don't blame him because he was short-circuited quite a bit. Being an ex-staff member, I couldn't refuse. It could be something that I worked on before.

Anyway, I went to the White House and had a conversation with him. Kissinger wanted to talk about who the next chief of staff of the Army was going to be because Westmoreland was leaving. I was amazed at his knowledge of the generals in the Army. Westmoreland and I are the same age and Abrams, who did come in, is a month younger. We were all contemporaries and had worked together. We knew each other like college classmates; some of us had been in combat together. I realized Haig had briefed Kissinger, but we went through the list of names that were being considered for chief of staff. It came down to Abrams' name. Kissinger didn't like Abrams. He said, "He is a drunk." Abrams wasn't a drunk; he was a fine combat soldier. He enjoyed a good, stiff drink at times, like a lot of soldiers do; but he wasn't a drunk. I talked about Fred Wyant, who became chief of staff later on. Fred had been my assistant in Steven's office. I brought him into the Pentagon. Kissinger said, "He is a public relations man." Well, Fred was a good public relations man when he ran that part of the army. He was also the best legislative liaison man they had and one of the best generals in the field. He gave the appearance of a lackadaisical attitude until you looked and saw the eagle in his eyes. Then I said, "We've got a young major general, who has great potential and could be a chief of staff, but you'd have to raise him up above others. His name is Bernie Rogers." Later he became chief of staff and is now commander in Europe. Henry looked at me and he said, "Do you think the country can stand two Rogers?" I looked at him and said, "Yes, if their tours of duty don't overlap." Then I realized Kissinger was trying to move Haig out of the White House and perhaps place him in line to be chief of staff. Haig was beginning to compete with Henry in the White House and Henry wanted Haig out of there.

Laird wanted Abrams. I'm convinced that Laird made a deal with Henry. He got Abrams if Laird would take Haig as vice chief. That's what happened.

It was a mistake on Nixon's part to let Henry short-circuit the basic machinery of government. It may be that it is difficult with rapid communications to get ideas across. But if the machinery of government is not used, you open yourself to a lack of data, lack of advice, and are apt to develop a mentality that only looks at one area of the information. Therefore the decisions may be tainted.

Was Nixon a good leader? He had all the capacities of being a great leader. He had a brilliant, retentive mind, and could make decisions if the information was properly presented to him. If his brilliancy was his strength, it was also his weakness. They say that an intelligent person will see twenty ways to solve a problem and a very intelligent person will see forty ways and therefore not make a decision. Nixon had some of that.

My initial impressions were that he was a man who had been a congressman for two years, a senator for four years, a vice president, and a governor, who fought battle after battle and felt surrounded by enemies, but should have known government. I came to the conclusion that he did know government, but he didn't like the practical nuts and bolts of it. He could do it but he didn't want to. It was like an auto enthusiast who loves to drive a car but detests putting in oil or checking the tires. In addition he was basically insecure and a loner. The loner within him would not let him exhibit the warmth that a leader must have sometimes to inspire people. He was insecure because of all his battles and because it was his nature. I think Henry was insecure as well and they sort of fed on each other.

Nixon detested face to face meetings. There are many examples. If a Cabinet man came in and told him something was going wrong and he needed help, Nixon would be apt to withdraw into himself and not listen. Agriculture Secretary Hardin used to complain about not being able to see the President; he couldn't get through the German guard: Kissinger, Ehrlichman and Haldeman. It wasn't their fault in many respects. It was the way Mr. Nixon used them but they also fed on him.

Mendel Rivers, who was a powerful top man on the Armed Services Committee in the House and was for Nixon's military policy, wanted to come down and talk to the President one time. He had some irons in the fire that he wanted the President to think about. Mendel said to me, "I want to come down to see the President but I have one condition: I will not come if he's got that damn Kraut in there"—meaning Kissinger. Mendel was very outspoken. My forefathers were German and French, so I don't have anything against Germans, but that was what Mendel said. I wrote that condition in the memorandum to the President, so it was arranged to have Mel Laird there instead.

Mendel came in and immediately began telling the President how he should do something. Nixon just withdrew within himself; he was very polite, listened; and then when we left, Mendel said to me as we went out the door, "Ken, I blew it, didn't I?" I said, "Yes, you did. You treated him like you would treat Lyndon." I said, "You know what Lyndon would have done." Mendel said "He would have told me 'Shut up and sit down. I'll tell you what you are going to do.' That's what Lyndon would have said." President Nixon could not do that.

If a senator was brought down to see him because he needed the senator's vote, Nixon would not say, "Senator, I must have your vote." He would say, "Now I hope you understand my position. Of course, you've got to make up your own mind, but please choose my position." Lyndon would have reached out clear across the table, clutched the visitor, and said, "Why?" Not that Lyndon was better than Nixon. Lyndon had an inferiority complex about the Defense Department and about Ivy League education or too much education. I suppose we all have inferiority complexes about some things.

What were Nixon's weaknesses, or failures? Well, his weaknesses were based on some of the items discussed earlier. He had a very retentive mind and could memorize a whole page and almost a whole speech. The first staff paper I had to give him was supposed to be in on Monday at about four o'clock in the afternoon. I worked all Sunday on it. Your palms sweat when you think about doing something for the President; you want it to be right. I had a paper all drawn up, conclusions, summary sheet, and tabs, and I was late. I called the office and was told, "Well, he is going to be here a little longer. Get it down here by five o'clock and it will be all right." He had to have it for a nine or ten o'clock meeting the next morning. I got there and he had gone. Somebody said, "We forgot to tell you, there is a small state dinner tonight and he has gone to prepare for that." Well, what to do? One of the old retainers there said, "Take it over to the residence down the hall." Where in the residence? I didn't know where. I wandered over and ran into a butler that I knew, who had been there with Johnson and Kennedy. He said, "Mr. BeLieu, what can I do for you?" I told him. He said, "Well, that's simple, give it to me, and I'll put it on his bed." "I don't want to put this on the President's bed. He'll come back from a dinner and be tired." "No, we do that all the time."

It was a thick paper with lots of tabs. The next afternoon it came back to me. He had read all of it that night, and put his remarks on it, "This is good," "I like this one," "We'll do it this way," and so forth. He had great abilities but didn't always seem to know how to bridge a gap between his own staff and the agencies which were the horses that had to pull the wagon. That was one of his fundamental weaknesses. He couldn't or didn't want to talk to a staff member, so the message often didn't get through.

It is too early to tell Nixon's place in history because we are just on the edge of history. History, to those of us who are old enough to have participated in this, is real. But every American who is twenty-one or younger only knows second hand about Mr. Nixon. There is a very revealing quote about Nixon:

> Here is a man with greatness who allowed himself to be involved in something that is a tragedy. A psychiatrist said, 'We are sometimes left with the picture of a divided man with lofty dreams and accomplishing wonderful things for the good of all, yet a man with an incurable chronic sense of insecurity and loneliness.'

It was said that he was cold, yet I never saw it. I never heard a profane word from him, and never saw his temper except once when he got mad at the chief of engineers for not doing something and he told me to tell him, in no uncertain terms, to do it.

Mike Mansfield had a luncheon for Nixon on the Hill to which I was invited. I have an artificial left leg that I picked up in Korea and sometimes I use a cane. This luncheon was in honor of the President and the top senators were there. Mansfield was trying to help Nixon with the Senate. I was using a cane when we got up to leave and the President looked at me and said, "What's the cane for, Ken?" Mansfield said, "Why, Mr. President, he's got an artificial left leg." The President put his hand on my shoulder because he had not known. One of the senators afterwards said to me, "I swear he had moisture in his eye." The man had a very tender trait but he didn't want to show it.

I don't know much about Watergate but I gave an order one time in combat to one of my subordinates which may be similar to what Nixon did to start Watergate. Crossing the Vire River in Normandy, I went back to the command post after being up all night and told my assistant, "The general is down there and I had to come back. Go down and make sure nothing happens to the general. Take care of him and see how far you can get." Now that was a stupid order—see how far you can get. He went down and got a Purple Heart. He got a minor wound in the leg and a Purple Heart and a tetanus shot. But I never gave an order like that again. I suspect that Nixon may have given one like that.

I've bounced around a lot of subjects but I would be happy to answer questions.

**MR. THOMPSON:** Who'd like to ask the first question?

**QUESTION:** I have one. Do you consider Nixon to be a good manager?

**MR. BELIEU:** No. My experience is that most politicians are administrative idiots. That is a harsh thing to say and not necessarily their fault. Using military terms, they've never commanded over twenty-five or thirty people at the most. Who was it that said, "You must have judgment based on bad experience," or something like that?

It may not be possible for a man to go through all the hurdles necessary to become President and become a good administrator at the same time. He must hire somebody to do that. That may be what President Reagan is trying to do with Donald Regan now, although he should not let him give speeches. The staff should be seen and not heard, in my opinion. Regan was not elected so he shouldn't give speeches. I wouldn't give a speech when I was in the White House. I talked to small groups but did not give a public speech or talk about any of the President's actions.

**QUESTION:** You mentioned courage. What were his other outstanding character strengths?

**MR. BELIEU:** Nixon had a desire for excellence. He had dreams that he thought he could fulfill and he had the courage to try them. He may have stumbled over the hurdles or didn't know quite how to get them done. However, the commanding general or the skipper on the ship is blamed for what happens in his command. So Nixon has to be blamed for Vietnam, as Haldeman said in his book. He should have gotten Vietnam over quickly, but he tied Congress up with the ABM (antiballistic defense). He had a great feeling for international events to the exclusion of domestic events, which the President can't afford to do. If a knight in armor can't keep his castle going, he shouldn't sally forth from it.

His strengths in terms of intelligence were great, but he stumbled on how to apply them in the administration. He had a good memory. He could remember details and events. For example, Senator Ellender wanted to come and see him, but he didn't want to see Ellender. I tried to talk the President into meeting with him three months in a row. One night several months later he asked, "What else on the Hill, Ken?" and I said, "Well, there's one." He said, "All right, I'll have lunch with Ellender." He had not forgotten.

**QUESTION:** I'm a little puzzled. If I understand you correctly, you judge Nixon to be strong in neither administration nor judgment about men. At the same time he got elected. A good politician must have at least one of these traits, and should have both.

**MR. BELIEU:** I don't disagree with his judgment about men as much as I disagree with his judgment of how to utilize them. Let's take Hardin in agriculture, for example. He was a very fine man but he couldn't get to see the President. The President tried to give orders through his staff. This is fine once good procedure has been established, but orders must be given eyeball to eyeball to start with.

Now how does the President get elected? It doesn't require any character to get elected. I think it is image-making today. The American people are so involved in watching television that we can't tell the difference between an actor and a leader. Some of our leaders can't tell the difference between a play and reality. It's an image process in the United States. "As a man thinketh in his heart" so is he, but the Lord looks on the inward and man looks on the outward side.

**QUESTION:** President Eisenhower was caught in a lie on the subject of the U-2 and Gary Powers. He initially lied because he thought it was in the best interests of the national security but then told the truth when it was obvious. What would be your observation about Mr. Nixon's character relative to telling the truth? How far do you think it was right to go in lying to the public?

**MR. BELIEU:** An assistant secretary of defense [Sylvester] made a remark that it was right to lie in defense of government. I don't think that is right. Ike did come clean on the U-2 business. Lyndon had a press conference every morning and I wrote the briefing paper for him on the day of the U-2 incident. It was a little note that basically said, "This machine gun diplomacy," meaning Russia shooting it down, "has got to stop." I didn't think we'd ever admit publicly to flying over Russia. Then Ike admitted that Gary Powers had done that, and Lyndon turned on me and said, "You shouldn't have let me say that."

You can't excuse the Watergate tapes. I've heard people say that Nixon's mistake was not burning the tapes. The mistake was in making the tapes. When I left the White House to go to the undersecretary of the army job, the President called me and we had a long discussion. All the time I was in the Army I was worried that those tapes might come out. He had asked my opinion of certain generals in the Army and I told him what I thought. When the President of the United States asks me a question, I give my unadulterated opinion. I was afraid as undersecretary that one of these days these tapes would come out for all the army to see.

You don't lie but you don't have to tell the whole truth. In a press conference, I get fearful sometimes about President Reagan's remarks because sometimes he is too frank. He should say, "I'm not going to discuss that subject today" and it would stop there. But every once in a while he feels he has a good thought and, bingo, it comes right out.

**QUESTION:** We have heard in prior discussions of Mr. Nixon's presidency about the difficulties in administration and organization. From an operating standpoint would you say that this was a fundamental reason for the disintegration of the operation?

**MR. BELIEU:** That is certainly one of the chronic problems in government. In addition, Nixon preferred paper work and to talk to subordinates rather than to peers. I went in with Jerry Ford for three months when he became vice president. He asked me to help him with the Senate and to come into the White House; I went in for three months. When I left I said to him, "When you go in that castle and the drawbridge closes you are not going to get the information that you have, had as a freewheeling congressman. You need a Kitchen Cabinet or a peer group that you can talk with." Nixon didn't have that. He developed a group who would sit around him and say yes. When they play "Hail to the Chief," give a twenty-one gun salute, and everybody stands up when you come in the room and nobody ever tells you to go to hell; you lose touch with reality. That was perhaps true of Nixon as President or any other President.

I had a driver in the Infantry. He told me one time. "The company commander didn't do as well this morning in inspection as he normally does." I almost sent the guy to the guard house. "What the hell do you mean?" "Well, you didn't. Two guys hadn't shaved and you didn't catch them." Such candor is necessary to bring a leader back down to earth. A leader can't stay in touch with reality if he doesn't have access to those around him.

**MR. THOMPSON:** Mr. BeLieu has spoken with clarity and courage in discussing issues that throw a light of all hues on a most vital subject. The only way we can understand our government is if we have this kind of oral history and reconstruction of what has actually occurred. Now that he knows where we are, we hope he'll come back.

# V.

# THE DEPARTMENTS AND THE WHITE HOUSE

# THE CABINET AND THE NIXON PRESIDENCY

## Robert H. Finch

**MR. THOMPSON:** It would be hard to improve on the late Theodore White when introducing a speaker. I thought you might like to be reminded of the way Teddy White, if he were here, would introduce Bob Finch. He wrote, "Finch's love affair with the American political process came to him naturally. His father was a World War I hero, an Arizona state legislator, and a cotton farmer who was driven from his farm to Los Angeles during the Depression. Finch had studied political science and history at Occidental College after the war, was elected student body president there, was chosen by Los Angeles Congressman Norris Poulson as his executive secretary in Washington, and found himself just down the hall from the office of young Congressman Richard Nixon. Their relation became that of an older brother-younger brother. Nixon would talk foreign affairs to young Bob Finch, of the political vulnerability Nixon recognized as a Republican in his support of the Marshall Plan, and of the dangers of unsubstantiated testimony at the hearings of the House's Committee on Un-American Activities. Finch was always on the sun side of Richard Nixon's character. Later when the men on the dark side cut Robert Finch's throat, Nixon defended him as a poet of politics."

Teddy White also wrote about the process of choosing Vice President Agnew, and Nixon's dilemma about the choice saying

> Nixon himself preferred above all others, Robert Finch of California. Finch was to him a

> younger brother, closer, more trusted, conspicuously more able and more visionary than any other man he had known over the years. He had telephoned Finch with a hard offer several weeks before the convention, but Finch felt he simply was not yet ready to carry, as he put it, the other end of the stick in a campaign as important as the presidency.

And there are other relevant passages in *The Making of the Presidency 1968* by Theodore White.

Lieutenant Governor and Secretary Finch had a distinguished military career, serving both as an enlisted man and as an officer in the Marine Corps. He returned to service during World War II and also during the Korean War. He became the head of the Young Republicans throughout Southern California and set up branches of the organization in close to twelve institutions of higher education, including Whittier College. He studied at night at George Washington Law School and received his law degree from the University of Southern California in 1952. He opened law offices in Inglewood, California, before being recalled by the Marine Corps. He decided to run for congress in southern Los Angeles County, won the Republican nomination in a district which had a three-to-one Democratic majority, and came within 2,000 votes of defeating Cecil R. King, who was a ranking member of the Democratic party. Thereafter he became the Republican County Chairman in 1955, the youngest county chairman in the nation. In 1956 he did advance work for Nixon, who was running again as vice president. He ran President Nixon's 1960 campaign and it is interesting to compare the tone and character of that campaign, between the two rising political stars Nixon and Kennedy, with subsequent campaigns that took on a different tone in the absence of Robert Finch at the controls. He chaired the successful Senate campaign of George Murphy against Pierre Salinger in 1964. He ran for Lieutenant Governor with Ronald Reagan in 1966 and won. In 1968, he was asked to consider nominations for the vice presidency and for attorney general but said that the social welfare field was his first love. Therefore, he was appointed secretary of health, education and welfare. So that brings us up to date within the Nixon Cabinet, and from here on it is up to Secretary Finch.

**MR. FINCH:** To discuss recent presidents of our nation, as Mr. Thompson has asked me to do, one must add to the presidential heritage of Virginia and Ohio, the emerging California phenomenon. As California surged to the forefront of states in post World War II America, California politicians came to play pivotal roles (as they do to this date) on the American political scene.

The political footprints of Hiram Johnson, Earl Warren and even Herbert Hoover loom large in any understanding of the California political theater. With its burgeoning, polyglot growth, California has established trends and personalities in American politics which have yet to be adequately chronicled.

First, allow me to refer to the reasons that led me to choose the position of Secretary of Health, Education and Welfare. You will recall the difficult and troubled times of the late sixties growing out of our involvement in Vietnam, which generated sharp controversy on many campuses. The whole question of how quickly that war could be brought to a close and how soon we could achieve the so-called "peace dividend" was central. In California we experienced the initial problems with the student unrest. As a member of the Board of Regents of the University of California, one of my roles was to work with Governor Reagan and try to stabilize and address that situation. I had a strong feeling for those concerns. When it was clear I could have one of several Cabinet positions, I talked to a number of people I respected and whose judgment I trusted, and they said that the department that was going to have to deal the most with the peace dividend in terms of medical care, welfare reform, and similar domestic problems was what was then known as "HEW". I recognized the enormity of the task, but that was the reason I selected that Cabinet position over others that were suggested to me.

This brings us to a point that I know you have discussed here before: How to organize the Cabinet to get things done. There have been a number of studies that deal with this issue. Probably the most sophisticated effort from a presidential standpoint came from the Ash Commission in which I was actively involved. Of course, I happen to agree with the Commission's conclusions. The Commission's starting point is the proposition that the Cabinet itself is too big, too structured, and wrongly so. It began and evolved as a Cabinet by constituency, that is to say, "labor," "defense," and so on. I believe it is necessary to organize our Cabinets by "function" rather than "constituency." Of course, the most recent and grievous example of that was Carter's reorganization of HEW, who in exchange for support from some educational unions, took education out of HEW and made it a separate department. In terms of federal resources alone, there is no justification for a separate Cabinet position for education. In terms of its importance as a generic subject, it may be justified, but not in terms of who pays the bill. The federal government pays less than ten percent of the overall expenditure by states and localities. For example, state budgets, state legislatures, and local resources in most states take care of community colleges and the state university systems. In effect, that makes of the Secretary of Education a spokesman or an advocate for a single group of people, the school teachers and school administrators. A Cabinet secretary, it seems to me, has to be somebody who is forced to make tough trade-offs.

If the organizational approach of the Cabinet changes to one based on function, mergers of resources and programs could take place. For example, a "national resources" department could result from the merger of the Department of Interior with the Department of Agriculture, and a "human resources" department from the merger of HEW and Labor, and so on. If the Cabinet is smaller, calls on the allocation of resources get tougher. If the number of Cabinet members is reduced, it would be a more collegial group. As things stand now, Cabinet meetings become a "show and tell" session depending on how each President wants to use his Cabinet. The President may have a Cabinet meeting if he wants to underscore a major issue or to launch something for public consumption. This was the case when we tried to organize welfare reform, for example. Nixon wanted to bring the rest of the Cabinet into the meeting because he knew there was a basic disagreement among his Cabinet members as to the approach. But also, the reduction in Cabinet size would allow the executive branch to submit a more orderly budget to the Office of Management and Budget. Lastly, it would force secretaries to make some trade-offs, and meet the new kind of budgetary restrictions that any new president will face following the approval of Gramm-Rudman.

I think that another concern we have is the ability of government actually to anticipate what is coming up. For example, take a basic program like the Social Security program or any of the Great Society programs. That was one of the problems that we had to reconcile when I was a member of the Cabinet because Lyndon Johnson had an extraordinary ability and got all of these very expensive programs of the Great Society approved by Congress. After a few months in office, it was clear that the estimates for the expenditures for Medicare and Medicaid had been greatly understated. They were going to cost massive amounts of money far in excess of the projections. So we were trying to implement that but make it manageable. The assumptions of many social programs, including Social Security, were that the number of people entering the market would increase, that the number of births would be larger than the number of deaths, and that more people were going on the payroll than leaving it. That was pretty much the justification of many of the original LBJ programs. In the late sixties and early seventies, without any of the indices giving us an advance indication, an extraordinary phenomenon took place. Suddenly the birth rate dropped, and all of these premises were then shaken, and all of the programs that were predicated on those assumptions were in trouble. Incidentally, I think that part of OMB's responsibility should be to attempt to anticipate these trends with finesse. I think we have acquired a capability of doing that to a much greater extent than was true in the past.

Richard Nixon is a part of this paradox and so is Ronald Reagan. The first, individual, intensely disciplined and intellectual; the second, one of the most relaxed, attractive and outgoing public figures in our nation's history. Nixon has always compelled attention; Reagan has inspired confidence through his wit, confidence and ease.

To underscore my assertion I must become anecdotal. I recall that in 1959, shortly after I had joined Vice President Richard Nixon as his chief of staff, we flew together on a commercial flight so that he could address a convention of sports writers in Chicago: a very tough audience! At that point, he was running well behind Nelson Rockefeller in the presidential polls and indeed, there were many who questioned whether Nixon would even seek the higher office of President.

Nixon, as we boarded, was thoughtful and subdued, pulled out the inevitable yellow legal pad and for the two-hour flight, scribbled furiously at his notes for his speech. I don't believe we exchanged any thoughts except when he asked if I recalled the first names of Joe DiMaggio's baseball playing brothers. In any event, Nixon's speech listing the players he had was seen and read about in each position on the diamond (with appropriate anecdotal comments) won a standing ovation when he concluded.

He gave the speech without notes and it was a triumph. Time and again over the years I was with him, I watched Richard Nixon focus his intellect, energy and remarkable memory and overpower a tepid or even hostile audience. When we were on the campaign trail, I never ceased to be amazed at his ability to recall names of individuals he met whom he hadn't seen for months or years.

Reagan, on the other hand, wins his audiences through his charm, wit, candor, and easy exposition. People now tend to forget that he has defeated some exceptional campaigners, beginning with his race for Governor in 1966 when he defeated an outstanding field of over six opponents in the Republican primary and went on to defeat Pat Brown, who derided him as that "actor."

Reagan, from his years in the entertainment field and on the lecture circuit for General Electric, has a rare gift for recalling funny incidents and stories which he rolls off with charm and polish. His sense of humor and timing are absolutely superb.

This disparity in style extends to the approach of both men in style of management. Nixon attacks a problem personally with enormous intensity, focusing on detail and options with a passion. Reagan, on the other hand, is more relaxed and casual and not given to quick commitment or decision-making. Time and again when I was his Lieutenant Governor, I would urge an appointment or a decision on a policy question and he would inevitably say—after extended discussion—that he would give me an answer the following day or after he "had slept on it." And he always did, even if it was not always the answer I hoped for.

While I have been requested to compare the presidencies of Nixon and Reagan, I think it only fair that you understand my perceptions as against other Presidents I have known in a limited way (or did not know), so that some measure of my credibility is established. My first exposure to the White House was in the late 1940s, when I attended receptions and functions. At that time the congressional staffs were not nearly as large as they are now, and Truman, reflecting his own background in the Senate, would invite congressional staff to such affairs. I saw President Eisenhower a number of times in settings either at the White House or Newport, Rhode Island and came to have great reverence for his under-regarded political skills and his "people skills." At the time, this ran contrary to a lot of then current observations of many of the press as to his being a "passive President." The more scholars dig into that presidency, the more they realize that his qualities of heart and mind were formidable, indeed.

I came to know Kennedy because his office in 1958 was in the old Senate Office Building directly across from the office accorded the vice president. At that time there was said to be no room either in the Executive Office Building or the White House for a vice presidential office and later, you will remember, it was Nixon who first insisted that a vice president be given that prerogative. In point of fact, Nixon had a smaller staff and budget as vice president than he received as a Senator from California. As both Kennedy and Nixon went through their respective party primary battles and before they were selected by their conventions, there was a perverse relationship that existed between office staffs and to a milder extent through to Nixon and Kennedy themselves. The two men had known and respected each other as House members, but I think their variation in political views and the nature of the political constituencies they had to advise drove them apart by the time they were ready to contest for the presidency in 1960.

Of other Presidents I have known, Lyndon Johnson had the most rampant ego and was the best manipulator of legislators we have ever seen in a President. He, as majority leader, came on so strong (and particularly irritated Eisenhower because he would always physically attempt to shake, touch and pat Eisenhower on the back. You could just see Eisenhower get red in the neck with his irritation.) But Lyndon was, of course, a dynamo as a President and managed to extract more legislation (for which taxpayers paid a greater price) than any other President with the possible exception of FDR, after whom he fashioned himself. In that regard, incidentally, I know both Reagan and Nixon regarded themselves as modest students of FDR; Reagan from his days as a working Democrat (voting four times for FDR) and Nixon just as an observer with an early political itch while he was still in the Navy.

I will only note in passing that Eisenhower's relationship with Nixon during the latter's vice presidential days was distant, in great part because of the "Checkers incident," but the maturing of the relationship through the two terms, the effect of that on the Eisenhower campaign for Nixon against Kennedy, and the later marriage of Julie Nixon and David Eisenhower all resulted in a warmth and mellowing between the two in the later years when Nixon became President.

Ford, I first knew because he was a young Congressman with Nixon and I advanced several visits on behalf of Jerry in Grand Rapids when Nixon was Vice President. He was very high on our potential vice presidential list in 1960. In mid-year, Nixon asked if I would garner reports on Ford's campaign stops around the country. They were mixed, but Eisenhower became the final factor in the ultimate choice in his pushing for Cabot Lodge as the nominee. Nixon had an inclination toward Congressman Walter Judd, who had been an old friend and knew that with his keynote speech, he had turned the convention on its ear.

I give Jerry Ford very high marks for the manner in which he handled the presidency after Watergate and he certainly did what needed to be done with respect to the very strained relationship between the presidency and the Congress. That was, of course, why Nixon named Ford as Vice President after Agnew resigned.

But coming back directly to the "one-on-one" comparisons of Nixon and Reagan, when you consider the many roles the President plays, you understand both of them have an awareness of "politics as theater." And while they are both confrontational, Nixon in his campaigns and with his dealings with Congress was a good deal harsher internally with his staff, but he was constantly having to manipulate and rework arrangements with the senior members and committees because the Democrats controlled both Houses. Reagan, from his years as Governor in California when the Democrats controlled the Assembly and Senate there (and particularly with a leader and a speaker like Jess Unruh, a very talented and tough guy) learned the lesson very quickly so that when he was elected, he very wisely came to Washington, D.C. before his inauguration and met with all of the key leaders in both Houses. That paid enormous dividends in getting his programs through for the next six years. And while he and Tip O'Neil needled each other back and forth, what was originally a low esteem in Tip O'Neil's eyes about what kind of a President Reagan would be, there came to be a very high degree of mutual respect between the two.

I think it is obvious that both Nixon and Reagan are "ultimate patriots," which means that they enjoyed the role of commander in Chief. I remember being with Nixon when he would order certain things done and, as every President had, he complained that he could not get any positive or quick action. With the military, of course, you always got a "Yes sir" and that goes beyond just a simple ego trip. Nixon from his days in the Navy, and Reagan from his own experience making films for the military, felt and appreciated the nature and the magnitude of World War II, and the necessity for keeping our defenses in good order.

Looking at both Reagan and Nixon as party leaders, the comparison is like apples and oranges. Both of them worked, had worked and continue to this day to work very hard for the Republican party.

Nixon came from a time when the Republicans were a greater minority than they are now, and on a tactical level he fought to get the conservative Democrats to come with him. Whatever race he was in, or contest or issue, Reagan would be far more theatrical, less controversial and just appealing as a "very reasonable man" through the success of his programs. But we really had to come through the 40s, 50s and 60s, Goldwater and all the excesses of the Great Society programs, before people finally realized that simply throwing federal money at programs wasn't going to work and the liberal syndrome the FDR coalition had welded had finally begun to come apart. And it is this that Reagan has been able to break very dramatically.

During the gubernatorial campaign, we established a pattern after we were elected which I recommended to George Bush, and they followed it. I had seen so many cases where either governors and lieutenant governors or presidents and vice presidents came apart. Their staffs would get jealous of each other, and infighting would go on. Just after we were elected, I asked him if we could set aside a lunch session every week, unless some other extraordinary problem came up. We would sit down and simply go over the problems and discuss issues or appointments or whatever. He maintained that policy with me, and now he is doing the same thing with George Bush. There is a weekly luncheon, when possible, on the President's schedule for just the two of them. For us, that was extraordinarily useful.

At the outset of that 1966 campaign, it was clear that if Reagan won as big as he actually did, he would quickly become a presidential candidate. I had run Nixon's campaign in 1960 and I was certainly convinced that on the foreign policy side, Nixon was much more experienced than Reagan. Reagan knew that I was supporting Nixon for President, but our personal relationship was very good and solid, and it always has been. Other members of the staff were convinced that it was in my interest to support Reagan for President in 1968 because I would become Governor. They thought that somehow I would shift from Nixon to Reagan. That never happened but Reagan never held it against me. It's that kind of relationship that I enjoyed with him. He also has this great sense of humor. Under

California law, when the governor leaves the state, he has to officially notify the lieutenant governor that he is going to be outside the state from whenever the plane crosses the state line to whenever it gets back, so that he can exercise the powers of governor. This happened a lot as Reagan's presidential campaign began to build up. So he would send me little notes and he would always put a P.S. of some kind on it, and it was always humorous. P.S.: "Solve something. Solve anything." That's pure Reagan.

To complete now my brief political profile of California I have borrowed heavily from U. C. Professor J. S. Holliday.

Richard Henry Dana told of his stay in California in his book *Two Years Before the Mast*, published in 1840. He found that the women of California preferred fine clothes to clean homes, and he suspected they obtained their finery by "immoral means." He wrote, "There are no people to whom the newly invented yankee word 'loafer' is more applicable than to the Californian."

Of all the images which have shaped national and world awareness of California, those from the Gold Rush years have been most persistent and influential. We are often reminded of the impressive economic and demographic statistics of that dramatic era. But I think we are unaware that it was during the Gold Rush years—when the gold seekers left their families "Back East"—that California offered its newcomers the freedom of anonymity.

In that reckless anarchical society of transient men in a hurry, everyone felt safe, far removed from the curiosity and censure of hometown eyes. That freedom has survived. Millions of men and women have come to California knowing that here they will be free to ignore the expectations of parents and grandparents, and the rules of Indianapolis and Philadelphia.

Another legacy of the Gold Rush—the exuberance of those years, the rambunctious energy and ambition of the goldseekers—became the hormonal source for California's confidence and optimism. No other state or nation had such a beginning, such a period of adolescent success and freedom. Think what it has meant to California's image, its spirit, and its psyche to have the 49'ers as founding fathers compared to the pilgrims. To have the wild, robust-better yet-sinful San Francisco as the mother city, compared to Boston or Philadelphia.

The Gold Rush for California has been like the Civil War for the South, a romantic era proudly remembered, giving distinction and identity. As the defeated soldier has symbolized the South, and the shared burden of a great loss has created a feeling of misfortune and denial among Southerners, the ambitious miner has symbolized California. The shared sense that anything is possible has created a feeling of confidence and great expectation among Californians.

Through the boom years of mining from 1850 to the turn of the century, California and San Francisco were synonymous. It was the capital of mining and trading empires, powerful and sinful San Francisco—that rough, masculine city-state—and it dominated national and world awareness of California.

That twin image began to change in the last decade of the 19th century and ever more rapidly through the first decades of the 20th century. Then, Los Angeles intruded for attention, sent out its own images, and in time became the dominant city.

Unlike San Francisco with its remarkable location, Los Angeles started without a single advantage: no harbor, no river, little rain, and isolated by deserts and mountains. Yet, in the beginning of the late 1880s that out-of-the-way village burst into national consciousness. The Southern Pacific Railroad and other real estate promoters launched one of the most intensive image-making campaigns in American history. Through handbills, posters, brochures, pamphlets, advertisements, magazine articles and books, they announced that Eden was for sale! A place of beauty, fertility and health.

The promoters who idealized Southern California created an identity and image for that region so long isolated from the rush, disorder, and power of Northern California. They sold a climate without discomforts, offering sunshine (pure and healing) and no snow, ice, sleet, or mud. It was a pacific utopia with the orange as its symbol and principal cash crop.

To promote oranges, when most Americans had never seen one, the growers and packers developed an advertising campaign, "Oranges for health, California for wealth." Exported in refrigerated freight cars, this new gold produced fabulous profits and the image of Southern California as an agricultural wonderland.

In 1982, the first oil well was started in Los Angeles. By 1907, 3,000 oil wells were pumping wealth in backyards, between houses, and from sites where homes had been removed. Prosperous with oil, confident of its future, ambitious to compete with San Francisco, Los Angeles needed what every great coastal city had—a harbor. But nature had provided only sandbars and mudflats. Not daunted, the city turned to its engineers and taxpayers to build what would become a great, man-made access to the world.

As Los Angeles entered the 20th Century with its reach to the ocean, San Francisco reached to the mountains. San Francisco's engineers sought to create a reservoir for the city's water system by damming the Hetch Hetchy Gorge near Yosemite. The destruction of this beautiful, granite-walled valley caused a bitter controversy, which introduced a new image of the Golden State. John Muir warned against the arrogance of science and technology and the assumption that man's errors will be healed by nature's bounty. Crying out that the growth of cities and the appetite of industries threatened their state's resources, beauty and beneficent environment, John Muir created the image of a fragile, endangered California.

There were other astonishments in the 1920s, best of all "Hollywood." A corps of columnists and magazine writers reported the movie peoples' dazzling salaries, their divorces, adulteries, seductions, wild parties, their yachts, stucco mansions and sunken bathtubs. New words and images "bathing beauties," "starlets," "boudoir" and "bungalows" conveyed new images of Southern California to millions of Americans and new expectations for their own lives in Michigan and Maryland.

Because the movie-makers used the Southern California locations, the old images became more vivid than ever. The American people saw palm-lined streets and lawn-fronted homes, romantic Spanish missions, broad ocean beaches, oil fields, orange groves, vineyards, farms, deserts, forests, and mountains . . . California, a land different from Michigan and Maryland.

Even during the Great Depression, the image of the Golden State—land of sunshine and year-round crops—attracted hundreds of thousands of destitute Americans who believed such a bountiful state would provide jobs, at least an escape from cold and suffering.

More than any other state, California felt the impact of the Second World War, immediately and long term—the evacuation and relocation of 93,000 Japanese-Americans living in California. Through the years of danger and of victories, the federal government spent $35 million in California. That incomparable stimulus revolutionized every aspect of the state's economy.

Men and women by the hundreds of thousands came to California to work in wartime industries, and millions of servicemen and women passed through training camps, ports of embarkation, Navy, Marine and Air Force bases. In 1943, the San Francisco Chronicle summed it up: "The second gold rush has hit the West Coast." For millions of Americans in service and in industry, wartime California was a place never to be forgotten—San Francisco, the greatest "liberty town" in the country; lonely women earning more money than their fathers back home; soldiers, sailors, marines, and airmen enjoying the freedoms of California. There had been nothing like it—not since the Gold Rush.

In 1950, The Korean War started. With peace an endangered concept and the Department of Defense an ever more important employer and investor, California gained a new image in the 1950s—as the science center of the nation, where Nobel Prize winners used modern physics to control atomic energy, where professors in their labs were allied with generals in the Pentagon. Millions upon millions of dollars were spent to build research facilities which made California preeminent in "pure research".

Scientists in agricultural research labs created new vegetables and new machines to nurture an agricultural economy unlike that of any other state of the nation—specialized, industrialized, mechanized, and irrigated. In photos, stories, and statistics, California sent out the image of a fecund Eden, fertilized by the energy, ambition, and genius of California's farmers.

The boasts and promises of promoters and builders were shouted aside in the 1960s by the angry voices of institutions and citizens echoing the warnings so eloquently and futilely expressed by John Muir. The Sierra Club, California Tomorrow, and the Save the Redwoods League, environmentalists, ecologists, radio and newspaper commentators, professors, and thousands of students made known their anxiety about California as a fragile, endangered environment.

But in Southern California, where the ratio of cars to people was one car to every 1.3 people, freeways reached out like a "cement octopus." In the words of historian Tom Watkins, "Enough freeway concrete was poured in Southern California to pave the State of Rhode Island. Rhode Island would have objected. Southern California loved it."

The anger and hatred that fueled the riots in Watts—the black city within the city of Los Angeles—flared up and burned painfully for six days and nights in August, 1965—smashing, burning, looting, snipers, the National Guard—and the image of black Americans filled with despair and a sense of denial and deep disappointment in the land of health and wealth.

With black anger there was student anger. "Look at those spoiled rowdies in California," was the attitude of many watching television and looking at newspaper and magazine pictures of student strikes and violence. Through the 1960s, California shocked the nation, its discontent feared as if contagious.

When Ronald Reagan ran for Governor of California in 1966, he characterized rebellious students as a "minority of malcontents, beatniks, and filthy-speech advocates." In California and beyond, his brand of leadership was seen as just what California needed, and some used the verb "deserved."

Before we get to questions and answers, there is another topic I'd like to discuss. I think all of us are interested in the whole process of what's going to happen politically in the post-Reagan years. As someone who was active in only one political party, I'm very concerned about the decline of two-party strength and the ability to recruit candidates, the credibility of the two parties and their inability to be responsible for policy. The increased power of political action committees (PACs), public campaign financing and the dominance of television have made it extremely difficult to build and strengthen political parties. Our two political parties have paid a great price for that and I am very much concerned. We'll see it in the "up for grabs" election coming up in 1988.

I think a remarkable phenomenon has already taken place. For example, one first wonders why Lee Iacocca has been running so well in the polls. We are not even sure what his registration is, yet the polls show that many would like him to be the Democratic nominee or the Republican nominee for President. After thinking about it, I've decided that it would be almost impossible for anybody to follow Reagan as the Great Communicator and do any better on television. But these trends tend to be cyclical. There is a host of candidates. Many problems that we're facing today in government involve just plain housekeeping. How do we improve and get our industrial productivity back? How do we approach the new world of global "high tech" and the whole host of problems that go with that? How do we cope with the problems of waste management? This whole set of problems will be on the agenda for the next President or presidents to follow. So, in thinking in terms of the need for "hands-on" management, we need a President who knows how to run something. Even in California, for example, Peter Ueberroth was suggested seriously and ran very strongly in the polls for the U.S. Senate because of the success he had in running the Olympics in 1984. That's a quality to watch as you look at the candidates for President on both sides in 1988. How will they attempt to show they can run something and that they can run the apparatus of government well? I think that's a kind of "sleeper" that's in the picture and will emerge as we go on.

**MR. THOMPSON:** Could I ask one question that you stimulated? In the oral history coverage that we've had of the Ford presidency, one issue that has kept coming up again and again was the split between the Nixon carry-over people and the Ford loyalists. Statements about who was right and who was wrong come from each group. The problem seemed to be there and everyone mentions it. I hadn't realized that there was a similar problem, or at least elements of it, in the Nixon presidency. I wonder if you would be willing to say anything about that?

**MR. FINCH:** First of all, I was going to mention Jerry Ford because he's one of my favorite office holders, and I think that he made a singular contribution to the stability of our whole form of government in dealing with Congress and the American people in the post-Watergate era. It is interesting to see how an idea gets planted and ten years later it comes to fruition. When Nixon got the nomination in 1960, you will recall that Kennedy picked Johnson, and we were trying to decide who the GOP vice presidential candidate would be. Ford was high on that list. Nixon had asked me to check on Ford to see how good a campaigner he was in the field. We did some checking, and we got mixed reactions because he was never a fire and brimstone type. I need to bring this up because I think it proves my point. You might recall that at the 1960 convention, Congressman Walter Judd made a stirring speech at the outset, the "keynote speech." The convention went crazy and wanted him on the ticket. There was a grassroots movement to have Walter Judd become the vice presidential candidate, particularly because there were those who thought that given his strong ministerial ties, he would be a strong factor with a Catholic candidate for President running on the other side. So there was a lot of agitation for him. Nixon liked Walter, and thought about him seriously, but what happened was that Eisenhower's influence was determinative. His strong endorsement of Lodge as someone for whom he had a lot of respect influenced Nixon and that's how it became the "Nixon-Lodge" ticket. Up to that point, Ford had been high on the list. The need to accommodate Congress prompted Nixon to bring Ford back to become vice president ten years later.

But there is always such a tension between successors and staffs and it raises two points. When Johnson came into office, he tried to heal any differences by retaining most of the key Kennedy staffers, and that didn't work. There was an historical problem there. Ford brought in some of his people, but even within the Nixon staff there was a division between the old and the new—those of us who had been with Nixon a long time and had gone through the 1960 campaign, and the new group that came in in 1968, the Haldeman-Ehrlichman group. In their eyes they had done what we couldn't do in 1960, not recognizing that it was a totally different ballgame. The 1960 election turned out to be almost fifty-fifty in the vote, probably the closest presidential election ever. The 1968 election was a political accident because both Humphrey and Nixon had about forty-two or forty-three percent, and George Wallace drained off the rest. So it would have to be called a less dramatic victory, but nonetheless it was a victory. So there was a division, and it began to exert itself in the Nixon staff. It was the "old and new guard" kind of thing. Sometimes it was philosophical and ideological but it is something to watch and you pay a high price for it. That also raises the last problem which we addressed: Was it good governance to take that team, whatever the team was and whatever the program was, that may have done a brilliant job in the election, and put them in the governor's office or the presidency to run the White House or to run the governor's office? My strong view on that is that it may be necessary to use the talent that have done a good job in the campaign, but that same group can't be allowed to totally exercise the responsibilities of governing. You want people who will take a broader view of things, reach across and heal gaps and not try to look back and say things like, "Well, since that legislator didn't support us, he will suffer the consequences." You need someone who is "building bridges" and not trying to put up walls. That's what the candidate runs into, and that is another thing to watch for. I regard someone like Bryce Harlow I regard as a "staffer for all seasons" who can take the long institutional view.

**QUESTION:** Do you have any insight you would care to share on the relationship between Mr. Nixon and General Eisenhower?

**MR. FINCH:** Yes, and that is another case where the staff during the Eisenhower-Nixon years created some of the problems. From the time of the Checkers speech, many White House staff in the Eisenhower office didn't want to see Nixon on the ticket again, particularly in 1956. They thought he was a liability. To add to all of that, in those days the Vice President didn't have an office in or around the White House, so proximity between Eisenhower and Nixon was limited. In point of fact, in 1958, when I joined Nixon's staff, we were in the old Senate Office Building. Kennedy was across the hall, and Nixon had a smaller office as vice president than he was entitled to as a senator from California. We were all stacked on top of each other, and the physical setup was terrible. Rose Woods had two offices in the Capitol, the formal office off the floor of the Senate and the little tiny basement office down in the bowels of the Capitol. So, Nixon wasn't getting any help from the White House staff until he built those bridges himself in the later stages of the second term. Leonard Hall was a very important factor in working with Sherman Adams first and later on with Jerry Persons, Bryce Harlow and others to help broker differences.

Eisenhower was never asked to campaign for Nixon. We probably should have used him more, but there were several problems. One, Nixon wanted to win it himself. He didn't want to be "in the shadow" of Ike in 1960 against Kennedy. Second, Mamie Eisenhower spoke to Pat Nixon and to me; she was worried about the President's health. Nixon was very much aware of that. Yet Ike made three important campaign speeches. But I don't even think that in itself was nearly as important as the economy's performance in the late stages of 1960. After the election Eisenhower was very unhappy. He said he felt he should have "done more" when we were closing down the administration. The close union that you asked me about did not really come about until the families had gotten final closure through the marriage of David and Julie. I saw President Eisenhower from time to time in Palm Springs, and I even saw him just a few weeks before he died when he was at Walter Reed Hospital. He still was saying at that time how much he regretted not participating more. He thought he could have done more and he might have been able to help carry the presidency in 1960. But he was also saying that everything came out all right in the sense that the two children had gotten together, and Nixon had finally been elected. That's really a short history of how long it took them to become close personally.

**QUESTION:** Mr. Finch, I was very much interested in your observation on the governance aspect. You referred to the traditions of the past and the communication with voters during the 1960s and 1970s. Possibly these factors are not going to prevail in the next elections and hereafter, because of the enormous threat of multiple television sets in everyone's home. Literally, there are millions of VCRs. The argument is not going to be whether somebody said something or not. There are going to be recordings of it all over the place.

I would also like to refer to the Cabinet's role in the administration. *Fortune* magazine has recently run an article on Mr. Reagan's administrative technique and said that he put good people in responsible jobs and allowed them to do their thing. He left them alone. A recent television program showed George Washington's administration and how he dealt with his Cabinet members, which to my way of thinking is comparable to what Mr. Reagan is doing now. He expected Cabinet members to conduct their responsibilities and work out differences and bring him solutions and not questions. You indicated some difficulties in Johnson's presidency when he tried to carry over people from the Kennedy administration. At least he gave the impression of personally making decisions on many programs and personally making the decisions and not overriding, not consulting, ignoring or even insulting Cabinet members. Considering the complexities of the government and the complexities of national and international issues, my question is how is it going to be possible to get a successor to Reagan if we don't adopt a realistic policy about governance? When the people in the country look to the President to make all these decisions and respond to political questions of enormous dimensions, how will the transition take place? How can we again elevate Cabinet members to the status that we have said they had in Washington's time?

**MR. FINCH:** It is not an easy question to answer. One alternative would be to compel presidential candidates to indicate in advance who their Cabinet members would be and start the briefing period. But I don't think any presidential candidate would want to make that kind of commitment, because he would offend more people than he would bring aboard that way. I regretfully have to say that with the size of the White House staff, the complexity of the problems that you have alluded to and the sheer magnitude of the demographic and financial problems at the White House level, I don't think there is any way that you can allow the President to deal directly with each Cabinet member the way each Cabinet member would like. The President is going to rely on different Cabinet members in terms of the political problems and on the basis of his relationship with each Cabinet member. The relationship will rise and fall depending upon what kind of problems the Cabinet member has, or avoids, and his ability to work with White House staff. The situation that arises is that somebody from the White House staff ends up being the broker on a day-to-day basis with each Cabinet officer and his problems. We have made different efforts to try to change that. We've tried to have "super Cabinet members," that is, to have three or four who would exercise their functions on a first among equals basis. We've tried to have Cabinet committees, i.e. a "domestic council" involving the domestic-related Cabinet members and a "national security council" for foreign policy. But none of these arrangements ever really worked. In the final analysis, unless further institutionalization takes place, it seems to me that it always comes down to how each president wants to organize the staff. I think it would be a mistake to try to set up legislation which required that the top domestic adviser, the chief of staff, or the foreign policy adviser must appear for confirmation before the Senate. I don't think that's the answer, because that just makes it tougher to get rid of them when the President wants to.

**QUESTION:** Is your recommendation to go from fourteen Cabinet members to nine?

**MR. FINCH:** Yes. In my view, any reduction would be important because once that reduction takes place, all of the rigid machinery and all the statutory mechanisms related to a given Cabinet position are also out. The toughest thing to do will be to try to reshape this. But it can be done. I think the greatest message for all of us out of this last tax bill is not whether you agree with the formula or anything else. It's that we finally divested interests from all these devices put into place in the Internal Revenue Code for so many years. Nobody thought they could be eliminated, but they were. We'll see whether it survives. It came out of the conference committee, but it's so difficult to try to shake Cabinet structure once it's in place because the Congress organizes its committees with that structure in mind and all of the private sector organizes its efforts in that way. You get this "triangle effect" that everybody talks about which is very real. We must work at it institutionally, but basically you always come back to what the individual president wants to do, and how he wants to operate. He is entitled to that freedom.

**QUESTION:** Mr. Secretary, President Carter had the problem of two voices speaking on foreign policy, Brzezinski and Cyrus Vance, and later Edmund Muskie. Is there any way that the National Security Council could be made less visible, less vocal, and more strength passed on to the presidency and the State Department?

**MR. FINCH:** That again comes back to the President. You had the same problem with Kissinger and Rogers in the Nixon years. But Rogers' role has been badly distorted. He is one of the brightest men around and everybody assumed that Henry finessed him badly. But Nixon played that just the way he wanted it. If he chose to use Bill Rogers, he did. If he chose to use Kissinger, he did. It would have been impossible to formulate and channel through the secretary of state the China policy that Henry could do behind the scenes through "back channels." Nixon was able to orchestrate that. I don't think there is any way you can institutionalize it. Indeed, prior to Nixon the National Security Council had uneven days, and there was a real question about whether it would be retained. It depends on the President. He has to support his secretary of state, but if he wants to elevate and allow his NSC adviser to have prominence, he will do it. If he doesn't, he won't be there very long. But in theory no head of the NSC should get into operations.

**QUESTION:** When you reorganize the Cabinet, have you thought of what I call a third level of government and of how we can put stability into this? The only area I know is health in the British system. I'm sure you've met Sir George Garber, who ran the British health system for 27 years. Ministers came and went, but one person directed the British health system during all the different governments. As I understand it, the only job in the U.S. that doesn't change is the director of the census, and that's metric. There is no problem there. You must have looked into the British system.

**MR. FINCH:** Yes, and as in most things British, they do some things extraordinarily better than we do. One is that they have a middle management career system where they keep very good people and whatever the change in governments, the basic management of affairs is sustained. There is some degree of continuity. At least on the health care side, and particularly in the research area, as the case of NIH and so on, my experience was that we are building a stronger and stronger core of solid career staff. I think that the past tendency of changing the personnel party-wise or of hiring new personnel on the basis of which administration is in office is diminishing. I know I resisted that strongly, even though I was a violent Republican partisan. I think there is a greater respect in the OMB for these kinds of career people who are necessary if we are going to get sustained talent, for example in the health care field. These folks are not partisan. There will be some other areas in which that is also true. But by and large, I would say that downstream, we are going to have to make some modifications about, and not preserve the present difficulties, which make it almost impossible to get rid of incompetent people in a rational, intelligent way.

**QUESTION:** We have heard other people in the Nixon Cabinet speak. I would like to know if you would be willing to speak on Nixon's tragic flaw, even though you were not there at the end of his regime? What did you think about the Watergate situation?

**MR. FINCH:** He above all people should have recognized that since he had both Houses of the Congress and a good portion of the press against him, he had to exercise great care in any political steps that he would take. That's why it was out of character for him to allow his "fortress" or "seige" mentality to develop and to take bad advice on whether or not the tapes or any memorabilia would ever get to the public or whether presidential privilege would allow him to retain them. I must say he came full circle on the question of "confidentiality." The day after we won the election in 1968, Johnson invited the President-elect and me to the White House. It was the first time we had been there since 1960. While Nixon was with Johnson, Joe Califano showed me around. Among other things, he told us about Johnson's taping system, which was hand-initiated. It wasn't "ongoing" or voice-activated like the system Nixon ultimately put in. Johnson's system was only in a few locations: the Cabinet Room, the Oval Office, and maybe one other place. So I told Nixon about that as we were flying down to Florida. He said, "Well, get rid of it. I don't want anything like that."

As you well know, it was taken out, but the senior staff later had a fascination with record-keeping and memorabilia. They wanted to have the best documented presidency **ever** and that was one of their compulsions. They wanted everything on tape. Actually, it turned out to be a lousy, second-class system, not even as good as LBJ's infidelity. That's why stenographers are still having so much trouble even trying to record it. That was a fatal mistake in judgment. You know, you can do an awful lot of business without having to put everything on paper, particularly with Xerox these days. That was just not the way I chose to operate. I think that they went too far. They were going to have the best record of what they felt was an important presidency, but every presidency is important. It was an attitudinal thing, finally, and the staff was not a collegial group. We were divided. Nixon, who prided himself on being a student of FDR, was fond of the way FDR used to make a series of multiple assignments. He asked a number of people to do the same thing, and he would then manipulate his own staff. He would do certain things with Colson, he would do certain things with

Ehrlichman, and he would do certain things with Haldeman. After a while that became counter-productive. It was a combination of managerial elements and misjudgments that helped bring Watergate about.

**MR. THOMPSON:** Could any of it have been avoided?

**MR. FINCH:** Of course, all of it could have been. I'm certainly not saying that if I'd been there it would have been any different. I'm just saying that it was a combination of miscalculations that came into play, as Nixon himself has said.

**MR. THOMPSON:** Almost everyone who visited the Miller Center to discuss the Eisenhower presidency said, "We all loved the President. We loved President Eisenhower." We are a little confused about Nixon because we've heard so many positive things about Nixon's leadership, but we're left with a kind of split personality picture. Many of your colleagues have said that they never heard the expletives deleted type of conversation, even though they worked with him for years. But a certain group did hear it and apparently responded to it. You get the sense that the atmosphere was poisoned with some. somebody drew the distinction between Nixon's emphasis on politics and his emphasis on governance, saying that for Nixon politics allowed no constraints or limits; there the end justified the means. In governance, and he knew government better than perhaps any postwar President we've had, there were constraints. Yet he kept politics and governance separate, according to this view, and in politics the kind of people that surrounded him and the atmosphere was a more sordid and questionable thing. Is there any truth in that?

**MR. FINCH:** Well, to put it against the 1960 versus the 1968 race, I probably was with him night and day in 1960, traveling with him as his campaign manager. Our relationship goes way back to when I first met him in the 80th Congress. I must also say that his day-to-day characteristics and language were absolutely and totally different than that which seems to be reflected in the tapes. I don't want to see it as simplistic as Teddy White's talking about a "good side" and a "sun side" or a bad side, but he did not like profanity used, although I remember he really would sometimes use some profanity. I don't think you can really generalize about that kind of thing. Whoever sets the tone between the President and the staff is what makes a great deal of difference as well. Nixon is a complex man and he operates on several different levels, but remember politics and political ends have always been his primary motivation. In my presence, he never advocated nor did we discuss anything that was marginal or illegal in that 1960 campaign. Quite the reverse. When some people seriously proposed including very sensitive issues in the campaign, such as the exacerbation of the Catholic issue in the South, we discussed it at length. He told me to monitor things to make certain that nothing like that happened and at his orders I put out a very stern directive to that effect. In the later stages and out of nowhere, however, without our foreknowledge, dear old Dr. Norman Vincent Peale put out a statement about how Popes might be running the country if Kennedy was elected.

I'm saying that I never saw the kind of dark mechanism in Nixon's mind or operations that some people have described. I have a massive respect for him up to this day. We had our differences, and sometimes he chose to go on with actions that were contrary to my advice. I couldn't expect that when I counseled the President I would win them all, but there came a point when it was clear that I was losing more than my share, and I wanted to get back to California. We had some other differences which we later patched up, but it was not because of anything that I saw that was fundamentally wrong, and I was certainly not aware of Watergate. Part of the problem was the nature and attitude of senior staff. Nixon was wrong not to stamp it out when it first appeared, when he first found out what was going on. That's the way I look at it. He also had, I believe, an excess of loyalty to Haldeman and Ehrlichman, saying, "Well, maybe they made a mistake, but I've got to protect them and as President, I can do it." That was probably his worst mistake, if indeed that is what happened.

**MR. THOMPSON:** The other thing one or two people have emphasized is his insecurity. You'll have to depend on the doctors for the terms, but people allude to the fact that he was overly anxious, a condition that ran through his career. People psychoanalyze it and go back to his relationship with his father.

**MR. FINCH:** That's not my line of work. But he lived through difficult times and he did come from a hard and humble background, as opposed to Kennedy. For many people that had something to do with the way he got into the debate and his discomfort or insecurity in that debate. I think that was perhaps some motivation all the way through. Didn't Lou Cannon once pose the question of how Reagan came from being a liberal Democrat supporting Roosevelt to the strongest conservative Republican of all? Cannon's response as I remember it was, "Well in the good years, when he got his first good salaries, he was paying in the ninety percent bracket." Reagan reacted violently, and said we are just taxing people too much. Reagan came from relatively humble circumstances. Yes, the background is something that counts strongly. Nixon was never easy with wealthy individuals in small groups. He became a very good campaigner with large groups, but he was never a "bon-vivant" and back slapper at any time.

**QUESTION:** Was President Nixon's drinking problem brought on by Watergate or did he have a problem prior to that time?

**MR. FINCH:** Well, from personal knowledge, it certainly was no problem during the 1960 campaign or while I was close to him when he was President. I know that Ehrlichman talked about it in his book, but I believe Nixon was careful to avoid drinking throughout his presidency, during the time I was there, any more than a glass of wine.

**COMMENT:** Alexander Haig was supposed to have taken over a lot of the duties of the presidency at the end because Nixon was said to have been drunk. That's why I brought up the question.

**MR. FINCH:** I would discount that very much, but I wasn't there. I don't know. You would have to ask somebody who was.

QUESTION: I remember a television broadcast by President Nixon during the Watergate crisis in which he said that since the American people had given him a mandate, he wasn't going to resign. He said that he was going to carry out that mandate. I got the definite impression that power interested him for its own sake. Did he have such a feeling or not?

**MR. FINCH:** I think so. As with all of us, I think that the feeling of a struggle was present. This had been the entire thrust of his life and explained his family's reluctance to see him resign. He was pulled back and forth, but he ultimately realized that the nation's security and other questions were coming into play and that he wasn't going to be able to deal with Congress and the overall situation. He was finally overwhelmed. I think it's simply the kind of thing he faced when there was a real question about whether the 1960 election had been won by fraud or questionable activities in Texas, Cook County, Illinois and Missouri. We supported taking the case to court because we felt we had all this proof. He thought about it for awhile, and the more he thought about it, the more he realized that we couldn't have the government of the biggest nation in the world at sufferance to a court proceeding. So he chose not to contest that election, even though he may have had good grounds. Ultimately he came, in my point of view, to the right decision.

**MR. THOMPSON:** May I ask the final question? We always ask people how they think history will judge a president. Can I throw a curve along with that question. How do you think history will judge your decision in terms of the role that Agnew played in the administration and Bob Haldeman and others played? You appointed Haldeman. Should you have been there to sit over him? Or, looking back, do you think that for personal reasons as well as for what was accomplished in HEW, that your decision not to take the vice presidency or the Attorney General's office was the right one?

**MR. FINCH:** In my own heart, and more importantly for my family, I am satisfied that I made the right decision.

**MR. THOMPSON:** And the President? How do you think history will judge him?

**MR. FINCH:** I think this country will make, as it has already done, positive judgement of his analytical abilities and his vision and judgment, particularly in terms of foreign policy. I don't see him serving in any official role in the future, but I think he will continue to give good counsel on the dynamics of foreign policy toward Soviet Russia and China and that he will continue to exercise a voice, a strong and positive voice that will be very helpful for whatever years he has left.

I enjoyed this discussion. Thank you very much.

# THE DEPARTMENTS AND THE WHITE HOUSE

## Earl Butz

**MR. THOMPSON:** Earl Butz was secretary of agriculture from 1971 to 1976. He was born in Indiana in Noble County. He did his undergraduate work at Purdue on a 4-H fellowship and got his degree there in 1932. Two things of unequal importance happened in 1937: he got his Ph.D., which was of minor importance, and he married his wife, Mariam Emma Powell, who had been a home demonstration agent in North Carolina. That was very important. He was head of the Agricultural Economics Department at Purdue from 1947 to 1957. He served in the Eisenhower administration as assistant secretary of agriculture. He returned to Purdue as dean of Agriculture and then vice president and dean of continuing education.

When he became secretary of agriculture in 1971, his primary goals were to keep America the best fed nation, to improve the farm economy, strengthen rural America, and support the free market system. He carried that message to all fifty states and around the world to more than fifty nations and a million and a half people. That is one of the reasons that we hoped very much that we could have an opportunity to talk a little bit today about the Nixon presidency and any other matters that he may want to discuss. It is a pleasure to have Earl Butz here today.

**SECRETARY BUTZ:** Thank you very much, Ken, for that nice introduction.

Nixon was a loner. He was very intelligent, I think perhaps one of the most intelligent men to occupy the

White House. I would classify him with John Kennedy, though I didn't know Kennedy that well, and I would probably include Woodrow Wilson. I would put Nixon right alongside them in intelligence. He was a great student of history. He knew precedents; he knew what governments had done and he knew where they had made mistakes. He had a staff around him that overprotected him and that finally got him into trouble.

John Ehrlichman was head of the Domestic Council and pretty close to the President. Ehrlichman had never been in politics; he'd been a Seattle lawyer. How he got that administration position I don't know, because I came aboard when the administration was two and a half years old. It got to the point where Ehrlichman would call and say, "This is what the President wants." You soon had to ask, "Is that Ehrlichman or the President speaking?" You were never quite sure. Haldeman operated in somewhat the same way.

Nixon liked to get written recommendations on issues under contention. Then he'd take them home and study them. He was a quick student and made his decisions that way. Ford was completely the opposite.

Watergate was an unfortunate incident; it is now becoming a footnote on the pages of history. When it does become a footnote, Nixon will emerge as one of our great Presidents, especially in foreign policy.

Like Nixon, Kissinger was also a brilliant strategist in foreign policy. He had a grand strategy of encircling of the Soviets. It came out time and again in Cabinet meetings. He always said, "Make the other guy look good at home. If you don't, he can't get you what you want. Find some way to make him look good at home." That reflects President Eisenhower's philosophy as well. I was in a Cabinet meeting with Eisenhower and Arthur Fleming, then secretary of HEW, the forerunner of HHS. One day Fleming was explaining how he was going to embarrass some member of Congress that he didn't like. He said, "I'm really going to turn the knife in him." The President looked up and said, "Arthur, when I ran the war I had three cardinal principles. *First*, never embarrass your enemy in public; it just makes him fight all the harder. *Second*, never impugn his motives. In his own mind he has justification for what he does. *Third*, and most importantly, never cut off his line of retreat. If you do that you've got to destroy him or he might destroy you. You are violating all three of those things when you try to embarrass a member of Congress." Ike said, "We can accomplish the same thing by letting him take a little credit too." This is one of Henry's long suits too.

Nixon chose Henry for National Security Council adviser and for secretary of state, two of the most important posts in our government. Henry had been a strong Rockefeller backer and had been publicly critical of Nixon. Someone, somehow, persuaded Nixon to choose Henry for secretary of state. It was a very wise choice, and Henry was a loyal and strong member of the team, though a bull-headed fellow. He had a global strategy, in sharp contrast to so many in government and in corporation board rooms these days.

These days decisions are apt to be made in terms of the opinion polls and the evening news. This means that there isn't a global strategy. The mob on the street or, in more polite terms, the pressure groups, make the decisions. Decisions are made with an eye to minimizing criticism. That is one of the great dangers to government, I think, and for corporations these days. We've got environmental groups, health groups, safety groups, the anti-air pollution groups, and all those others that will attack you if you impinge on what they think is their jurisdiction.

How do I think future historians will judge the Nixon presidency? It is hard to say. Harry Truman frequently made me very angry when he was President. I'm now convinced he is emerging as one of our great Presidents. I think history will list Harry Truman among our top half dozen Presidents. He made me fighting mad when he fired General MacArthur, but he was right. You only have to make a half dozen great decisions to be a great President. Harry decided to use the atom bomb. It was a major, controversial decision that ended the war. It probably saved hundreds of thousands of American lives. When the communists came marching down through Greece, he moved the fleet up to the eastern part of the Mediterranean and drew the line. He didn't send a note to the United Nations to ask if he could do that. When the communists invaded South Korea, he acted immediately. He didn't send a note to the United Nations saying "Debate this and give me a vote on it." He did, however, report to the United Nations what he had done. I think in retrospect he made a great decision.

Was Nixon a great President? Yes, except for Watergate. He had too tight a ring of advisers. In the election of 1972 he carried every state except the District of Columbia and Massachusetts.

Ehrlichman's and Chuck Colson's goal in that election was to get a hundred percent unanimous election. They almost made it. But they disassociated the Nixon campaign from the Republican party. Money didn't go to the Republican party; money went to the Committee to Re-elect the President (CREEP). The National Committee was an adjunct to this campaign. A unanimous vote for the President would have been unique. But they were ruthless in going after it.

There was a hate relationship between the press and Nixon. It was mutual; he didn't like the press, and they didn't like him. As a matter of fact the press will get anybody in Washington. The press looks for cracks and conflicts and they'll play them up. If one hundred years ago today Tom Edison had come into this room, a room lighted with oil lamps and flickering candlelights, and said, "I've just invented a new incandescent bulb that will light this room with the brilliance of noonday," we would all have been excited. We would have rushed home and tried to figure out how to get such an invention for our own homes. Then we would have tuned into the evening news and heard, "Good evening, this is the evening news. Lead story tonight: Disaster just hit the candlemaking industry!" All the positive things go by the wayside. That's not news. It's disaster in the candlemaking industry that is news.

The Nixon resignation was a traumatic thing. It had been coming though for some time. Just prior to it, a military man, General Al Haig, White House chief of staff, had the reins in his hands. That is the time when, in other places, military governments take power. There was a power vacuum when Nixon resigned. I think the nation will never know how much it owes to Al Haig for holding things together during that very, very difficult time. I can never praise Al Haig enough for being an American, an upholder of our constitutional system, and a military man who subordinated the military to the civilians. I don't think history has properly put that in perspective.

When Rogers Morton and I were talking about the transition that afternoon, Al Haig said, "I've talked to Ford; he is actually ready to take this over. This change is inevitable. I've been trying to brief him because the vice president is never fully briefed." After all, in the American system, what is the vice president's role? He has no role other than that he votes in the Senate in case of a tie. Each morning upon awakening, the first thing the vice president says is, "Did the President live through the night?" If the answer is "yes" he goes about his routine. That was the problem that Harry Truman faced when Roosevelt passed away. It was a difficult time in government. At that point, Truman didn't even know about the development of the atom bomb. He was completely on the outside.

When Nixon was President, he said "I'm going to try and use the vice president" because he had been vice president under Eisenhower. He knew how sterile the vice presidency is. He said he was going to use the vice president, but he didn't. Agnew, his first vice president, had to resign. Then they chose Ford. Ford was not closely involved in decision-making. Then Ford chose Rockefeller, who was controversial. He was too liberal for the right wing of the Republican party. Rockefeller was a nice chap, but he was never really on the inside at the White House.

Why is this the case? Everyone in the administration soon learns how power flows in the White House. The vice president has a staff, and the President has a staff. The departments learn that the decisions are made within the President's staff. The vice president's staff is kept informed, but the President's staff is the locus of decision-making. The bureaucracy knows that, and the bureaucracy of course survives every secretary and every vice president. The staffs that do the work know their way around and know the power flow. I think it is one of the shortcomings of our presidency that the number two man really isn't equipped to take over.

How does he build himself up? How does he sell himself to the public? I do not know. Why do I hear statements to the effect that George Bush would not make a good candidate for President? On paper, George Bush has impeccable qualifications to be President. He has good experience. The guy is terrific. He'd make a great President. But why do I hear comments around the country, "I don't think he'd make a good candidate?" How do you build up a vice president's image while he stands in the shadow of the President? We have a President who casts a long shadow and it's impossible to build up a vice president, no matter how good he is. If you make him look better than the President, then you get in trouble. Somebody cuts him off. Even with a weak President it won't work. I think that's one of the faults of our system. We don't have anybody really equipped to takeover and carry on.

The tragedy following Watergate was the drawing up of new rules governing political contributions. They have resulted in these tremendous Political Action Committees (PACs) whose sole purpose is to buy influence in Washington. Up on the Hill, there are endless numbers of committees and subcommittees. Every senator in the Republican party in this Congress is either chairman of a committee or a subcommittee. After January, every Democratic senator will be chairman either of a committee or subcommittee. Each committee has two staffs; the majority staff and the minority staff. These committees have to find something to do. The best thing to do is to hold a hearing. It's newsworthy to have a hearing and to get a Cabinet member or some of the White House staff to testify before the camera. Thus, the purpose of the committee staff is to get its principal on the evening news. If they can do that they have the day made.

Unfortunately, that's the way Congress operates. It makes the news, and I'm not being facetious when I say the goal of the staff is to get the committee chairman on the evening news because the Senate is now the best springboard for the presidency. It is not good for government that this is taking place.

**QUESTION:** Two of the people who have been here have said that Cliff Hardin resigned because he couldn't get access to the President. Cliff denies that. He hasn't been here for the Nixon series but we've talked with him. Did you have that problem?

**SECRETARY BUTZ:** I think everybody has that problem. It's a question of how often you want access to the President. You can't take trivia to the Oval Office. If you do, they soon shut off all access. You've got to reserve your time with the President for major issues. You can't afford to waste it on the mundane. I didn't have any problems but sometimes there is a problem getting past the staff. You have to convince the White House staff that what you want is economically and politically right. Sometimes that's difficult to do. Sometimes you've got to pull in some outside influence. One of my goals when I became secretary was to learn the power structure on the Hill, out in the country, and in both the Republican and the Democratic parties. I went out and campaigned for some of those characters, and they became beholden to me. When I needed a little pressure on the White House I could call them up and say "Look, can you put your testimony on that side?" Of course, that tactic should not be used too often because you are not kidding anybody on the Hill either. But sometimes you simply have to do it.

What a pleasure it has been meeting with this group.

**MR. THOMPSON:** We thank you for a stimulating and provocative discussion.

# VI.

# FOREIGN
# AND
# DEFENSE POLICY

# FOREIGN POLICY AND THE BUREAUCRACY

## Michael Raoul-Duval

**MR. THOMPSON:** Michael Duval is managing director of the First Boston Corporation, an international investment bank with headquarters in New York. He is responsible, with the firm's executive and management committee, for the commercial real estate business of First Boston. Both the general counsel and the governmental affairs staff of First Boston report to him.

Mr. Duval is a graduate of Georgetown University and of the United States Marine Corps. He has a California University law degree. He joined the Department of Transportation as an attorney in 1967, came into the Nixon White House in 1970, became associate director of the Domestic Council in 1972, and continued in that capacity until 1974. He became special counsel to President Ford in 1974 and occupied that position until 1977, when he was appointed vice president for industrial products activities and later senior vice president of Mead Company. He will discuss the role of the bureaucracy in the Nixon foreign policy.

**MR. DUVAL:** Thank you, Ken. I'm somewhat intimidated by that introduction. I didn't think anybody could remember that much about someone else. I'm having a hard time now remembering all that about me. I commend you for it. I might say there are four great educational experiences I've had in my lifetime: the Jesuits, the Marine Corps, Haldeman and Rumsfield; and they were all about the same!

*Michael Raoul-Duval*

I spent seven years in the White House, about half that time in the West Wing, and the balance in the Executive Office Building. That's a long time. I can understand what Sakharov and others have gone through in their lives—that's a long time to be in such a position. Fortunately, I was young and single, and I think that those are the two most important factors to surviving that long in the White House, particularly at the time when I was there. At least a portion of that time it was literally open warfare, and the only good news was that you knew if you got the grenade out of the foxhole it would hit an enemy, no matter what direction you threw it.

I can remember going to work when they surrounded the White House with buses. It was during the Vietnam riots. They would take the old DC transit buses (they finally found some good use for them) and park them all around the White House, bumper to bumper. That sort of became the outer wall; the Secret Service and the White House police were the inner wall. It was an interesting way to go to work each morning.

I served two Presidents and in a lesser way a third. Both Presidents found me by accident, so I got there by circumstances which to this day I can't figure out. I didn't come in through the campaign or by having been associated with one of them before this election. There is, I think, a message there. I ended up in fairly responsible, senior positions with both Nixon and Ford. Clearly this was true in the case of Ford, and in the case of Nixon you can judge for yourself. In both cases, I had a lot of direct, personal contact with the chief executive on substantive and political issues, such as reelection campaigns, yet I had had no prior relationship with either man. I think the message is that when a candidate does become president, the nature of the job requires him to reach out and bring in whatever help he can find to accomplish things. Old friends and kitchen cabinets tend to fall by the wayside very quickly. I think that is the reality which shapes a president's team.

My experience ranged from policy to politics, from substance to logistics, from domestic to foreign, and I've been across all those boundaries. I think that is the case with most people who serve presidents closely. They tend to get thrown in where the problems exist.

I was in government when Richard Nixon was elected President. I also worked for Kennedy very briefly in 1960, and then sort of dropped out of politics totally until a well-known Democrat steered me back in after I came out of law school in 1967. I ended up as an attorney representing the newly formed Department of Transportation and was involved in the aircraft controller strikes and many related issues when Nixon was elected President. I was apolitical in the sense that although I voted and had some interest in politics, I wasn't clearly identified as a partisan. As such, I was surprised in 1969, when, as I was thinking of leaving government, I got a call to go up to the White House.

I was asked to come to the White House because Nixon, with Haldeman's direction, was putting together a team of advancement whose primary function was to do foreign advances and then also be there as a cadre to help in the 1970 election, the off-year election. It turns out that John Volpe, who was secretary of transportation, had recommended me. I don't know if that was his way of getting rid of me as far as transportation was concerned or if he was just doing me a favor, but I ended up walking into the White House, was interviewed by Dwight Chapin and Ron Walker—people I had never heard of before—and I said to myself, "This is insane; they don't know if I am a Democrat or a Republican or a mouse." But they did interview me, and I ended up doing advances for Nixon in 1970. Nixon, of course, had tried to have an influence on the 1970 off-year elections, but he failed miserably, and probably hit one of the lower points in his presidency in terms of popularity and in terms of his ability to get things done.

For reasons which I'd have a hard time explaining, I was selected to go to China with Ron Walker in advance of President Nixon's visit. By that time, I had made three or four other trips abroad for Nixon. He deeply distrusted the State Department, but I don't think that distrust ran to Bill Rogers personally. I think Kissinger clearly had a rivalry going with Rogers. Nixon absolutely distrusted the State Department and I think with some cause. There were not only ideological and political differences, but there was a bureaucratic stagnation that was deeply entrenched. Not all of it was liberal but some of it was. For example, many

State people were pro-Taiwan, and that was an obstacle for Nixon's Far East policy, an area where he made some very bold initiatives. If any plans got out, the State Department would instantly leak it to the press, the coalitions against it would form, and the policy would be killed before it could be implemented. So Nixon managed foreign policy very much through his own staff, which was fundamentally built under Haldeman. Nixon even had some questions about the NSC staff functioning as a back channel of the State Department, and so he constructed a new management structure in order to get things done in the foreign policy arena.

It showed up in some interesting ways. When we'd go to a foreign country we'd work with the ambassador, but, depending on who the ambassador was, we would establish a channel through the CIA to the White House. Basically, we'd cooperate with the ambassador and try to have a very good personal relationship with him, but the fact of the matter was that all of the decisions were taken through these back channels directly to the White House, deliberately cutting State Department channels out of the communications.

When I went into China in 1972, Kissinger and Haig, in two separate trips, had preceded me. It was extraordinary, in every aspect. When we landed at Shanghai Airport they had cleared the airport of all people and all aircraft. Our C-141 landed and it was like landing at Chicago's O'Hare and having it absolutely cleared except for soldiers along the runway facing outward with machine guns and a five-man delegation with posters and flags walking down to meet you. It was bizarre.

In a strange way I developed some close friendships in China, including the current ambassador from the PRC [People's Republic of China], Han Xu. I also feel that of the foreign leaders that I was privileged to meet while working for Richard Nixon and Gerald Ford (and I met many heads of state), without any doubt the most powerful one was Chou Enlai. He was in a class completely by himself. Probably the next closest was Anwar Sadat, but down the ladder.

The next major event, of course, was the SALT I Treaty, and we went to Russia and Poland for that. It was vintage Nixon. First, he came home from China and went up to Canada because Bill Rogers had committed him to go. He hated Prime Minister Trudeau, and there are a lot of stories I could tell you about how he tried not to have to see Trudeau. It was unbelievable. Here he is on a head of state visit, and he refused to go and meet Trudeau alone. He felt Trudeau was using him purely for domestic political purposes, and he didn't trust the man. We went through all sorts of maneuvers to try to avoid a major diplomatic incident, and in the process didn't succeed very well.

Then we went to Moscow for the SALT I agreement. The extraordinary thing is that at the time that SALT I was coming together (and it clearly was going to be the crowning achievement of Nixon's first term although China was the more symbolic achievement), President Nixon lobbed a few bombs into Haiphong harbor and hit a Russian ship. It was an act of war, and we fully expected the Russians to cancel the summit. Since I was in Warsaw at the time along with U.S. Ambassador Walter Stoessel, I was called at midnight to the foreign minister's office, and he said, "Now we want to begin to work with you on the planning of the President's trip." This was the first indication we had that the Soviets were going forward with the summit and would sign SALT I. I think, frankly, the Russians thought Nixon had a screw loose and they were terrified that he would do something drastic. That was the bargaining leverage that President Nixon had over the Soviets and it was effective.

We went through the 1972 election. You've had other people here to talk about it, so you know how much money was spent, that it was highly organized, and that the election was probably over by the time of the Democratic convention. There was no way that McGovern represented the interests of the people of his party; the Eagleton episode was a disaster. I met with Mayor Daley between the time of the nomination and the time of the election, representing the White House and Transportation policies, and he said that President Nixon could be guaranteed that Illinois would be carried for him. So I think that this was a measure of the feelings within the Democratic party about the nominee of their party.

After the election and by virtue of my role with the domestic council, I was involved in the Super Cabinet experiment. First of all, we were faced with how not to do a transition from a first term to a second term. The incredibly incompetent mismanagement of that by the President—I don't blame Bob Haldeman—soured a lot of very good people.

The seeds of Watergate had already been sown and were beginning to expand throughout the inauguration. Jeb Magruder, Hugh Sloan and others were beginning to feel the initial pressures of it. We went through that whole period of euphoria, having come off the largest mandate in history or close to it, and then began to deflate slowly as the corrosive effect of Watergate took hold.

An important impact of Watergate—a story which is not often told—is how it so distracted the President that domestic policy was managed by relatively unknown White House staff during a crucial period in our history. There were some very important policy issues on the desk of the President. First, we were losing a war for the first time in our nation's history. Second, we were entering the worst recession in our nation's history. And third, the successful formation of OPEC would prove to be catastrophic for us.

OPEC, in historical perspective, was probably the most important event that occurred in that time frame and can be understood by looking at its economic impact. The successful cartelization of oil resulted in the largest transfer of wealth in the history of the world, including transfers of wealth that have occurred because of war. That enormous dislocation and the implications that flowed from it in terms of alliances, changing standards of living and quality of life, and the potential for friction among allied nations and people was enormous. It also was one of the very few world crises of major proportions that could have been managed successfully by us. The fact is that from the time it occurred in 1973, until 1978 or 1979, it was not addressed in any comprehensive way except for Ford's 1975 State of the Union message. By 1973, President Nixon was totally consumed by Watergate and simply didn't focus on anything else. There was no mechanism for dealing with it, although there were some very good people like Bill Simon, Frank Zarb and others who tried to get their hands on it. I also tried to deal with it because I had responsibility for energy policy in the Domestic Council at that time. The fact of the matter was that at the time when leadership was needed from the President, it didn't come. The Congress, of course, had only one focus, and that was Nixon and Watergate.

The other point is that during that time there were some significant domestic decisions. If you look at the domestic policy record on transportation, economics, and health and human services, many little things which were important to the constituencies involved were dealt with well. But those decisions were taken without active involvement by the President.

Memoranda would be written by the Domestic Council or by the National Security Council. There were only two ways that things went to the President: with Henry Kissinger's signature or with Ken Cole's signature. Three of us could sign for the Domestic Council: Jim Cavanaugh, Ken, and myself. But once Haldeman was forced out and Haig became chief of staff, Nixon insisted that we as staff put our own recommendations on them and not just summarize the issue with the recommendations of the Cabinet and the like. Before Watergate we would never put our recommendations on them. Our role was that of an honest broker. On every single issue that I am aware of that went up from the Domestic Council, the President acted on whatever our recommendation was. He did so even in one case when the entire Cabinet was against the recommendation. That became an enormous burden on us. We tried to be as honest as we could in presenting things, but I think fundamentally the President simply was not focusing on policy at all because he was totally consumed by Watergate.

On August 10, 1974, at nine o'clock in the morning we went into the East Room, and President Nixon resigned in that emotional speech. Then we walked to the South Lawn's diplomatic entrance, where he got into the helicopter and left. I then went back to my office, and as I was walking through the West Wing, all the photographs of Nixon were being taken off the wall. That was an extraordinarily emotional thing.

I think there are a couple of points of wisdom that I would like to end on, and then we'll get to your questions. One is, there are two quotations that have stuck with me—quotations from people whose counsel over the years I've learned to respect. One is Bryce Harlow. During the depths of the Nixon problem I had lunch with Bryce, and we were talking about the inevitability that Nixon would be impeached or leave and about how to manage the country through that period. Bryce said, "Mike, it's my experience with presidents that inevitably their greatest weakness turns up in the area of their greatest strength because they simply aren't distrusting enough about that area. They don't focus on their strengths. They apparently think: 'I'm good at this area, so I don't have to worry.'" I think if you apply that to Nixon, Johnson and Carter and to a lot of others and you can see the wisdom of the observation.

The second one applies to the process of government itself and is something that was said by another person who became a friend of mine in those times. That was Lane Kirkland, who is the head of the AFL-CIO. Lane was always there when we needed him on a foreign policy question and I became a great admirer of his. Lane's comment that sticks in my mind is, "All problems are caused by solutions." Those two points, I think, should give a little humility to anybody who gets into this arena. No matter how important the problem that you are working on, no matter how brilliant the solution, it won't last long in this world that we live in. If you apply some basic principles of integrity and common sense, they will guide you through. Don't try to come up with permanent or easy solutions because they all will have two sides by the time they get to the Oval Office. I don't think people should try to look for the perfect and long-term answers to things. I just don't think they exist.

Having seen many people in seven years come and go, Duval's law is that in Washington, D.C. your rate of descent is two times your rate of ascent, and I think the people who are the most successful are the ones who keep their heads down, build up some experience and wisdom, act modestly and with some humility, get the job done and move on to the next one. The final point that I'll make is this: it is very clear to me, particularly in this age when the United States is no longer dominant in any sense of the word, that people really do matter, that whom we put in key positions matter.

**MR. THOMPSON:** There are many things that would be interesting to explore with Captain Duval. For example, he was commanding officer of the RAID Team that came within thirty miles of . . .

**MR. DUVAL:** Thirty miles and, I guess, about thirty minutes of . . .

**MR. THOMPSON:** . . . rescuing Diem in Vietnam when that rescue mission was called off. But from that time to the present he obviously is one of these people that he talked about who does a succession of jobs well and continues to get called on, both in the public and private sectors. Who would like to ask the first question?

**QUESTION:** Let me pick up the observation you made about the Russians or the Soviets thinking that Nixon really might be a little bit crazy. Haldeman talks about this as a "madman" theory, that it was a conscious decision on Nixon's part to seem irrational at times in order to get action. Did you have that sense?

**MR. DUVAL:** Well, Nixon said that to me a couple of times in an elevator. He said, "Well, they obviously think I'm nuts, and that's good. That's what I want them to think."

There is a particular incident that may answer the question in terms of Nixon's mind and thinking. It is a little bit risque. I don't know how to censor myself, so I'll give it to you the way it is. You heard about the time during the Vietnam mobilization demonstrations in Washington when Nixon got up at five-thirty in the morning and took the valet, Manola Sanchez, walked out of the White House, and said to the Secret Service guy who was on duty, and half asleep, "I'm gonna go down to visit the demonstrators." Can you imagine this poor guy? He was probably the new rookie from Des Moines who just came onto the White House detail, and here is the President of the United States and he says "I'm going."

Nixon got into the car—there's always a car there—and left. There were two Secret Service agents with him, and they were radioing for everything, you know: "Send in the

101st and the 82nd." Nixon drove to the Lincoln Memorial, got out of his car, and roused up a guy who was asleep in a sleeping bag on the monument grounds. The guy looked up and obviously thought he had had a little too much of a controlled substance the night before, but it actually was the President. Nixon got into this silly conversation on football and all that, but that was his way of trying—you know he is a very shy person. Well, pretty soon, of course, the word went out and these guys began rolling out of their sleeping bags and tents to see what was going on. The Secret Service was getting scared to death. They finally convinced Nixon to get back into his car, and they started to drive away. As the car pulled off this guy with a beard ran up to the window and went like this (extended his middle finger), right in the window, right at Richard Nixon. Nixon looked up, looked around—there was no one around—no press people so he gives the finger right back to the guy. He turned to Manola, smiled and said, "That s.o.b. will go through the rest of his life telling everybody he knows that the President of the United States gave him the finger, and nobody will believe him." He was very, very conscious of how he appeared to others, and he used that.

**MR. THOMPSON:** You know the other version of this. Dean Rusk was walking along the Black Sea with Khrushchev. Khrushchev was starting to get more and more threatening until Rusk said, "I'd think twice about that, Mr. Secretary. You know those American people; they do the craziest things."

**QUESTION:** Could you comment about Mr. Nixon's decision-making process?

**MR. DUVAL:** Yes, Nixon's decision-making process was a paradigm that is worth following. It's like most things that get sullied because of an external event that prompts you to say, "I don't want to have anything to do with it because Nixon's name is on it." It was probably the most efficient and effective decision-making process that has ever existed in the White House.

My wife was in the Reagan White House in the first four years as a television adviser and because of her and of

Jim Baker and a lot of the Ford people there that I knew, I saw a lot of things. I saw the Ford decision-making process, which became more like the Nixon one after the initial problem we had with the Ford staff from the Hill, which was incapable of making a decision about anything. I know what was involved in the Johnson administration because I was in it. I knew Joe Califano and I knew some of the people who were close to Johnson. This perspective has convinced me that the Nixon decision-making process was by far the best and for the following reason.

It basically recognized that any decision that gets to the Oval Office doesn't have a clear right/wrong, best case/worst case scenario to it. Every alternative carries with it a balance of good points and bad points, and the decision will be a trade-off. For every decision made, for every action taken, you will pay a price. Some constituency group is going to be hurt; some option is cut off; some other nation is hurt. So it is a balancing act. The Nixon decision-making process was designed to put in front of the President the broadest array of analyses of the issue, the most honestly stated opinions, with a sort of advocacy element coming from the constituency groups, including outsiders, Cabinet members, and Hill members. The decision-making process then came down to one of two sources: it either came through the Domestic Council which had high level, well geared, good people, who were very apolitical, nonideological, substantive, driven, young, and not tied to any constituency group, but there to serve the President in the process of making good decisions. Or there was the analogue of that over on the national security side. Policy options came to the President in a disciplined manner so that he was able to recognize the implications of the options he might choose. By and large, that's how decisions got made, through a very disciplined process.

It has been said that Nixon wasn't big for one-on-one conversations, whereas Ford was visceral in that sense. I do think that the Nixon White House worked for him. Every decision-making process, every management system in the White House has to be geared to two things: number one, the character and the characteristics of the President himself and how he normally operates. Number two, the point in time that the administration is in. Is it the point in time when it is just coming into power and therefore developing alternatives, setting priorities, sorting out what it should do? In this case, you use basically the decentralized system of management. If you have been there a while and you are implementing policy choices that have already been made, you need a more centralized system of management. So I think you have to design your system according to those two realities, but I think the Nixon system came as close as you can come to being an honest broker and a good decision-making policy machine.

**QUESTION:** Mr. Duval, I was intrigued by your statement about Chou Enlai. He was a unique individual, particularly so given the Chinese hierarchy. Can you elaborate on that? Did he deal much with Dr. Kissinger in discussions with him? Could you give us more background information on him?

**MR. DUVAL:** It was very clear to me that Chou operated in a most unstable environment yet with absolute control. That was the single thing in China that impressed me the most. The instability of the environment was occasioned by the domestic instability within China, including the Lin Piao problem. The fact was that Mao was clearly close to the point of senility. It was the old transitional problem of going from an absolute and dominant leader—who had become, in essence, deified but who couldn't exercise leadership anymore—to the cults that had built up around him, including the one led by Mao's wife. It involved the inherent instability of China itself in terms of its physical proximity to the Soviet Union, the xenophobic relationship and the clashes on the borders. So the fact that there was sort of a ring of war around China created political instability within China, influenced by the inherent instability in the relationship that was developing between the United States and China. There were no touchstones; there was no precedent in their eyes. They viewed themselves as a new nation; they viewed the United States as an old nation because, in their minds, their history starts with the revolution.

Through all of that the man who was not number one, Chou, but who was in absolute control—control to the point where he knew all of us who were there by name as well as something about us—made every significant decision. We could see that and we understood that. I had the sense that he was one of the very few people who could deal with Richard Nixon as a peer, that Nixon couldn't get around him in a sense of being more glib or more manipulative or more cunning, that Chou was personal and engaging but in absolute control. Chou recognized that he was riding a nation of eight hundred and fifty million people that was coming out of the stone age, relative to the nations around it. This powerful leadership was grounded in his own personal strength, intellect, wisdom and farsightedness in plotting the moves and keeping things in his extraordinary, direct personal control. I have never seen anything like it. Also, I trusted him. There was something about him; I absolutely trusted him. I thought he would be the hardest person in the Chinese delegation to negotiate with but when you agreed on something there wasn't anything hidden. You understood what it was, and you lived by it. I never had that feeling about any of the Soviets.

**QUESTION:** How much interest did Nixon have in trying to save John Mitchell? According to John Mitchell's wife, they conferred nightly about Watergate at the time Nixon was taking the position that he was unfamiliar with all that was going on. I've often wondered, since Mitchell was his campaign manager, if he tried to save John Mitchell's face longer than he should have.

**MR. DUVAL:** There certainly is no doubt in my mind that Nixon wanted to save Mitchell as long as he could. You'd need a lot better psychologist than me to tell you whether he was acting in Mitchell's behalf or his own behalf, you know, the shield argument. But there are a couple of other things that are worth keeping in mind. Number one, Martha Mitchell clearly had a serious drinking problem and it was a very sad situation. John Mitchell loved her very much. John Mitchell is one of the most misunderstood public figures that I've ever known. He is one of the most gentle, unassuming, humble men that I've met who got to the level of the Cabinet. His public image is of this gruff, stand-up-to-the-demonstrators type. But he really did love Mrs.

Mitchell, and she was calling reporters at midnight, telling the whole thing. It was part of his problem. I think Mitchell did know about the break-in plans. I think Mitchell was distracted from what was going on. If it hadn't been for Mrs. Mitchell, he probably would have just taken strong action to deal with it and gotten the thing over with. I suspect, therefore, that the President did protect Mitchell and to a large degree out of compassion but also to a very large degree out of self-preservation.

**QUESTION:** Do you have any idea whether Mitchell gave the order on the plumbers? Haldeman and others have said, "No one knows who gave the order," but privately one or two have said "It could have been John Mitchell."

**MR. DUVAL:** I didn't even know there was an argument about that because I think the evidence that came out in the trial is fairly clear that he was at the meeting when Gordon Liddy presented the plans and said, "Go ahead," but I guess there is some question as to whether or not Magruder was supposed to control it. To me the whole thing gets sort of silly. If you are going to hire somebody and you are running for President of the United States you shouldn't hire a guy who puts matches on his hand and carries a gun around. But they had him there because they wanted somebody like that. So I really don't care who gave the order. Mitchell was clearly responsible. Magruder was responsible. Nixon was responsible. There is no doubt about that.

**MR. THOMPSON:** You mentioned Bryce Harlow. A week ago I drove to Harpers Ferry and interviewed him, so we have him on tape. I'm sure he has told you this theory. It would be interesting to have your reaction to it. His theory is that beginning with Roosevelt, but particularly with Roosevelt's successors, you got an augmentation of the size of staff. You got an exporting of powers out of the departments into the White House. You've given more and more authority, as he put it, to smaller and smaller people and, therefore, by the time of Lyndon Johnson you ought to have had a Watergate for Lyndon Johnson because of the small people that were running the office. But it got delayed. He told about how some in the Republican party were working on projects that would have thrown a shadow over not only Billy Sol Estes but all the others, including Johnson. They didn't quite make it but then with Nixon, given all the opposition to him, this long-range tendency of putting little people in the White House finally led to Watergate.

**MR. DUVAL:** There is a lot of truth in that. I would put it this way. The pressures are so great, the world has become so complex, and the nation is managed from the perspective of a chief executive versus the perspective of legislative consensus-making basis. There is so much that you have to manage in today's world that goes past you or that has to be dealt with so quickly, that you don't have time to deal with things like lack of trust because there is a spotlight on you. There are leaks to the press and there are conflicting interests and what-not. You tend to find presidents, and I think the current President is a clear exception but Carter was not, who are not willing to pay the price of wisdom. They are not willing to surround themselves with people who bring wisdom and experience to decision-making roles. The price you pay for that is they tend to stop you, force you to think, and so they slow you down. And guess what? They tend to tell you what you don't want to hear a lot. You get on this fast bandwagon and you are not willing to pay the price of wisdom. I think that is a very serious problem. How anybody could manage an organization of any importance with the likes of a John Dean or a Jeb Magruder, who albeit now is a minister and a wonderful human being but at the time was a punk little kid and so was I, is beyond me. Fortunately, I had a low enough role that I couldn't do any damage. I also happened to have been trained by parents and others who kept me out of trouble and taught me some ethics. But there were people in there who had no business with that level of responsibility, none whatsoever. The reason they were there was because Nixon didn't want people telling him what he didn't want to hear.

I think the single most important lesson for the President of the United States that I learned watching Ford and Nixon very closely, and reinforced by what Carter lacked and doubly reinforced by what I see in Reagan, is that inner tranquility that comes from knowing what you are good at and not good at and being comfortable with both. Ford had it and Reagan has had it; Nixon did not have it (but may now); and Carter did not have it. If I would make a single judgment, it's the presence of that inner sense, that gyroscope that no matter how many times you spin that person around or walk him around he comes back on track and keeps going. It is being at peace with yourself, liking yourself, and being comfortable with yourself. You get there, I think, by experience and by doing things. I think that is part of it, but I wouldn't give much credit to going through the House of Representatives or the Senate versus being the chief executive of a state. I don't think it matters too much.

**MR. THOMPSON:** One final question. We've asked everybody: how do you think history will judge the Nixon presidency?

**MR. DUVAL:** I think the judgment of history on Richard Nixon will be very mixed. There will not be a clear-bottom line. I suppose that it will always bottom line a little bit to the negative side but there will always be very strong positives, very major negatives, and it will net out based on the biases of the person making the judgment. As time passes the Nixon administration will increasingly become known for and known in a positive way due to the quality of some of his people. You have to remember that the White House staff in the first six months of the Nixon presidency consisted of the likes of Pat Moynihan, Bryce Harlow, and Arthur Burns.

**MR. THOMPSON:** We thank you for a most illuminating discussion.

# THE MAN AND FOREIGN POLICY

## Hugh Sidey

**MR. THOMPSON:** We are pleased to have a session with Hugh Sidey on the Nixon presidency. This is Mr. Sidey's twentieth anniversary as the author of the presidency column of *Time* magazine. He began his career in Greenfield, Iowa writing for a small paper, *The Adair County Free Press*, and afterwards for the *Omaha World-Herald*. In 1955 he joined the staff of *Life* magazine and in 1958 he joined *Time* magazine and began his column on the presidency in 1966. He was also head of the Washington bureau of *Time* magazine. He is the author of a number of books on presidents including *John F. Kennedy, President, A Very Personal Presidency, Lyndon Johnson in the White House, Portrait of a President* and other writings.

For a variety of reasons including the unavailability of key figures we've given more attention to Nixon's domestic than to his foreign policy. This is ironic given the major contribution President Nixon made in foreign policy. Fortunately, foreign policy is an area that Hugh Sidey has analyzed over the years. He has continued his contacts with Richard Nixon and has had recent opportunities to visit and talk with him. For all these reasons we are delighted to have him with us today.

**MR. SIDEY:** I don't cast myself as the ultimate authority on Richard Nixon. However, I've had a long exposure to him starting back in the mid-fifties when I began to cover the Senate and he was the vice president; and I've followed him ever since. I take some credit in having stimulated *Newsweek* to put him on their cover that said "Nixon is Back." I was able to do so because I was one of those early ones who finally got him to come out of his shell after Watergate. In fact, he granted his first interviews to a reporter from the *Christian Science Monitor* and myself at San Clemente. These interviews fascinated me. He is an absolutely sinister human being, but fascinating. I'd rather spend an evening with Richard Nixon than with almost anybody else because he is so bizarre. He has splashes of brilliance. He is obscene at times; his recall is almost total; his acquaintanceship with the world's figures is amazing. He is a fascinating human being.

I started seeing him with some regularity then and wrote a few pieces about our meetings. Steve Smith, one of the *Time* editors in New York, got intrigued through me because I kept saying, "You ought to talk with this man; he is slowly opening up." Smith left *Time* and went to *Newsweek* about six months ago. I think he was the one who put him on the cover.

Just recently, I was up in New York for the service commemorating the career of Theodore White, author of *The Making of the President.* It was a very moving ceremony. We had gathered out in front of the synagogue. Larry O'Brien was there with others from the Kennedy period. I stood there and remembered Teddy White's first years as a reporter. I knew him very well in those days. The last time I saw Teddy White was in the summer of 1984 at the San Francisco Democratic Convention when we had lunch. In the course of this lunch he said, "Do you realize that my entire political and literary career has been based on Richard Nixon? Not John Kennedy, not Lyndon Johnson, not the Democrats. The central figure in all my books is Richard Nixon, except for my autobiography *In Search of History* which went back to China." In all White's political books, Richard Nixon had been either a player or an event. The arguments were about RIchard Nixon or on something that he did. White added, "He more than any other figure has dominated my life, twenty-five years of political reporting." And that is probably true for all of us. He has been the central political figure, whether you like him or not, hate him or not. My point here is that he has probably shaped more events than any other figure, in either a positive or negative way.

So let me take you back a little. I met him in the mid-fifties up on the Hill and he was a loner from the start. Now I didn't go back to the California years like Herb Klein and others. When I arrived he was vice president and he had that wonderful office off the Senate chamber. He also had another office over in the Senate Office Building. Lastly, he had a hideaway. He was secretive even then. He used to sneak around those places. Of course he had to sit up in front of the Senate, but when he was off duty you would see that hunched figure trying to skulk off down the back ways of the Senate. It was a terrible effort to get to him, since he didn't like the press even then. Unlike Earl Mazo and some biographers, I didn't go into it but I sensed that as a young reporter he didn't like me, he was hostile. So as a young reporter I didn't like him. There was a hostility yet everybody recognized his ability. He had survived the McCarthy period, the Pumpkin Papers, that whole bit. And that was not without its merit; I think we all recognized that and yet there was something that was unpleasant about it. We didn't like the way he had done it. I don't know if we were too idealistic, if we were too young. At that time, I was in my twenties, maybe that was the problem. But we just didn't like him. The feeling was mutual and I could sense it.

Years later Henry Kissinger once said something to me that haunts me and makes me feel terribly bad. I don't know what to do about it. Sitting in those last traumatic days of Watergate with Kissinger in the White House, he told me, "Can you imagine what this man would have been had somebody loved him?" I said, "What do you mean?" He replied, "Had somebody in his life cared for him. I don't think anybody ever did, not his parents, not his peers. There may have been a teacher but nobody knows, it's not recorded." Finally, Kissinger said, "He would have been a great, great man had somebody loved him." The lack of love may be the clue. He was suspicious of everybody, even in those early days.

Throughout those years there was a certain admiration for him because he confronted issues in a brutal manner. It was just straight on, Richard Nixon. He used to talk about it; he was the gut fighter and he was rather proud of that. He worked hard; he was chosen as vice president.

Obviously the people in politics found that there was a certain virtue in all that.

My first extended campaign with him came in 1958. He was the lone political fighter. Eisenhower was sick and wavering at that time, indifferent to politics. Nobody in his Cabinet wanted to be caught out there because they knew it was the off-year election. They knew it was going to be a disaster. The only guy out there was Richard Nixon. I remember, it must have been early September, when we climbed on a Convair and flew for the next six weeks solid. We went to Alaska, and to every state we could, together with Pat and the girls. Nixon was isolated from us. He had a red curtain that separated this little cabin. He never gave up, night and day. I remember the defeats in Nebraska, Montana, Alaska—he lost them all. He didn't win one of those places he went to. It was a disaster. The last night of the campaign Nixon finally talked to us. He wasn't, as I said, gregarious. There was a hostility still.

On the airplane, we gathered around Nixon and he said, "Well, boys, I think it's lost." He was very candid about it. He had given everything he had and then he gave us the figures. I forget, but I think the Republicans lost fifty seats in the House that year. He just took it as a matter of fact. I don't recall if we had any sympathy for him in that election. Again, there was that constant battle between us and him. Phil Potter of the old *Baltimore Sun* was on board; he hated his guts and thought he was terrible. He used to go around with his poison telling us all what an awful man he was and we generally believed it. This was just another chapter in that unfortunate relationship between Richard Nixon and the press.

As vice president, he didn't get treated very well by Eisenhower. In eight years, Eisenhower never asked him to the private quarters. The vice president of the United States was never upstairs in the White House! At that time, I think the tradition of an elite was still lingering, with people like Robert Lovett, John McCloy, Jim Forrestal, and the Dulles brothers. That was a very elite group, highly cultivated, thoughtful, well connected, well educated, calm, discreet, everything that Nixon wasn't. I don't think he felt very comfortable with them ever. He knew them, got along with them, but his friends were still Californian friends: Bob Finch, who came to run his campaign, and Herb Klein, who was his press secretary. He did become a friend of Bill Rogers when he got into trouble on the Checkers matter, the fund. There were some people around town whom he reached but they were the old hard-line political types such as Mel Laird. The real elite didn't take very kindly to Richard Nixon and I suppose he felt some hostility towards almost everybody.

Afterwards, he went out to California; I didn't really follow him then, but that was more of the same. We were not going to have Nixon to kick around any more. He felt it was the press's fault, and everything went wrong. Finally, Pat Brown beat him.

I think something happened there. Nixon has never told me when he began to read Charles de Gaulle but I think it may have been then. General de Gaulle had this great theory that nobody is a great leader unless he has been in the wilderness, unless he has been rejected by those that he wants to convince, unless he has been put out to pasture and he gathers up his strength and comes back. For Nixon it really worked. I think of those years when Nixon wandered around the world as a Pepsi Cola salesman and a lawyer, and nobody paid any attention to him. He was alone; now and then an aide would go with him. Some of my bureau chiefs, who were out there in the various cities said that he would come in to town—he was a former vice president—and he would ask to see the head of state, whether he was in Kuala Lumpur, Algiers or some far away place. In most cases they wouldn't see him. He was out of power, he was a has-been; they didn't like him very much. He'd see anybody who'd see him. He didn't care. He'd see the second officer, vice president, whatever they would have out there, and sometimes it would end up being the fifth and sixth power, but he kept going. He'd talk to them all.

When he got to the White House he knew virtually every leader of every country in the world because some place along the line he'd ended up as a reject with that guy. It paid off in the end. They'd toss him to this fellow or that and six or twelve years later, this fellow would be elected president or prime minister of a given country and he'd be Nixon's pal.

He came back in the campaign of 1968. He did reach a certain equilibrium with himself and he did read more than ever. He was a much more relaxed candidate and also, honestly speaking, the times were right for him. In Washington we had become thoroughly disenchanted with Hubert Humphrey. The was had taken its toll. It was apparent—at least to some of us—that Hubert, great heart and mind that he was, simply was not going to manage this monster that had gotten out of hand. He didn't know what to do. He was tinged by Vietnam and Lyndon Johnson's paranoid leadership. Everything was wrong and in came Richard Nixon. By then, he had an incredible organization, all the money he needed, and an idea of what he wanted to say and do and he got it. There wasn't really anything startling about that campaign. I guess the Chicago upheaval was as much a part as anything, but it wasn't unexpected. There were so many problems in politics and in the streets that almost anything could happen. Richard Nixon remained cool and aloof. Ehrlichman, Haldeman and those people didn't deal that much with the press, but they controlled debates. I don't even know if they had debates in 1968, I can't remember. I think Nixon turned them down. I don't think there were any at all. I think he said, "No, I don't want to get into that after the Kennedy experience." And he made it stick.

So here we were in this new campaign with great weariness and Nixon took over. It was a very formal presidency, not much relationship with the press, certainly no buddy-buddy relations. He was remote and still bitter and vindictive, yet he recognized that he needed the media and he tried to use it as much as possible. He would play favorites. I can recall that the press never got to see him or rarely got to see him. I can also recall that before one of his first overseas trips, when he decided to fly to Iran, visit the Sixth Fleet in the Mediterranean and then go to Yugoslavia, he suddenly granted me an interview. By then, *Time* was the only American publication of wide international circulation and he knew we were going to put him on the cover so he granted me an interview because he wanted to use us and say what he wanted to say before he left on his trip. That was alright and we took it on that basis. He was good at that and he would open up under those conditions, but for the most part he was far removed. He understood us; he understood our deadlines; he understood how to manipulate us. Those first four years of Nixon in the presidency were pretty successful.

However there was that latent hostility. We didn't like the way Nixon looked; we didn't like the way he acted; we didn't like the way he talked, but we couldn't deny his achievements in foreign policy. In one sixteen month period he stopped the war in the Sinai, started the opening to China, began arms talks with the Soviet Union and decided to get out of Vietnam. There isn't any modern president who has achieved so much in foreign policy. It's astonishing when you look back on it.

But still, despite our great respect, there was also dislike of his manner, his style, the person; he was still an insecure and very curious fellow. I remember once the reporters were taking pictures of him and tried to get him to relax. His public relations personnel finally got him to appear on the beach at San Clemente but he showed up with a white shirt and tie and his Air Force One jacket. He was walking along with the dog and the tide came in and he was up to his knees in water. Any normal fellow would have looked down and sworn like Johnson and lifted his pants, but Nixon was so flustered and so uncertain that he walked along in the water with his shoes on. He kept walking along the water as if he came down there every day with his wing tips on; he slushed in the water. It was the silliest looking bit I've ever seen on television. Nixon was still that way. He couldn't somehow quite face the world yet, but he had moments when he tried.

I got a call one afternoon after I had written a piece about Vietnam that he liked because I basically supported Nixon's effort to pull out through a tough position together with negotiations to turn it over to Vietnam without yielding right away and without just saying that we were going to walk out. Nixon called me about three o'clock in the afternoon and obviously he had been drinking, since he couldn't talk very well. He said, "I just want to tell you that's a great piece. Come on down for the weekend. I'm going down with Bebe Rebozo and we're going out to the Virgin Islands. Bring your wife and we'll have a weekend." The prospect of it horrified me. As much as I like presidents, that sounded so bad. I accepted finally and said, "Well, fine, Mr. President." Within two hours Ron Ziegler called me and said, "Forget that; you've been disinvited." So on occasions, Nixon would try to leap out of his shell but it never worked. However, he tried.

When he left this country, a change would come over him. He obviously felt better abroad than in this country; there was something about being overseas that was much more pleasant. I don't know what it was. One of the people who traveled with Pat Nixon said that the same thing happened to her. The instant the airplane crossed the Continental Divide, she was a different woman, as if released. She was funny, witty, irreverent about Richard Nixon and someone fun to be with. When the plane came back, when it crossed the Continental Divide she was in her little cocoon again and the same happened to him. When we were in France, I remember he invited me to dinner with de Gaulle. It was a great experience. I was standing next to the door, with my rented white tie and tails, and in came Nixon with de Gaulle. He grabbed me and introduced me to de Gaulle. He was an entirely different Nixon. Everything was warm and gracious. "Meet de Gaulle," he told me and added, "Great man of our time, General de Gaulle." I wondered to myself, "Who is this guy?" But he would change back.

On another occasion we went to Tito's birthplace and boyhood home. Isn't it funny? All these figures have their boyhood homes and they restore them and then they lie about them, they sit there and lie. It's not only our Johnson, with the boyhood home, the birthplace and the monument to him down in Texas. Richard Nixon went up with Tito who had done the same thing. It was like Johnson City, Texas. It was Tito's boyhood home. It was raining, just terrible rain, and I was sticking my head through the window, watching Tito and Richard Nixon talk about their boyhoods. Richard Nixon was telling the hamburger story about how poor the Nixons were and how they had to eat hamburger. Also, he told the story about the pony he wanted but never got. He kept telling it over and over again. Well, he told it to Tito, but Tito beat him. Tito said, "We had eleven kids who were in this room." He showed where everybody slept. By then, Nixon saw me sticking through the door and he grabbed me and pulled me in. "I want you to meet Tito, meet Marshall Tito." Suddenly, out of the blue, this strange impulse to be one of the boys appeared but it never lasted, it went away.

I suppose it was a presidency that was bent on tragedy, and in between these little things he tried. When Watergate started, everything soured and there was just no hope. He tried to get me banned from Air Force One and he bugged all those other people. He was a contemptible figure in those days. He may have understood the world but he didn't understand the oath of office he took. The crimes, the arrogance, and the idea that he could do whatever he wanted backstage and conceal it were terrible. Yet his amazing amount of achievement in the world is still there. The bitterness, particularly in the last days, and the drift in government were all bad. Of course the media made the most of it. Honestly, the media was nearly hysterical. We never had such a story. Probably it was as if somebody said, "It was like feeding the sharks, the more you got the more you wanted." It did get out of hand. I think there is no question about it. It went further than it should have but it was an incredibly complex, fascinating story, the only one like it we'd had in two hundred years. At that moment the media was just beginning to feel its power. Television had come of age finally. The amount of money that we could devote to this sort of thing and the numbers of people had increased by geometrical proportions. So Nixon was driven from office. It was a sad, sad moment for the country, for him, and for everybody. Yet I must confess that during the period there was a certain exhilaration and perversity that always exists in Washington, no matter which crisis is involved. There are people who love crisis. People in government like it. There is something about it: the challenge and the problems. I suppose war is like that, that's why people go to war. There is this kind of odd feeling.

In Watergate the feeling was with us. I can recall standing in Lafayette Park in August 1974 as Nixon prepared to go on television to say that he would quit the presidency. The White House correspondents were there: Dan Rather for CBS, Frank Reynolds for ABC and Tom Brokaw for NBC. Dan Rather just loved it. He never had so much fun. He was out there in the spotlight; thousands of people had come to see Dan Rather in the flesh. It took on an extraordinary dimension.

Then Nixon retired to San Clemente and for five or six years he lived in bitterness there. He granted me his first interview when he decided on the comeback. I guess it was after Carter when he finally began to come out again. We had that first tentative interview. He now has regular dinners at Saddle River with three or four people; he entertains some correspondents and he continues to travel. Richard Nixon is still a most extraordinary man. I guess he's given up the martinis but the first time I went he was a little tiddly before the evening was over. He had a couple of martinis. He always has a Chinese dinner in memory of his great moment on the Great Wall. Then after dinner we drank that dreadful Mai Tai. If you've been to China you know it tastes like kerosene. Nixon drinks it, one right after the other, and he really does get a little bombed. But let me tell you, he is absolutely amazing. In my judgment, he has a better grasp of world power than any man on the scene, except Kissinger. The two seem to see eye to eye on it. He keeps up through his travels, his writings, and his reading, and he also is a very practical man. He understands the personalities, the realities; sincerely, there is nobody who equals him in terms of his grasp of the world. My lament is that Reagan doesn't pay much attention to him. He calls up the White House but, as Nixon says, with Reagan things go in one ear and out another in most instances. Nixon is more moderate than Reagan is and more realistic about the necessity to talk to our adversaries. I think Nixon's views would benefit Reagan if he were to listen.

He is still around and he is in reasonably good health. It may seem that he has more influence than he actually does in terms of foreign policy today. There is no doubt that he is a personality in the world and in this era of show business that we have created, he has a place on the stage but his impact on actual policy is probably less than we suggest. Nevertheless, I suspect he is going to be one of our elder statesmen for many more years and I suspect not much is going to change. If he were in the room today he would be reasonably polite but he would also be kind of nasty. He would say a few things that would jolt everybody but be immensely intriguing.

**QUESTION:** Which is the best book on Watergate? Secondly, do you have any idea who "Deep Throat" was?

**MR. SIDEY:** Regarding the second question, I don't have a specific answer, but Al Haig is one of my candidates. I don't really know in the end. I tend to reject the theory that it was a composite. I know Woodward a little bit and I don't think he would make it up, although it is possible. I tend to think it may be somebody startling like Al Haig, who was head of the NSC at that time.

I don't know if there is a single book on Watergate that I could suggest. The one that sticks in mind is still the first one by Woodward and Bernstein, which presents their episodes. Through its narration, it captured much of Nixon. There is also the second book that they wrote about the aftermath. These two books combined might make as good a story as any. There are a lot of reasonably good studies on Watergate. I like the immediacy of Woodward and Bernstein. They were on the scene and they saw it. I think they were unfair in some ways but the story is interesting. I guess it's a movie now.

**QUESTION:** I'm rather intrigued with your discussion of Richard Nixon's background, his lack of being loved and his view of the establishment. Did it ever strike you that there is an enormous resemblance between Richard Nixon as a person, his knowledge of life, people, the establishment and government, and Lyndon Johnson?

**MR. SIDEY:** Yes, there are some similarities. Although I am not a psychiatrist or a psychologist, I saw some of those same overtones of inferiority, resentment, the chip on the shoulder and the feeling of "once I get into power, I'm going to grind your faces into it; I'm going to make you suffer."

I remember talking to McGeorge Bundy one time. After Kennedy's death, he was still head of the NSC for a little while. When I went to see him, Bundy couldn't hack it. He came from Boston and had all that blue blood in his veins. It was a little more than he could take to be around Lyndon Johnson. I don't blame him because unless you were weaned in that world it is hard. Bundy talked to me one day very thoughtfully about it and he said, "His problem is this feeling that because he didn't go to Harvard he can't contend in this world." He then added, "Yet, the fact of it is he is about as bright a man as I've ever run into. But lacking the credentials, he can't quite bring himself to believe that he is that good."

I remember very shortly thereafter, when Johnson became president, I went to see him. I knew him very well because I had written about him when he was majority leader. Once there, he told me, "Well, Hugh, there I was around the Cabinet table today. You know I took count. Around that Cabinet table were two boys from Harvard and a man from Columbia, three from Yale, and a Ph.D. from Stanford, and one little old boy from Southwest Texas State Teachers College. I just want you to know." He never got over it and I must say that the Kennedys were just dreadful to him. Bobby was especially terrible. They were contemptuous and they were mean.

**QUESTION:** If we could generalize at all, in the last twenty years we've had two presidents and perhaps three if you count Jimmy Carter, who came out of very humble surroundings, who got to the top of the heap politically and who were driven out of office. What does it say to you about the way we choose presidential candidates?

**MR. SIDEY:** The generalization is true. The process of choosing and the way we let these people come up to it is probably the most troublesome thing that we've got going in our system. I don't have an answer on how to solve the problem, I really don't.

**QUESTION:** I would like to return to the subject of Nixon's grasp of the world, which you defined as unparalleled. I wonder if you would develop that idea further and give us some idea as to how he developed his insights.

**MR. SIDEY:** He could talk about a subject and he brought clarity when he'd talk about it. I think it was based on his own kind of scholarship. He really did work at things. He read, traveled, and compiled. He wrote letters; he watched everything he could get in on so there was quite a fund of knowledge. Kissinger once told me that one of the shocking things about becoming National Security Adviser was to observe that when he sat down to negotiate with these so-called world statesmen, they knew so little about what they were talking about. When he sat down with world leaders, half of them hadn't been to the countries they were discussing. Nixon was different. He had been many places and Saigon was a street scene to him. Frequently the French negotiators hadn't been there but with Nixon it was a street scene. He knew the people, sights and sounds and he felt it. Also, he had guts, as in the case of his trip to China.

Lyndon Johnson was different. One night, while he was in office, I was in his study. Johnson was drinking, as he always did. We were having a conversation. Sometimes he would talk for hours. He'd talk things out and tell you about them until you were groggy. I remember this night he was talking about China and he said, "I'd like to sit down with them. I'd like to sit down with the Chinese. You never make a deal until you get two at a table. You got to talk to people in order to understand them." I said, "Mr. President, why don't you?" He replied, "My diplomats tell me I can't. They just tell me this isn't the right time, all my diplomats tell me we can't do it." You know what Nixon would say if somebody told him about the diplomats' opinions; you couldn't print it. He'd just tell them to stick it in their left ear. That is what he did with China. He said, "I'm going to do it." He read the Snow article that came out in *Life*, picked out that little nuance in the article, and said, "I think they are ready." He listened to others who had been there and he decided that this was a move he could make.

After he came out of the shell in the very first interview, I made the following comment, which actually was my wife's comment, not mine. I said, "Mr. President, it is kind of an enigma for us that in the minds of many people in the world you are the incarnate of evil. You've been thrown out of office and you've done all these bad things, and yet people are saying you have a better grasp of the world now and you are more honored for your foreign policy than anybody. On the other hand, Jimmy Carter who was a man who was supposed to be the incarnate of good, who walked among the people in his sandals and brought love, is rejected now. He is condemned and reviled. How do you explain that? I paused and watched him. Nixon looks like an evil person. He has a hunch. On that occasion his nose and eyebrows were going up and down, and he looked evil. He took a long time to answer and it was rather incoherent but what he said was: "You've got to be a little evil to understand those people out there. You have to have known the dark side of life to understand those people. I only know half a dozen corporate chief executives that I would trust in a room with a healthy Brezhnev. Yet, I know twenty or thirty labor leaders I'd let in there." It was a view of the world. It all kind of figured. He didn't trust anybody.

When we first went to Moscow on the first day, he figured he was being bugged, and he was right. So, he met with Kissinger in the car. They sat outside in the car with the motor running and the radio on and they talked. All of these little bits and pieces that he picked up in this rather incredible career came together to give him a realistic view of the world and the people involved in it.

I remember that in the 1974 trip to Yalta, Nixon got along with Brezhnev. In turn, Brezhnev liked him. He took him out in his speed boats; he took him in his cars. I remember talking to Kissinger afterwards about how these two old rascals got along together. There was some bond there in which Brezhnev would talk about his father and his tough childhood and Nixon could relate to that and also talk about his own experience.

**QUESTION:** Previously, you said that nobody loves Nixon. Does he love his family? Is there any warmth toward his family?

**MR. SIDEY:** That's a good question and I can't answer it for sure because several years ago I'd have answered negatively. But of all the presidential kids I've known, kids of seven presidents now, Nixon's daughters are the best. In my judgment, Tricia and Julie meet the standards of public behavior as well as any of them, maybe not better than Margaret Truman, but certainly better than the rest. They have been dignified through the worst of times. During Watergate they didn't turn on their father. They gave him support, yet they didn't endorse what he did. Therefore, there has to be something there. Now between Nixon and Pat, his wife, I don't think there was any kind of a human bond. There had to be something, but I don't understand it. She is never in public. Whenever I've gone up there she is not there anymore. She kind of followed along with him and he used her in campaigns, but once he got in the White House that was the end of it.

I'm told by curator Clem Conger that Pat Nixon did more to redecorate the White House than any of the First Ladies. She got more objects, but nobody gave her credit for it. Nixon didn't give her credit for it. He doesn't talk about her much now. So I don't know. I'm mystified by that. Obviously with the daughters there is some kind of a bond although there are no public displays of great affection. I think that they get together now and then.

I have asked myself if Nixon has a real love for the country. In the past, I would have answered negatively. I would have also said that his driving force was simply ambition. Lately, I've changed my position. I believe that deep down he did care about this country in a strange way. The same happens with Lyndon Johnson, who was the biggest liar and crook I've known. He took everything that wasn't nailed down at the White House. With tax funds we paved runways in Texas for him and fixed up hog sheds into hangars. Who else in modern public life could take a little radio station and make a twenty million dollar empire? Nobody said a word about this. What that man did was just outrageous. Yet when you sat down with Lyndon Johnson his real concern for the country would come out.

**NARRATOR:** We thank you for our discussion.

# RECONSTRUCTING THE NIXON FOREIGN POLICY

## Helmut Sonnenfeldt

**NARRATOR:** We're pleased to welcome you to a Forum with Helmut Sonnenfeldt, one of this country's authorities on American foreign policy. He began his career in the Department of State in 1952 and concluded that service in 1977. During the mid- to late 1960s, he was director of the Office of Research and Analysis for the U.S.S.R. and Eastern Europe. He left the Department to become a senior member of the National Security Council staff from 1969 to 1974 and returned in 1974 as counselor in the Department of State until 1977. He is currently a guest scholar at the Brookings Institution. He recently returned from a trip to Moscow. His mastery of the Soviet and East European field has not only earned him recognition among scholarly specialists in the field, but he is also credited with being the author of the Sonnenfeldt Doctrine. I don't know many people who have had doctrines named for them, but the Sonnenfeldt Doctrine is testimony to the force of his thinking and conceptualizing on foreign policy.

Mr. Sonnenfeldt was born in Berlin, Germany and came to this country in 1944, becoming a naturalized citizen in 1945. He is a trustee of Johns Hopkins University, a director of the Corning International Corporation, and an associate of the Lehrman Institute. He has taught and lectured at the School for Advanced International Studies of Johns Hopkins University and at many other institutions. His interest in problems abroad and knowledge of theories of foreign policy is substantial. We're pleased to have him with us to discuss the Nixon presidency and foreign policy drawing on first-hand experience. He is uniquely qualified to review, revisit and perhaps reconstruct the Nixon foreign policy.

**MR. SONNENFELDT:** Thank you Ken. I thought that I would make some brief introductory remarks about how I happened to become part of the Nixon White House and reflect on that experience and his foreign policy.

I had been in the Department of State for many years when Nixon was elected President in 1968 and selected Henry Kissinger as his National Security Adviser. I had known Kissinger since the end of the Second World War when we were discovered by the same *guru,* who thought that we were promising young men and he should take us on. Kissinger went on to become a well-known professor at Harvard, but he was also a consultant to the government. We were in contact officially from time to time but we also stayed in touch on a personal basis.

When Kissinger was appointed, he was essentially given a free hand by Nixon to put together his own staff and he went about doing that. I think there was only one exception and that was Mr. Richard Allen, later the first National Security Adviser to President Reagan, who was appointed to the staff. He had worked in the Nixon campaign in 1968. In fact, he had worked in several Republican presidential campaigns. He apparently had expectations of becoming the National Security Adviser himself but Nixon chose otherwise. He did appoint him, however, as a deputy assistant to the President. Kissinger had known him only fleetingly. The rest of the group was recruited by Kissinger through various personal acquaintances. In my case, coincidence had it that the State Department put forward a list of people that they thought might serve on the National Security Council staff and I happened to be on that list.

The selection of the National Security Council staff in 1968 by Kissinger on the basis of his criteria of what and whom he wanted caused some difficulties as time went on. The staff Kissinger put together was a mixed lot of people, some from within the government, some from the academic community and some from other places. Very few if any had any special credentials as either Nixon Republicans or as Republicans at all. Kissinger picked people essentially on the basis of their particular knowledge of issues and for other reasons. It was the only part of the White House staff in the Nixon presidency that was selected in this fashion. Most of the other assistants to the President put their staff together based on political involvement in Republican politics, especially in the Nixon campaign. It did in fact prove possible to get people who had both the substantive qualifications and had worked in the Nixon campaign and in Republican politics. But in the case of the National Security Council staff these political credentials were very much secondary, if indeed they figured at all. That caused some suspicion and bad blood in other parts of the White House and some friction between Kissinger and other people on the senior White House staff. Kissinger also selected a few people who at one time or another had aroused the suspicions of J. Edgar Hoover, who objected to their selection. That caused problems later on when the famous wiretap issue arose.

I actually went to the White House somewhat reluctantly, in part because the previous eight years in the Kennedy and Johnson administrations had seen an enormous growth in the size and influence of the National Security Council's staff and a change in the role of the National Security Adviser. Until McGeorge Bundy became Kennedy's special assistant for National Security Affairs, the people who held that job in the White House were essentially very able and experienced staffers, such as General Goodpaster in the Eisenhower administration, who had very low profiles and were rarely seen or heard in public. Their staffs were relatively small and their function clearly was one of coordination, moving the paperwork along and staffing the various committees that were set up. This did not exclude their giving presidents direct advice when asked, but the staffs were small and low profile.

In the Kennedy administration the making and the administration of foreign policy, and in some respects defense policy and national security policy, came to be concentrated more in the White House in substantive fashion than had been true in the Truman and Eisenhower administrations. This became an issue, particularly between the Department of State and some of the people on the

National Security Council staff because it cut into the traditional role of the secretary of state and of the various departments, divisions or bureaus which had been the principal places where policy recommendations originated and where policies, once decided on through mechanisms of the presidency and the executive branch, were implemented. But in the Kennedy and Johnson administrations, much of this shifted into the White House and many of us who served in the State Department had reservations about the wisdom of that.

It's not surprising that this should have been the case. I felt that this movement was a trend that should not be encouraged and perhaps should be reversed. I was totally wrong in judging how Nixon saw the presidency and his role in foreign policy. In any case, I overcame my reluctance. But when I discovered the extent to which President Nixon wanted to have policy-making and even policy execution concentrated in the White House, sometimes even to the exclusion of the secretary of state and the Department of State, I had even more misgivings.

I discovered this in the first month of the Nixon administration when the President decided to go on a trip to Europe to consult with our NATO allies. While preparation for that presidential trip did very much involve the Department of State and the Department of Defense and the other departments of the government, it was clear that the whole strategy of the trip—the planning for each stop, and for the conversations that the President was going to have with the other leaders in these various countries—was going to be handled largely from the White House. Participants were kept down to a very few, and in many cases officials from the Department of State and even from the embassies were excluded.

It was Nixon's view that he could only conduct policy as he wanted to in complete privacy without people around taking notes and then passing them around the government bureaucracy, the press and the Congress. So it became clear early in that administration that initiative and activity were going to be concentrated in the White House. Nixon, of course, felt very confident of his judgments in foreign affairs. He had had a lot of experience as vice president in travelling around the world. He had kept up wide ranging contacts with world leaders while out of office.

Incidentally, one of your questions is about my acquaintance with Nixon. I had not really known Nixon, although I had met him a few times when he was vice president. I served in a relatively junior capacity in the State Department then and had no direct contact with him. But he clearly had significant experience in dealing with foreign leaders and knew most of them far better than his chosen Secretary of State, Mr. William Rogers. He had seen them while he was out of office and they had been willing to receive him and listen to his views. So his first trip to Europe as President was actually a return to see old acquaintances in his new capacity. But he felt that whatever business was going to be transacted, whatever confidences were going to be shared, they should remain confidential. A lot has been written about the problems created by this secrecy, and sometimes deviousness, *vis-à-vis* the rest of the government.

There is a problem here that reflects the fact that our executive branch is not permanently organized on the basis of statutes or regulations or even rigid tradition. In this respect it's quite different from the British Cabinet and other systems. It depends heavily on the personality, style and preferences of the president. We've seen this again and again. Organizational structures in the White House change, styles of operation change, methods of decision-making change. Under our system, in the field of foreign affairs, the president can make decisions as he chooses on behalf of the executive branch. Of course, he is subject to constraints by the Congress and other parts of the government as required by the Constitution, but within the executive branch he is paramount if he wants to be.

In the Nixon administration the National Security Council, an agency set up by statute in 1947, had purely advisory meetings. They were not decision-making meetings and there is nothing that obligates the president to take a vote around the table and say, "The ayes have it; that's my decision." There's nothing that requires the president to call a meeting and present the agenda and close the meeting by saying he's heard all the arguments and positions and this is his decision.

The president can call meetings of two people, three people, seven people, or ten people or whatever he wishes. He can tell three people what his decision is, he can tell nobody what his decision is or he can tell a hundred people what his decision is. These things are not written down anywhere and there is no particular tradition of how to do them most effectively or how to do them best under our system. On the big issues that concerned him, Nixon chose to keep the circle of those who were in on the decision process very narrow. This didn't mean that he didn't consult and ask the views of lots of people within and outside the government, of foreigners and Americans alike. He was quite open and he read quite a bit in these particular fields. When it came time to make decisions, he would do so in his own way and in his own time.

Nixon, unlike President Eisenhower and to some extent President Truman, preferred not to get agreed-upon recommendations from within the government. He wanted to hear the arguments and he didn't want to have precooked decisions that were bargained out in the bureaucracies and among Cabinet officers and then presented to him in such a way that he could only accept or reject them. He preferred to have a more open-ended way of having issues presented to him. Above all, he didn't want his subordinates to bargain with each other and confront him with consensus views. One reason for this was that he didn't want phalanxes of Cabinet officers forming little coalitions in his administration underneath the presidency which would be very hard to crack on some other occasion. What this usually meant in the National Security Council staff was that we worked extremely hard to crystalize issues and positions for Kissinger in the first place and then with him for the President.

The President wanted to know what the arguments were, who stood for what, what agency favored this, that and the other. Many things, of course, one could predict because they were well-known agency positions. Then he would form his own judgment, based on any number of considerations. I can't speak with any great expertise on that because I wasn't in the room with him when he balanced off relationships among and between his various subordinates, political fallout in the Congress, electoral as well as personal considerations and a number of other factors that go into this rather mysterious process of rendering judgments and decisions and setting directions.

But a great deal of the function that we performed—and Kissinger in this respect was a very rigorous and hard taskmaster—was to array the arguments and, not just the verbal arguments but the reasoning behind the arguments on particular alternatives or options, to present them to the President for the tough job of selection. Sometimes he would postpone; sometimes he would straddle; sometimes he would remain ambiguous; sometimes he would decide one thing in a formal way and do something else privately.

The next problem was to see that, whatever the decisions were, they would be carried through as the President had decided. That was very often difficult because the President himself didn't necessarily spell out in detail what he wanted done and how he wanted to do it. You had to get some sense of what the intent was in a given decision so that in its implementation, you could conform to the intent of the decision. Many times that took a sixth sense, but after a while it became clearer because you got accustomed to it. But you had to get some sense of the direction and strategy that went into the particular decisions. Then you had to keep an eye on the rest of the government as it carried on with the decisions. No matter how brilliant or numerous a National Security Council staff or White House staff may be, it is still very small compared with the rest of the government.

For many decisions, you need many parts of the government to carry them out. Some you can do secretly and quietly with just a few people, such as carrying a message to another head of state. Many other things require congressional action or public explanation and may get dragged on for many months. Other decisions obviously cannot be carried out by a handful of people, so they are delegated to the Cabinet departments and other parts of the government. That's where it becomes very important from the standpoint of a president who is purposeful and wants to see his policy pursued, that the decisions don't get diluted and distorted in the process of execution as they get transmitted down the line. This is particularly true in the case of decisions that go against the recommendations of some particular department. There's nothing a bureaucracy knows how to do better than to take a decision that goes against its own recommendations and, in its implementation, transform it into what the bureaucracy wanted in the first place.

So the White House staff, the National Security Council staff, Cabinet officers and others have the task of trying to keep the essential integrity of decisions and policies as intended by those who made the decisions. For example, most of the major instructions and telegrams that went to our ambassadors or representatives at international conferences from the Department of State had to be cleared by the National Security Council staff and that sometimes meant dozens and dozens of messages a day and hundreds of messages a week.

The problem of moving that process along without causing a bottleneck, especially when some decisions required fast, prompt action, was another one of those procedural problems which were quite important in practice. These were the basic functions that we performed to help the decision process: presenting as objectively and faithfully as possible the different attitudes, views and ways of looking at an issue and of dealing with them so that the President could make his own choices, and interpret and implement and watch over the implementation.

There were of course more painful aspects of this. Policies fail and strategies go awry. The United States isn't in control of events as much as we'd like to be. Other actors are heard from and you have to see how you are doing and go back and ask yourself whether the strategy is right, the decisions are "doable," whether there were effects that hadn't been anticipated and were adverse to our interests and concerns. How do you go back to the president and say, "Look, you've got to think about this one again and see what we do next." This, of course, was a constant problem during the Vietnam war. The war was a major public issue in this country fifteen to twenty years ago, and the question of revising policy, changing strategy, choosing other ways of dealing with a problem presented itself constantly because the public, the Congress and foreign governments continued to raise the issue. It became an agonizing set of problems for the President and his advisers.

In other cases it wasn't always that obvious. President Reagan, to take a case that's well known, ran into a problem in this regard with the famous gas pipeline question with the Soviets. His own instincts and most of the advice that he received called for trying to prevent the building of the gas pipeline from Siberia to Western Europe, and trying to stop foreign concerns that got technology and equipment from American firms from transferring these to the Soviet Union. Over time that issue became so politically costly to American interests that, whatever the merits of the original decision may have been, it required revision.

That's the sort of thing that happens all the time, frequently in much less visible ways than the case I have just cited. In the end, it becomes very much a function of the relationship the president has with his own staff and with his Cabinet officers. At some point people have to go in and see the president, or perhaps the president observes the unfolding of a policy and will take the initiative himself. But in the Nixon case, any questions about whether things were working as planned—what to do next, how to adjust the strategy—were very much a matter of a small circle of individuals. As members of the National Security Council staff we were not directly involved except to the extent that Kissinger, who was much involved directly with the President, sought our advice and used our expertise to buttress his own arguments.

The work we did was essentially work for the National Security Adviser, and I think this is the case and has been the case with other National Security Council staffs. A president cannot possibly see all the members of the staff or even all the senior members of his staff on a continuous basis. He can have staff meetings if he's so inclined. Most presidents sooner or later get tired of that because it's very time consuming. Presidents tend, therefore, to have a few senior advisers work directly on various issues with staff assistance. That certainly was the case in the White House set-up that I was familiar with from 1969 to 1974.

The last year and a half of the Nixon presidency was, of course, heavily taken up by Watergate. I actually left the National Security Council staff in January of 1974 to become counselor of the Department of State. Kissinger in the meantime had become secretary of state. So I was not in the White House in the last few months of the Nixon presidency. But from a foreign policy standpoint, one of the difficult, serious and delicate problems was to continue to conduct the foreign policy of the United States with authority and assurance, while the President became increasingly preoccupied with the travail of Watergate and his authority was increasingly sapped.

In retrospect, I think that Kissinger and General Haig, who became chief of staff in the White House toward the end of the Nixon administration, deserve a great deal of credit—and I think will get it—from historians for holding the government together, enabling it to function even though it was increasingly clear that the President was severely handicapped in decision-making and in getting Congress to go along with him on a whole series of issues. In many respects this was a unique situation. I suppose that when a president is severely disabled, as President Wilson was physically disabled, something similar happens, although those were simpler times and the involvement of the United States in international affairs was much less pervasive at that time than when we were engaged in a full-scale war, as we were in Vietnam in 1973 and 1974, and a host of other issues, including leadership roles in our structure of alliances and other international institutions.

To some extent our jobs in that period had to do with maintaining the credibility of the presidency within the government and also *vis-à-vis* foreign governments, the press and the Congress. I remember very vividly the crisis that arose over the Yom Kippur War in October 1973, when at one point a threatening message from Brezhnev was received from the Soviet ambassador in Washington. The Israelis had failed to abide by the timing of a cease-fire and were continuing to operate militarily against an almost encircled Egyptian army in the Sinai Peninsula. The Soviets sent a seemingly threatening message about a joint American-Soviet military intervention to stop the Israeli effort to defeat and humiliate the Egyptians despite the fact that there had already been an agreement to institute a cease-fire.

Response to that Soviet threat was a very serious matter and a group of the President's senior advisers spent all night trying to decide how to handle it. The decision eventually involved the alerting of some American military forces and a rejection of the Soviet proposal for joint military action and, on the other hand, some continued pressure on the Israelis to abide by the cease-fire decisions that had been made. When these decisions, particularly the alerting of our forces, became known the next morning, the question was raised immediately in the press whether this had been a crisis artificially created by Nixon in order to demonstrate his indispensability in the context of the then gathering storm of Watergate. This was October 1973 so it was almost a year before his eventual resignation, but Watergate was in the news and very much a preoccupation at the time.

Even though a great deal of the material has since become available—people have written their memoirs and participants in these decisions have spoken out about it—I don't suppose the suspicion has been completely dispelled to this day that this was an action taken by the President of the United States which was unjustifiably harsh or drastic and which was essentially designed not to serve a national interest but his own particular personal interest in the difficulty. My own view at that time was an outgrowth of my participation in the debates and discussions that night. In helping to make assessments of how serious the Soviet threat was and, participating in the examination of various options we had, I was convinced then that these were valid decisions. In fact, Nixon didn't participate in most of those discussions and approved the recommendations early in the morning of the following day. I have always felt that decisions were made on the issues at hand rather than in terms of the President's own personal considerations. That is perhaps a more dramatic example of the kind of problem that we had to deal with in the declining phase of the Nixon presidency in 1973 and 1974.

I've previously said it's difficult to anticipate the judgment of historians. Sometimes what historians say five years after an event may be quite different from what those same historians may say ten or fifteen years later and quite different again from what yet another group of historians may say many years after the event. Having had the opportunity to serve fairly close to the seat of power, I would say that it is extraordinarily important for later judgment that as much effort be made while it is possible to get the testimony and views of the participants in particular decisions and processes.

If one has available only the documents that were written at the time, I think the results can be extremely misleading. I'm afraid that many documents, memoranda and papers, especially in our government, are written with multiple audiences in mind. Therefore, they are not incontrovertible evidence as to the views of the author. Sometimes they are written for mundane purposes like trying to look good in getting a promotion. Even leaving that venal aspect aside, however, our government, particularly in the last twenty-five or thirty years, has been a particularly leaky one. Since the invention of the xerox machine there is really no sanctity to anything that's put on paper. One almost has to assume that anything that's written will sooner or later fall into hands or come before eyes that it wasn't intended for. Therefore, I have great reservations about the validity of written documents. I think that any historian who tries to reconstruct events has to do so with extraordinary caution, subtlety and effort with attention to other factors than the ostensible ones that are the subject of a particular document. That's almost impossible to do fifty years later if you have nothing but the written record.

This does put an enormous burden on people who try to reconstruct events, and in a way it is frustrating. Of course it's an invitation to constant revisionism. It's simpler to make judgments concerning the effects of decisions, regardless of how they were arrived at and how complex particular papers or conversations were at the time. I suppose in the end when historians judge presidents like Nixon or any president for that matter, they will look at the effects. They will look at the fortunes of the country and see what shape it was in when they started and what shape it was in when they ended, what legacy was left for the successors.

All-in-all, our nation held up very well in the foreign policy field in particular, given the enormous complexity of the Vietnam War, which was one of the most painful experiences that we've had in modern history in this country, and the extraordinary convulsions associated with the Watergate events, convulsions that didn't, however, really go to the roots of our constitutional system. We came through with the national interest in pretty good shape.

**QUESTION:** One of the things we wondered about is who are the best people to approach in supplementing the documents. For example, what three, four, or five people are most crucial in any attempt to get our views straight, say, on the wiretap issue? Can you identify people?

**MR. SONNENFELDT:** I was a "tappee" but not a tapper. I probably was the most frequently and longest tapped person in the government in the Nixon administration. Wiretaps and bugs were one means by which people were investigated as far back as the Truman administration for routine security clearances and updates, let alone suspicion of some wrongdoing. I don't know what I can add on that subject. I think the main actors in decisions that led to that particular episode, like Hoover and people in the FBI that were involved, are no longer with us, but others are. I don't know whether they have anything squirreled away that they haven't told us yet about those decisions. I suppose they have and I think there will be some things that eventually will come out and shed additional light on just how and why it happened.

I would only remark on that subject that while it was a pretty common practice, I felt it was not a particularly effective device for trying to discover leaks or wrongdoing. It was a pretty common practice in this country in the postwar period at least, and it therefore did not especially surprise me that it had been resorted to in the case of the plumbers and the Pentagon Papers as well as the other leaks. It was part of the investigative technique that was common in the government. It was loosely and badly handled. Far too much reliance was placed on random conversations. What happened in the Nixon administration was an extreme form of what had been going on as a matter of routine.

**COMMENT:** The question was asked earlier regarding how we get the supplemental documentation of written records. I think you are doing it through these forums. That's been one of the great developments in your effort here. Not everything is in a written record. You are getting an awful lot in these meetings. It's doing just what you pointed out should be done.

**MR. SONNENFELDT:** I think the presidential libraries are also doing oral histories. I've been out of the government for seven or eight years now and out of the White House for longer than that, yet I still get many graduate students and others who come through the office with their tape recorders. I try to help them from memory as much as I can. I can't go and do a research project every time a Ph.D. student comes along. But I try to refresh my memory, and I think most of the people that have been involved in one way or another try to do that. Some people write memoirs and they have to be properly weighed and assessed given the frailties of human beings when writing about themselves.

I should say in this regard that I think the Kissinger memoirs are an extraordinary achievement. They're in one sense self-serving and apologetic and they withhold information. But in that *genre* of writing, they are extraordinarily candid, open, full and complete. He's been subjected to criticism for using materials that were withheld from others. That's another matter. Whether these public documents should be there for the initial private and personal use of the individual or whether they should be made equally available to all legitimate scholars and observers is a complicated issue. But Kissinger is first of all a historian so he has the historian's technique. He was involved to an extraordinary degree in the affairs of our government and he's a perceptive and sensitive figure. He did keep very substantial records, including records of telephone conversations. Secretaries are no longer permitted to listen in on telephone conversations, but we still transact an extraordinary amount of business on the telephone. So I think he did quite a remarkable job. Historians will pick it apart and journalists have already picked it apart, but I think it will survive as a central part of the record of the Nixon administration and, when he gets around to it, the Ford administration.

**QUESTION:** Which Kissinger guides us best? The one who headed the NSC or the one who told us the secretary ought to coordinate foreign policies?

**MR. SONNENFELDT:** If you want the secretary of state, under the President, to guide the country's foreign policy, you've got to get yourself a secretary of state who's capable of doing it. You've got to organize the Department of State in such a way that the secretary of state has an instrument with which to do it. If you pick a secretary of state who doesn't have the ability, for whatever reason, or turns out not to have it even if you thought at the beginning he did, and if the Department of State insists on being cumbersome and bureaucratic, the President will get his business done where he can. So I don't take that particular argument as seriously as I did at one time.

One of the problems in the State Department is that the geographic bureaus have their own view of the national interest. Unless you have an extraordinarily competent secretary of state and unless he has an inner group of people who would cut through the way the bureaus interact and argue with each other and hone decisions to the lowest common denominator in order to satisfy everybody, a president is bound to be impatient. I don't really know what the final answer is because we do have the bureaus in the State Department in order to be expert on particular parts of the world. That makes integration hard.

Someone made the comment about Jeane Kirkpatrick and the Falklands crisis noting that she was taking the position of Argentina. Whether Jeane did or didn't do this, the Latin American bureau in the State Department is going to have a lot of sympathy with how the Argentines look at the Falklands. The European bureau and the rest of us who have spent our lives putting together NATO are going to have a lot of sympathy with the way the British look at the Falklands. You need a secretary of state and a president to say this is how it's going to be. If you don't, then you have no overall view of what the national interest is. It's a tough issue to settle.

The President has to say, "I've been elected by the American public, and the buck stops here. I'm getting all kinds of advice. I'm going to do it this way." Yet the next thing we know somebody pops up and says he overrode the Joint Chiefs of Staff (JCS) who unanimously told him not to do it. Or someone will say he overrode his entire Cabinet, or he overrode five out of six Cabinet officers, or he had the Senate Foreign Relations Committee in there and they told him not to do it and he did it anyway. We've got to make up our mind whether we want a president who sometimes puts his foot down and says, "This is how I'm going to do it because this is what I think is right for the country," or whether we want a president who says, "This guy says this thing; this guy says that thing; I'd better sort of thread the needle." I don't think there is a finite answer for that problem.

**QUESTION:** British experience has been that prime ministers want to pick out of Department of Defense and Foreign Office people those who tend to be regarded as generalists who can see the thing as a whole because the prime minister has to see the forest rather than the trees. There is a strong tendency, I think, in English prime ministers not to rely on people who have spent all their lives dealing with Latin America or the Arab world or Russia, but rather those who are generalists.

**MR. SONNENFELDT:** I know the English Cabinet system is quite different from our system. For one thing it carries on from prime minister to prime minister. We don't have such institutions, not in the White House at least. I have long been in favor of having a small corps of people on the National Security Council staff who do in fact have appointments that overlap the presidential term, much as the chiefs of staff of our military services and the chairman of the Federal Reserve System. I think it would be helpful to do that. It would require some legislative changes but I would welcome having three or four people that couldn't be fired. I don't suppose there's anything to stop Mrs. Thatcher from consulting anybody she wants to, but you have a tradition that's more firmly established. You have a system that, partly because of a permanent undersecretary who gets carried over from administration to administration, tends to integrate these things a little more efficiently than ours. So there are some differences.

**QUESTION:** You've observed other NSC staffs. You were part of one that had some unique characteristics. Roger Morris and others have written books about Kissinger's conduct of the office. Herbert Butterfield used to say that whenever he heard the intellectuals or scholars had taken a government position, he got a particularly bad headache. That's one view reflecting the suspicion some people have of the Roger Morris types. On the other hand, Kissinger evidently thought he would gain more from having these exciting people around him than he would lose. What's the balance sheet in that regard?

**MR. SONNENFELDT:** The Kissinger crowd was mixed. Some came out of the academic world, and some came out of government. There were some *prima donnas*, most of whom didn't last very long, and some people whom I guess would be called team players. I don't know that there's ever a wholly optimal mix. I do begin to wonder, however, about the wisdom of having prominent academics as national security adviser. One shouldn't generalize because there are obviously going to be prominent academics who can do an extraordinary job. There's a role for prominent academics or people that come out of the world of thought and intellectual endeavor rather than just out of the world of bureaucracy, politics and action. I think there has to be a good mixture. You can't let the urgent drive out the important all the time. You've got to keep a balance. You can't live from hand-to-mouth and you can't have the day's events so control you that you can't try to shape them. All that requires a mixture of qualities and purpose.

In normal circumstances it's a good idea for the national security adviser to be a largely nonpublic figure and for the secretary of state—assuming he has the qualities and depending very much on the president—to be the spokesman of foreign relations for the president and for the administration to that extent that the president is not. The secretary of state must testify in the Congress—the national security adviser can't do that—and he should be the one who makes the major public speeches and who has periodic press conferences.

Academics have a tendency to want to get on the air. They have a tendency to spin grand theories about the world and the shape of things to come. Occasionally, one encounters an academic who is articulate and has thought a lot about issues but knows very little about how to make things move in a complex government and bureaucracy. This person may think that by enunciating a grand concept he has thereby created a policy and he can move on to the next grand concept. In fact, nothing happens even though he has brilliantly enunciated the policy.

Generally speaking, academics are more inclined to do that than politicians or hardened bureaucrats or whatever you want to call the people that come up in careers that require not only thinking and articulating but also doing. Without overgeneralizing and allowing for the exceptions of which there will be many, we are better off having secretaries of state as public explainers and promulgators of policy with the President who must himself under our system be the principal spokesman.

**QUESTION:** You rightly worry about the ability of historians and academics, some fifty years after the event, to reconstruct what was really happening when a certain issue was before the country. I wonder how very different that position is from that of politicians trying to decide what is really happening now in Washington on any issue of the moment. It seems to me that all histories differ because people remember different things. It isn't that they're lying or that they're arguing for particular audiences. Rather what's going on at any particular moment is itself comprised of multiple factors. It's here that the worried academic tends to come forward with schemes for reforming the government and trying to get foreign policy views accepted. But what's going on in the decision-making process in Washington is much more haphazard than I would wish.

**MR. SONNENFELDT:** I don't disagree with you and I certainly wouldn't disqualify academics from coming forward with ideas of how better to arrange the decision-making process or the government. In fact I would be inclined to turn more to some types of academics in this respect than to bureaucrats or certainly to a mixture of the two. I was being slightly facetious on a slightly different point and that is the natural proclivity of the academic is to think, as the saying goes, that the use of conceptual terms is salutary in itself in giving a sense of direction and in helping the president and other actors to shape their own ideas. There is a strong temptation on the part of articulate intellectuals to confuse enunciation with policy.

**QUESTION:** I take that point. My purpose was not to defend academics who can defend themselves. My worry is for the politicians.

**MR. SONNENFELDT:** The question of what an issue is and how to deal with it is very elusive at the moment that it arises. Sometimes you get a perspective on it with hindsight and sometimes things that seem extraordinarily important at the time move on into a more appropriate perspective.

**QUESTION:** But don't you lie awake at nights worrying that people are making major decisions without being as well informed as they might be?

**MR. SONNENFELDT:** I don't lie awake at night worrying about that because it's endemic. I don't know of a way to correct it totally. You can't know everything, and of course it's the essence of decision-making, especially in these areas, that when you wait long enough so that you can be sure you know everything the issue has passed you by. You've got to make decisions with incomplete information and you've got to act on hunches. You've got to do the best you can with what you know or think you know at the time. That's why we elect people the way we do and why, when we select them for appointed positions, we try to find people who can make good decisions on incomplete information.

I myself have never spent nights awake wondering whether I made the right decision the day before. In my case it was more giving the right advice because I was only rarely in a place where I could actually make a decision that moved people or did things in a non-recallable fashion. But that's a question of temperament. There are a lot of people, including Kissinger incidentally, who after some major decision would chew the cud for days as to whether it was right or not. While that sounds very salutary because it shows that such people aren't quite as arrogant and self-assured as they are pictured as being, it can also go too far. You can gnaw yourself to death. At least one should wait and see what the results are and try to change matters later. I myself don't think it's good to make decisions and then spend the next month tearing yourself apart as to whether you made the right decision.

**NARRATOR:** I know all of us would like to go on indefinitely discussing these issues. This experience with Helmut Sonnenfeldt is something we have observed before. Whenever he takes part in discussions, new areas are opened up and fruitful dialogue occurs. I know I speak for all of you in thanking him for being with us.

# AN AMBASSADOR'S PERSPECTIVE

## Kenneth Rush

**MR. THOMPSON:** Kenneth Rush is a lawyer, industrialist and public servant. He has had a long and distinguished career in business and government. He was a member of both the Nixon and the Ford administrations. Under Nixon he served as ambassador to the Federal Republic of Germany from 1969 to 1972 and under Ford as ambassador to France from 1974 to 1977. He was a member of various presidential commissions on food, trade, wage and price stability, and urgent problems. He was deputy secretary of state, secretary of state *ad interim*, and deputy secretary of defense. He was also president of Union Carbide and chairman of its general operating committee.

Early in his career he taught at the Duke Law School and one of his students was Richard Nixon. He is a graduate of the University of Tennessee and holds a J.D. from Yale University. Since leaving government he has served on numerous boards and committees, has been chairman of the Atlantic Council for eight years, and co-chairman with Edmund Muskie of the Joint Atlantic Council—Former Members of Congress Committee that reviewed presidential-congressional relations and foreign policy. Wherever he has served, presidents, corporations and advisory groups have turned to him for leadership and wise counsel. It is a privilege to have Secretary Rush with us this morning to discuss the Nixon presidency.

**AMBASSADOR RUSH:** Thank you very much, Ken. I thought I would discuss, in general terms, my personal relationship with President Nixon. That reminds me of a Russian story. When I was ambassador to Germany and was involved in negotiating the Berlin Agreement, my counterpart in the Four Power talks was Abrasimov, the Soviet ambassador to East Germany. One day I was upbraiding him because he wouldn't discuss details; he wanted to talk in generalities. I told him we'd never get anywhere unless we got down to the real problems of access and maintenance of the ties between Berlin and the FRG. "Well," he said, "that reminds me of a story. There was a man lying in the streets of Moscow dead drunk. A policeman came along and kicked him and said, 'Get up, get up.' The drunk looked up and asked, 'Where am I?' The policeman said, 'You're on Gorky street.' The drunk said, 'Leave out the details, what city is it?'" I will leave out the details and give you a few highlights of the history of my relationship with President Nixon.

In 1936 I was offered a job teaching law at Duke. One of my students was Richard Nixon. He impressed me very much. He was second in his class scholastically. He was president of the student body and editor of the *Duke Law Review*. He was a brilliant man and obviously popular. He and two other students who were short of funds had built a little cabin in the Duke forest where they lived to save money.

During the years between 1937 and 1969, I didn't see Nixon much and we didn't really stay in touch. He had gone back to California and I was in New York City. While he lived in New York City in the 1960s we occasionally played golf and had lunch together. One night in 1969 at a private dinner he asked me if I would be on his Industry Advisory Committee. This was before he was nominated for President that year. I said, "Yes." I donated a total of three thousand dollars to his campaign. After he was elected President, according to Ehrlichman's book, *Witness to Power*, "Nixon yearned to recruit his old law professor Kenneth Rush; perhaps he could join the Cabinet or direct the CIA."

I was sitting in my office in the Union Carbide Building in New York City in May of 1969 when Peter Flanigan, the President's assistant and a friend of mine, telephoned. He said that President Nixon wanted me to be ambassador to the Federal Republic of Germany. This call was in accordance with Nixon's custom of having one of his assistants initially approach a perspective presidential appointee to avoid the undue pressure involved in the President's making the first approach directly, an illustration of Nixon's considerateness. I thought over the offer and my first reaction was quite negative. Here I was in my late fifties and leading a very interesting life as President of Union Carbide. Acceptance would mean a complete upheaval in my life. I knew it meant putting control of my financial affairs into a blind trust and I realized the other negatives of going into government. But then, after talking it over with my wife, I decided to accept, a major factor being my high regard for President Nixon and my desire to help him achieve his objectives.

During my period of about three years as ambassador to Germany, the major event was the negotiation of the Berlin Agreement. I'll give you an illustration of how the White House worked at the time. I saw the President whenever I came to Washington, but never through appointments made by the State Department. Henry Kissinger would tell me that the President wanted to see me. I would go over and see the President. Henry would be with us at times. Both Henry and the President told me about how meek the State Department was and how it couldn't keep secrets. They had strong feelings about the need for secrecy in diplomacy. They told me about China, about the prospects for détente with the Soviet Union, and about their hopes for an agreement on Berlin because, without a Berlin Agreement, there could be no détente with the Soviet Union.

I'm a great admirer of Henry Kissinger, an extraordinarily brilliant statesman, and Bill Rogers is a friend of mine. But Henry had a deep suspicion of the loyalty of Bill Rogers and the State Department to the President. Henry was a master at manipulating the media, through leaks and otherwise. This sometimes resulted in the leaks from Henry being attributed by President Nixon to State or Defense. President Nixon would then get more and more suspicious of State and Defense and tell them less and less. This meant that more and more Henry was the only one who fully knew what was going on with regard to foreign policy.

The Four Power talks on Berlin continued for almost eighteen months, but for a long time we weren't getting anywhere. I talked to President Nixon about it. Then in February, 1971, I was called back to Washington, and John Mitchell, a friend of mine, arranged for me to have dinner with him and Henry Kissinger at Mitchell's Watergate apartment. They raised the question whether I could somehow conduct secret negotiations with Abrasimov to try to work out an agreement. I was all in favor of this because we were making no progress in the Four Power talks. Secret talks were approved by President Nixon and arranged by Kissinger through Dobrynin. I couldn't *really* negotiate with Abrasimov because he was a hardliner; he didn't seem to want an agreement. Also, he didn't speak English and my Russian is non-existent. Later, we worked out the idea of my having the secret talks with Mr. Falin, the Soviet ambassador to Bonn. He spoke excellent English, and we could easily meet for our secret talks. Wily Brandt was very much in favor of this, particularly since *Ostpolitik* depended on securing a Berlin Agreement. So I negotiated the Agreement with Valentin Falin in Bonn although I had some sessions with both Abrasimov and Falin in Potsdam.

Bill Rogers, the secretary of state, didn't know much about the secret talks that had resulted in a complete draft of agreements for the official Four Power forum. Bill Rogers is one of the finest men I've known and a longtime friend of Nixon. We had some very serious problems, however, because of his ignorance of the secret talks, complicated by the fact that Abrasimov tried to sabotage these talks until he was stopped by Brezhnev. This complete secrecy resulted in a situation in which, just as we were getting acceptance of the secret draft through the Four Power forum, Secretary Rogers sent me a cable to stop everything, that much of what I'd done was wrong and that he was going to call in the ambassadors from the other powers and inform them to this effect. I ignored the cable, the negotiations were completed, and I sent a cable to Bill Rogers saying in effect, "Wait until I get back to discuss the agreement with you. You are wrong about its violating the National Security Decision Memorandum which I have operated under."

One of Nixon's traits was that he didn't want to take up unpleasant things with anyone. For example, he didn't want personally to fire anyone. He did it through others. He is a sensitive and considerate man, contrary to what many people might think. He did not want to talk to Secretary Rogers directly about the Berlin Agreement and hear Rogers' objections to some of what I had done with Kissinger's approval.

After returning to Washington, I had my meeting with Bill Rogers and his assistants in the State Department. We were in the middle of a rather heated argument about the whole thing when a telephone call came from John Mitchell out at San Clemente: the President wanted to see me there. I went out to San Clemente the next day and had a good talk with President Nixon. He approved everything. I then had a press conference saying the President had approved the Agreement. He issued an approving statement and that was that. Throughout, Kissinger was a tower of strength. I kept him fully informed of the secret negotiations and he very skillfully handled the Washington end and gave me unqualified support.

The Berlin Agreement was signed on September 3, 1971. President Nixon wanted me to come back to Washington. Once again John Mitchell talked to me and told me that President Nixon wanted me to be deputy secretary of defense, succeeding Dave Packard. Dave Packard had felt compelled to resign because in his confirmation hearings he had agreed to donate to charity the difference between the value of Hewlett-Packard stock when he became deputy secretary of defense and the value of the stock when he left. The stock was about forty when he went in. It had later dropped to about twenty, so he was right; then it was up to forty-two and he was out nineteen million dollars. So he resigned immediately. Within a matter of months it went to about ninety-two.

The Defense Department is unique in that the deputy secretary has all the powers of the secretary and one of them has to be in Washington at all times because of the nuclear trigger. So the secretary, Mel Laird, couldn't leave Washington while the post of deputy secretary was vacant.

When John Mitchell told me that the President wanted me to be deputy secretary of defense, he also stated that the President had authorized him to tell me that the President, if he was reelected, was going to appoint me to be secretary of state at the beginning of his second term. The saga of how I became "The Secretary of State who never was," as Haldeman referred to it in his book, is outlined in Kissinger's *Years of Upheaval*, in Haldeman's *The Ends of Power*, and in Erlichman's *Witness to Power.*

Once I got in Defense I found the intrigue was as pervasive between the White House and Defense as it was between the White House and State. Secretary Mel Laird had announced that he was resigning at the end of Nixon's first term, and because Mel had opposed the invasion of Cambodia and some other policies concerning the Vietnam War, the President would rarely see him privately. Instead Nixon would call me over to the White House and I then would go back and tell Mel everything. Even the press thought that Mel had been over to see the President. Mel is a wonderful man, but he also is an intriguer and could mislead the press at times. He and Henry also had serious differences. I was the one caught in between. It was the toughest year I ever had. Mel and I worked well together though and, all in all, it worked out pretty well.

Then after his 1972 reelection, Nixon asked for the resignation of all top officials so that he could have a clean slate. Bill Rogers wouldn't give his resignation. According to Bob Haldeman's account in his book, Henry all along had been backing me to be secretary of state in order to get rid of Rogers. President Nixon called me out to Camp David and told me I was to be secretary of state at the beginning of the second term. Bill asked to stay on until May, 1972, so that it wouldn't look as though he had been ousted by Henry. Nixon consented. During the interim, I became deputy secretary of state and Bill Casey, who was to become deputy secretary, became undersecretary for economic affairs.

Then Watergate hit with a bang. Kissinger gives an account in his book, *Years of Upheaval*, of how he was designated as secretary, so I won't go through that. Nixon appointed Kissinger reluctantly. Instead of telling me directly, Nixon had Al Haig and later Bill Rogers tell me that Henry had said he wouldn't stay with the administration unless he became secretary. Henry had become a hero to the press and much of the public, although there were charges that he was deeply involved in wiretapping. This shows how brilliant he is because the press, which hated Nixon, was all for Kissinger. Al Haig said that the President felt that for his survival he had to make Henry secretary of state.

After the announcement of his appointment, one of the first things Henry did was to ask me to remain as deputy secretary. Henry continued also as assistant to the President for national security affairs and, as a unique twist, Nixon made Henry sit in the chair of that position at Cabinet and National Security Council meetings. I always sat on Nixon's right in the chair of the secretary of state, the ranking Cabinet officer. That naturally galled Henry, and it didn't help our relations very much. Nixon usually wouldn't have Cabinet meetings when Henry was in town.

At the first Cabinet meeting after Henry had been designated, Bill Rogers had resigned, but Henry hadn't been confirmed; so I was secretary of state *ad interim* for several weeks. At one Cabinet meeting and before the whole Cabinet, Nixon turned to me and said, "Ken, wouldn't you like to have your Cabinet chair?" I said, "Well, I'm not going to be acting secretary long enough for that, "Oh, yes, you ought to have it," he said. So I said, I'll be glad to have the Cabinet chair." He evidently felt very guilty about the whole thing. Nixon later wanted to bring me into the White House, and I came very close to catastrophe. Henry was shuttling in the Middle East following the Yom Kippur War in 1973, so I was administratively running the State Department. The week before Christmas 1973, Al Haig called and said that President Nixon wanted me to come over to the White House, be in the Cabinet, on the National Security Council, and be "the defender of the President." My title would be counsellor to the President. He said that President Nixon wanted to concentrate on running the presidency. I was to take over everything having to do with Watergate. I said, "Well, Al, if he wants me to do it, I suppose I have no choice." Later the President called me over and I talked to him. I said "I haven't practiced law for years; I never was a criminal lawyer." Well, he didn't want me for that purpose. He wanted to have the lawyers work for me. I was to take everything having to do with Watergate off of him. I said, "Well, who is going to run the State Department?" Nixon asked, "Who is more important, me or the State Department?" I said, "Well, obviously you are." So I said, "Well, all right, I'll do it." I was sure that he was innocent, that he was too savvy to get involved in a thing like Watergate.

Later Al Haig called and said the President wanted to announce the appointment at once. I said, "Have you told Henry?" Al said, "No." "Well, that's very unfair, isn't it? Here Henry's shuttling in the Middle East and you are announcing this without even telling him," I said. "At least you ought to tell him." Al said, "He's coming back Saturday and I'll talk to him." Henry called me Sunday morning and asked if I wanted to do this. I said "Heavens no, Henry. That's the last thing on earth I want to do, and if you can help me out of this one I'll reciprocate in any way possible." He said he would do what he could. He called me back later and said he hadn't made any headway.

Al Haig called me later that day to say that the President wanted to announce the appointment on Monday. That meant it would be on television on Christmas Eve. I said, "Well, it's crazy to announce this kind of appointment on Christmas Eve. At least let's wait until Wednesday after Christmas." He said he'd go talk to the President. He came back and said that the President agreed. I didn't hear anything further on Christmas Day. The press conference was to be at noon on Wednesday, the day after Christmas. At 11:30 I called in my staff and told them what was going to happen. Then we started listening in on the press conference and nothing was being said about it. In the middle of the conference Al Haig called me. I said, "Al, is this being announced today?" "No," he said. Henry had gone to see the President and had said that whatever the President wanted should be done. But Kissinger had continued that if I left State, he could no longer carry on the shuttle because there was no one else to run the State Department. The President had decided that the best interests of the country came first, so he would leave me in the State Department.

However, the President still wanted me in the White House, and in May, 1974, he had Al Haig ask me if I would become counsellor to the President for economic policy. I was to be the President's primary adviser, spokesman and coordinator with regard to domestic and international economic policy. One reason for my appointment was the confrontational situation between Bill Simon, secretary of the treasury, and Roy Ash, director of the Office of Management and Budget. With my title and grant of authority from the President, I was supposed to be able to control them plus the other Cabinet members. I said, "Yes, I will take the job."

Watergate was a very traumatic time. While counsellor, I saw Nixon frequently. Throughout that period we never talked about Watergate. He had private offices in the Executive Office Building where we would often sit and talk about the economy and foreign policy. He always talked business. He never wanted to talk trivial stuff. He was perfectly calm throughout. We would go out on the Sequoia about twice a week. I'd go to Camp David on weekends. I never saw President Nixon take more than one drink. Now all he takes is a glass of wine. So if all these drinking stories are true, I never saw any evidence of it and, in fact, I know that they are false.

When we were in San Clemente in the summer of 1974, the opinion came down from the Supreme Court that some of the tapes must be released. Then we knew the end had come. I was not really involved in the resignation, but I saw him on other matters during those final days. I saw him in the White House the last day of his presidency and heard that very emotional speech he gave just before he flew off to California and private life.

Later, in September, 1974, President Ford appointed me ambassador to France. One day while I was at my desk in the Paris embassy I had a call from President Nixon. He wanted to give David and Julie a trip to France and wondered if I would find a nice villa for them, not a chateau but a pleasant place along the Riviera. I said I would. We had a chat and then he said, "Why don't we stay in touch by writing and otherwise? Then I can be informed about your mission in France and I'll give you my views." So we corresponded frequently throughout my period in France. I've now decided to give my official papers to the Hoover Institution and the Nixon Library to be located at San Clemente. Included in these papers is this extensive correspondence with President Nixon which, I think, will be interesting to historians.

When I came back from France after Carter became President, Nixon started having small dinners at his house in New York City and later at Saddle River in New Jersey. He invited my wife and me and about four other people to an early one. Later he turned them into more serious affairs, without wives present, for discussion of important national and international issues. He also resumed making speeches and other public appearances and has gradually come back into the mainstream. He has written several books, including *The Real War* and *The Real Peace.* He has thoughtfully sent me an autographed copy of each one.

**QUESTION:** Since we are in another age of summits, and you were ambassador to Germany and negotiated with Berlin, could you give us some insights from your experience on how Mr. Nixon viewed the process of dealing with this tough bunch of Soviet leaders?

**AMBASSADOR RUSH:** President Nixon's basic philosophy was that our competition with the Soviet Union was permanent. The Soviet Union represents a system of dictatorial power vested in its self-appointed rulers where for all practical purposes power comes from the top; the people are oppressed and a favored few get the best of everything. Our system is based on the concept that power comes from the people, that the people can change policy and remove officials and that they have the freedoms that we all value so much. These two systems are always going to be in conflict no matter what they are called, whether you call it communism, dictatorship, "the divine right of kings," or whatever. In the nuclear age where we can destroy the world, we have to learn to get along with the Soviet Union and conduct the competition between the systems in a way that avoids actual confrontation that might lead to nuclear war. That was Nixon's great purpose. But the concept is not appeasement. In concentrates on areas of mutual interest where each is better off by easing tension and settling issues rather than through confrontation. That was his approach with regard to both China and the Soviet Union.

He also believed that we should not make an agreement for agreement's sake, but only if the agreement is mutually beneficial. An agreement that is too much in our favor is just as bad as an agreement too much in theirs because they won't live up to it; it just creates acrimony. He also believed that when you are dealing with a secret society, at times you have to deal with them secretly. It is awfully hard to do everything openly. With our open society, some secrecy is often necessary for progress with closed societies. For example, if President Nixon had announced publicly his objectives with regard to China you would have had the old upsurge of emotions about Taiwan; those who supported Taiwan most were his own supporters. He'd never have gotten anywhere. The Congress and the press would have started to debate, emotions would have been aroused, and nothing would have been accomplished.

Nixon was able to bring about rapprochement with China by handling it secretly, followed by favorable publicity through the impact of television on his visit to China. He did it all in a way that caused a minimum of dissent in this country and didn't reopen the debate about Taiwan. Presidents Carter and Reagan have maintained Nixon's China policy because it is a wise policy. The same thing was true with regard to détente with the Soviet Union; that was Nixon's idea after the secret negotiations on Berlin. We'd never get anywhere if we kept arguing and arguing among ourselves because in that case people like Richard Perle in the Defense Department, for example, who contend that any agreement with the Soviet Union is a bad agreement, might be able to block a policy of moving from confrontation to negotiation. Nixon is basically a very secret man. As President he liked to make decisions and he felt that the decision process can be destroyed by too much openness too soon.

**QUESTION:** I wonder if I might follow up with a footnote. Ambassador Rush, will you give us some of President Nixon's insights on that Berlin accord? It seems to me to be one of the most durable and effective agreements achieved in the entire Nixon administration. What did you have working in your favor that made it possible?

**AMBASSADOR RUSH:** We had, first of all, Brandt's *Ostpolitik*. The Moscow Agreement, which Brandt had negotiated and signed in August of 1970, was conditioned upon a Berlin Agreement. The Moscow Agreement recognized that there could only be changes in the existing borders of Europe by peaceful means. The Soviet Union considered this to be a substitute for a formal peace treaty. There has never been an overall peace treaty after World War II. The second thing was that Brezhnev and the government of the Soviet Union saw great benefits for themselves in trade and economic matters if they could establish better relations with us. The thing that was preventing the agreement was deep suspicion on both sides. There were many people on our side who felt that any kind of Berlin agreement would be bad, that the Soviet Union was out to use this as a means of finally getting control of Germany. The Soviets, in turn, had their deep suspicions of us.

We were able to dispel Soviet suspicion. Once both sides decided that an agreement was possible, I pressed hard to get the best terms possible. It has worked out well for the past fifteen years and I hope it will continue to be effective during the years to come.

**QUESTION:** Did you have any feeling about whom Abrasimov was speaking for?

**AMBASSADOR RUSH:** Abrasimov was determined to prevent the Berlin negotiations from going through the Dobrynin-Kissinger channel. Kissinger tried several times to get something through the Dobrynin channels but without success. This was obviously because of infighting in the Soviet Union. Falin told me that he had a direct line to Brezhnev and Gromyko, as I had to Nixon and Kissinger, and that Abrasimov was a party man, not a diplomat.

**QUESTION:** Ambassador Rush, you told us about Mr. Nixon's problems with his secretary of state and his secretary of defense. He also had problems with his vice presidential nominee. Do you understand those problems as errors in judgment or do you think he was threatened by people in high office because they conceivably could be candidates to replace him and that Mr. Kissinger, being born outside the country, was not in that category? How do you account for this feuding?

**AMBASSADOR RUSH:** I don't think that there was any such threat. Bill Rogers had no possibility of being nominated for President. He didn't have any political base. I don't think Mel Laird did either. President Nixon wanted to be his own secretary of state in charge of his own foreign policy. Foreign policy, the Vietnam War, and the Defense Department were inextricably interrelated. Laird had opposed the invasion of Cambodia and that's when he lost favor with Nixon. Tom Moorer, chairman of the Joint Chiefs, and Mel Laird were not very close. Mel was bypassing Tom to get to General Abrams, our commander after Westmoreland in Vietnam, and this was known to Nixon. Mel had a very strong influence on the Hill. The President felt that Mel was undermining him on Cambodia and various other aspects of his policy for Vietnam, which Mel would not have done, even though he was opposed to aspects of the policy. The President never had anything personal against either Laird or Rogers that I know of. Kissinger and Nixon had the idea that if Rogers came in on policy decisions the State Department would know about it, it would then be leaked and the whole policy would be destroyed. Again Nixon felt that if his policy with regard to China and the Soviet Union became public too early, this policy would be destroyed by leaks and by political controversy. So he wanted to keep it as tightly held as possible.

It was a case of the President being dedicated to trying to achieve the benefits of what he felt was the correct foreign policy. He felt, unjustly I think, that Mel and Bill Rogers were not cooperating on this. Of course, Henry wanted everything to go through him. The way the National Security Council was organized helped achieve this. Committees were the action groups, not the NSC itself. Henry was chairman of the committees. The Verification Panel had SALT; the Washington Special Action Group had

Vietnam and crisis situations; the Senior Review Group had the Defense budgets and all that. But the members of those committees were not the secretary of state or the secretary of defense, but rather the deputy secretary of state, the deputy secretary of defense, the chairman of the Joint Chiefs, the head of the CIA, and, on special things like the SALT talks, the head of ACDA or later on the head of the negotiating team, Alexis Johnson.

Therefore, the recommendations going to the President through Henry from these groups, which were the action groups, did not include the secretaries. We'd discuss everything there and Henry could go to the President and say this is what the committees have recommended. The secretaries weren't in on the committee discussions. It was a very clever way of keeping the secretaries from participating in the decision-making process until it reached the National Security Council, by which time the President had pretty well made up his mind. It was a process of organization which was very cleverly designed to try to keep the President in direct control.

**MR. THOMPSON:** The deputies didn't report back?

**AMBASSADOR RUSH:** Oh, yes, I would go back and tell Mel Laird everything that happened the minute it took place.

**MR. THOMPSON:** By then the report had gone up.

**AMBASSADOR RUSH:** We had had the discussion. If Mel wanted to he could step in and try to stop it. But stopping something after that is much harder than it is when it has just started. In the Defense Department we would always discuss issues ahead of time as much as possible.

**QUESTION:** Do you think that would have changed if there hadn't been Watergate and you had become secretary of state? If Kissinger had stayed would you have been another Bill Rogers?

**AMBASSADOR RUSH:** First of all, Kissinger had some problems with Nixon. Following Nixon's re-election in

November, 1972, Nixon lost a lot of confidence in Kissinger after Henry's "Peace is at hand" speech just before the election and after the debacle of the peace process after the election. You remember that President Nixon started the "Christmas bombing" of Vietnam then. He would call me to go over Henry's telegrams of his negotiations in Paris with Le Duc Tho during the crucial December 1972 period. He was very critical of Henry's conduct of the negotiations. He told me that he didn't know whether he was going to keep Henry or not. Henry's book tells you something about this too. The only question was whether Henry would be there or wouldn't be there. He was somewhat out of favor with the President. Now if he hadn't been there then of course being secretary of state would have been a very desirable job. If he had been there the question is whether I would have had the same treatment that Bill Rogers had because Bill Rogers was a good friend of President Nixon too. But Henry and I got along very well, and Henry wanted me to be secretary of state. I don't know what would have happened. We'll never know.

**QUESTION:** You mentioned you were convinced early on that President Nixon was not in any way involved in the Watergate situation. You explained that to yourself by saying you were just convinced that he was much too bright to get involved in anything like that. Do you think you radically misjudged him from his early days?

**AMBASSADOR RUSH:** Watergate was one of those things like the pimple that becomes a cancer. I would say frankly that the political tactics of Nixon were no worse than those of Johnson or Kennedy or a lot of others. Nixon had developed a distrust of the press. The press hated him from the very beginning of his political career when he first defeated Jerry Voorhis for Congress and later Helen Gahagan Douglas for the Senate, and then destroyed the hero of the eastern liberal establishment, Alger Hiss. Then he was the hatchet man for Eisenhower. The liberal press developed a hatred for him that was unbelievable. I ran into it all the time. Then one thing that really capped the climax was when Abe Fortas was prevented from being chief justice by a Senate filibuster. Abe was very close to

Johnson; he made Johnson. He is the one who was the successful lawyer for Johnson in the court challenge after Johnson won the Democratic nomination for Senator by some seventy-eight votes and when, in one county, there were several hundred more votes for Johnson than there were people living there. Abe went all the way to the Supreme Court with the case. He won it and he was Johnson's closest adviser.

But Warren made the mistake of resigning as chief justice a little bit too late. The Republicans filibustered until Nixon was elected. Then John Mitchell found out about Abe. Abe was the hero of the eastern liberal establishment, even after that. But it turned out that Fortas, while he was a justice on the Supreme Court, had gone down to see Louis Wolfson in jail. They entered into a consulting contract which would pay Abe $20,000 a year, or if he died, his wife for her lifetime. When this came out Abe had to resign. He was in Yale Law School with me—a very smart man. All this increased the hatred of Nixon tremendously. You remember how they went wild in defeating Haynesworth for confirmation as a justice of the Supreme Court to succeed Fortas. The establishment press' hatred of Nixon was unbelievable.

The emotionalism of the Vietnam War fed on that too. By way of contrast, the press loved Jack Kennedy; he couldn't do anything to destroy himself. They would cover up for him no matter what. Everybody knew about his sexual peccadillos but nothing ever came out about it in public while he was President.

President Nixon thinks that Martha Mitchell's problems and John's worry about her caused John not to veto this Watergate stuff. Anyway, John is the sort of man who would just smile at stupid ideas instead of decisively saying, "No, you can't do that." I think Liddy and the others thought they had *carte blanche* to go ahead, so they did the wiretapping in the Watergate. President Nixon was in Moscow at the time. He obviously didn't know anything about it. When he came back, he was awfully busy. When he heard about it, unfortunately, the first thing he said was, "Well, let's keep quiet and see if we can't ride this through." That started the whole sequence, but such serious results would not have happened if the press hadn't hated him so much. They adopted the tactics that Hitler had used, "If you just keep repeating and repeating and repeating something, even if it is a lie, people will begin to believe it." In the press, particularly in the *Washington Post*, variations of the same story, like the Hughes story which had been printed much earlier, came out over and over again. They'd bring out that Mrs. Nixon had accepted all kinds of jewels—things that were absolutely untrue. The press was determined to get him. This is politics; if you lose out in a revolution, as Louis XVI did, you lose your head. It was the same sort of feeling towards him. It was just one of those things that happens in politics.

**QUESTION:** Isn't it true that the Soviet Union approached the United States and the United Kingdom in 1969 about a so-called preemptive attack on Chinese nuclear facilities?

**AMBASSADOR RUSH:** I have heard that story but I only know what I've read.

**COMMENT:** When I was in China some of the Chinese officials expressed their appreciation for Mr. Nixon, not only for his policy but they made reference to this incident and what a wonderful thing he did.

**AMBASSADOR RUSH:** I have no firsthand information on it. All I know is what I've read.

Incidentally, I might tell you a story that Abrasimov told me. He was in China for years and knew Mao in the middle fifties. Mao would call him at night. Mao said the reason he did that was that while the Americans were awake, he didn't dare sleep. Mao was convinced that the United States was going to invade China. He said that when the Americans did come in, he'd have a thousand soldiers who would surround each American soldier; he'd have a thousand times as many soldiers as we did. He would thereby neutralize our forces and win the war.

**QUESTION:** One speaker criticized Nixon's administrative ability. He had some rather caustic remarks about Nixon as administrator as vice president. I had always thought of Nixon, from outward and visible signs, as one who seemed to have a good administrative view of the presidency. I wonder if you could comment on Nixon the administrator.

**AMBASSADOR RUSH:** As an executive, I think he had a lot of good qualities; as an administrator, I'd say that he did not excel. There was too much chaos. Many people in power promote friction; they encourage the divide and conquer concept. They do not encourage the formation of a cohesive working team, so they are the only ones who can decide anything. Their power comes from the fact that their teams can't work together. We didn't have that with Nixon. But if a good administrator is someone who has people working together in harmony toward a common objective, then I'd say he was not a great administrator because he believed in working primarily in secret and in keeping anyone who didn't have to know from knowing. Thus, the vital sense of participating was missing among many of the staff.

In a large corporation, you have people around you that you can trust. You delegate power and if they don't come through, you fire or move them. In government you have an entirely different thing. The President may make a decision and then those opposed to it will try to undermine it. They'll try to get the Congress to undermine it and then the press.

When I was deputy secretary of defense, I'd have a small group in, let's say, on some procurement matter involving maybe large sums of money. I would make a preliminary decision and sign it. It was supposed to be in complete secrecy. Within hours, I'd start getting calls from the chairmen of committees on the Hill, the ones who had lost out. Pressure began the minute you signed it, ostensibly in complete secrecy. But I would not give Nixon a high grade as an administrator.

**MR. THOMPSON:** Would you give him high grades for his knowledge of the economy and the way the economy worked?

**AMBASSADOR RUSH:** I'd give him very high grades in foreign policy, which is his primary interest. He also took a very keen interest in the economy because the strength of foreign policy depends upon the economy. During those last months, about every two or three weeks, I would have top industrial leaders come in and meet with Nixon. They were much impressed by his grasp of economic issues. He knew the economy in a profound way.

You will remember the oil conference of 1974 that we had where Jobert, the French Foreign Minister, got into a serious debate with Kissinger. Nixon gave a speech to the delegates about the economics of the oil picture. After it was over I was walking out with Helmut Schmidt. He said that it was the most brilliant speech he had ever heard. Nixon didn't use a note. He knew the complete economic setup of the entire world on oil. He is a profound student; he knows economics, but his great interest is foreign policy.

**MR. THOMPSON:** Was that foreign policy interest apparent at Duke when he was a student?

**AMBASSADOR RUSH:** No.

**MR. THOMPSON:** How did it get started?

**AMBASSADOR RUSH:** I think he was always interested in politics. The more interested you are in politics—unless it is local politics—the more exciting foreign policy is. The place where you can do something is in foreign policy. You can tackle the farm problem or the trade deficit or the monetary structure but it is like attacking a pillow—you push in here and it comes out there. In foreign policy you have the fate of the country at stake; that's the exciting part of international political life.

**MR. THOMPSON:** It is fitting that Mr. Newman, a member of the Executive Committee of the Miller Center, ask the final question.

**MR. NEWMAN:** In looking over your career, Mr. Rush, with several different positions serving the President and thinking in terms of structuring an efficient governance perspective, to what areas would you give top priority?

**AMBASSADOR RUSH:** If you think of the origins of our country, the Founding Fathers did not want any one branch of government or any person to have too much power. So they diffused the power. Power was diffused between the states and the federal government. Getting the states to ratify the Constitution was of course a very difficult thing. All powers not given expressly to the federal government were to be reserved to the states. At the federal government level, the idea was to diffuse power between the executive and the legislative so that you wouldn't have too strong an executive. The judiciary gradually assumed more and more powers because they took on the job of interpreting the Constitution.

The power is now so diffused that the executive can work for years to negotiate a SALT agreement, SALT II for example, and then it cannot be ratified by the Senate. We have to tell the world we've got an agreement but we can't ratify it. Then we announce that we'll live up to it anyway. So we have all the burdens of this agreement without the benefits. Under SALT II the Soviets were going to destroy hundreds of ICBM's and make other concessions; we didn't get any of that because we didn't ratify the agreement. If anyone makes an agreement with us they don't know whether it will be ratified or not. We say we will back a country like South Vietnam; Kennedy said so; Eisenhower said so; Johnson said so; Nixon said so; and Congress says no. Near the end, Congress wouldn't even appropriate money for South Vietnam to purchase ammunition.

When I was ambassador to France, Henry Kissinger and I talked to President Giscard d'Estaing of France about Angola. He agreed secretly that if the U.S. would supply the money, he would supply the helicopters, the mobile equipment and the like for the anti-communist forces in Angola. Then Congress passed the Clark Amendment saying no money could be spent in Angola. So France was left holding the bag. Questions arise as to our credibility and reliability.

We must continue to be the world leader; whether we can continue with this kind of disarray is unknown. If I were suggesting changes, I think that we should study the French system of a strong president, a premier who is head of government and a parliament to which the premier is responsible. But the respective powers and responsibilities of the president and the premier are ambiguous where the president does not control the parliament. So there may be weaknesses when that condition arises.

In our system no one in Congress is elected to represent the national interest. A Senator represents only his state; a Congressman represents his district. One can change parties, as Wayne Morse and Strom Thurmond did. There is little party discipline. Therefore sectional and special interests dominate the thinking of the members of Congress. Some do rise above it, at least part of the time. Churchill in effect said of democracy that it is a bad system, but it's the best there is.

**NARRATOR:** We are grateful to Kenneth Rush for his thoughtful discussion. We hope he will continue to have an interest in the Miller Center. We shall cherish his encouragement and support. Thank you very much.

# VII.

# RENEWAL

# NIXON IN EXILE

## Stephen Hess

**MR. THOMPSON:** We are pleased to welcome you to a Forum with Stephen Hess, a Senior Fellow of the Brookings Institution since 1972. He is the author of one of the early books on Nixon written jointly with Earl Mazo called *Nixon: A Political Portrait.* He is also the author of books on the Washington reporters, on organizing the presidency, and, with the late Malcolm Moos, on the story of the political campaigning of presidential candidates entitled *Hats in the Ring.*

He was born in New York and educated at the University of Chicago and Johns Hopkins. He served as staff assistant to President Eisenhower and deputy assistant for urban affairs in the Nixon administration. He has continued to lecture and write and has had both domestic and international experience, having been an alternate delegate to UNESCO and to the United Nations in the mid-seventies. He is respected by political scientists and researchers and, best of all, he knows how to write.

**MR. HESS:** Ken's introduction suddenly reminded me of General Eisenhower's favorite cartoon from the old *Saturday Evening Post.* It showed a man at a lectern saying, "Our next speaker needs all the introduction he can get." You gave it to me, Ken, and I appreciate it.

**MR. THOMPSON:** I'm also reminded that you wrote a book on political cartoons.

**MR. HESS:** Oh, yes, that's right.

Writing the Nixon biography also reminded me of one of life's most horrible moments. My colleague Earl Mazo and I were interviewing Nixon for what would be a verbatim appendix to the book. We were in his study at his home in New York at 62nd Street and Fifth Avenue, and he was sitting there with a hassock in front of him on which there was a soft pillow. We had two tape recorders; I put one under the pillow on the hassock to be a little less obtrusive. The other tape recorder had a special two hour tape. We started the interview and, about ten minutes into it, I saw the tape snap, but I felt very confident because I had the second one hidden on the hassock. We got back to our hotel room and played the tape but there was nothing on it. The pillow had muffled the sound. We called him up and Nixon was very nice about reconstructing the more important parts of the conversation over the phone. If you happen to find the book, there is such an interview.

**COMMENT:** You mean, he didn't have a tape himself?

**MR. HESS:** I always vowed that I would never write a book or give a talk that might be called, "Presidents Who Have Known Me." And here I am. I don't know; maybe it is Ken's persuasive powers; maybe it's just that time has passed, but I want you to know that I feel a little uncomfortable, even after all these years. I do feel, as I think you probably feel, too, that many of us belong to another era in which we didn't repeat private conversations in public. Our mothers lectured us on not telling tales out of school. I never talked publicly about Richard Nixon before, but I do think now that my recollections should be part of the historical record. This will be very tame compared to what others have said.

The trend towards memoirs does trouble me, as I think it should all of us. In government today, everyone seems to have their million dollar book contract. Everything is spoken for the record, and I think we are all poorer for that. We probably don't have the sort of give and take that we had when I entered government in the Eisenhower years. In fact, I can recall very well that when we left government the staff generally considered that the only staff person who had a right and obligation to write his memoirs was Sherman Adams, because he had been personally attacked. Otherwise, the record would be written by General Eisenhower. When one staff member, Bob Gray, actually wrote an innocuous little book called *Sixteen Acres Under Glass*, we were all shocked. To think today we are reading David Stockman on the machinations of Reagan's first term shows how far we have come in public morality.

When Ken suggested a title and a subject, I gave a counter-suggestion, which he was gracious enough to accept. That was, "Nixon in Exile, 1961 to 1968." I am not going to focus on the Nixon presidency, but I hope that what I say may suggest some things that will help us think about Nixon.

The period from 1961 to 1968 was the only time during which my relations with Mr. Nixon were very close. I worked for him from the spring of 1961, when he had returned to California, until he started to get ready for the 1966 congressional elections, which were important to him in building future support. At that point he hired Pat Buchanan, a young man from the *St. Louis Globe-Democrat*, as his permanent staff person. Until then I was the person who was most likely to be called upon if Nixon needed speech material or help writing a newspaper column, which he had for a while, or assistance with magazine articles.

In 1965, we had been on a big swing around the country for Lincoln Day Republican dinners. Nixon always had a volunteer advance man. In this case, it was a geologist named John Whitaker, who later became secretary to the Cabinet and undersecretary of the Interior. The plane stopped to refuel in Buffalo on the way back, and Mr. Nixon and I got out and walked along the air strip. When we came back, I said to John, "Well, RN asked if I would join him full time in New York, and I said that I wouldn't." I had a lot of books in me that I wanted to write. I had been assistant to other people for a long time and I just felt that I couldn't make that move. Whitaker said, "Well, that's going to change your relationship with him." I said, "What do you mean?" He said, "You said no to him." Nixon and I were always cordial after that, and I was involved in his administration, but I think that John was right. I never had quite the same relationship with Nixon.

*Stephen Hess*

Let me first say, as someone who was a ghost writer to Mr. Nixon, and in fact to two other presidents and various other public people, he was by far the most satisfactory person for whom I ever wrote. It's a very difficult relationship, as you can imagine. Probably it can be best described in psychological terms. Usually a person who can afford a speech-writer has a considerable ego but the presence of a speech-writer represents a need which the person is apt not to want to recognize. Relationships can be very strained, as many of my colleagues from other administrations have told me.

With Nixon it was quite different for a variety of reasons. The first one probably had to do with Nixon's regard for the writing process. He himself found it very difficult but very satisfying writing *Six Crises*. I did not work on the book, but he told me at that time that it was one of the hardest and most satisfying things that he had ever done. So he had a respect for writers and I think that was important.

The second thing was that he was deeply involved in the process of writing speeches, articles, and newspaper columns. It was a special relationship which would tend to lead to friendships. In contrast, I can recall talking to one person who had been a speech-writer for Lyndon Johnson. This may not be true of all of his speech-writers, but in describing the way that he did it, he said he simply wrote the speech. If Johnson liked it, he used it verbatim, word for word, changed nothing. If he didn't like the speech, he threw it away. Now that was not the foundation of a great friendship, but my working with Nixon on speeches really was. We worked very well together.

Also, I found it easy to write for Nixon, because he had a distinct style. I spent two and a half years as a speech-writer for Eisenhower, and I found it very difficult. I did not understand his cadence, his rhythm. Of course, it was at the end of the administration and he had had a stroke. He could not handle certain sounds as well as others. I would change the sentence structure to try to accommodate the way I knew he could handle something. He would always change it back to ways which were difficult, but ways he had learned sixty years before. With Nixon, although I did not have the time to watch him do five or six speeches a day because I was busy working on the next day's speeches, I would make a point of going to at least one speech each day. I wanted to be sure that my ear stayed accustomed to the rhythm of his voice and his qualities. So it was a good relationship in that way too.

He was very generous with his praise, which was a very unusual quality. I can remember Jimmy Carter had asked me for some help during the (1976-77) transition, because I had just recently written a book called *Organizing the Presidency*. His secretary called me one day on some matter and said, "You know that memo you sent to him yesterday? He wrote 'Good' across the top." She didn't quite understand why I wasn't more excited that he had written "Good" across the top. She explained, "He just doesn't write 'Good' across the top. This is very unusual." But Nixon was very generous with his praise.

Less important, but indicative of his nature, was that he also compensated me generously for my work. He was the only employer in my life with whom I never set a price, never had any formal contracts of any sort. The reason was very simple: he would send me a check for something that was far more than I would have asked or thought I deserved. I once questioned him about that. He seemed a little embarrassed and said, "Oh well, I would just pay it to the government anyway." In fact, it was his rule of thumb that on a magazine article he would send me half. For example, he would get $10,000 for a *Saturday Evening Post* article and send me a check for $5,000. Remember we are talking about 1962 and 1963, and for $5,000 you and your wife could take a trip to Europe *and* remodel your home. If I had written the article under my name, I would probably have gotten $1,000. So if I say something sharp about Richard Nixon, I do want to make sure at the outset that I have voiced my respect and debt to him for those years and my appreciation of his generosity towards me.

Since Ken's first question inquires how the association with Nixon began, I should start by saying that when the Eisenhower administration was over on January 20, 1961, I had two clients within a few months, Eisenhower and Nixon. I opened a little office to service them in different ways and for very different reasons. My Eisenhower account, if you will, was the result of the Republican National

Committee wishing to keep Eisenhower alive politically for its own purposes. To do that, there were a lot of things that had to be done—mail had to be answered, messages had to be sent and so forth. Eisenhower felt that he had earned retirement, so he had gone back to Gettysburg. This was before the days that former Presidents were given staffs. Back then, if they wanted a staff they paid for it out of their own pocket. In this case the Republican National Committee had agreed to foot the bill for Eisenhower, so I set up a little operation and the mail was bundled up at Gettysburg and sent down to Washington on a Trailways bus. We had people who sorted it and answered the letters.

The arrangement with Nixon was of a very different sort. The transition back to California was, for him, a very difficult one. California had become his voting address, but was not spiritually his home any longer. He had been away far too long. He had been in Washington fourteen years as a member of the House of Representatives and Senate and eight years as vice president. Even before that, of course, he had been in the Navy in World War II. When he came out of the Navy he almost immediately ran for public office. So it was very difficult for him to be back in Los Angeles. Nixon read the *New York Times*, the *Wall Street Journal*, the *Los Angeles Times*, but he missed the feel of Washington. It wasn't the gossip he missed because he wasn't a great gossip. He missed the touch and tone of the place. I was asked to do a newsletter for a readership of one and describe Washington to him week by week. As time went on, I took on other assignments as well, but basically that is what he wanted of me.

I remember one thing I did just because I had the time, and it seemed to be something politicians might like. Each week I would gather a list of honors and events involving people who were friends or political acquaintances of Eisenhower and Nixon. If I read in the paper that somebody's daughter was getting married, or that someone received an award, I would draft a little letter for either Eisenhower or Nixon, and they had the option of sending it. Suddenly all over Washington, I would bump into people who had received these "wonderful little notes" from Eisenhower, and were intent on telling me how thrilled they were. I thought that was very nice.

In Nixon's case, I did not hear anything until he came back to Washington for the first time. In those days all the major law firms didn't have Washington offices. Nixon actually used Bill Rogers' desk at his law firm. We met to discuss what he wanted of my operation. In the course of the discussion he said, "Oh, don't bother to send those notes to me. I really don't want to be remembered as a person who recalls people's birthdays." What a contrast! Here on the one hand was Eisenhower, considered a babe in the woods politically. Yet, the apolitical former President instinctively knew the utility of this personal touch. On the other hand, Nixon, often considered the quintessential politician, rejected this service.

That incident started me thinking, and I have never changed my view that Nixon was a very unnatural politician. He once told me about an incident that occurred when he was a student at Duke University Law School. As you recall, he was there during the height of the depression. During a boiling hot North Carolina summer, Nixon worked for a professor who had not been able to get his textbook published commercially. He was going to have it mimeographed, and then the students would have to buy it. Richard Nixon's summer job was to crank the mimeograph machine. That was before the days of Xerox, and it was an inky, dirty job. He did it in a windowless, airless room. He cranked all summer long. He said to me that in effect it all came down to ends and means. The end was getting a law degree. Anything that he had to do—cranking that mimeograph machine in that airless room—had to be done so that he would get his law degree. I always thought that going through the hoopla of politics was for Nixon rather like that.

For so many politicians the gratification they get from the crowds, the laying on of hands and all of that, really is why they go into politics. For Nixon, it was the means to the end, which was public service, and particularly, as it turned out, public service in foreign relations. Somehow I think it would have been more appropriate for Nixon to have been secretary of state and not to have gone through this glad-handing routine. It so often seemed that the words were somewhat out of place with the gestures. He was not a natural politician, although he worked very hard at it, and could occasionally be very good at it, I should say.

When Nixon decided to run for governor, it was incumbent upon me to go out there at least for several months during the primary. I will always be struck by the ironic undertones of the whole campaign. After all, as I just said, I didn't think this was spiritually his home anymore. I can clearly remember when he got out there and started to practice law. He was basically what is called "a rainmaker." It was his job to help bring in clients, to massage them, and so forth. He said to me one day, "If I have to play golf with Randy Scott one more afternoon, I think I will go out of my mind." Remember the old cowboy star, Randolph Scott? He may have used Scott symbolically, at least I hope he did. But it was just this: he was not emotionally or intellectually prepared to spend his afternoons doing anything but talking to world leaders. It was very tough on him. Now suddenly, he was going to run for governor of the state.

I think there were two reasons he ran, one more important than the other. The lesser, although not unimportant for a person who had no independent wealth—in many ways this was a serious problem for him—was that his financial backers told him that they could not continue to raise the sort of money he needed to maintain the fairly sizeable staff of an active politician if he was not running for something. That was the nature of the game and that troubled him. He was feeling very good about making so much money for the first time. He was very proud of the fact that he was building and could afford for the first time a nice home. It was in Truesdale Estates above Beverly Hills. As an Easterner it didn't impress me because I did not have any knowledge of Beverly Hills real estate—how little you get for so much. There were houses on either side, and when he put the driveway in the front and the swimming pool in the back, there literally was not one more inch of land. But Nixon knew the price and he was very proud of his new home. The first five times I visited the house, he would take me on a tour, forgetting, I guess, that he had done it already. We would stand out at the swimming pool and look across the mountains. He would say, "On a clear day, you can see Catalina." It was almost a joke. The smog was hitting us in the face, we couldn't see the other end of the swimming pool, but he would say that, and I would nod. Then one day we went there with Paul Keyes, a friend of his who was the producer of the "Jack Paar Program" and subsequently the chief writer of "Laugh In." He was a great comic writer. We were standing there, and Nixon was telling us about what we could see on a clear day, and right next to his house they were building another house. It just had the wooden frame up, and Keyes turned and said to Nixon, "That's a lovely house, but wouldn't it be a little hard to heat?" Nixon gulped, and never again took us on a tour. He was proud of these possessions. He had a right to be.

At any rate, the first reason was that not being independently wealthy, he could not pay for a staff which he needed. The second reason was that he needed an excuse not to run for President in 1964. He needed a bomb shelter to hide out in so that he could run for president in 1968. Think of the irony of that. The thought was quite obviously that if he could not have defeated John Kennedy in 1960, he would certainly not stand a chance against the incumbent Kennedy in 1964. Understanding this, the Republican party, particularly those who had other ambitions, would have tried to use Nixon as a sacrificial lamb. He had to devise a way that would preempt his running for President. Being governor of California, promising the people that he would serve his term, was such a way.

I should say that although years later I heard many advisers of that time claim they told Nixon not to run, my impression was that most people told him to run. Among other things, many of us being from Washington, the East or at least not from California, grossly underestimated Pat Brown. Brown, to us sophisticates, seemed a very bumbling sort. In fact, I can remember during that campaign one Sunday in the fall, Pat Brown was on a program like "Meet the Press." Bob Haldeman, Bob Finch and myself were watching it at the Nixon house. Nixon didn't like to see his opponent on television. He left the room and we watched. He came back in and said, "How did he do?" We had a field day. "Oh boy, he is an easy target . . . He missed that . . . He stumbled over that fact . . . He didn't get that nuance right." We were going on and on when Julie Nixon came in. She had been watching in another room. She was about thirteen or fourteen. She said, "Oh, he was marvelous. He was terrific!" She saw through fresh, unsophisticated eyes. She told us all we were wrong and she was right.

When Nixon ran for governor, Pat Brown effectively convinced California, as he said, that Nixon just wanted to double park in Sacramento on the way back to Washington, that Nixon wasn't serious about keeping his pledge not to run. That compounds the ironies, since this was one thing that Nixon was serious about: he did *not* want to go back to Washington at this point. But we could see from our own polling that this was a very effective argument. More compelling than that, Brown had been a good governor. It was very hard to build a major theme. He had been particularly good on the water question: how to get water from northern California to southern California. We found one scandal of sorts, but it was so minor that it would have been ludicrous to drag out this story about some political friend of his who had had a contract to run the Squaw Valley concessions, or something like that. So, in the absence of a major issue, we had to develop a collection of minor themes, which is a very bad way to run a campaign. We had to hope that the collection would add up to one major theme. It didn't.

We still had high hopes, in part because our crowds were terrific, as you would expect. After all, Nixon was a celebrity. He worked very hard campaigning and running for governor of California, which was about to become the most populous state. The actual campaigning in a very big state is harder than running for President. When you run for President, there are many more buffers. People also recognize that they can't go up to you and tell you their problems. A presidential campaign is on a level that can be conducted with about as much civility as you choose. You can race around the country if you want and touch hands at airports, but you don't have to. Running for governor is a different thing. The governor is your person, and the state was large enough so that on a typical day we could wake up in Los Angeles, do a noon speech in San Francisco, a dinner speech in San Diego, and be back at home in bed in Los Angeles. It was a physically brutal routine.

The turning point for Nixon, as I recall, was the Cuban missile crisis. I think that was October 22, 1962. We were in an Oakland hotel and there was Rosemary Woods, myself, and Richard Nixon sitting there watching John Kennedy tell us about this most serious threat. Nixon turned to me and said, "We are finished. We just lost the election." Now this was, I think, November 5th, so there were some two weeks left in the campaign. I said, "What do you mean? What has this got to do with us?" Nixon had a theory of peaking. Nowadays politicians use the word momentum, but it was virtually the same. He was building up to something, and if you got it right, you would peak on election day. If you got it wrong, you peaked before election day, or as in his own election in 1960, you peak after election day. He felt that was what happened—that this was like a guillotine, a knife cutting down. He felt that no one with this tremendous threat ninety miles away from our borders was going to be focusing on local or state events after that. He may or may not have been right but he was convinced, and at least two other people knew of this conviction. Obviously, neither Rose nor I were about to say anything, even to anyone on the staff.

Election day came and I was packing my office to go back home to Washington. Nixon called to say goodbye since he doubted that he would see me that night, or have much time at any rate, and wanted to thank me. I said, "You still think you are going to lose?" "Yep," he said, "I think I'm going to lose." That night I did go to the headquarters, and I wrote a concession statement for him. I didn't even go in to see him, I just sent it in and went home to bed. I woke up at about 10:00 a.m. and there he was on television marching in to give what became "My Last Press Conference." I was shocked. After all it wasn't a surprise to him that he was going to lose. In later years I never talked to him about why he did that. I assume it was just the tremendous frustration of what he saw as the early end of a public career which came so close to the presidency.

Eventually Nixon moved to New York. A move to New York was clearly another signal that he was finished politically. It was an era in which we did believe strongly in having a political base. New York was Nelson Rockefeller's political base. There was no political motive in Nixon's moving to New York. He moved to New York, partly to get away from the fallout of the disintegrating California Republican party. If he had stayed in California, he would have had to spend much of his time putting the pieces back together. He abandoned elective politics for what he saw as the fast-track in business and law. "Fast-track" was a word he repeatedly used. For him, New York was the place where people worked harder, were smarter, and became more successful than any place else. He figured he would get on that fast-track himself. When one thinks of the sequence of events after that, how he got from here to there, how he got to be the 1968 candidate and President, it's truly amazing.

Let me just say one other thing about the time in New York because it is a little bit of Nixon history that perhaps hasn't come out. In 1964, we were contemplating giving Theodore White a run for his money. He had written a marvelous book, *The Making of the President 1960.* Richard Nixon was about to sign a book contract with Doubleday as the analyst of the 1964 election. The premise was that it would be marvelous to have someone who had gone through it himself and was no longer a politician explaining to the rest of the world how the process works. I was supposed to be the legman, organize all of the research, manage a staff, etc. We were going to meet in New York on November 23, 1963, to go over this and make the final arrangements with the publisher. Richard Nixon was flying back from Dallas, Texas that day after giving a speech the night before. I was to meet him later at his office on Wall Street.

That afternoon, I was in a restaurant in downtown New York with a Doubleday editor. A waiter came up and said something about the President being dead. He happened to have a heavy Italian accent and we thought he was telling a joke. We didn't think it was funny. We went out and learned the truth from a television set in a store window. I quickly called Rose Wood and said, "What should

I do?" She said, "Get to his apartment. He will be coming in directly, I'm sure."

Nixon got off the plane and got into a taxi at LaGuardia airport. On the way in, at a red light, somebody from another car called, "Did you hear that the President has been shot?" He got home, and the doorman confirmed that the President was dead. I arrived a couple of minutes later. Nixon has said to interviewers that his recollections at that moment were of his friendship with John Kennedy, and their service in the House together. But when he opened the door for me—the first person of his circle to see him—I can assure you that to me, his reaction appeared to be, "There but for the grace of God go I."

Nixon was very shaken. He got out his attaché case and took out the Dallas morning paper which had a story about a press conference he had had the day before. He had talked about how the people of Dallas, when they disagree, should have respect for their political adversaries. This related in part to an incident in which Adlai Stevenson had been heckled and spat upon in Dallas. He was saying to me in effect, "You see, I didn't have anything to do with creating this." He was very concerned then that Kennedy had been assassinated by a right-winger, and that somehow Nixon would be accused of unleashing political hatred. I remember that he made two immediate calls. The first one was to J. Edgar Hoover, who assured him that to the best of their knowledge the assassin was a left-winger. Nixon was, I think, somewhat relieved. The second call was to Eisenhower, who was at the Waldorf Towers, and Bob Schultz said he was taking a nap and he wouldn't wake him. Then we sat around that afternoon and prepared a statement for delivery before the TV cameras that were now downstairs.

The next morning on my way back to Washington, I stopped by at the Nixons. By this time, the politicos had gathered. Len Hall, Cliff Folger, and others were already assessing how this event would affect or recreate the possibilities of Nixon running for President. But of course, as we know, Barry Goldwater got the nomination and his overwhelming loss somewhat cleared the Republican dockets. Other Republicans of Nixon's caliber had chosen not to campaign very hard for Goldwater or not to campaign at all.

Nixon, on the other hand, had worked very hard for Goldwater and Goldwater was grateful, as was the right flank of the Republican party. In 1966, Nixon again did an amazing job of campaigning for a Republican congress and in the process built a lot of political capital for himself. Then a whole series of events occurred. It was incredible. There was Richard Nixon, the man who had tried to find a bomb shelter so he wouldn't have to run for president in 1964, so he could be the candidate in 1968. He had been defeated in California, moved away from a political base, had no national organization, and yet became a candidate and then President of the United States. It's a remarkable story of endurance, perseverance, and a good bit of luck. So with that, let's turn to comments or questions.

**QUESTION:** Mr. Hess, you have been around Washington for a long time. What mindset do you think prevailed in the Nixon White House—I was one of his appointees—that convinced them that they could keep secrets in the city of Washington?

**MR. HESS:** Well, let me say, I left the administration at the end of 1971 and know none of the events first hand. I imagine much of their attitude was naive. I guess I could account for it in other ways, too. However, I was truly shocked by a lot of what I, along with the rest of the world, found out was going on. To give you a very simple example of how surprised I was, I had never heard Nixon curse. In the hundreds and hundreds of hours I spent with Nixon, often alone, the Nixon of the "expletive deleted" never emerged. When I think about it, I think that reflects a Nixon who compartmentalized things and categorized people. You were the intellectual or you were the political apparatchik. He dealt with different people in very specific ways, so that in fact, none of the most substantive people or their staffs, whether they were right of center or left of center, whether an Arthur Burns or a Pat Moynihan, were in any way implicated in the Watergate thing.

Let me stress that there was a whole side of Nixon that I clearly knew nothing about and clearly I am not a good source for that question. But I do think that certain things happen and have the potential of happening in any

White House. It has to do with the size of the place. So often a President is coddled and pandered by his staff. When you look at the Eisenhower staff, with the one exception of myself—an absolute fluke, a twenty-five- year-old who got there by accident—it consisted of people who actually stepped down to work in the White House. The place was full of former governors; Sherman Adams was just one of many. It was full of former presidents of major corporations, Clarence Randall of Inland Steel, etc. These were people who could have easily said, "Mr. President, you are wrong." Now Eisenhower tended to have people around him who agreed with him, so I don't mean that "Mr. President, you are wrong" was often said. But clearly they would have, that's the kind of men they were.

Looking at the Nixon White House, and other White House staffs, you see people who are in the best jobs they have ever had in their lives. For example, take the Carter staff. I think there were probably two Atlanta lawyers who made at least as much or more than they made on the White House staff. Yet it was characteristic that staff people then were at their top earning power. How does a person formerly making $15,000 and now suddenly making $50,000 walk in and say, "President Carter, I think you are wrong." It is very hard.

Nixon had an awful lot of people on his staff who fell into this category, though not all by any means. Yet, strangely, Nixon was very proud of the fact that he had the youngest White House staff in history. When I was on the Eisenhower staff, I was the only person in my twenties, and maybe there were a couple of people in their thirties. You look at the Nixon staff, and my own staff at that time, the Urban Affairs Council, and it looked like a kindergarten. We had people twenty-one, twenty-two, or twenty-three-years-old with huge portfolios. If it had ever gotten out that the District of Columbia, which in some ways was the smallest piece in our portfolio, was virtually being run by a twenty-two-year-old, it would have caused a scandal. Nevertheless, Nixon was very proud of having this bunch of bright young people, but he paid a price for it. He got a lot of energy, which in my judgment was often counterproductive because it moved a lot of problems into the White House that shouldn't have been there. He certainly didn't get wisdom. Occasionally you get a Bill Moyers, who at twenty-nine was a top aide to Johnson. I don't know how you make somebody that wise that young. It is not to be expected. We had a lot of energetic, bright but not very wise people on that staff.

Wisdom is an important commodity because there are so many situations that call for careful judgment. I can remember many times with Nixon during the 1962 campaign, when he would be incredibly frustrated and say, "Do x." I would think to myself, "That's really not a very good idea. I think I will wait until tomorrow and ask him again if he wants to do that." I would ask him the next day, and he would say, "No, forget about it," and go on to something else. Well, that isn't likely to happen in a White House staff of this size. Relatively few people see the president. A president signs off on something and so it gets done; and not to do it immediately is insubordination.

**QUESTION:** Didn't Nixon already have the reputation of being a somewhat ruthless hatchet man as witnessed in the Helen Gahagan Douglas campaign? Did that come through at all in your association?

**MR. HESS:** I do not feel that the 1962 campaign was particularly ruthless. In campaigns of that size there are gross acts that are performed, but almost always performed by silly people. By that I mean people around the fringes decide to put out a pamphlet or decide to do some sort of dirty trick. These tend to be done by both sides. So in the 1968 campaign you could point to incidents which, if Nixon indeed orchestrated them, he should not have been proud of, and probably the same with the campaign against Pat Brown.

My perspective in 1962 was different from that of most of the other people in the campaign. I was physically with the candidate every minute, which means that the campaign looked very different. The candidate was off making speeches, shaking hands, and was not involved in that sort of thing. The candidate shouldn't be involved in details anyway. For that he should rely on his campaign manager.

**QUESTION:** What part do you think the debates had in Kennedy's win over Nixon?

**MR. HESS:** Well, when an election is that close, everything decides it, not just the debates. I assume the debates changed some minds; they certainly were dramatic. We know that people who heard them on the radio rather than saw them on television felt differently. Nevertheless, it may have made a difference just as five or six other factors may have made a difference. It was an honorable thing for Richard Nixon to do; he was the incumbent as vice president. I think his agreeing to debate—it had never been done before—probably surprised the Kennedy people.

So much has been written about the debates, I have nothing special to add. Clearly, Nixon was the old high school or college debater. Kennedy was the one who more quickly understood the powers of this new medium. He also quickly realized who the audience was that he was addressing. It was not his opponent on that stage, but the people at home. Nixon certainly did not look well. We know he had injured his knee, how he had lost so much weight and the problems with his makeup. More than that, we know from every day that we turn on television how important these visual images are. It's the nature of television and it played a role in the debate. I don't even remember the details they discussed—Quemoy and Matsu and so forth. But the debate was certainly not a plus for Richard Nixon.

**QUESTION:** Dr. Knight Aldrich, a psychiatrist, had an interesting exchange with Elliot Richardson when he was here. Richardson's thesis was that Nixon could never forget his background, and he was forever anxious or insecure.

**MR. HESS:** Well, I think there is no question that Nixon could not escape his past. I don't know if anyone can. Things came up constantly that were repetitions of the past. Even in the 1962 campaign when he knew he was going to lose and he had to reach out and grab at something, he grabbed at what had worked for him once before—the Checkers speech. He gave another Checkers speech, but there was no reason for a Checkers speech this time, so it fell flat.

Of course, it is true of all presidents that when they can no longer run for re-election, they run, as it is said, for the Nobel peace prize. They run for their place in history, and Nixon was no different. The irony is that Nixon, the one who was most concerned about his place in history, will probably end up being the second most written about president of the twentieth century. Only Franklin Roosevelt surpasses him.

I'll tell you a little story about Nixon and his ties to his childhood. I was deputy assistant to the president for urban affairs for the first year, 1969. Basically, that meant I was chief of staff to Pat Moynihan, and by the end of that year the White House had been reorganized, and I became national chairman of the White House Conference on Children and Youth.

When I left government at the end of 1971, someone thought that it would be appropriate for me to bring in my family and formally say goodbye, given my long history with Nixon. The event was scheduled for a late afternoon, the last appointment of the day. There was a helicopter outside, ready to take him to the airport where he was to board Air Force One for Canada and a meeting with Trudeau. Nixon, as we all know, was not very good at small talk. We had exchanged gifts and as we got up to leave, he asked my eight-year-old son Charles, "What is your favorite subject in school?" My son surprised me; he said "Geography." Nixon's eyes lit up and he said, "That was my favorite subject too." He said to my son, "Travel when you are young. Don't wait until you are old; it's too late then." He illustrated his point by doing a little routine in which he was an old man with a cane walking down a ship's plank to visit China for the first time, realizing that he is too old to enjoy the experience fully. My son's eyes got bigger as Nixon continued with, "Even if you have to borrow money, *go*! Travel!" By this time the helicopter was buzzing and the military aides were frantic but Nixon would not stop. He continued talking—China, China, China. He showed my son the little bonsai plants that he had been given by the Chinese government. We were there forever while he talked about his youth, geography, moving around the world, his dreams, and so forth.

I think maybe in other people, in healthier people for all I know, we move on to the next stage. Childhood and its accompanying dreams and aspirations fade, become a memory. But I do think you are right if you are saying that that stayed very much with Nixon and was real to him.

**QUESTION:** I once asked why President Nixon recorded conversations. Elliot Richardson told me his theory. Nixon was of humble origin and was interested in making his name in history. Therefore, he made the recordings to leave them for the historians to judge. The advent of Watergate confused everything.

**MR. HESS:** I would move that around just slightly. I am convinced that he did the taping as a historical record, but not in that sense. I don't think they would ever have been in the National Archives. They were his record from which he was going to write his memoirs. I think *that* was what it was all about. I don't think it ever entered his mind that they would become public property. It was not the tapes that he was leaving to history; it was the history from the record which he was going to transcribe as he saw fit. Presidential memoirs are very strange animals. Nixon's would not have looked like those tapes at all, but the tapes would have been terribly important to him in the reconstruction of events. That is how I see those tapes.

**MR. THOMPSON:** Could we ask one last question? You've graphically described his 1960s recovery. How has he again managed another dramatic recovery in the eyes of a substantial portion of the American public? How does one explain that? What is there about him? Is it his knowledge, or is it that others are just so average by comparison?

**MR. HESS:** I think it is a combination of a man, Richard Nixon, who never gives up, and a nation that easily forgets. I think it reflects our lack of a historical memory, if you want to put it that way, or our generosity and willingness to make amends, if you look at it another way. Also, Nixon remains an interesting and useful figure. He writes books, makes speeches, and what he has to say is worth listening to. He has quite skillfully reconstructed himself once again. Perhaps it is for the betterment of the United States if we want to take advantage of his wisdom. It's not an insightful psychological wisdom. He is not willing to say, if indeed he needs to, what it was that created Watergate and the downfall of his administration. But on an intellectual level he is willing and anxious to impart what he thinks the lessons were in Vietnam, in détente, in the opening to China and in dealing with the third world. We should take advantage of that. He is a resource.

**QUESTION:** It seems to me you have described a split personality: a person that is fine when he is winning and calls on the hit men when he's losing. In the instances you have described to us, except in California, he is always winning. Did you know of any of the hit men?

**MR. HESS:** I knew some of the younger people, Egil Krogh, Ed Morgan, people who had gone to jail. Of course, I knew Erlichman and Haldeman. Some of them have written quite well about the situation, including, in his own way, John Dean. They were very, very ambitious. They did things that they thought would be supportive of their careers and pleasing to their employers. Jeb Magruder also wrote a particularly interesting book, I thought. Some of the younger people have been quite insightful. Their "case histories," though, are much more simplistic, based on "Yuppie" ambitions perhaps.

Some of them have paid a price for it. I don't know whether Chuck Colson really has religion or not, but I think by this time we probably should believe that he has. Other people have learned from that experience and my sense among some of the younger ones is that it could have happened to an awful lot of people. I don't mean to just anyone, but take Krogh, for example, who was the one involved in the plumber operation. His commander-in-chief told him that this was in the interest of national security; he was twenty-eight years old. Who was he to say that it is not in the interest of national security? I think there was some of that going on as well.

I like to think that I could not have been tempted. I once said to my cousin Carole, "I've been in public life so long and I've worked for all these presidents, yet no one has ever tried to bribe me. Why is this?" She said, "Oh, it's simple. It's body language. They know they couldn't." I hope she's right. But these were great temptations for very ambitious and often very young people.

**MR. THOMPSON:** You've never felt that the atmosphere was sinister in the circles in which you worked, or that somehow this kind of thing was encouraged in a different way than it had been, say, in the Eisenhower administration?

**MR. HESS:** Well, in the course of this series, you've had many people talk about domestic affairs and relatively few on the foreign side. In 1969 I was involved in domestic affairs. Moynihan had his shop of people and I was the Number Two. Arthur Burns had his shop and Marty Anderson was his Number Two. We had very different agendas. We had a great deal of leeway because the President was basically interested in foreign policy. I can remember when Moynihan first went to the Hotel Pierre to meet with the President-elect. When Moynihan and I had dinner later that night, he could not get over the things that Nixon said that he didn't know. Moynihan, kidding, said, "I would have bluffed it." But the President-elect did not know much about basic domestic programs. He was really consumed by international affairs.

It was almost Rooseveltian in the sense of staff conflict, although I think it was sometimes by accident. He created two shops, one with this Harvard professor and one with a Columbia professor. Both were men of great knowledge and wisdom and they built strong staffs. We fought it out quite honorably for the President's mind and soul. We sent memos back and forth, and in 1969 I felt that I was in worthy combat. In the end, we won some and we lost some. We won what we cared about most, which was the Family Assistance Plan. That was the first time a President had ever proposed what would have amounted to a guaranteed annual income for poor families—not individuals but poor *families.* It was a massive program which we felt was important. I think the Burns people's major priority may have been revenue sharing. They won on that one. It was that sort of combat. When we were replaced, we were replaced by the apparatchiks. You could say that we lost and they won because the administration started a different phase.

In a sense, whether or not they were the wrong people was not the question. The administration was moving into a second phase. Usually a president devises a staff system upon entering the White House, and then he turns to other things. But the problems change and the people change. Yet presidents rarely make sure that the two are compatible. In this case, we had finished what was the creative part of the administration. By August 7, 1969, when he gave his speech to the nation on his domestic agenda, we were, in a sense, all out of a job. We were clearly not the people who were going to get this thing through. We were not the congressional lobbyists or the wily bureaucrats. We were a group of itinerant intellectuals who had wandered in and fought it out. The President had accepted a bit here and there, and was now satisfied that this was his program. He was looking for somebody who could move his program to the next stage. The next stage included Erlichman and others. We, the stage one people, soon left the White House.

**MR. THOMPSON:** We thank you for your searching review of an important period in the Nixon political career and in his presidency.

# VIII.

# HISTORY'S JUDGMENT

# THE NIXON PRESIDENCY: SOME MITIGATING CIRCUMSTANCES

**Raymond K. Price Jr.**

During the final week of Richard Nixon's presidency, hostile crowds stood a triumphant deathwatch outside the White House gates. Inside, the few of us who were privy to the secret that he was moving toward resignation went about the grim business of preparing it. Just as the Watergate battle had looked very different from inside, so too did its denouement.

I delivered the first draft of his resignation speech with this note:

> Aug. 7, 1974
> Memorandum for: The President
> From: Ray Price
> Subject: Resignation Speech
>
> A first draft is attached. I'll be working on additional thoughts for it.
>
> As I believe you know, I think this has become a sad but necessary decision in the circumstances. But I do hope you'll leave office as proud of your accomplishments here as I am proud to have been associated with you, and to have been and remain a friend. God bless you; and He will.

Americans still find Richard Nixon endlessly fascinating, partly because they find him so puzzling: such a seeming bundle of contradictions and conundra. He has been a major national figure for almost 40 years now, a central part of the political experience of three generations. Few leaders in history have gone so high and been flung so low. And yet he has endured. Now, 10 years after his flight into exile, he once again beams from the television screen, exchanges visits with heads of state, holds forth on national and world affairs—and is listened to with respect.

The explanation for this involves not only the particular qualities of Mr. Nixon, but also the unique circumstances of his presidency.

From start to finish, Richard Nixon's was one of the most fiercely embattled presidencies in the nation's history. The fact that this contributed to his downfall has itself contributed to his comeback.

In domestic terms, the 1960s were the second most disastrous decade in U.S. history, following only the 1860s, ravaged by an actual civil war. It was Mr. Nixon's lot to inherit those passions: the verbal and physical violence, the escalation of hate, the riots and assassinations, the burning cities and bombed campuses. And he did so in the midst of a bitterly unpopular war, faced with an opposition Congress, at a time when "adversary journalism" was reaching the zenith of its fashionable acceptance and the nadir of its professional standards. In a real sense, the battle that brought Mr. Nixon down was the final struggle of that tortured era.

Domestically, the middle third of the 20th century was a time of escalating expansion and centralization of government. Mr. Nixon saw this as having reached a dangerous and debilitating point. He was determined to reverse it, which put him on a direct collision course with many who had a vested interest in the existing distribution of power.

But his overriding concern was the role of America in the world. Here, the picture was more complex.

When the United States sought to halt the tide of Soviet advance in the first tense years after World War II, it had the power, it had the will, and it had the cooperation of the European allies. By the time Mr. Nixon took office, America's will had been eroded, the Western alliance was in disarray, and the Russians had built their military strength to a point at which the American strategic advantage was all but gone.

Mr. Nixon set out to create a new "structure of peace" that could hold Soviet ambitions in check within the constraints of what was politically possible and militarily credible. One of his first acts as President was to set in motion the process that eventually led to a new relationship with China and thus a new balance of forces in the world.

Another was to repair the NATO alliance, and particularly to end the destructive U.S. rift with his friend Charles de Gaulle. A third was to begin working toward a new kind of relationship with the Soviet Union, in effect creating new "rules of engagement" for what both sides recognized would continue to be a competitive relationship, but in which both sides would also confine that competition to means that would avert a major armed conflict.

An intricately interwoven fabric of economic and other arrangements was designed, in part to raise the cost to the Russians of adventurism that the United States would consider unacceptable; and these were used at the same time to induce the Soviet leaders to accept agreements on control of nuclear arms.

But all of this required a firm show of American strength, at a time when retreat and withdrawal were clamorously in fashion. The more strong measures he took to make peace possible in the longer term, the more he inflamed those who marched under the banners of "peace" in the shorter term.

Leonid Brezhnev was a tough adversary; the relationship worked because he recognized that Nixon was also tough. Each knew that neither would let the other get away with anything. And so they were able to bargain in cold terms for their respective national interests—recognizing that some of those interests were irreconcilable, but also that there were large areas of mutual interest, not least the avoidance of mutual suicide.

# NIXON'S REASSESSMENT COMES EARLY

## Raymond K. Price Jr.

It took thirty years for Herbert Hoover, long reviled as a modern Caligula, to be reassessed. It took 20 years for Harry Truman, the only president whose Gallup approval ratings in office dropped lower than Richard Nixon's lowest. The reassessment of Mr. Nixon is well underway after only 10 years.

This should not be surprising, for two reasons. First, the pendulum of history swings more rapidly now. Second, the attitudes that prevailed 10 years ago were spawned by a spasm of national hysteria, and hysteria does not last. As it fades, people begin to search once again for perspective.

In the public's mind, "Watergate" came to mean vastly more than a break-in at Democratic national headquarters and a subsequent clumsy cover-up. Wild charges flew in all directions, breathless hints were rushed onto the airwaves; 16 months of relentless pounding, the most intensive coverage ever given any story in the entire history of the republic, created a climate in which even the most outlandish charge had only to be made in order to be believed.

The crowds that gathered outside the White House in the final week of the Nixon adminsitration looked in and saw what they perceived to be unprecedented corruption of power and a threat to their liberties. We insiders looked out and saw what we perceived to be a system run amok—a special prosecution force recruited lopsidedly from Kennedy and McGovern political organizations; on Capitol Hill, partisan congressional committees brandishing subpoenas, furiously leaking unsubstantiated allegations and abetted by an opportunistic media claque. And we saw all the unfinished work of forging a structure of international relationships, designed to keep the peace through the perilous final decades of the 20th century, being cast almost casually to the Watergate winds.

In the years since, passions have cooled. The achievements and sins of the Nixon administration are beginning, like those of other administrations, to be weighed together in the same historical balance. Myths persist, but truths are catching up.

Richard Nixon is no devil; neither is he a saint. But most Americans have a basic, gut recognition that a saint would make a disastrous president. The job descriptions are different. Americans hire presidents to look after the nation's interests in a brutal, dangerous, lawless world. A president has to be concerned with the morality of process, but even more so with the morality of consequence. Every act, every decision, has consequences, which may reverberate halfway across the country or halfway around the world. The worst thing a president can do is to be so paralyzed by propriety that he shrinks from bending the rules when the nation's security reuires it.

Those past presidents whom Americans hail as "strong"—Abraham Lincoln, Theodore Roosevelt, Franklin Roosevelt—all bent the rules, Lincoln most egregiously of all; but history sanctioned their acts on the grounds that times required it.

The successful president is idealistic in what he seeks, but often crafty, duplicitous, scheming, conniving in the ways he pursues it—because the essence of his job is to prevail over a sea of conflicting interests in order to advance the national interest. He has to create and manipulate a constantly shifting mix of coalitions first for one purpose and then for another, edging the country, however indirectly, toward his vision of its future.

In presidential terms, the true idealist is the one who does not shrink from getting his feet into the muck, if necessary, in order to make things better in a harsh and imperfect world. In war, America gives medals of honor to men who cover themselves in blood and slime, risking all, doing what in another environment would be repugnant to every moral sensibility, because in that environment it becomes necessary, not to the man but to the nation. Yet a soldier's responsibility for his country's safety pales before that of a president.

Strong leaders arouse strong passions. Typically, those most extravagantly admired are also the most extravagantly detested.

Like him or not, Mr. Nixon is what the French call *un homme sérieux*, a man of large vision who knows the world and whose views carry weight. However grudgingly, even those who hate his guts respect his mind; even those who disagree most vehemently know that he thinks before he speaks.

In an age that exalts the trivial, Richard Nixon is one of the last of the true heavyweights.

This, in the final analysis, is why he endures, and why many who cheered his downfall find themselves, to their own surprise, perversely glad to find him back.

# NIXON'S FOREIGN POLICY: THE N.S.C. AND THE STATE DEPARTMENT

## Joseph J. Sisco

**MR. THOMPSON:** It's a pleasure to introduce for the final Forum in the Nixon series a man who has been a close, personal friend for many years. Joseph Sisco is Doctor Joseph Sisco and we labored together as long suffering graduate students at the University of Chicago. He was a legend there and he remains a legend in his present work and activities. Others have been tapped as potential leaders in foreign policy almost from birth, but Joe Sisco made his way and achieved his success through dint of hard work mastering and sticking with the subject. As graduate students at the University of Chicago, we used to comment about the fact that one of the brightest students in the graduate group had spent two years at a junior college and then finished his degree at a very fine liberal arts college, Knox College in the midwest. McGeorge Bundy and others followed different paths through private schools and Yale and Harvard. Joe Sisco was at the top of the graduate student group, not only in international relations but in the Soviet field, where he did a good deal of his work and mastered economics as well.

There are a number of other things that illustrate my point. I won't belabor it, but he was a science teacher.

**DR. SISCO:** Take another ten minutes, Ken. I'm enjoying it all.

**MR. THOMPSON:** It's all true. He was a science teacher; he had a newspaper job for a while. He did a number of these things. Usually the student moving rapidly through graduate school doesn't have to do such things, but they proved good preparation for future activities.

To come to his foreign policy role, Joe Sisco was associated with the Department of State from 1951 to 1976. I remember a recurrent phrase that was used when people were talking about what we were doing in the U.N. or in the Near East or wherever it might be, whether it was the Rogers plan or strategy in the General Assembly or the Security Council. My friends and his friends, leaders like Joseph Johnson used to say "If you want to know what we are trying to do, ask Joe Sisco," and that continued through his career. He held high positions in the government beginning as deputy assistant secretary, assistant secretary, and then finally undersecretary for political affairs, a position that four major figures were considered for and every one of them—Phil Habib, Walter Stoessel, David Newsom and Sisco—ultimately fell heir to that position. However, from that group Joe Sisco emerged as undersecretary in 1974.

He has won numerous awards: the Rockefeller Public Service Award, the Civil Service League Award, and many others. He was president and chancellor of American University in Washington. He serves today on five corporate boards in his consulting agency work, and that consulting work is a story in itself. Today he is involved in the leadership of an agency that provides economic, political and social advice to groups that are working in China, the Soviet Union and other countries all over the world. It is most fortunate in this oral history that we can have Dr. Joseph Sisco as our final speaker.

**DR. SISCO:** Ken, thank you. You've been very kind as usual and very generous. I have no hesitation in telling this group that there is no one of my former classmates for whom I have greater respect and greater affection than Ken. I know what he's done here in what I consider to be a monumental project of historical significance which many students of the future will be able to avail themselves. And therefore, Ken, I'm extremely pleased to be able to make whatever little contribution I can.

*Joseph J. Sisco*

In talking about the Nixon presidency, I'm keenly aware that I'm among experts here today. I feel a little bit like the man who could talk about nothing else except how he survived the Johnstown flood. Everywhere he went he talked about how he survived the Johnstown flood and lo and behold he died. He went up through the Pearly Gates and he was welcomed by Saint Peter who said, "First day, easy schedule, tea at four p.m., and of course you will be expected to make several appropriate remarks." He said, "Fine." He said "I'm going to talk about how I survived the Johnstown flood," and this took Saint Peter aback and he said, "Are you sure you want to talk about this?" He says, "Yes, I'm sure." Saint Peter said, "Well, all right, but bear one thing in mind, Noah will be in the audience."

I served in the Nixon administration. He appointed me Assistant Secretary for Near Eastern and South Asian Affairs shortly after he was elected President, and therefore I went through that early phase of the Nixon administration's organization and decision-making process. I've served under half a dozen secretaries of state and a half a dozen presidents. Organization is something that has to be a reflection of where the United States is in the world as well as the predilections and the general comfort of the president himself in whatever system has been adopted. If you look at it historically, FDR started the process of not necessarily consulting fully his own secretary of state. I saw firsthand how McGeorge Bundy and Dean Rusk operated the relationship between the National Security Council and the State Department and it worked well and then subsequently, Walt Rostow, Henry Kissinger and others.

Our most productive periods, historically, have been periods of strong executive leadership supported by a bipartisan Congress. If you look at our current situation and go back to the early days after World War II, it was an America that was supreme from a military point of view. We helped rebuild the world after the war on the assumption that world stability was in our own interest, and it was and is. We were by far the number one power economically. We then helped to rebuild Western Europe and Japan. In that period from World War II up to Vietnam, there was a real consensus in executive-legislative relationships focused both on domestic and external policy. When you look at foreign affairs, it is Vietnam and Watergate that fractionalized that consensus.

It is in the aftermath of Vietnam and Watergate, at least in the last six years—and I don't mean this to be a partisan remark—that we had begun to restore a certain amount of executive leadership to the presidency as an institution and to restore that pattern of cooperation that fractionalized the post World War II consensus and weakened the presidency as an institution. There is no way in which America could lead effectively on the basis of a so-called resurgent Congress of 535 would-be secretaries of state.

So one of the sad dimensions of the current situation is the weakening of the presidency. The presidency was basically at a nadir at the end of the Carter administration reflected in the impotence of the United States in the whole Iranian hostage issue. In the last six years, the presidency as an institution has been strengthened. Now we face the kind of Iran crisis in institutional terms, no matter how this Iran hostage business comes out. Unfortunately it is going to set us back. There is no way in which the United States can lead successfully unless we are able to restore a pattern of strong executive leadership and a bipartisan Congress to give direction, certitude and predictability to American foreign policy. One should also add domestic policy. There was a time in the nineteenth century when you could make a sharp distinction between domestic and external policies. You can't do that today. The needs of the military front line are inextricably linked with the financial bottom line. The distinction between politics and economics cannot be made today as it might have been made in the nineteenth century.

Now to go back to the Nixon administration. *First*, organization was the reflection of how President Nixon saw the position of the United States in the world. He thought strategically, not in technical terms. He saw American leadership in foreign affairs as number one, and he saw the world primarily through the prism of how does one manage Soviet power and the overall U.S.-U.S.S.R. relationship. He had a monumental disinterest in domestic policy. I know that you've heard from Ehrlichman and others, but from my vantage point the Richard Nixon that I got to know found domestic policies a bore. Every president seems to come to office not knowing or forgetting that American foreign policy is an amalgam of continuity and change. Every president feels, based on the presidential campaign, that he has to reinvent the wheel. He has a transition to make from being the leader of a successful campaign group and the simplicity of the campaign rhetoric to suddenly realizing he is president of all Americans. He has the job of governing rather than winning an election. Richard Nixon, I think, understood what the world environment was all about. He did come into the presidency with considerable knowledge of foreign affairs, having traveled widely, having been the vice president and knowing something about these problems and with a sense of priorities. He recognized that the Soviet-American relationship was the number one item on the agenda. He is unique in this respect. With most of our presidents in the post-World War II period, their strengths were on the domestic side. In the case of Richard Nixon his initial strength was on the external side, on the foreign policy side, and he viewed foreign policy strategically.

*Secondly*, the organization that was adopted was a reflection of a combination of Richard Nixon's and Henry Kissinger's personalities. Richard Nixon came into the presidency with a deep suspicion of the bureaucracy, a chip on his shoulder insofar as the State Department was concerned. He was not an individual that was comfortable in a room with a lot of people. He was fine in a formal setting on television or in a speech where there were thousands of people and he read a text. But as to group situations, he was much better in a one-to-one, one-to-two or one-to-three situation. In fact he disliked the National Security Council meetings at which there would be no more than a dozen of us to discuss an issue. He was not entirely comfortable in that kind of a setting. He liked the notion of a one-on-one with his NSC adviser.

He was a strong leader. Therefore, he wanted the major leadership elements and pulsations in foreign policy, and particularly the focus of Soviet-American relations, to be closely held with a large measure of initiative stemming from the White House. While he appointed a very close friend, Bill Rogers, as secretary of state, it was decided that the structure would be reorganized from the previous administration and the so-called interdepartmental committees would be under the National Security Council group, meaning Henry Kissinger. However there were any number of subgroups that were formed on individual problems, whether it was Africa or the Middle East, and all of the various agencies participated. In the last analysis, any of the papers that developed options ultimately came to Henry Kissinger's desk as part of the overall review. He basically decided how these papers were presented to the President, if they were presented at all. A number of times he wrote critiques of them and indicated whether a formal meeting of the National Security Council was necessary or desirable.

You can draw a sharp contrast between how Nixon operated the National Security Council and how, say, President Johnson did. President Johnson had what was called the informal Tuesday group and many decisions were made by eight or ten people around lunch on Tuesday. Most of the time you went into a National Security Council meeting under President Johnson it was largely a show; that is, individuals were either assigned or were expected to make a presentation. Johnson pretty much knew ahead of time what he wanted to have come out of it and therefore it frequently was not a serious give and take in terms of the substantive issues at the formal National Security Council meeting. That, I think, is at one extreme; in other words, it was largely perception rather than reality.

With Nixon it wasn't quite that. The meetings were carefully prepared; the various Cabinet members were given a full opportunity to express themselves. But rarely was a decision taken formally around the table and conveyed at the conclusion of that particular National Security Council meeting. Instead, the President would say, "I'll reflect on this." What had occurred frequently is there had been a prior meeting between Kissinger and the President on the various options. They had discussed in what direction they may or may not have been leading or had received a recommendation from Mr. Kissinger. It's not that the National Security council meeting could not at least theoretically change whatever predilection they may have had because there were fairly free discussions in the NSC meetings in which I participated over the years. By the same token, Kissinger and the President would get together and they would then decide either before or after the NSC meeting, and a written decision would be conveyed to the various Cabinet members.

The gray area is to what degree was the President leading, to what degree did Mr. Kissinger press it in a certain direction. It is clear that Mr. Kissinger's predilection for running foreign policy from the national Security Council converged with the President's view that matters should be held in a limited number of hands. There isn't any question in my mind that Henry Kissinger strengthened the predilection of President Nixon in this direction because it meant a greater concentration of power for the National Security Council mechanism as against the Cabinet members on a particular given issue. There really wasn't basically any difference of approach between the President and Kissinger in this regard.

In fairness it has to be said that Kissinger held two positions. When he was National Security Council adviser, he organized it in such a way that the focal point there was on the NSC staff, and at the same time a duplication of the diplomatic process in the State Department was put together at the White House level. He and his people were seeing ambassadors as regularly as the secretary of state, with the latter frequently not knowing either that the meeting had taken place or what happened at that particular meeting. I am being utterly frank because one has really to look at how the thing actually occurred if we are going to arrive eventually at some kind of a balanced picture as to how these things got done. There was considerable duplication of diplomatic activity. A number of operations involved the channel from the ambassador to the White House as well as to the State Department. Secretary of State George Shultz recently expressed shock that Ambassador John Kelly had communicated with the White House, and he didn't know anything about it. I could have told him a little bit about what happened in some other administrations in this regard. In fact, every ambassador that went out in the field—I can remember it as clear as could be—would be told by the National Security Council adviser, "Remember that you serve at the pleasure of the President. You are the President's representative, not the secretary of state's." Therefore, what was encouraged during that period was, if something was particularly sensitive, that a channel be established between an embassy and the White House directly. I don't know of any comparable period where there was as much of that going on, even though we would all agree there are certain things that have to be limited to two or three people and are so sensitive, particularly in the intelligence area or some new diplomatic opening, that you can't spread it around the bureaucracy. Kissinger felt strongly that's the way it ought to be done. This was the kind of thing that strengthened Nixon's propensity for secrecy, his suspicions of the bureaucracy and his reserve about getting involved in large group meetings.

Now the interesting thing is that if you read the two volumes of the Kissinger book, you will find that when he became secretary of state, subsequently, he had a change of heart. He decided that really now the secretary of state should be the principal adviser of the president, and the NSC adviser should be a coordinator, an individual who assures that the president is properly informed, and that the options are presented to the president. He underscores the importance of the NSC monitoring foreign policy. After all, one of the things that has changed and impacts on the organization of foreign policy is that it is a much more complicated and complex world than in the past. Every agency in Washington has a piece of the foreign policy action. As President Truman indicated: he thought that once he took a decision things would go forward. He discovered very soon that they don't go forward and, therefore, obviously there is need for a National Security Council adviser and staff. I'm not suggesting that our organization as such is a bad organization. In fact, it is being emulated in many other countries. The NSC mechanism is essential in this world of communications revolution and need for quick decisions. It is needed in the world of complicated foreign policy issues that touch upon every facet of our society. The focal point has to be right there next to the president, and don't ever underestimate the law of physical proximity and bureaucracy. There has to be a coordinating point. The NSC sees this across the board and coordinates it. No secretary of state can do this. No Cabinet member can do this in a satisfactory way. But this should not mean an NSC staff essentially or duplicating the operations responsibilities of the Department of State.

So for all of the changes that we have seen, the system has worked best when you've had individuals in the NSC job who viewed it as a coordinating function and as an administrative function, making sure that information is conveyed rather than a National Security Council that's gotten itself into trouble, as today, by getting into covert operations where it doesn't belong or, in the days of Kissinger, when it was almost frequently duplicative of what the State Department is mandated to do under our constitutional system. Then he became secretary of state and said, "Well, in retrospect, I've looked at this and I realize I didn't run it this way." He was very frank that the secretary of state should be principal adviser. What most people don't realize is that the situation began to rub. For a while he wore two hats. He was the National Security Council adviser and the secretary of state. Ford decided that he couldn't carry water on both shoulders. So Brent Scrowcroft became the National Security Council adviser. Some of us that lived through this began to see the irritations that were developing between Secretary of State Henry Kissinger and National Security Council Adviser Brent Scrowcroft because the shoe then was on the other foot.

But in terms of decision making, I've wanted to wrap this around a little broader setting. There is much more I could say but I'd rather begin to address your questions.

**QUESTION:** Would it be practical, in order to avoid the duplication that you mentioned and still keep somebody close to the president, to elevate the secretary of state to become a more or less personal adviser and establish policies for the department but let it be run say by an undersecretary and then have the secretary of state close to the president and make that his primary duty?

**DR. SISCO:** The closest we got to that was in the relationship between Dean Rusk and George Ball in the

Kennedy-Johnson administration. Rarely has a secretary of state been willing to appoint a number two individual as his alter ego. George Ball came close to that with Dean Rusk. Dean Rusk felt he had to focus on the advice he was giving the President on Vietnam. I don't want to suggest that he gave up the leadership of running the department, but in operational terms I would say that the suggestion that you make has a great deal of sense to it. There is no way in which you can eliminate or downgrade or should downgrade the role of the secretary of state as the principal adviser and the principal spokesman for American foreign policy. The advantage that the NSC adviser has had historically is his work in coordinating and doing the job in the White House and keeping the president informed. He is not subject to any testimony whatsoever before the Congress, whereas the poor secretary of state is not only worrying about telegrams that go out to 150 countries but he has diplomatic and representational responsibilities. Above all, he has enormous responsibilities in explaining and justifying policy on the Hill, which I found, as undersecretary of state in the top career post, took more and more of my time as well as that of the secretary of state. Theoretically your number two or number three or even number four, who is an undersecretary for economic affairs, ought to be able to do much to relieve the secretary of state of the operational load along the lines that you've indicated. I think there is more that we can do in this regard without necessarily making any formal changes. As secretary of state some have understood: if I'm going to maximize my capacity to provide advice to the president, I'm really going to have to have someone that I have full confidence in who can run this whole huge bureaucracy and relieve the load in a very considerable degree. Too few secretaries of state have been willing to approach it from that point of view. When Henry Kissinger became secretary of state, he did not approach it from that angle. He was a hands on secretary of state in every major respect.

**QUESTION:** I have a question that relates to the secretary of state with regard to the complexity of world problems and continuity. Why don't we have more secretaries of state who have been career ambassadors?

**DR. SISCO:** Here you have to look at our electoral process and our system. One of the mistakes that a number of careerists make is that they tend, perhaps in their focus on the substance of foreign policy, not to recognize the political dimension of policy in domestic terms. Our foreign service traditionally is training people who do the job abroad, although that's changing. My feeling has been that what we ought to be aiming at is developing a greater number of so-called political executives. These are professionals but they are political executives in the broadest context. When a president is elected, he comes in with more or less knowledge of the outside world. I can tell you that he always comes in thinking that the international problems are more susceptible of solution than domestic problems because most of our presidents, with the exception of President Nixon, knew more about domestic issues than they did about foreign policy issues. However, expertise is not synonymous with wisdom.

The strength of American foreign policy is inherent in the political process. As such, if you are going to have an effective American foreign policy, it has to be led basically by a politician in the best sense of the word. I would have no quarrel with the appointment of people to the job of secretary of state who have very good knowledge of foreign affairs. I would cite someone like Cy Vance, for example. Cy had been deputy secretary of defense and a practicing lawyer. He has had a strong and continuing interest in foreign affairs. Cy Vance reflects the combination of an individual who did a few things politically, locally, in order to be chosen as a Democrat. By the way, Dean Rusk is also an example of this. Dean Rusk, after all, got into the domestic, political process in a very small sort of way in Scarsdale, New York, and elsewhere. Ken, you lived there at that time. He was identified as a Democrat and yet there isn't any question of his expertise. He had been assistant secretary for UN affairs and deputy undersecretary. So that there have been certain appointments where people have been experts in the best sense of the word, as well as political executives, and I think you need a combination of both.

**QUESTION:** To what extent would you say that the organizational and operating procedures and indeed the foreign policy of the Nixon administration was the result of Mr. Nixon's own profound understanding of foreign problems, and to what extent was he simply responsive to Mr. Kissinger?

**DR. SISCO:** There is no overall judgment that I can give you that can capsulate that because you really have to look at it on an issue-to-issue basis. The strength of Henry Kissinger is that he had knowledge of foreign affairs, and he had a remarkable talent for thinking not only strategically and conceptually but tactically as well. That's a very unusual synthesis in a man. It is a rare quality. Some have been thinkers up in the clouds and who did not know how to go about putting it together bureaucratically. Kissinger was a remarkable individual and is a remarkable individual. I happen to think, for all the differences of view that I had with Henry over the years, he is probably the number one foreign policy talent in the world today. I pay him that compliment. He had some strong views. The first two or three months of the administration, he cranked up thirty-five different studies on thirty-five different major problems, drawing on State Department and National Security Council studies. The only thing that he was not given responsibility for was the Middle East, largely because Mr. Nixon had appointed Mr. Rogers, and he wanted to be very sure that Mr. Rogers as secretary of state had his own little niche. Henry resented this; there wasn't any question about it. He didn't know too much about the Middle East. He had not gone there very often. Therefore, the struggle between the NSC and State not only got mixed up in policy differences, but likewise in differences in terms of ambitions and turf, and all the usual things that one associates with Washington.

I would say that issue by issue more and more the President took the recommendations of Henry Kissinger and that the portrayals that one reads frequently about the President's predilection on something has to be examined on a case by case basis. It's not that Mr. Nixon wasn't knowledgeable, but when you begin to focus on these issues in great detail, they sometimes begin to look a little different than had been expressed on the campaign trail. Nixon was not a voracious reader. I don't mean that he wanted a brief piece of paper on the pattern of President Eisenhower. Based on his military experience, President Eisenhower had tremendous confidence in John Foster Dulles. The National Security Council mechanism was largely a coordinating mechanism then under Bromley Smith and the President liked to get one sheet of paper which said, "Here are the options and here is what I recommend."

I can recall on a number of occasions Mr. Dulles picking up the telephone and saying, "Mr. President, we've just had a meeting, here's what we've considered, and my recommendation is this," and I can recall Ike saying, "Foster, fine." I'm not suggesting that President Eisenhower approached these things superficially, not at all. But in one-on-one meetings between Nixon and Kissinger there isn't any question in my mind that nine times out of ten Henry gave the President what his view was. I'll put it this way. At least as many times, it was a pulsation from Kissinger to the President rather than vice versa. I can't be more precise than that; one would have to look at the documentation on each one of these decisions. One has to give Henry his due. He knew his man and therefore he built not only his position, but he built a solid base of confidence. In our system, you are only as strong an NSC adviser or a secretary of state as the president entrusts you with his confidence in that particular job.

You take my friend, George Shultz, today. He has gone through a difficult period and a number of us can admire the position of principle he has taken. On the other hand, we should be under no illusions. You cannot adopt a position on the Iran matter which is at odds with the President and not have it affect your personal relationship with the President of the United States. Therefore, the question of trust and confidence is absolutely key and Henry had a remarkable ability in this regard. Kissinger approached foreign policy making in a small group or one-on-one, the system with which President Nixon was very comfortable. President Nixon on the whole is a very confident man in the field of foreign affairs. He knew enough about it to know generally the direction in which he wanted go. And he didn't get into a lot of the details.

The contrast between the "in" box of Jimmy Carter with all those detailed studies and examining things in great detail in contrast to the clean "in" box and clean desk of President Nixon is startling. That says something about how these presidents operated. You have to be comfortable in your own system. Nixon was certainly very comfortable and Henry did an absolutely unbelievable job in this regard.

**QUESTION:** I wonder who was the originator of the most important foreign policy of the Nixon administration, namely, the opening to China. Was it President Nixon or was it Henry Kissinger? I understand that actually the originator was the President and that, for reasons of not offending the Soviets, Mr. Kissinger denied some information to the President. This was the message from the Pakistani leader from Mao to Nixon that Mao would be open to better relations. Only later when a more definite message came did Kissinger pass it on to Nixon. I don't know whether this is correct.

**DR. SISCO:** I don't know about that dimension, but I'm very clear in responding to your fundamental question. In my judgment the initiative for the opening of China came from the leadership of President Nixon himself, and not Henry. For one thing Henry did not feel himself to be sufficiently secure in that job at an early stage to recommend this kind of a fundamental break. One has to think about the twenty or thirty years of hostility towards Communist China. The whole McCarthy period was a difficult period for anybody who thought there ought to be an opening or the beginning of a two-China policy.

President Nixon clearly felt that he, with a strong reputation as an anti-Communist, could do what Hubert Humphrey could not have done if Humphrey had been elected president as a Democrat. So Nixon deserves tremendous credit. Insofar as the initiatives *vis-a-vis* the Soviet Union or the whole detente approach, Mr. Nixon is number one, not Henry Kissinger. He recognized not only that we have to manage power, but we've got to try to work this thing out with the Russians by means of negotiations.

In my own case, when I was appointed assistant secretary for Near Eastern affairs, I was called in by the President. He said, "Joe, I want you to do one thing; I want you to develop some options. I want to test the Soviet Union in its policy in the Middle East. Do they want a policy of controlled tension or do they want a policy of trying to work this out with us? I want you to develop the recommendations." He told me this firsthand, right in his office. I said, "Fine, Mr. President, we'll develop our recommendations in this regard." This was not Henry Kissinger, this was Richard Nixon. So that in the whole detente structure of trying to work things out, the China opening and the Soviet dimension, one has to put Mr. Nixon number one with Henry obviously agreeing and supplying the information and contributing philosophically and otherwise. But President Nixon, as you look at his administration, will go down in history for having taken some very important leadership initiatives largely at his own behest in the first instance. Henry's views in this regard paralleled the President's.

**QUESTION:** I have an organization question about how the executive branch can be better organized to deal with crises. If you take three examples—Watergate, the Challenger disaster and the current Iran situation that we face—all were unforeseen. Some of them were even unforeseeable at the top. In two of the three we are faced with the hemorrhaging of political power by the President. What intrigues me is the inability of the President to cut his losses when faced with such a tremendous problem. It has been suggested that the Challenger disaster was handled differently in that before it became politicized, the President was willing to create a presidential commission that dealt with the problem very adequately apart from the political process. I'm curious if it is possible to consider better organizing the government to handle crises or if it is simply a matter of *ad hocing* it and is it the individual president involved who controls these things?

**DR. SISCO:** I'm not sure I can really answer your question very satisfactorily. When you look at the Challenger situation I think it was handled very well politically. The unique feature of the Challenger crisis is that it was essentially a domestic problem and not one like Iran where our relationships with our allies in the Middle East were involved and where the problem is one of credibility of the administration saying one thing and doing another. The Challenger thing was handled extremely well and my former colleague, Bill Rogers, did an outstanding job as the head of that commission. In the tussle between Kissinger and Rogers within the framework of the Nixon administration, because of the strength of the Kissinger personality and his political position, a good many people have tended to denigrate the capacities of Bill Rogers. But Rogers is a tough, shrewd, pragmatic, problem-solving attorney. Granted that he did not have the knowledge that Kissinger had, and granted that he approached it like a lawyer in the sense of problem by problem solving, with less knowledge at the beginning. But he was a man who is tough; he had eminent good sense; his instincts were extremely good; and when he got hold of a problem, he was able to manage it and manage it very well.

I don't honestly think it is a question of how we can organize ourselves better. Government is people. As I look at the current National Security Council under MacFarlane and Poindexter, one of the problems is not only the size but also the caliber of some of the people the National Security Council staff. The NSC staff of the last three or four years does not measure up to that which existed some years back.

However, ironically it's under Henry Kissinger that more and more of the military were brought into the National Security Council staff. Let me elaborate on this. We need good military on that National Security Council staff. We need that dimension because so often with foreign policy you've got to worry not only about the State Department but about the Defense Department. There is a security element; there is a political element; there is an economic element. However I don't believe it's a desirable thing to put a military man at the head of the National Security Council staff. I will make one exception, Brent Scowcroft, who in my judgment developed the broad capacity that is required. This is no criticism of the military. I knew John Poindexter and I know Bob

McFarlane. They are good military officers. Poindexter was number one in his class, a nuclear physicist. But that's not the job for a Poindexter or a Bob McFarlane. You need people with political breadth and knowledge because our system is multidimensional. Not only is it a question of coordination and negotiating within the bureaucracies but there is a whole public media dimension, a congressional dimension, let alone the worldwide audience. Another difficulty is that we have tended to go the other way by appointing National Security Council advisers whose ambitions were not limited to being National Security Council advisers. Not only was that true of Henry Kissinger, but it was certainly true of Mr. Brzezinski. Both wanted to be secretary of state. So you've got a situation where that National Security Council adviser not only is seeing foreign leaders diplomatically but, lo and behold, he is on American television every Sunday morning.

Yet I don't believe that the National Security Council adviser should be subject to the consent of the Senate. I think that would be wrong. The president needs a National Security Council adviser who provides him with confidential advice. He should be able to exercise the right of executive privilege. But he has got to be an individual who is broadly gauged politically and economically. These are people that are hard to find.

Al Haig, for example, was part of the system of bringing up military in the NSC staff to deputies and then eventually to the head of the National Security council staff, all started by Henry Kissinger. There were reasons why he did that. One of them was that he worked best with individuals who could carry out and implement basically what he wanted. I don't say this in any negative sense; Henry knew the direction in which he wanted to go. Therefore, that gave a premium to certain individuals. We have had a spate of military people in this job, and I don't think it's a sound practice.

**QUESTION:** One of the things that increasingly bothers us in Britain is the capacity of the legislature in this country to hamstring foreign policy. It means that your allies don't feel that there is a foreign policy that they can support. I wondered how President Nixon dealt with the Hill?

**DR. SISCO:** First, it is a very untidy system, there is no question about it. I like to think it is still the best and the most effective. We are not a parliamentary government. It is presidential leadership and there isn't any question that our leadership position has been undermined by the recent Iran crisis. What our friends and our adversaries expect from the United States is predictability, certitude and direction. In too many cases, in the aftermath of Vietnam, the President took one position, and it was not sustained by the Congress. That's why I underscored early that there is no alternative to strong presidential leadership. Our system is Jeffersonian. It works best by political negotiations between the executive and the legislature. The effective president is able to organize himself as well as his administration so that the pattern of cooperation that was so characteristic from post-World War II to roughly Vietnam is restored. That is partly a function of the strength of the president politically; for example, Ronald Reagan winning the kind of massive victory that he did in this last election. This manifests itself into political realities and strength on the Hill, and therefore what the president can achieve. And that's why this present Iran-Contra crisis is so bad; it has weakened the presidency once again as an institution.

With Richard Nixon, the fractionalization came about over Vietnam but then began to pervade every foreign policy issue. It led to a loss of credibility. Up to that point, Nixon had adopted the position that he wanted to get out, that we needed to Vietnamize the problem, and that we needed to turn it over to the South Vietnamese. One of the critical turning points was the secret bombing of Cambodia which had such an adverse impact on the Hill. Henry Kissinger will never be forgiven either by the ultra conservatives for his policy of detente or by the liberals for the policy that he pursued in Cambodia. So historically he is caught between these two crossfires.

In the earlier phase, Nixon's congressional relations were very good. It's not only that Nixon himself played a substantial personal role. He would call the leadership in and he did a good job briefing the leadership around the table. But in the earlier periods, the Congress was so organized that if you could talk to the key leaders on both sides of the aisle plus the relevant committee chairmanships, they could say, "Mr. President, we agree with what you are trying to do." Then these people could produce the votes up there on the Hill. No longer. That certainly was not the case during later stages of Vietnam and Watergate. Since then, we have had some return of the pendulum so that we no longer have the young, resurgent Congress of the immediate post-Vietnam period, which brought chaos and unpredictability in the executive branch and in the Congress. There is a good deal more organizing that the Congress itself needs to do to put its own house in order. What have in the Congress today are different clusters of support on different issues so that for every foreign policy issue you say, "All right, who are the key people?"

Let's take, for example, arms control. I hope I'm not being unduly naive. As I never do lose hope. I would hope that a man like Senator Sam Nunn can now pull this thing together so that the executive branch and the Congress can move ahead, not only in terms of what portion of the budget ought to be allocated to defense but also on the positions we take in the arms control negotiations.

In the Nixon administration the briefings were informal. There were briefings by Rogers and the State Department and by Mel Laird, who was a very fine defense secretary and the epitome of the politician in the best sense of the word. He would have made a tremendous president. He was able to do everything that needed to be done for the Nixon administration in terms of the Defense budget. So there were good people both at the Cabinet level as well as in the White House, a lot of talent. Nixon picked good talent. The congressional liaison was effective on the whole up to the time that the bleeding began over Vietnam and the whole unnecessary coverup over Watergate. Then the whole thing fell apart. So one has to look at the Nixon administration in two phases.

**QUESTION:** Dr. Sisco, during President Nixon's administration there was a short conflict between Pakistan and India. Why is it they supported Pakistan instead of India?

**DR. SISCO:** That was a pretty painful chapter. I was intimately involved and there were some very strong differences within the U.S. government at that time. Let me put it quite baldly. The State Department took the position that we were tilting too much to Pakistan at that time, and that there were things that we could do diplomatically to ameliorate the situation and hopefully avoid the war. By the same token, it has to be said very clearly that as we look at this thing in retrospect, Indira Gandhi and the Indian government had made up its mind that it was going to cause the break with East Pakistan, which is Bangladesh today. That was the policy of the Indian government, and we had no significant leverage to prevent it. We became very concerned about the intelligence reports indicating that there had been at least discussions within the Indian Cabinet and the Indian hierarchy that the Indo-Paki episode should be used to destroy irreparably the military capacity of Pakistan. So we became very concerned about a fundamental change in the balance of power in the area even though we knew that we couldn't prevent the break by East Pakistan because Indian policy was set in that regard. We began then to focus on what it was that we could do politically and otherwise in order to bolster the Pakistanis to prevent what might have been irreparable injury to Pakistan itself.

A number of us quite frankly felt that the intelligence reports that were coming in this regard were exaggerated. While there was no disagreement about assisting Pakistan at that juncture, the dangers of Pakistan being snuffed out seemed exaggerated. They were used to justify the tilt in that direction, and that's where all the policy arguments came about.

But our support for Pakistan goes back a long way. It goes back to the alliances which were put together by Mr. Dulles. There isn't any question that the U.S. problem with India has been that India has viewed itself, understandably from its own point of view, as the number one power in the subcontinent. It has felt all along that the United States has never, as explicitly as they would have liked, recognized that supremacy and therefore we have tended to support Pakistan.

From a strategic point of view, our overall interests are and were to maintain a stability in the area that does not offer the opportunity for a superpower confrontation. We've done better at certain times than others. Our relations with India today are somewhat improved over what they have been. But the fundamental problem is, what should American policy be *vis a vis* India and Pakistan, relative to the situation in the subcontinent? You can't decide that merely on a regional basis. There is the question of overall relationships with the Soviet Union as well as with Communist China.

**MR. THOMPSON:** Could I ask a final question? What happened in terms of the morale of the State Department as you saw it when the NSC augmented its role in the Kissinger era? What happened to Mr. Rogers? How did he cope with what he must have seen as a drift of power away from State? We've worked with him recently on the Commission on Presidential Transitions. One thing he doesn't want to talk about is the State Department and the NSC problem. We are a little bit embarrassed at the moment that others on the Commission want to add something to the text and he apparently doesn't want to do that. What is the human price when you begin to export powers out of the major departments and into an agency like the NSC?

**DR. SISCO:** I can tell you this very first hand. Bill Rogers and his wife Adele—and his wife was one of the best secretary of state wives that we've had since World War II—took it very stoically. Bill Rogers is a man of great dignity, and a man who has scratched to get where he is. He was not an individual born with a golden spoon in his mouth. He became a practicing attorney, attorney general and then secretary of state. Decorum, dignity and courtesy in the best sense of the word are things which Bill Rogers attributes great importance. Therefore, the humiliations—and they were numerous—that were heaped on this man have scarred him indelibly. You don't forget an experience like this. I've known about what you've just said, namely, his unwillingness to talk about it because it is to this day still too painful. That's how deep it went and particularly when ridicule was heaped upon him in our press. He was not as ineffective a secretary of state as our press made him out to be. He was a man of eminent good sense and wisdom. I know of certain instances where in an NSC meeting he was able to ameliorate and to deflect some actions that might not have been in the interest of the United States. The experience he went through as secretary of state should not have happened to any individual whether as the head of a corporation or the secretary of state. Therefore, you cannot exaggerate the human dimension of this. One would have to cite not only the dozens of incidents that are known, but the eight dozen incidents that aren't known because they came up in the day-by-day interactions between the State Department and the White House. All you have to do is read the two volumes of the Kissinger book and Henry makes no bones about it. The President gave Bill Rogers the responsibility for taking the lead in all of the Middle Eastern policy, and all the way along that book cites chapter and verse as to how Kissinger and the NSC sought to undermine the policy. He was very frank about it. It was the one area that the secretary of state had responsibility for and therefore Kissinger was not able to exclude Rogers from that sensitive area as he was the China initiative, Vietnam and a number of other things. So what you say does not surprise me at all.

**MR. THOMPSON:** One final question that we always ask is how do you think history will judge the Nixon presidency?

**DR. SISCO:** Unfortunately, you cannot divorce Nixon foreign policy from the overall Nixon administration. Clearly, if you were trying to evaluate the President exclusively in foreign policy terms, and you cannot, then I would have to say that he was one of the best and one of the most effective Presidents that we've had in the post-World War II period. He was knowledgeable and sound. After all, we remember the opening to China and the whole policy of detente, if nothing else. It was also the period where in the Middle East we achieved two disengagement agreements between the Arabs and Israelis and laid the groundwork for Camp David and the Egyptian-Israeli Treaty. While there is more of a quarrel over Vietnam, I am satisfied that he was trying to move in the direction of disengaging the United States. He didn't move rapidly enough, the debacle occurred, but that got complicated because there was a weakening of the presidency, a destruction and deterioration in public opinion at home and in Congress. We lost Vietnam as much, in my judgment, as a result of the loss of public support at home as we did on the battlefield itself. This is an old view but I happen to hold it. So in foreign affairs, you've got to say that Nixon will historically come out reasonably well. But to the extent we got into Watergate and the cover-up, you get into the weakening of the presidency. We are still suffering from that today. We still have not restored the position of the presidency and the support that is absolutely essential if America is to maintain a reasonable role of leadership in a more complicated world.

**MR. THOMPSON:** I am sure all of you would agree that this has been one of the clearest and most forceful presentations we have had on the Nixon presidency. Those of us whose association with Joe Sisco goes back a number of years aren't a bit surprised. As a graduate student, a U.S. Army officer, or the president of a major university, this same forcefulness has manifested itself. When he decides he wants to return to his first vocation of scholar in international relations, we hope he will come here and write his book at the Miller Center.

**DR. SISCO:** Thank you very much.

# CONCLUDING OBSERVATIONS

Few presidencies evoke the intensity of response and reaction generated by the Nixon presidency. In part, the emotions surrounding that administration arise from disputes over the facts. From disputes over personal questions such as "Did he have a drinking problem" to "What were his relations with Henry Kissinger" or "Who gave the order to the plumbers," the historian struggles with contending testimony and interpretations. The same is true of Nixon's approach to the organization of the government. On one hand, few presidents can match his preparation for governing the nation. He had performed many of the tasks of the presidency especially during the illnesses of President Eisenhower. He knew and was respected by foreign leaders, many of whom he had met in foreign travel during his years in exile. Yet some witnesses to this oral history make clear he was not a good administrator, had difficulty ordering the relationship of politics and governance and lacked credibility with large segments of the American public.

He was experienced but insecure and competent but neither trusted nor trusting. He was the architect of the most promising foreign policy approaches yet also the author of security and intelligence structural arrangements that were to haunt American foreign policy to the present day. He brought an array of outstanding public servants into the government, as Leonard Garment relates, but they worked under a cloud of suspicion and distrust that hung over his administration and culminated in Watergate. It would seem he performed best in adversity, as he confided to Gary Wills; his downfall came after an unprecedented landslide victory for a second term. His attempt to build a new "structure for peace" was cut short by the fateful end of his presidency.

It may be possible to continue the catalogue of this "seeming bundle of contradictions and conundra," but no single observer can do it justice. The justification for a broad based review of the Nixon presidency with more than twenty intimates and associates is the benefit of diversity. We need to collect and organize every possible fragment of information available on the Nixon presidency if we are to understand it. Even with Nixon's early restoration, of which Raymond K. Price writes, many thoughtful persons remain skeptical, baffled or perplexed. It may be personally satisfying, as it doubtless was for Mr. Price to write the President in an August 7, 1974 Memorandum accompanying the first draft of a "Resignation Speech": "God bless you; and he will." Yet lasting historical judgments require more than personal expressions of confidence.

Will there ever be an authoritative study of the Nixon presidency to help bring full understanding where little now exists? President Nixon's unwillingness to participate in free and open exchange in an oral history such as that of the Miller Center does not encourage this hope nor does the absence, despite repeated invitations, of some of his key associates. Memoirs alone will not provide the necessary source material for an authoritative study because the majority represent something approaching special pleading prepared in self-justification of the writer's actions. Lacking a true dialogue and genuine debriefing with a jury of informed questioners, we are thrown back on those who are public spirited enough to participate in a serious oral history.

The Miller Center pays tribute to the participants in this review who, without monetary gain or political advantage and often at considerable personal sacrifice, took part in a search for the truth about the Nixon presidency. Until the day that new and better forms of oral history appear, future public servants and the hard-pressed citizenry striving to make sense of the deeds of his government will be dependent on efforts such as these. The Center has devoted itself to this enterprise out of conviction that success in governance rests on wider and deeper knowledge of the presidency. With the publication of this volume, the Center will have published studies of postwar presidencies from Franklin D. Roosevelt through Richard M. Nixon. We expect to continue these histories through published works and unpublished source materials made available by the participants to future scholars and historians. Within six months, the Center anticipates the completion of the Ford presidency oral history, a project which has been underway over the past two years.